CAREERS IN CRIMINAL JUSTICE

AND RELATED FIELDS:

FROM INTERNSHIP TO PROMOTION

Sixth Edition

J. Scott Harr
Concordia University St. Paul

Kären M. Hess
Normandale Community College, Bloomington, Minnesota

With contributions by Christine Hess Orthmann
Orthmann Writing & Research, Inc.

WADSWORTH
CENGAGE Learning™

Australia • Brazil • Japan • Korea • Mexico • Singapore • Spain • United Kingdom • United States

WADSWORTH
CENGAGE Learning

Careers in Criminal Justice and Related Fields: From Internship to Promotion, Sixth Edition
J. Scott Harr, Kären Hass

Acquisitions Editor: Carolyn Henderson-Meier

Editorial Assistant: Lee Kamilah

Media Project Manager: Ronda Robinson

Marketing Manager: Michelle Williams

Marketing Assistant: Jillian Myers

Marketing Communications Manager: Tami Strang

Project Manager, Editorial Production: Abigail Greshik

Creative Director: Rob Hugel

Art Director: Maria Epes

Print Buyer: Linda Hsu

Permissions Editor: Bob Kauser

Production Service: Pre-PressPMG

Text Designer: Christine Orthmann

Copy Editor: Pre-PressPMG

Illustrator: Christine Orthmann

Cover Designer: Yvo Reizebos

Cover Image: Yvo Reizebos

Compositor: Pre-PressPMG

For product information and technology assistance, contact us at **Cengage Learning Academic Resource Center, 1-800-423-0563**

For permission to use material from this text or product, submit all requests online at **www.cengage.com/permissions**
Further permissions questions can be e-mailed to **permissionrequest@cengage.com**

Library of Congress Control Number: 2008943014

ISBN-13: 978-0-495-60032-9

ISBN-10: 0-495-60032-6

Wadsworth, Cengage Learning
10 Davis Drive
Belmont, CA 94002-3098
USA

Cengage Learning products are represented in Canada by Nelson Education, Ltd.

For your course and learning solutions, visit **academic.cengage.com**

Purchase any of our products at your local college store or at our preferred online store **www.ichapters.com**

Printed in Canada
1 2 3 4 5 6 7 8 12 11 10 09

Dedicated to J. Scott Harr, 1955–2008

Scott Harr, our dear friend and colleague for nearly two decades, died unexpectedly in the fall of 2008 as this text was nearing completion. In addition to being an associate professor and chair of the Criminal Justice Department at Concordia University–St. Paul, Scott was uniquely qualified as the lead author on this book, having experienced every facet of finding employment and building a career in criminal justice and related fields. He had been a social worker, emergency medical technician, firefighter, police officer, school liaison officer, attorney, private investigator, emergency management director, and chief of police. Although deeply devoted to the law and to teaching, mentoring, and writing, his deepest passion was his family—wife Diane, daughter Kelsey, and son Ricky. We will truly miss his warm smile, his honesty, his sense of humor, his work ethic, and his joy for living.

The verse Scott had chosen to post at the top of his Concordia home page aptly sums up the high esteem in which he held the role of peace officers and those who seek this calling in life: "Blessed are the peacemakers for they shall be called the children of God." —Matthew 5:9

BRIEF CONTENTS

CONTENTS

FIGURES

TABLES

INSIDER'S VIEWS

INTRODUCING THE CENGAGE LEARNING
CRIMINAL JUSTICE ADVISORY BOARD

The entire Criminal Justice team at Cengage Learning wishes to express its sincere gratitude to the hardworking members of our Criminal Justice Advisory Board. This group of skilled, experienced instructors comes together once a year to further their driving mission, which can be summed up as follows:

> This collaborative group of publishing professionals and instructors from traditional and non-traditional educational institutions is designed to foster development of exceptional educational and career opportunities in the field of criminal justice by providing direction and assistance to the faculty and administrators charged with training tomorrow's criminal justice professionals. The Advisory Board offers Peer support and advice, consults from both the academic and publishing communities, and serves as a forum for creating and evolving "best practices" in the building of successful criminal justice programs.

The members of our Advisory Board have the wisdom, expertise, and vision to set goals that empower students, setting them up to capitalize on the field's tremendous growth and expanding job opportunities. According to the U.S. Bureau of Labor Statistics, employment for correctional officers, law enforcement officers, investigators, and security officers is projected to increase at a rate of 9–26% over the next eight years. Add to that the growing number of jobs available in other parts of the criminal justice system—case office, youth specialist, social services, and more—and one can begin to get a true sense of the vast employment opportunity in the field. Helping today's students unlock the door to exciting and secure futures is the ultimate goal of everyone associated with the Wadsworth/Cengage Learning Criminal Justice Advisory Board.

Included on the board are faculty and administrators from schools such as:

Brown College
Florida Metropolitan University
Globe University/Minnesota School of Business
Hesser College
John Jay College of Criminal Justice
Kaplan University
Keiser University
Rasmussen College
South University
Western Career College
Western Carolina University
Westwood College

Again, the Wadsworth/Cengage Criminal Justice Team would like to extend our personal and professional thanks for all that the Advisory Board has enabled us to accomplish over the past few years. We look forward to continuing our successful collaboration in the years ahead.

We are always looking to add like-minded instructors to the Advisory Board; if you would like to be considered for inclusion on the Board, please contact Michelle Williams *(michelle.williams@cengage.com)*.

FOREWORD

Abraham Lincoln once said, "Prepare yourself for the day opportunity presents itself, and you will be rewarded." The process of entering a career in criminal justice or private security usually consists of several steps to "prepare yourself."

Philosophical questions regarding your goals must be resolved by practical approaches. As an applicant, you will be seeking to reach one of your most important goals in life. Whatever the situation, success is more likely to be realized if you are prepared to present yourself in the best possible manner to a prospective employer. Different expectations are held by employers and future employees in a situation where there is the beginning of a career.

This book is a genuine contribution to the future of young Americans seeking employment in such careers as law enforcement, juvenile justice, corrections, or any of the numerous areas within the private security profession. J. Scott Harr and Kären M. Hess have been heralded by many as being the best in providing information, guidance, and direction to those seeking a career in the public or private sectors of the criminal justice system. The authors give applicants a realistic, factual approach in conveying to the reader "this is what it's all about."

The past and present dynamics of seeking employment projected into the future suggest great optimism for applicants who pursue careers and job hunting with a positive attitude. This book goes as far as our knowledge takes it today. It is the best resource for the 21st century and gives the aspirant an enlightened, positive approach to job seeking in these highly competitive fields.

Henry M. Wrobleski
Former Coordinator of Law Enforcement
Normandale Community College

PREFACE

Welcome to *Careers in Criminal Justice and Related Fields*, 6th edition. This book serves a dual purpose. First, it provides an in-depth look at the vast array of job opportunities in criminal justice and related fields. This book discusses career opportunities throughout the criminal justice system, including law enforcement and other first responders; the practice of law, courts, corrections; and related local, state, and federal agencies. It also discusses career opportunities within the private sector because private security, risk management, and other private sector work and law enforcement are complementary professions.

The second purpose is to teach the skills and strategies you can use to obtain the job that seems the best fit for you. Whether you are a college student or reading this book on your own, whether you are seeking your first job or are already employed but want to change jobs, or want to move up in your current position, this book has much to offer.

This book was written for individuals throughout the country and is, therefore, general. Each state has different laws you must be aware of, for example, laws regarding licensure requirements and use of polygraph testing. In addition, every employing agency will have its own requirements, for example, what areas in a background investigation will be of particular concern or what types of physical agility testing will be given. Searching for a job actually becomes a job in itself. The first step is to develop a personal job-hunting strategy. However, this job-hunt strategy should not control you—you should control it. A planned strategy will make the entire process more tolerable, successful, and even enjoyable.

ORGANIZATION OF THE TEXT

The first section of the text gives a general overview of the world of work (Chapter 1). This is followed by a discussion of career opportunities as first responders in law enforcement, public safety, and related fields, the most visible components of the criminal justice system (Chapter 2); opportunities in courts and corrections (Chapter 3); opportunities in private security (Chapter 4); and factors to consider when selecting a career (Chapter 5). This section concludes with a look at internships and how to test the waters (Chapter 6).

The second section focuses on preparing for the job search, including physical fitness and testing (Chapter 7), other tests that might be encountered (Chapter 8), desirable attributes to develop and present (Chapter 9), and the résumé (Chapter 10). This section concludes with a critical component of being prepared—facing the risks of failure and building upon them should they occur (Chapter 11).

Section Three presents very specific job-seeking strategies to help you land your "dream job." These strategies are important during the application process (Chapter 12), when presenting yourself (Chapter 13), and during an interview (Chapter 14).

The fourth and final section discusses how you can succeed on the job once you get it, including making it through probation (Chapter 15) and enhancing your chances for promotion (Chapter 16). The final chapter addresses job loss and change and how you move through such setbacks (Chapter 17).

MAJOR FEATURES AND BENEFITS

Each chapter begins with a series of thought-provoking questions for you to think about to prepare yourself for getting the most out of each chapter. Possible answers to these questions are highlighted within the chapter, which can be used to compare your thought with those of other authorities and the authors.

Throughout the book you will be asked to become actively engaged with the topic being discussed, to write down your ideas and plans. Such instances will be indicated like this:

 You are also strongly encouraged to keep a journal for this purpose. The more you interact with the ontent in this book, the more you will get out of it and the more effective your job-search strategy is likely to be.

Each chapter has relevant *Insider's Views*—brief, personal essays written by individuals in the field. The *Insider's Views* are based on experience and give a variety of perspectives on what is or might be important in seeking a career in law enforcement, corrections, private security, or related fields in criminal justice, as well as learning how others have succeeded. The idea for these personal contributions resulted from the enthusiastic reception of speakers sharing similar ideas at our job-seeking seminars. Most job seekers never get a chance to find out what really goes on in the minds of those doing the hiring. The *Insider's Views* fill this void. Repetition occurs within these personal essays. Although the individuals were asked to write about their experience with the topic of the chapter, many felt compelled to add information and advice about other areas as well. As areas are repeated, you will come to realize the critical aspects of the job-seeking process. Every contributor talks about them. You may also find some contradictions with what is said in the text. Use your own judgment as to whose advice you feel suits *you* best. Often no "right" answer exists.

Each chapter concludes with a series of *Mind Stretches* to get you thinking about the topic as it relates to your particular interests and talents. Again, to get the most out of this book, *do* take time to work through these Mind Stretches, either mentally or in your journal.

Let your first reading be only the beginning. As you get into your job search, use the book as a reference. Also, libraries and bookstores have a tremendous amount of information on the many important aspects of job seeking. Keep practicing your skills such as working up great responses to those "most commonly asked" interview questions. Look at interviews that do not result in a job as opportunities to practice your interviewing skills. Continue to role-play interviews whenever you get the chance.

Experts say that most people will have between *five* and *twenty* careers—not just jobs, *careers*—during a lifetime. The job-hunting process is, indeed, never-ending, so become skilled at it.

NEW TO THIS EDITION

Each chapter has been streamlined and updated with the latest references available. Based on feedback from students, instructors, and reviewers several new topics have been added.

➤   *Chapter 1 Employment Trends: The World of Work*—Added a discussion on the importance of education.

➤   *Chapter 2 First Responders: Careers in Law Enforcement, Public Safety, and Related Fields*—Added a new section on emergency management as well as on disqualifications and updated all Occupational Outlook Handbook (OOH) information.

➤ *Chapter 3 Careers in the Courts, Corrections, and Related Fields*—Updated all *OOH* material; included a new section on the benefits of licensure, certifications, and education; and added potential disqualifiers.

➤ *Chapter 4 Careers in Private Security*—*OOH* updates throughout, added disqualifiers, expanded discussion of privatized corrections and public/private partnerships leading to potential career opportunities, added bodyguards, and executive protection as employment options.

➤ *Chapter 5 On Choosing a Career: Knowing the Job and Yourself*—New contribution by David Axt and added a flow diagram of the decision-making process in selecting a career path.

➤ *Chapter 6 Internships: Testing the Waters*—Clarified paid vs. for-credit internships, expanded where to look for internships using the Internet and resource books that list hundreds of thousands of possibilities, reinforced importance of presenting oneself at every stage of the process, added new "dos and don'ts" for interns, and added a trilogy of *Insider's View*s on internships.

➤ *Chapter 7 Physical Fitness and Testing*—Added Illinois Law Enforcement Training and Standards Board physical fitness standards as an example, updated U.S. Marshals fitness standards, updated ways of maintaining fitness, and expanded application beyond so as to apply to other areas of criminal justice and related fields.

➤ *Chapter 8 Other Forms of Testing*—Added information by Diane Harr, PhD, on testing, added Minnesota POST Learning Objectives to reflect the professional development expectations of applicants, added a discussion on preparing for the application process by meeting with business owners and citizens, and added a new section on employment personality tests.

➤ *Chapter 9 Attributes of Successful Candidates*—Added information on the importance of college and online courses, expanded computer and writing skills section, and the discussion of ethics.

➤ *Chapter 10 The Resume: Selling Yourself on Paper*—Addressed e-communication and "netiquette," added a discussion on the length of résumés, and expanded the discussion of following up and thank-yous.

➤ *Chapter 11 Preparing for Not Getting the Job*—Emphasized importance of staying positive and added a discussion of strategies for maintaining finances during the job search.

➤ *Chapter 12 The Application Process: Finding and for Jobs*—Expanded the discussion of e-communication, added a new section discussing practical and safety issues pertaining to online ads, and expanded the networking and personal inquiries sections.

➤ *Chapter 13 Your Job-Seeking Uniform: Presenting Yourself as the One to Hire*—Updated the primacy effect, emphasized the "dos and don'ts," and added a discussion on getting feedback on how one appears.

➤ *Chapter 14 The Interview: A Closer Look*—Emphasized looking at the interview from the employer's perspective, added an explanation of "behavioral" interviews, and added a new section on the dangers of accepting a position without being sure it's the right one for you.

➤ *Chapter 15 At Last, You've Got the Job—Congratulations!*—Added a discussion on "paying your dues"; added information on generational issues; and included two additions from a new 2008 resource, *Police Recruit Magazine*.

➤ *Chapter 16 The Career Ladder: Insights into Promotion and Job Change*—Expanded on the benefits of preparing for more than a single promotional opportunity to capitalize on unexpected opportunities that may present themselves and reemphasized the benefits of college for those seeking promotion. Greatly expanded the discussion of assessment centers and added a new graphic: The "10 C's" of promotability; and included information obtained from experts specifically for this chapter, including Jim Ollhoff, PhD, Susan Stanek, PhD, and Sgt. Ron Neirenhausen.

➤ *Chapter 17 Job Loss and Change: The Road Less Traveled*—Emphasized the importance of dealing with feelings, especially for a group of traditional "less emotional" types, and added a discussion on not making things worse.

We wish you the best of luck in your job search. Here's to developing the skills and a strategy that will get you the job you really want.

J. Scott Harr
Kären M. Hess
Christine Hess Orthmann

ACKNOWLEDGMENTS

We wish to personally express appreciation to the criminal justice, security, and other professionals who have contributed to this book, which is richer because of their personal sharing:

Russell M. Anderson, Field Supervisor and Investigator, Wisconsin Alliance for Fair Contracting

Richard D. Beckman, Sergeant, Cloverdale (California) Police Department

Brian Beniek, Officer, Plymouth (Minnesota) Police Department

Jack R. Cahall, Past Chair, Crime Abatement Committee, New Orleans, Louisiana

Jim Chaffee, Director of Security, Walt Disney Pictures and Television

Jim Clark, Chief, Eden Prairie (Minnesota) Police Department

Dennis L. Conroy, PhD, Sergeant and Director of the Employee Assistance Program, St. Paul (Minnesota) Police Department

John H. Driggs, Licensed Clinical Social Worker, St. Paul, Minnesota

Timothy E. Erickson, Assistant Professor, Metropolitan State University

Lawrence J. Fennelly, Sergeant and Crime Prevention Specialist, Harvard University Police Department

Joe Guy, Officer, Roseville (Minnesota) Police Department

Marsh J. Halberg, Attorney, Halberg Defense, Edina, Minnesota

Sheldon T. Hess, MD, General Internist, Health Partners

Robert B. Iannone, CPP, President, Iannone Security Management, Inc.

Gil Kerlikowske, Police Commissioner, Buffalo (New York) Police Department

Molly Koivamaki, Emergency Management Coordination, Eden Prairie (Minnesota) Police Department

John Lombardi, Professor of Criminal Justice and Criminology, Albany State College

John J. Maas, Deputy Chief, U.S. Probation/Pretrial Services Officer, South Dakota

Brenda P. Maples, Lieutenant, Memphis (Tennessee) Police Department

Robert Meyerson, Trooper I, Minnesota State Patrol

Linda S. Miller, former Sergeant, Bloomington Police Department and Executive Director, Upper Midwest Community Policing Institute

Ron Nierenhausen, Sergeant, Elk River (Minnesota) Police Department

Richard J. Obershaw, Grief Center, Burnsville, Minnesota

Marie Ohman, Executive Director, Minnesota Board of Private Investigators and Protective Agents

Penny A. Parrish, Public Information Officer, Minneapolis (Minnesota) Police Department; Parrish Institute of Law Enforcement and Media

Richard W. Stanek, Sergeant, Minneapolis (Minnesota) Police Department

Michael P. Stein, Chief, Escondido (California) Police Department

Albert J. Sweeney, Captain Commanding, Training and Education Division, Boston (Massachusetts) Police Department

Timothy J. Thompson, Director of Safety and Security, University of St. Thomas

Kenneth S. Trump, Assistant Director, Tri-City Task Force Comprehensive Gang Initiative; Director of Safety and Security, Parma (Ohio) City School District; National School Safety Consultant

Luis Velez, Captain, Colorado Springs (Colorado) Police Department

Henry Wrobleski, Former Coordinator, Law Enforcement Department, Normandale Community College

Monte D. Zillinger, Special Agent in Charge, Burlington Northern Railroad

Thanks also to the three internship contributors for Chapter 6: Sgt. Darren Juntunen, currently with the Minnesota State Patrol; Officer Jason Weber, currently with the Owatonna (Minnesota) Police Department; and Eric Clinton, a senior majoring in criminal justice at Concordia University St. Paul.

We also wish to thank the reviewers of this text and its various editions for their helpful comments and suggestions: Frank P. Alberico, Joliet Junior College; Tim Apolito, University of Dayton; DeWhitt Bingham, Heartland Community College; Jerald C. Burns, Alabama State University; Robert H. Burrington, Georgia Police Academy; Dean J. Champion, Minot State College; Paul V. Clark, Community College of Philadelphia; Dana C. DeWitt, Chadron State College; Marge Faulstich, West Valley College; William J. Halliday, Brookdale Community College; Debbie Hansen, Oregon Youth Authority; William E. Harver, Widener University; Robert Ives, Rock Valley College; Vivian Lord, University of North Carolina—Charlotte; Joseph Macy, Palm Beach Community College; Charles E. Myers; Aims Community College; James E. Newman, Rio Honda College; Daniel W. Nolan, Gateway Technical College, Kenosha; John M. Paitakes, Seton Hall University; Carroll S. Price, Penn Valley Community College; Heidi Samuels, Mountain State University; Dave Sexton, Clatsop Community College; Gregory B. Talley, Broome Community College; Joy Thompson, University of Wyoming; and Rosalie Young, State University of New York at Oswego.

We wish to acknowledge Christine Hess Orthmann for her research; writing; and careful, accurate manuscript preparation; Dr. Diane Harr for her assistance reviewing the initial manuscript; Abigail Greshik, our production manager at Pre-PressPMG.; and Carolyn Henderson Meier, our editor at Wadsworth/Cengage Learning for her encouragement and assistance.

Both authors would like to thank Henry Wrobleski for his influence on both of their careers and professional endeavors. Henry was the kind of friend, colleague, and mentor whom everyone should experience, and the kind we should strive to be to others.

Scott would like to acknowledge the following colleagues from Concordia University St. Paul: President Robert Holst, Vice President Robert DeWerff, Dean Bruce Corrie, and Associate Dean Craig Lien. Thank you also to Richard and Marie Lacy and Reed S. Harr. Scott would also like to acknowledge the support of his wife, Diane, and children, Kelsey and Ricky, with whom he has always shared his dreams. They provide more support than they realize, and their continued interest in these projects and patience throughout help make them happen. Their smiles, laughter, and demands that he put the work down and listen to a new flute piece or new juggling routine helps keep priorities in check.

Kären would like to acknowledge the support of her husband, Sheldon, and children, Christine and Timothy.

Without the patience and encouragement of our families, efforts such as this text could never come to be.

ABOUT THE AUTHORS

The authors of this book are committed to the advancement of the professionalism of criminal justice and related fields. Both Scott and Kären have been teaching college-level law enforcement classes for many years and have a number of other criminal justice–related texts on the national market. Their joint publications with Wadsworth include *Criminal Procedure* and *Constitutional Law for the Criminal Justice Professional*, 4th edition.

Scott was employed in various areas of the law for his entire working life. He had been a social worker and a youth worker. For over 11 years he served as the chief law enforcement officer and public safety director for a suburb of the Twin Cities and served as a police officer for two other cities before that. In addition, Scott served as a firefighter, emergency medical technician, and emergency management director. He was licensed as a lawyer, police officer, and private investigator, and founded Scott Harr Legal Investigations in 1985. Having taught as community faculty at Normandale Community College, and served as resident faculty at Metropolitan State University School of Law Enforcement and Criminal Justice, he was, at the time of the writing of this edition, the Criminal Justice Chair at Concordia University St. Paul (Minnesota). He sat by governor's appointment on the Minnesota Peace and Police Officer Standards and Training Board (POST) and chaired the POST Training Committee. He also served on the Anoka/Champlin Fire Board.

Kären is the executive director of Information Age Communications, Inc., and president of the Institute for Professional Development. She holds a PhD in English and a second PhD in criminal justice. Kären conducts in-house workshops on writing effective reports and has also published extensively. Wadsworth publications include *Community Policing: Partnerships for Problem Solving* (4th edition), *Criminal Investigation* (8th edition), *Criminal Procedure, Introduction to Law Enforcement and Criminal Justice* (9th edition), *Juvenile Justice* (4th edition), *Management and Supervision in Law Enforcement* (4th edition), *Police Operations* (4th edition), and *Private Security* (5th edition).

She is a member of the Academy of Criminal Justice Sciences (ACJS), the American Correctional Association (ACA), the International Association of Chiefs of Police (IACP), and the Police Executive Research Forum. In addition she is a fellow in the Textbook and Academic Authors' Association (TAA) and is a member of its Foundation Board of Directors.

SECTION ONE

THE CHALLENGE

There are two things to aim at in life;
first, to get what you want; and,
after that, to enjoy it.
Only the wisest . . . achieve the second.

—_Langdon Smith_

Nothing great was ever achieved without enthusiasm.

—_Ralph Waldo Emerson_

Before beginning your job search, you should fully understand what you are getting into. Work is so vitally important that choosing a career deserves far more effort than many people can give. By taking an educated look at the actual world of work, you begin a _realistic_ job search. You've probably read startling statistics about the rate of change facing employees and the job market. These dramatic changes are directly affecting, and will continue to affect, the service sector, including employment in criminal justice and private security services. Chapter 1 addresses how these changes have affected the job market and what the career you're seeking might look like in the 21st century.

Chapter 2 discusses careers in law enforcement—the most visible and familiar component of the criminal justice system—and other first responder positions, examining where employment opportunities exist on the federal, state, county, and local levels. Chapter 3 looks at careers in the courts and corrections. The field of corrections is rapidly expanding due to a growing intolerance of repeat offenders, the "three strikes and you're out" approach, and the mandatory serving of sentences. Included in this chapter is information on careers in probation and parole.

Chapter 4 explores careers in the private sector. Privatization is a continuing trend, with private security growing much faster than any segment of the criminal justice system. Numerous career opportunities are found in the private security profession, including not only the familiar security officer but alarm services, armed courier services, executive protection services, private corrections, and the like. Chapter 5 examines the steps for choosing a career and what factors to consider. It helps you look at the entrance requirements in light of your background, experience, and personal likes and dislikes. Finally, Chapter 6 explores the topic of internships and the benefits that come from trying out the job before investing yourself 100 percent in the pursuit of a particular career.

If, after reading this section, you are convinced that a career in criminal justice, private security, or a related field is for you, read on. The rest of the book provides strategies and techniques to help you get the job. These fields are demanding, as is the road to employment.

You have made an important decision by taking this step to develop your job-search strategies. Let's get started!

CHAPTER 1

EMPLOYMENT TRENDS: THE WORLD OF WORK

Most of our adult lives are spent working. Taking into account commuting time, overtime, thinking about our jobs, and worrying over work, we spend more of our waking hours in the office, at the factory, on the road, behind the desk, than we do at home.

—The Joy of Working, p. ix

Do You Know:

➢ What the hierarchy of needs is?
➢ What role work has in meeting our needs?
➢ How many job and career changes the average person will make in a lifetime?
➢ How our labor force is changing in terms of age, race, and gender?
➢ Why it is crucial to keep current with technology?
➢ What factor education will play in future work?
➢ What job areas will expand?
➢ What the projections look like for jobs in criminal justice and security?

INTRODUCTION

Work. For most of us, work is a large part of who we are, occupying a vast amount of our time and, to a great degree, shaping how we view ourselves. The fact that you have invested your time, energy, and money into working with this book says it is important to you, too.

This chapter examines why work is so important to people, what needs it fulfills, and how these needs may change. It then presents a brief history of how work has evolved to its present state and some of the massive changes that have occurred, including the impact of technology. This is followed by a look at the changing job market and jobs of the future, including the need for more education as well as growth trends in the service sector. This chapter concludes with a discussion on keeping up-to-date on the job market and employment trends.

THE IMPORTANCE OF WORK

Working *is* important because it provides you with income, but work is so much more than just a paycheck. Work helps form your identity, and it makes a statement about who you are. Well-known psychologist Abraham H. Maslow developed a hierarchy of needs, which ranges from the most basic physical needs to the most complex self-actualization needs (Figure 1–1). Once people's needs are

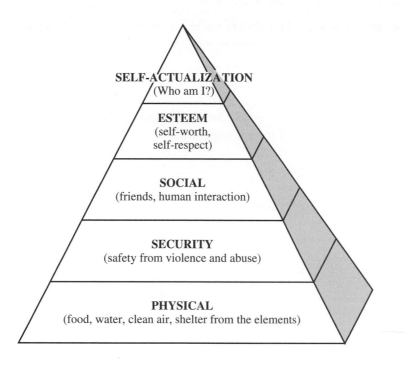

FIGURE 1–1 Maslow's Hierarchy of Needs

satisfied at the lowest level, they are able to move up the hierarchy to the next level. According to this rather simplistic hierarchy, work meets *all* five levels.

> According to Maslow's simplified hierarchy of needs, physical needs are the most basic of human needs and self-actualization needs are the most complex. Security, social, and esteem needs fall in between.

These needs and their job-related counterparts in a *satisfying* job are often as follows:

➤ Physical: Good working conditions, rest periods, labor-saving equipment, sufficient income, heating/air-conditioning

➤ Safety: Safe working conditions, good supervision, job security, training in survival

➤ Social: Feeling of belonging to a "job family," agency/department/organization spirit, after-hours get-togethers, picnics, softball games

➤ Esteem: Challenging job, promotions, titles, community recognition, awards

➤ Self-Actualization: Opportunity for growth and development, discretion/decision-making authority, contributing to society/organization

> Work has the potential to meet all five levels of human needs; however, only truly *satisfying* jobs will actually fulfill every level.

Think for a few minutes about what's important to *you* in the career you select. Which level(s) of need will influence you the most? Jot down your responses in your journal.

WHAT'S IMPORTANT ON THE JOB

What's important to you as you consider your career? Several factors are listed below. Rank them yourself, using 1 for most important and 17 for least important.

_____ Amount of feedback given about your job performance

_____ Amount of freedom you have on your job

_____ Amount of pay

_____ Amount of fringe benefits

_____ Amount of job security

_____ Amount of praise you get for a job well done

_____ Chance for getting a promotion

_____ Chance for taking part in making decisions

_____ Chance to accomplish something worthwhile

_____ Chance to do something that makes you feel good about yourself

_____ Chance to do things you do best

_____ Chance to learn new things

_____ Friendliness of people you work with

_____ How you are treated by your supervisor

_____ Opportunities to develop your skills and abilities

_____ Resources available to do your job

_____ Respect you receive from people you work with

Think carefully about your top rankings and how well they would be met in your chosen field. Again, record your thoughts in your journal.

Work satisfies so many human needs that those who find themselves without meaningful employment usually experience a sense of loss. If your work is unfulfilling, your needs must be met elsewhere or anxiety, frustration, or even depression may result. If you are suddenly unemployed, as in the case of an unexpected layoff, your lifestyle may become seriously disrupted. Losing a job and being unable to find other work has driven some to such self-destructive behaviors as alcoholism, other substance abuse, and even suicide. Truly, work is important as something positive to meet your needs—not only your financial needs, but also your identity and self-esteem needs.

For these reasons it is important to give careful thought to what work you pursue. This book will help you decide what you want to do with your working life. You will have a chance to look at what is important to you and what you have to offer employers. Many people spend more time planning their next vacation than they do planning what they're going to do for the rest of their lives. To do so is risky.

A brief look at the evolution of work in the United States is revealing.

A BRIEF HISTORY

You may be familiar with Toffler's "three waves" theory, which compares ocean waves to the three sweeping changes in society:

➤ The Agricultural Revolution

➤ The Industrial Revolution

➤ The Technological Revolution

The first wave, the Agricultural Revolution, occurred about 8000 B.C., sweeping aside 45,000 years of cave dwelling. The second wave, the Industrial Revolution, came around 1760, turning our landscape from "amber waves of grain" into smokestacks. This second wave was not without its resistors. A group of workers, called Luddites, systematically destroyed machinery they saw as a threat to manual laborers. But the wave engulfed America, forcing many farmers into factories as blue-collar workers in the new era of industrialization.

A decade ago, Pulley (1997, pp. 15–16) noted that the Industrial Revolution affected more than just how and where people worked—it changed the way people identified with each other and viewed themselves. Whereas the Agricultural Age saw family members working in the fields together, the Industrial Age separated families, sending its members, young and old, into the factories to labor as nameless "cogs" in the massive machine: "As people spent more time in the factory than with the family, the importance of work grew. Increasingly it became the principal source of people's identity. . . . The workplace became the main organizing feature of our life and the source of our identity, status, income, and affiliations. And by the 20th century, identity became specifically tied to *organizations*."

Over time, these organizations became increasingly "paternalistic," taking care of their employees by providing benefits such as health care insurance and retirement pensions as well as rewards for company loyalty, such as bonuses, watches, plaques, and dinners. Pulley (p. 16) contends: "Out of this grew the implicit and pervasive understanding between workers and organizations that is now coming apart at the seams—the belief that hard work and loyalty will be exchanged for promotions and job security."

Gradually, the dominance of factories and industrialized business ebbed and a new era was born—the "information age." This third wave, the Technological Revolution, began in the mid-1950s and again changed the face of the American workplace. Brains rather than brawn became important, and white-collar workers began displacing blue-collar workers. Again, resistance occurred. As the Luddites had done before them, many people rebelled against computers, fax machines, voice mail, iPhones, web cams, and the like. But the third wave *is* here.

OUR CHANGING WORK WORLD

One result of this third wave has been the virtual end to the one-company career path so common in previous generations. No longer does the American workforce toil under the assumption that hard work and loyalty will be rewarded with job security. Those who do find themselves shocked and unprepared for the hard truths of today's employment trends.

The Bureau of Labor Statistics (BLS), under the U.S. Department of Labor, is a valuable resource for anyone keeping tabs on the changing face of the American workforce. The BLS is the principal fact-finding agency for the federal government in the labor economics and statistics, and data regarding employment in the United States is accessible through the BLS website at www.bls.gov. The *Occupational Outlook Handbook,* referred to from this point on as the *OOH*, is a biannual publication prepared by the BLS, available online at www.bls.gov/oco, that provides career information to individuals making decisions about their future work lives, including descriptions of what workers do on the job, working conditions, training and educational requirements, earnings, and anticipated job prospects in a wide range of occupations.

Many statisticians are cautiously optimistic about the future for employment: "During the most recent decade-long economic expansion, the civilian unemployment rate fell from 7.5 percent in 1992 to 4.0 percent in

2000, the lowest reading in 30 years" (Su, 2007, p. 29). With the baby boomer generation poised to retire, in addition to various other national and international factors, the Bureau of Labor Statistics predicts an increase of 0.8 percent in the civilian work force between 2006 and 2016 (Su, p. 29). This trend appears to hold for younger generations as well. Nonfarm payroll employment is projected to grow at an annualized rate of 1.0 percent between 2006 and 2016, rising from 136.2 million to 151.1 million, an increase of 14.9 million jobs.

However, with job turnovers continuing and news of mass layoffs perpetually present in the media, the future can seem discouraging. Hall (2008, p. D1) reports: "A 52-month streak of job creation ended in January [2008] with the loss of 17,000 jobs. People are taking longer to find work, and long-term jobless are a great share of the unemployed." Economic setbacks that may have influenced employment include the September 11, 2001, terrorist attacks on America, corporate accounting scandals, and the war in Iraq. Hall (p. D2) suggests: "Like much in economics, labor statistics are vexing because they can be seen as a glass half empty or half full."

And for those who continue to seek employment, change may inevitably follow. Job change is not necessarily bad. In fact, it has become the norm and is all the more reason to develop a strong job search strategy. According to a BLS news release, the average person born in the later years of the baby boom held ten jobs from age 18 to 38. More than two-thirds were held in the first half of the period, from ages 18 to 27.

> Statistics indicate the average person is likely to make more than ten job changes and five career changes in a lifetime.

Demographic Trends

The workforce will increase by 12.8 million, or 8.5 percent, to 164.2 million between 2006 and 2016 (*OOH*). "As the U.S. population ages, the labor force will grow more slowly during the next decade; the older labor force is projected to grow more than five times faster than the overall labor force, which will become ever more racially and ethnically diverse" (Toossi, 2007, p. 33).

According to the *OOH*, the baby boomers (ages 55 to 64) will increase by 30.3 percent, or 9.5 million. Those ages 35 to 44 will decrease by 5.5 percent; those 16 to 24 will decrease by 1.1 percent. It is predicted that in 2016 the workforce will consist of 12.7 percent in the 16 to 24 age group, 64.6 percent in the 26 to 54 age group, and 22.7 percent in the 55 and older age group.

An important trend affecting employment is the growing proportion of minorities and immigrants. This increasingly diverse population has not only required an expanded range of goods and services, but it also has produced corresponding changes in the size and demographic composition of the labor force. According to the *OOH*, White, non-Hispanic persons will continue to make up a decreasing share of the labor force, falling from 69.1 percent in 2002 to 64.4 percent in 2016, yet remaining the majority of employees. Hispanics, the fastest-growing segment of the workforce, are projected to account for an increasing share of the labor force from 13.7 percent to 16.4 percent, making up 29.9 percent of the workforce. The percent of Asians has increased from 4.4 percent to 5.3 percent, and the Black percentage has grown from 11.4 percent to 12.3 percent.

> The labor force in America is undergoing many changes, including an increasing percentage of older people, minorities and immigrants, and women.

Important demographic changes have also resulted from shifts in basic societal values, norms, and conditions. For example, before the Technological Revolution, American families were generally categorized as warm, secure units with both parents living at home with their children. However, as the twentieth century progressed, divorce rates soared and an increasing number of families became categorized as blended or single-parent families. The disintegration of the "traditional" family and weakening of family values have been credited with contributing to numerous social ills, including crime, increased drug use, and a diminished sense of connection with and responsibility to the community and society in general. Another trend observed throughout the twentieth century was the declining view of childhood as a carefree time and an increasing rate of children committing violent crimes and being victimized.

Vital Skills for Job Seekers at Any Level

Basic skills are required by employers at every level. The successful job seeker has more than these basic skills. The more marketable skills, abilities, and experiences that set an applicant apart from the rest, the better the likelihood of getting hired. This includes education, training, special talents or knowledge, community service, and past job experience.

As discussed, the U.S. population in general is becoming increasingly diverse, with language barriers presenting a formidable challenge in many professions, particularly those geared toward public service. Many employers now actively seek applicants who speak more than one language. Other expected or necessary skills result directly from continuing technological advances, which are occurring so rapidly it can be difficult to keep up with the changes. For example, basic computer experience is now merely the starting point, with advanced skills reflecting a person's willingness to learn and ability to adapt. Computer skills should be continuously improved. Forsgren (2004) asserts that it is no longer enough to know answers: "Educated people are those who have the information literacy skills to know how and where to seek answers using technology and how to present their findings at an expected professional level." Job applicants of today and the future need more than just the keyboarding skills required in the past.

> Technology is a powerful, rapidly changing force in today's working world. To stay competitive and ensure your value in the workforce, you must keep current with technology.

Formerly, basic skills or a basic education such as a high school diploma was sufficient for acceptable employment. As economic, political, social, and technological factors affect an increasingly complex world of work, the basics restrict a person's hiring, and advancement, more than ever. According to the BLS: "Millions of job openings are projected for high school graduates over the 2004–14 decade . . . . But jobseekers will probably need training beyond a high school diploma, particularly if they want a job with high pay. That training could include taking a few college courses, getting an associate degree, training on the job in an apprenticeship program, or taking vocational classes at a technical school" ("The 2004 to 2014 Job Outlook," 2006).

A Need for More Education

New service industry jobs will require enhanced skills and proficiencies, and many will demand successful applicants to possess college degrees and other certifications. According to the *OOH:* "Education is essential in getting a high-paying job. In fact, for all but 1 of the 50 highest paying occupations, a college degree or higher is the most significant source of education or training."

The BLS states: "Education is an important determinant of labor market outcomes. The more education a person has, the more likely he or she is to be in the labor force and the less likely he or she is to be unemployed. The proportion of persons 25 to 64 years old with some college (or an associate degree) more than doubled between 1970 and 2006. The share with a bachelor's degree and higher also more than doubled over the period. In contrast, the share of the labor force with less than a high school diploma declined markedly" (*Charting the U.S. Labor Market in 2006*). As statistics show: "The higher the education level, the lower the unemployment rate" (*Charting the U.S. Labor Market in 2006*).

A person's capacity to earn more can be directly related to their level of education: "Average annual earnings of individuals with a bachelor's degree are more than 75 percent higher than the earnings of high school graduates. These additional earnings sum to over $1 million over a lifetime" (Hill et al., 2005).

It is projected that more than half of the new jobs created over the next decade will require an educational level beyond high school. Criminal justice and security agencies nationwide are also raising applicants' educational requirements. To stay competitive, you must seek higher education.

According to *Occupational Outlook Quarterly* online: "Bright prospects are expected to continue for college graduates, especially for those who prepare for careers with lots of job openings. Data consistently show that, on average, college graduates earn more money, experience less unemployment, and have a wider variety of career options than other workers do." The importance of education is discussed more fully in Chapters 8 and 9.

A LOOK AT JOBS OF THE FUTURE—WHERE WILL YOU FIT IN?

In the twenty-first century, interest has heightened in looking ahead at what our world of work might be like. Certain trends, some already discussed, are pointed out repeatedly:

➢   The labor force will continue to grow.

➢   Women and minorities will account for a greater share of the workforce.

➢   Blue-collar jobs will decline slightly.

➢   Rapid growth will occur in jobs in the *service sector* (which includes criminal justice and security).

➢   More education will be needed for more jobs.

Growth in the Service Industries

The *OOH* (p.2) reports: "Total employment is expected to increase from 150.6 million in 2006 to 166.2 million in 2016, or by 10 percent. The 15.6 million jobs that will be added by 2016 will not be evenly distributed across major industrial and occupational groups. Changes in consumer demand, technology, and many other factors will contribute to the continually changing employment structure in the U.S. economy."

Between 2006 and 2016, government employment, not including employment in public education and hospitals, is expected to increase by 4.8 percent, from 10.8 million to 11.3 million jobs. Growth in government employment will be fueled by an increased demand for pubic safety, but dampened by budgetary constraints and outsourcing of government jobs to the private sector. State and local governments, excluding education and hospitals, are expected to grow by 7.7 percent as a result of the continued shift of responsibilities from the federal government to state and local governments. Federal government employment, including the postal service, is expected to decrease by 3.8 percent. Figure 1–2 illustrates the projected percent change in total employment by major occupational group from 2006 to 2016; Figure 1–3 depicts the projected number of jobs that will exist by 2016 in each major occupational group, created either through growth or replacement needs.

As these two figures show, many new jobs created in the next decade will be in the service industries, which include the protective services of law enforcement, corrections, firefighting, private investigation, and security. Protective services occupations are projected to increase 24.7 percent between 2002 and 2012, adding a total of 769,000 new jobs in this sector (Hecker, 2004, p. 88). In addition: "Half of the growth is projected for government, and nearly two-fifths is projected for rapidly growing investigation and security services" (Hecker, p. 99). The BLS's *Career Guide to Industries* (2004) reports: "The attacks of September 11, 2001, will increase demand for police, firefighters, and other emergency personnel; however, budgetary constraints may force spending cuts in other areas, slowing overall employment growth."

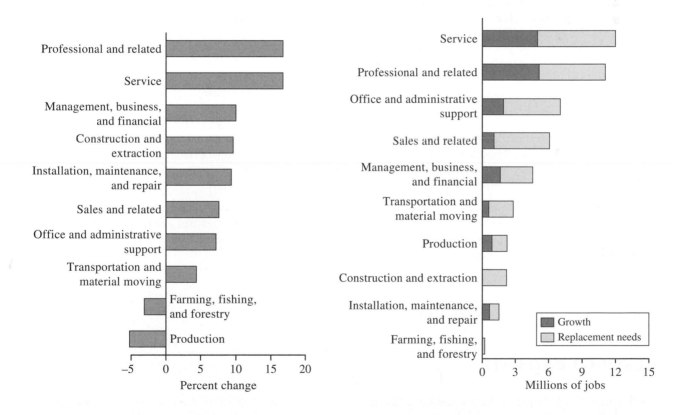

FIGURE 1–2   Percent Change in Total Employment by Major Occupational Group, Projected 2006–2016

SOURCE: *Occupational Outlook Handbook, 2008–09 Edition.* Washington, DC: Bureau of Labor Statistics, 2007. Online: www.bls.gov/oco/images/ocotjc06.jpg.

FIGURE 1–3   Number of Jobs Due to Growth and Replacement Needs by Major Occupational Group, Projected 2006–2016

SOURCE: *Occupational Outlook Handbook, 2008–09 Edition.* Washington, DC: Bureau of Labor Statistics, 2007. Online: www.bls.gov/oco/images/ocotjc10.jpg.

Farr and Shatkin's compilation of the *Best Jobs for the 21st Century* (2004, p. 124) analyzes a variety of job factors, such as annual earnings, percent job growth, and annual openings, and lists the following as the "Best Jobs for People Interested in Law, Law Enforcement and Public Safety":

> Lawyers; correctional officers and jailers; paralegals and legal assistants; security guards; highway patrol pilots; police and sheriff's patrol officers; police patrol officers; sheriffs and deputy sheriffs; nuclear monitoring technicians; emergency medical technicians and paramedics; first-line supervisors/managers of correctional officers; private detectives and investigators; first-line supervisors/managers of police and detectives; forest fire fighting and prevention supervisors; municipal fire fighting and prevention supervisors; child support, missing persons, and unemployment insurance fraud investigators; criminal investigators and special agents; detectives and criminal investigators; immigration and customs inspectors; police detectives; police identification and records officers; and arbitrators, mediators, and conciliators.

> The employment outlook for police detectives is expected to increase faster than average for all other occupations through 2008. U.S. Department of Labor estimates call for an increase of approximately 90,000 detectives, but this number also includes police officers and special agents. . . . An area of particular growth is the investigation of the various forms of computer fraud.

Regarding corrections officers (p. 115):

> The prison population has more than doubled in the past 10 years, and this growth is expected to be sustained for the near future. The increasing number of prisoners means there will be a strong need for new corrections officers. Employment in this field is expected to increase much faster than the average for all jobs. . . . The ongoing war on drugs, new tough-on-crime legislation, and increasing mandatory sentencing policies will create a need for more prison beds and more corrections officers.

The employment outlook is equally positive for security consultants and technicians (pp. 331–332):

> Employment for guards and other security personnel is expected to increase faster than the average through 2008, as crime rates rise with the overall population growth. The highest U.S. Department of Labor estimates call for more than 1.25 million guards to be employed by 2008. . . . A factor adding to this demand is the trend for private security firms to perform duties previously handled by police officers, such as courtroom security and crowd control in airports.

Trends in the changing workforce show service-producing industries, including criminal justice and security, will account for much of all job growth. Furthermore, protective services will remain one of the fastest-growing industries throughout the next decade.

Occupational Outlook Quarterly (Fall 2006, p. 36) asserts: "Workers who keep the public safe from crime, disasters and fire are projected to be in high demand."

KEEPING UP-TO-DATE

As discussed, savvy job seekers must have sharp information technology skills. Never overlook the power of the Internet to enhance your job- or promotion-seeking strategy. To this end, an excellent source for keeping current on jobs and employment trends is the *Occupational Outlook Handbook* (*OOH*), already mentioned and available online at www.bls.gov/oco/. Completely revised every two years by the U.S. Department of Labor, this resource covers more than 200 occupations and, for each career, describes work activities and environment; earnings; number of jobs and their location; and types of education, training, and personal qualifications needed to have the best prospects. BLS projections of employment to the year 2012 are used to assess what kind of job opportunities future entrants to each occupation should encounter. It also includes a list of sources of state and local job information. The *OOH* is available in paper, hard cover, and CD-ROM and can be purchased at any U.S. government bookstore or by calling the office of the Superintendent of Documents in Washington at (202) 783–3238.

BLS supplements to the *OOH* include the *Career Guide to Industries* and *Occupational Projections and Training Data*. The *Career Guide* covers forty-two diverse industries and highlights some occupations not covered in the *OOH*, discussing the nature of the work, job qualifications and advancement opportunities, job outlook, and earnings. *Occupational Projections and Training Data* provides the statistical data supporting the information presented in the *OOH*. Education and training planners, career counselors, and job seekers can compare more than 700 occupations on factors such as employment change, self-employed workers, earnings, and the most significant source of education or training. Users will also find awards and degree data by field of study.

You might also want to check with your local library, state agencies, and employment offices, as well as your state department of education, state job services agencies, and state labor departments.

CONCLUSION

The days of picking one career and sticking with it for forty years are over. Statistics show the average person is likely to make more than ten job changes and five career changes in a lifetime. Trends in the changing workforce show service-producing industries, including criminal justice and security, will account for most of the job growth. Furthermore, these services will remain one of the fastest-growing major industries during the next decade. It is also projected that more than half of the new jobs created over the next decade will require an educational level beyond high school. Criminal justice and security agencies nationwide are raising applicants' educational requirements. Therefore, to stay competitive, you must seek higher education and keep current with technology.

INTRODUCING THE INSIDERS' VIEWS

A supplement to this book is a collection of short articles written by men and women whose careers have intersected criminal justice and related fields. Each guest writer's contribution, called *An Insider's View*, presents a unique perspective about jobs in criminal justice or related fields and how to obtain them. The contributors' backgrounds and credentials are quite varied, including police officer, sergeant, captain, and chief; railroad police agent; probation/parole officer; private security manager; crime prevention specialist; gang task force member; director of safety for public schools; attorney; professor; medical doctor; and businessman. They also include perspectives from both sides of the interview table—those looking to be hired and those doing the hiring. Whichever angle a particular writer pursues, think about the important insights given from those "on the inside."

At the end of each chapter, you will find an *Insiders' View* with relevance to the topic(s) just covered. For this first chapter Timothy Erickson introduces you to the "World of Work" as it applies to criminal justice and security professionals.

WHAT YOU'LL NEED TO SUCCEED IN THE 21ST CENTURY

Timothy E. Erickson

Assistant Professor
Metropolitan State University

In the early 1900s August Vollmer, Chief of Police in Berkeley, California, had a vision that included a place for college-educated peace officers within law enforcement. Since the days of Vollmer, this vision has been revisited periodically through such events as the *Wickersham Report* of the 1930s and the *President's Commission on Law Enforcement and Administration of Justice* in the 1960s. In fact, the cry for college-educated peace officers has come from several quarters, but until rather recently, few real efforts have occurred to make this vision a reality.

During the 1970s the federal government spent substantial amounts of money in LEAA grants to help working peace officers attain postsecondary education. In 1977 Minnesota became the first state to require as a state standard, a minimum level of postsecondary education as an entry requirement for the peace officer position. In 1989 two separate proposals were introduced at the congressional level which would provide resources directed toward programs designed to provide college-level education for peace officers.

While these efforts are laudatory, the law enforcement profession has only been slowly nudged to the precipice. It is time for individual practitioners to take proactive steps to ensure this vision for themselves. In other words, peace officers need to "fish or cut bait."

The increasing complexity of the issues in our society—issues individual peace officers must address—has become an incredible burden. Rapid advances in theory, knowledge and technology, rapidly changing demographics, and newly developing and evolving social problems ranging from ecology to global political realities—all point toward the need for continual growth in peace officer education.

In addition, peace officers interact daily with other professionals in the criminal justice system, all of whom have at least one undergraduate degree. Most have graduate-level educational experiences. Add to this the fact that the educational level of all citizens is increasing dramatically (approximately 40 to 60 percent of current high-school graduates will go on to some form of postsecondary education experience), and it becomes clear that if peace officer education does not at least keep pace with these changes, individual officers will be "left in the dust."

All of the preceding information aside, individuals entering law enforcement professions owe it to themselves to aspire to higher educational levels and commit to lifelong learning. This is important for several reasons.

First, broadly based, postsecondary liberal arts education prepares individuals for a wide range of professional opportunities both within and outside the law enforcement profession. Recent research indicates that most adults will have the opportunity to make major career changes anywhere from three to six times during their life spans. It would be tragic if those choosing law enforcement as one of their careers were not in a position to have similar opportunities.

Second, although no scientific or empirical evidence indicates that increased education results in increased performance levels of peace officers, numerous recent perceptual studies report that citizens have more confidence in and esteem for more highly educated officers.

Third, law enforcement executives are constantly expressing the need for more officers who have:

➤   Well-developed verbal and written communication skills
➤   Excellent critical-thinking and decision-making skills
➤   Highly developed ethical and moral standards
➤   The ability to analyze complex public policy issues and social trends

Such attributes are developed in the broad-based, interdisciplinary liberal arts curriculum available through postsecondary educational experiences.

Finally, and perhaps most important, postsecondary education will prepare peace officers to grow personally. If allowed to, the law enforcement environment can become a narrow, isolated, cynical place, not unlike a prison. Postsecondary education, continuing education, commitment to lifelong learning and an appreciation for diversity can help peace officers keep the walls from closing in on them.

We in law enforcement do not have the luxury to wait for our agencies or our governments to provide education for us. We must recognize that education is as important to our "officer survival skills" as our firearms and other weapons training. Education does not need to be a state mandate or a department policy. It can be our individual choice, a gift to ourselves. No group of professionals is more deserving.

Timothy E. Erickson *is a returning professor at Metropolitan State University in Minnesota. He has been employed in the field of criminal justice for over thirty years, serving as a police officer, police sergeant, and sergeant investigator for the St. Paul (Minnesota) Police Department and as the chief of police for the Arizona Western College, Campus Police Department. He also served as the education coordinator for the Minnesota POST Board. Mr. Erickson is also a licensed secondary education teacher and holds both MAT (broad-area social science) and MSE (educational counseling) degrees.*

 MIND STRETCHES

1.   Imagine you have a crystal ball—what changes do you see in the world of work five years from now? Ten years from now? Fifty years from now?

2.   What role do you think education will play in the future?

3.   Do you think work will become more specialized or more generalized in the future? Why? How will your job goals be affected?

4.   What do you think will happen to current age limitations on jobs? Why?

5.   What jobs do you think will become more necessary in the future? Less necessary?

6.   Is your community changing? How? What about neighboring communities?

7.   Why do you think more people don't pursue advanced education or specialized training? Are these reasons legitimate?

8.   Recognizing that our entire society is always changing, what importance will you place on continuing to grow and change yourself?

9. Is always striving to improve yourself important to you? Is there a danger in not continuing to grow and change?

10. Can you think of jobs that do not now exist but will within the next 10 or 20 years?

REFERENCES

Career Guide to Industries, 2004–05 Edition. Washington, DC: U.S. Department of Labor, Bureau of Labor Statistics, 2004. Available online at www.bls.gov/oco/cg.

Charting the U.S. Labor Market in 2006. Washington, DC: U.S. Department of Labor, Bureau of Labor Statistics, August 2007. Available online at www.bls.gov/cps/labor2006/intro.pdf.

Farr, Michael, and Shatkin, Laurence. *Best Jobs for the 21st Century,* 3rd ed. Indianapolis: JIST Publishing, Inc., 2004.

Forsgren, Laurel. Concordia University Saint Paul (Minnesota). Personal interview, February 25, 2004.

Hall, Kevin G. "U.S. Workforce under the Worst Stress in Seven Years." *Star Tribune,* February 19, 2008, pp. D1–2.

Hecker, Daniel E. "Occupational Employment Projections to 2012." *Monthly Labor Review,* February 2004, pp. 80–105.

Hill, Kent, Hoffman, Dennis, and Rex, Tom R. *The Value of Higher Education: Individual and Societal Benefits (with Special Consideration for the State of Arizona).* Arizona State University, October 2005.

Occupational Outlook Handbook (OOH), 2008–09 Edition. Bureau of Labor Statistics, U.S. Department of Labor. Washington, DC: U.S. Government Printing Office, December 18, 2007. Available online at www.bls.gov/oco/.

Occupational Outlook Quarterly, Fall 2006. Available online at www.bls.gov/opub/ooq/2006/fall/art03.pdf.

Pulley, Mary Lynn. *Losing Your Job—Reclaiming Your Soul.* San Francisco: Jossey-Bass, 1997.

Su, Betty W. "The U.S. Economy to 2016: Slower Growth as Boomers Begin to Retire." *Monthly Labor Review,* November 2007, pp. 13–32.

Toossi, Mitra. "Labor Force Projections to 2016—More Workers in their Golden Years." *Monthly Labor Review,* November 2007, pp. 33–52.

"The 2004–14 Job Outlook for People Who Don't Have a Bachelor's Degree." *Occupational Outlook Quarterly*, Fall 2006. Updated February 15, 2007. Available online at www.bls.gov/opub/ooq/2006/fall/art02.htm.

CHAPTER 2

FIRST RESPONDERS: CAREERS IN LAW ENFORCEMENT, PUBLIC SAFETY, AND RELATED FIELDS

The opportunity for public service through law enforcement work is attractive to many because the job is challenging and involves much personal responsibility.
—*Occupational Outlook Handbook*

Do You Know:

➤ What percentage of time is spent on patrol or doing routine paperwork and how much time is actually taken up with chases and shoot-outs?

➤ What local agencies you might consider when seeking employment in law enforcement or a related field? County agencies? Tribal agencies? State agencies? Federal agencies?

➤ Where the greatest employment potential is usually found?

➤ How common promotions are in law enforcement?

➤ Why specialization within the law enforcement profession is important?

➤ How specialized training or expertise may benefit a law enforcement professional?

➤ How job prospects look for those interested in the field of juvenile justice?

➤ What the availability is of international jobs in law enforcement?

➤ What nonsworn civilian career options exist for those interested in law enforcement?

➤ What other careers are available to those interested in public safety and first response?

➤ What might disqualify a person from a position in the fields discussed in this chapter?

INTRODUCTION

This chapter discusses the largest, most visible component of criminal justice—law enforcement—beginning with what law enforcement entails in reality as opposed to what is often seen in movies and on television. Next, employment requirements and the outlook for careers in this field are discussed, followed by an up-close look at the variety of employment available in law enforcement and an explanation of where specific opportunities exist at the local, county, tribal, state, and federal levels.

Salaries for various law enforcement positions, as well as fringe benefits and promotional opportunities, are presented next, followed by a look at advanced jobs and specialization within the field, international job opportunities, and a variety of nonsworn civilian jobs that support law enforcement. The chapter then looks at other first responders and a discussion of public safety career opportunities in the fire service, emergency medical services, and emergency management. It concludes with a discussion of what might disqualify a person from these positions.

IS LAW ENFORCEMENT OR OTHER EMERGENCY SERVICES FOR YOU?

In order to make informed decisions about your career, you must gather facts. Some of this information comes from within. Do you possess the personal attributes needed to be a police officer? Can you give orders? Can you take orders? Can you remain calm under stress? Can you treat people professionally and apply the law equally? Can you work the hours under the conditions required by the job?

You also need to consider objective, external data. Much of what happens within law enforcement is not common knowledge. Consequently, many people considering employment in law enforcement may find themselves relying on inaccurate data. Unless you have a personal friend or relative in law enforcement, you are likely to obtain what you know about the field from where most people do: television or the movies.

Because of the popularity of police investigators and detectives, movies and television shows about them are abundant. But the primary goal of such shows is to entertain, not to educate. Sensationalism is much more likely than realism. A major public misconception about police work is that it is primarily oriented toward catching criminals. *NYPD Blue, CSI, Cold Case,* and other television dramas about law enforcement depict police continuously involved in high-speed chases, exciting and dangerous shoot-outs, and other dramatic criminal-catching activities. Even "reality" shows such as *COPS* are misleading because they suggest there is nonstop action when that's just not the case.

> The law enforcement profession is grossly misrepresented in television shows and movies. In reality, about 80 percent of duty time is spent on patrol and doing routine paperwork. "Action" such as investigations, high-speed chases, shoot-outs, and other dramatic criminal-catching activities consume only about 20 percent of duty time.

Selecting a career based on fiction means setting yourself up for disappointment. No one knows better than those in the profession that television shows and movies don't exactly "tell it like it is." The uniforms, the cars, the equipment, the apparent prestige, and the legal authority create a romantic ideal. Don't be fooled. Take a hard look at the law enforcement profession in order to make realistic, informed decisions about your future career.

The *Occupational Outlook Handbook* (*OOH*) notes forty-hour workweeks are typical for law enforcement officers, although paid overtime is common. Because most communities require round-the-clock police protection, officers (typically junior officers) are needed to work the night, weekend, and holiday shifts. Also, keep in mind that you will not begin your career as a detective—it may be a goal that takes many years to achieve. Other significant points to consider when exploring a career as a police officer, detective, or special agent include:

➤ Police work can be dangerous and stressful.

➤ Competition should remain keen for higher-paying jobs with state and federal agencies and police departments in affluent areas.

➤ Opportunities will be better in local and special police departments that offer relatively low salaries or in urban communities where the crime rate is relatively high.

➤ Applicants with college training in police science or military police experience should have the best opportunities.

Large urban departments may offer the widest variety of positions.

The possibility of officer assaults and fatalities is one aspect of the job many prefer to not think about. Nonetheless, grim statistics attest to the danger law enforcement officers face on the job. According to the National Law Enforcement Officers Memorial Fund (NLEOMF) website, 186 law enforcement officers across the nation were killed in the line of duty in 2007, compared to 145 the previous year. The year 2007 saw the greatest number of police officers killed in a single year other than 2001 when 72 were killed in the September 11 terrorist attacks, making the total number killed that year 239. The nonprofit Central Florida Police Stress Unit website states: "Law enforcement officers face many types of danger in their career. On average somewhere in America, a law enforcement officer is killed in-the-line-of-duty every 54 hours" (www.policestress.org/main.htm). In addition to the annual average of 165 deaths, law enforcement officers suffer an annual average of 56,292 assaults and another 16,138 injuries per year.

Another hazard of police work involves communicable diseases. Officers called to the scene of an accident may come in contact with blood or other bodily fluids. Officers attempting to arrest or contain drunken, high, violent, excited, or otherwise "altered" individuals may be bitten, scratched, spit on, or worse, increasing their chances of contracting diseases, some of which may be fatal. Many agencies now make hepatitis vaccinations available and have regular HIV testing for officers involved in needle pricks and other high-risk incidents.

Law enforcement officers often pay another price that doesn't make the headlines or the evening news, yet one that still destroys lives. Police work can take an emotional and psychological toll because of the impact shift work has on officers and their families and the high-stress situations involved in the accidents, assaults, and criminal behavior they routinely witness on the job. Stress is law enforcement's 'hidden assailant'" (www.policestress.org/main.htm). Long-term stress is not only destructive but may be fatal in police work: "When individuals are overwhelmed by occupational stress, they suffer from increased chronic stress, depression, heart disease, stomach disorders, alcohol and drug use and abuse, divorce, and even suicide" (Morash et al., 2006, pp. 24–25). Kelly and Martin (2006, p. 95) note: "Suicide is a permanent solution to a temporary problem." Unfortunately: "Police commit suicide at up to three times the national average and are eight times more likely to kill themselves than to become a victim of a homicide" (Fox, 2007, p. 352).

This information is presented not to discourage you from considering a career in law enforcement but to raise awareness about some potential hazards of a very worthwhile profession. Caution, alertness, and good judgment are critical, possibly lifesaving, qualities every good officer should possess. Other personal characteristics such as honesty, integrity, and a sense of responsibility are especially important in law enforcement. You must also consider the level of education, training, and other qualifications necessary to apply for a law enforcement position.

EMPLOYMENT REQUIREMENTS

According to the *OOH*:

> Civil service regulations govern the appointment of police and detectives in most states, large municipalities, and special police agencies, as well as in many smaller jurisdictions. Candidates must be U.S. citizens, usually at least 20 years old, and must meet rigorous physical and personal qualifications.

Physical examinations for entrance into law enforcement often include tests of vision, hearing, strength and agility. Eligibility usually depends on performance in competitive written examinations and previous education and experience.

To be considered for appointment as an FBI agent, an applicant must be a college graduate and have at least 3 years of professional work experience, or have an advanced degree plus 2 years of professional work experience. An applicant who meets these criteria must also have one of the following: a college major in accounting, electrical engineering, information technology, or computer science; fluency in a foreign language; a degree from an accredited law school; or 3 years of related full-time work experience. Most other federal law enforcement agencies require either a bachelor's degree or related work experience or a combination of the two.

The Need for Higher Education

As law enforcement is increasingly viewed as a profession, education has also become increasingly important. Although policing has come a long way from a job traditionally filled by men returning from the military, because they could shoot a gun and take orders, the educational requirements for applicants or those seeking promotion is not entirely agreed upon. Different states and employers view the desirability of college, and how much college, differently.

According to the *OOH*: "Applicants usually must have at least a high school education, and some departments require 1 or 2 years of college coursework or, in some cases, a college degree. Law enforcement agencies encourage applicants to take courses or training related to law enforcement subjects after high school. Many entry-level applicants for police jobs have completed some formal postsecondary education, and a significant number are college graduates. Many junior colleges, colleges, and universities offer programs in law enforcement or administration of justice."

Currently, only 1 percent of all police departments require a four-year degree (Carlan, 2006, p. 59). In some states, such as Minnesota, a two-year college degree is required. A U.S. Department of Justice study reported that in 2000, approximately 37 percent of large police agencies required applicants to have some college when applying, compared with 19 percent requiring some college just ten years prior in 1990 (Schanlaub, 2005, p. 79).

Research shows that furthering one's education results not only in higher-paying jobs but also in making a candidate more successful in being hired and promoted. In addition to the critical-thinking skills, maturity, discipline, and goal attainment ability required of college graduates, a degree is a way of setting oneself apart from other applicants and providing future options: "Officers with bachelor of arts degrees are excellent employees who use less sick time, are involved in fewer traffic collisions, are disciplined less often, and receive more commendations" (Bostrom, 2005, p. 18). Napier (2005, p. 94) goes further in asserting: "When we rationally look at what is required of law enforcement today, it is clear that higher education is not a luxury, not simply desirable, not a bonus—it is a necessity."

The *OOH* reports: "Applicants with military experience or college training in police science will have the best opportunities in local and state departments. Applicants with a bachelor's degree and several years of law enforcement or military experience, especially investigative experience, will have the best opportunities in federal agencies."

EMPLOYMENT OUTLOOK

A career in law enforcement looks bright now and in the foreseeable future for those with the desired attributes and proper qualifications: "Employment of police and detectives is expected to grow 11 percent over the 2006–2016 decade, about as fast as the average for all occupations. A more security-conscious society and population growth will contribute to the increasing demand for police services" (*OOH*, 2008). The overall increase in security awareness at all jurisdictional levels makes this an excellent time to consider work in these fields.

The *OOH* goes on to suggest: "Overall opportunities in local police departments will be excellent for individuals who meet the psychological, personal, and physical qualifications. In addition to openings from employment growth, many openings will be created by the need to replace workers who retire and those who leave local agencies for federal jobs and private sector security jobs. There will be more competition for jobs in federal and state law enforcement agencies than for jobs in local agencies. Less competition for jobs will occur in departments that offer relatively low salaries or those in urban communities where the crime rate is relatively high."

LAW ENFORCEMENT—UP CLOSE

What the public, and often those initially considering a career in law enforcement, thinks police work is can be far from the reality of the job. Although most associate the job with wearing a uniform and driving a squad car, the following examples from the *2008 International Association of Chiefs of Police Membership Directory* exemplify the tremendous variety of jobs that exist in law enforcement at both entry level and promotional levels:

Animal Control Worker
Arson Investigator
Attaché
Bailiff
Ballistics Expert
Booking Officer
Campus Police
Chaplain
Chief of Police
Chief of Staff
Commander of Field Operations
Commissioner Communications Officer
Community Safety Coordinator
Community Service Officer
Computer Crime Specialist
Conservation Officer
Crime Lab Technician
Crime Prevention Specialist
Customs and Border Protection Officer
Data Processing Specialist

Deputy
Deputy Chief
Detective
Detention Officer
Director of Research and Development
Director of Scientific Service
Director of Standards and Training
Document Specialist
Drug Recognition Expert
Emergency Management Coordinator
Evidence Technician
Explosives Technician
FBI Special Agent
Fingerprint Technician
Firearms Instructor
Forensic Scientist
Gaming Enforcement Agent
Gang Investigator
Inspector

Instructor
Insurance Fraud Investigator
Intelligence Officer
Investigator
Jailer
Juvenile Specialist
K-9 Handler
Narcotics Agent
Operations Specialist
Patrol Officer
Personnel Specialist
Photographer
Pilot
Police Attorney/Legal Advisor
Police Psychologist
Police Surgeon
Polygraph Operator
Professor
Psychiatric Advisor
Public Information Officer
Public Relations Officer
Public Safety Director

Radio Communications
Railroad Police
Records Management Director
School Resource Officer
Scientist
Secret Service Agent
Security Specialist
Serology Specialist

Sheriff
Street Crimes Specialist
Superintendent of Police
SWAT
Traffic Officer
Training Director
Transit Police
Treasury Agent

Trooper
Undercover Operative
Undersheriff
U.S. Marshal
Water Patrol
Witness Protection Agent

Examining the makeup of today's police culture, Scoville (2008) discusses the changing demographics of those entering the profession of law enforcement. The increasing number of women, people of color, openly gay individuals, more highly educated people, and those who are older when they begin their path to becoming police officers continues to challenge the stereotype of what and who law enforcement officers are, both within the profession and in the public eye. Perhaps because police agencies today better reflect the makeup and diversity of the communities they serve is one reason research indicates a more positive public perception of law enforcement than existed thirty years ago (Scoville, p. 42).

The opportunities for employment and a successful career continue to increase for people who just decades ago may not have considered or thought they had a chance to pursue their dream in this field. Responding to the question "Who wears the badge in twenty-first century America?," Scoville provides an encouraging response: "We are everyone and no one individual. Beneath the uniform we are as diverse as we are unified. Each and every one of us is a dichotomy. Who we are depends upon how closely you choose to look at us. Like a mural created with hundreds of thousands of mosaic tiles, the ranks of law enforcement officers in this country project an image that is viewed differently by each individual that gazes upon it" (p. 19).

WHERE OPPORTUNITIES EXIST

When looking at law enforcement, consider the basic jurisdictions in which you might work. Different law enforcement agencies have different jurisdictions, defining where they work and what they do. For example, although Secret Service agents are federal law enforcement officers, they do not perform traffic enforcement. The following descriptions of local, county, state, and federal law enforcement positions are adapted from *Introduction to Law Enforcement and Criminal Justice* (Hess, 2009, pp. 17–24) and the *OOH*.

Local Agencies

Throughout the United States, 12,766 local police departments were operating during September 2004 (Reaves, 2007, p. 1). Full-time employment by sworn personnel increased overall by 3.4 percent between 2000 and 2004 (p. 3).

Local agencies and offices with law enforcement responsibilities include (1) township and special district police, (2) the constable, (3) the marshal, and (4) municipal police.

Township and Special District Police. The United States has thousands of townships, which vary widely in the scope of governmental powers and operations. Most townships provide a limited range of services for predominantly rural areas. Some townships, often in well-developed fringe areas surrounding a metropolitan complex, perform functions similar to municipal police.

The Constable. Several states have established the office of constable, especially in New England, the South, and the West. The constable is usually an elected official who serves a township, preserving the peace and serving processes for the local justice court. The constable also may be the tax collector or be in charge of the pound, execute arrest warrants, and transport prisoners.

The Marshal. In some parts of the United States, a marshal serves as a court officer, serving writs, subpoenas, and other papers issued by the court and escorting prisoners from jail or holding cells in the courthouse to and from trials and hearings. The marshal also serves as the bailiff and protects the municipal judge and people in the court. In some jurisdictions, the marshal is elected; in other jurisdictions, the marshal is appointed.

Municipal Police. The United States has thousands of municipal police jurisdictions, employing hundreds of thousands of police officers, all with similar responsibilities but with limited geographical jurisdictions. Municipal police departments were the largest employer of law enforcement personnel in 2004, with about 573,000 or (53 percent) of the nearly 1.1 million employees nationwide (Reaves, p. 2). The least uniformity and greatest organizational complexity are found at the municipal level due to local autonomy. The majority of these police forces consist of fewer than ten officers, yet this is what most people think of in terms of law enforcement.

County Agencies

County agencies with law enforcement responsibilities include (1) the county sheriff, (2) the county police, and (3) the county coroner or medical examiner.

The County Sheriff. Many state constitutions designate the sheriff as the chief county law enforcement officer. A total of 3,067 sheriffs' offices existed throughout the country in 2004 (Reaves, p. 1). The sheriff is usually elected locally for a two- or four-year term and may appoint deputies to help provide police protection as well as to (1) keep the public peace, (2) execute civil and criminal process throughout the county, (3) maintain and staff the county jail, (4) preserve the court's dignity, and (5) enforce court orders.

The hundreds of sheriff's departments vary greatly in organization and function. In some states, the sheriff is primarily a court officer; criminal investigation and traffic enforcement are delegated to state or local agencies. In other states, notably in the South and the West, the sheriff and deputies perform both traffic and criminal duties. The sheriff's staff ranges from one (the sheriff only) to several hundred, including sworn deputies and civilian personnel. A major difference between sheriffs and municipal police departments is that sheriffs often place greater emphasis on civil functions and operating corrections facilities.

The County Police. The county police are often found in areas where city and county governments have merged and are headed by a chief law enforcement officer.

The County Coroner or Medical Examiner. The coroner's principal task is to determine the cause of death and to take care of the remains and personal effects of deceased persons. Approximately 2,000 medical examiners and coroners' (ME/C) offices provided death investigation services across the country in 2004 (Hickman et al., 2007, p. 1). The coroner need not be a medical doctor or have any legal background to be elected. In some jurisdictions, however, the coroner has been replaced by the medical examiner, a physician, usually a pathologist, who has studied forensic science. Still other jurisdictions are using medicolegal death investigators or deputy coroners, to be discussed shortly.

Tribal Agencies

Somewhere between the county level and the state level of law enforcement is the tribally operated agency: "As of June 2000, American Indian tribes operated 171 law enforcement agencies that employed the equivalent of at least 1 full-time sworn officer with general arrest powers. In addition, the Bureau of Indian Affairs (BIA) operated thirty-seven agencies providing law enforcement services in Indian country" (Hickman, 2003, p. 1). The broad range of public safety services and functions provided by tribally operated agencies include responding to calls for service, engaging in crime prevention activities, executing arrest warrants, performing traffic law enforcement, serving court papers, providing court security, conducting search-and-rescue operations, and operating jails (Hickman, p. 1).

Tribal law enforcement agencies provide a broad range of public safety services and functions.

Criminal jurisdiction is a major difference between tribally operated agencies and their state and local counterparts. Jurisdiction over offenses in Native American country may lie with federal, state, or tribal agencies depending upon the particular offense, the offender, the victim, and the offense location. Furthermore: "While tribally operated agencies and other general purpose police agencies provide a similar range of services, a major difference between them is the land area served. . . . In terms of land area, some tribally operated agencies may be more like county or regional police departments" (Hickman, p. 2).

State Agencies

State agencies with law enforcement responsibilities include (1) state investigative agencies, (2) state fire marshal divisions, (3) state Department of Natural Resources, (4) driver and vehicle services divisions, (5) Departments of Human Rights, and (6) state police and highway patrol agencies.

State Investigative Agencies. State investigative agencies place investigators throughout the state to help investigate major crimes, organized criminal activity, and the illegal sale or possession of narcotics and prohibited drugs; conduct police science training courses for peace officers; provide scientific examination of crime scenes and laboratory analysis of evidence; and maintain a criminal justice information and telecommunications system.

State Fire Marshal Division. Designated state fire marshals investigate suspicious and incendiary fire origins, fire fatalities, and large-loss fires; tabulate fire statistics; and provide education, inspection, and training programs for fire prevention.

State Department of Natural Resources (Fish, Game, and Watercraft). Conservation officers investigate complaints about nuisance wildlife, misuse of public lands and waters, violations of state park rules, and unlawful appropriation of state-owned timber. They also dispose of big-game animals struck by motor vehicles, assist state game managers on wildlife census projects, and assist in identifying needed sites for public access to lakes and streams. The Department of Natural Resources also issues resident and nonresident boat licenses and licenses for hunting, fishing, and trapping.

Driver and Vehicle Services Division. The motor vehicle section registers motor vehicles, issues ownership certificates, answers inquiries, licenses motor vehicle dealers, supplies record information to the public, and in some states registers bicycles. The driver's license section tests, evaluates, and licenses all drivers throughout the state; maintains accurate records of each individual driver including all violations and crashes occurring anywhere in the United States and Canada; interviews drivers whose records warrant possible revocation, suspension, or cancellation; records the location of every reported crash; assists in driver education efforts; and administers written and road tests to applicants.

Department of Human Rights. The Department of Human Rights enforces the Human Rights Act, which prohibits discrimination on the basis of race, color, creed, religion, national origin, sex, marital status; status with regard to public assistance; or disability in employment, housing, public accommodations, public service, and education.

State Law Enforcement—State Police and Highway Patrol. Some state police enforce all state laws; others enforce primarily traffic laws on highways and freeways and are usually designated as state highway patrol. A major difference between the two officers is that state police generally have more investigative duties than the highway patrol.

Usually, state police work within jurisdictions on request or in following up on their own cases. State police typically have specialized units of special agents or criminal investigators, plainclothes detectives who investigate various violations of state law such as drug trafficking.

Most state patrol agencies enforce state traffic laws and all laws governing operation of vehicles on the state's public highways. Officers usually work in uniform and drive marked cars and motorcycles. Duties include (1) maintaining preventive patrol on the highways, (2) regulating traffic movements and relieving congestion, (3) investigating traffic crashes, and (4) making surveys and studies of crashes and enforcement practices to improve traffic safety. (*Note: Highway patrol,* although still used, is becoming less common, with many states replacing the term with *state patrol.* Although their training emphasizes traffic-related matters, state patrol officers are trained in all areas of professional law enforcement.)

State officers seeking additional specialization should research their state's specialized units, such as canine units, aircraft units, special response and tactical teams, investigation units, and executive protection teams. Sources of further information regarding state law enforcement careers are provided at the end of this chapter.

Federal Agencies

Reaves and Bauer (2003, p. 1) report: "As of June 2002, Federal agencies employed more than 93,000 full-time personnel authorized to make arrests and carry firearms." In 2002, women and minorities accounted for 14.8 and 32.4 percent of federal officers, respectively.

Prior to September 11, 2001, the primary federal law enforcement agencies were housed under either the Department of Justice (DOJ) or the Department of the Treasury. Following the terrorist attacks of 9/11, however, President George W. Bush decided twenty-two previously disparate domestic agencies needed to be coordinated into one department to better protect the nation against threats to the homeland, thus creating a new federal agency called the Department of Homeland Security (DHS, www.dhs.gov). The DHS now oversees a variety of law enforcement agencies that were previously within either the Department of Justice or the Department of the Treasury, such as the Bureau of Customs and Border Protection, the U.S. Secret Service, the Bureau of Citizenship and Immigration Services (formerly the Immigration and Naturalization Service, or INS), and the U.S. Coast Guard. Other DHS agencies with investigative and law enforcement roles include the Transportation Security Administration (TSA), the Office of Inspector General, and the Federal Computer Incident Response Center.

The Department of Justice is the largest law firm in the country, representing U.S. citizens in enforcing the law. Numerous federal law enforcement agencies exist within the DOJ, including the Federal Bureau of Investigation (FBI); the Federal Drug Enforcement Administration (DEA); the U.S. Marshals Service; Federal Bureau of Prisons (BOP); Bureau of Alcohol, Tobacco, Firearms and Explosives; and Office of Justice Programs (Juvenile Justice, Office of Community Oriented Policing Services [COPS], Victims of Crime, Violence Against Women, and more).

The Internal Revenue Service (IRS), under the Department of the Treasury, also has agents involved in law enforcement activities.

Federal agencies to consider when looking for a job in law enforcement or a related field include (1) the Bureau of Customs and Border Protection; (2) the U.S. Secret Service; (3) the U.S. Citizenship and Immigration Services; (4) the U.S. Coast Guard; (5) the Transportation Security Administration; (6) the Office of Inspector General; (7) the Federal Computer Incident Response Center; (8) the Federal Bureau of Investigation; (9) the Federal Drug Enforcement Administration; (10) the U.S. Marshals Service; (11) the Federal Bureau of Prisons; (12) the Bureau of Alcohol, Tobacco, Firearms and Explosives; (13) the Office of Justice Programs; and (14) the Internal Revenue Service. Other federal career avenues to pursue include (1) the Federal Aviation Administration; (2) the Bureau of Diplomatic Security; (3) the U.S. Mint; (4) Postal Inspectors; (5) the Bureau of Indian Affairs Office of Tribal Justice; (6) the Forest Service; (7) the National Park Service; (8) military services; and (9) the Federal Law Enforcement Training Center.

In addition to changing the placement of several agencies on the government's organizational chart, the emphasis of many agencies has changed. For example, fighting terrorism has replaced drug enforcement as the U.S. Customs Service's first responsibility.

The Bureau of Customs and Border Protection (CBP). The CBP is charged with protecting the more than 8,000 miles of international land and water boundaries surrounding the United States and has agents stationed along various points of entry to the United States (ports and along the Mexican and Canadian borders). On a typical day, CBP agents perform many diverse tasks to ensure homeland security, flow of trade and compliance, inspections at ports of entry, and seizures of illegal drugs and contraband. CBP enforces, in addition to its own statutes, more than 400 provisions of law for forty other federal agencies.

The U.S. Border Patrol is the mobile uniformed law enforcement arm of the Department of Homeland Security (DHS) responsible for combating illegal entries into the country and the growing business of alien smuggling. The Bureau of Immigration and Customs Enforcement (ICE) brings together the enforcement and investigative arms of the Customs Service, the investigative and enforcement functions of the former Immigration and Naturalization Service (INS), and the Federal Protective Service (FPS) as part of the DHS.

The U.S. Secret Service. The Secret Service was established in 1865 to fight currency counterfeiters. In 1901 it was given the responsibility for protecting the president and vice president, their families, heads of state, and other designated individuals; investigating threats against these protectees; protecting the White House, the vice president's residence, foreign missions, and other buildings within Washington, DC; and planning and implementing security designs for designated national special security events. The Secret Service also investigates violations of laws relating to counterfeiting of obligations and securities of the United States; financial crimes that include, but are not limited to, access device fraud, financial institution fraud, identity theft, and computer fraud; and computer-based attacks on our nation's financial, banking, and telecommunications infrastructure.

The U.S. Citizenship and Immigration Services (USCIS). USCIS officers are responsible for adjudicating and processing various applications and forms, such as petitions for the immigration of relatives and workers, work authorizations, adjustments of status, requests for asylum, and naturalization necessary to ensure the legal immigration of people and their families to the United States, from initial stages through their transition, to permanent residence, and finally citizenship.

The Coast Guard. The Coast Guard helps local and state agencies that border oceans, lakes, and national waterways. The Coast Guard's mission is multifaceted and involves maritime safety (search and rescue, recreational boating safety, international ice patrol), maritime mobility (aids to navigation, icebreaking services, vessel traffic/waterways management), maritime security (drug interdiction, alien migrant interdiction, protection of fisheries resources, general maritime law enforcement, law/treaty enforcement), national defense (homeland security, port and waterway security), and protection of natural resources (marine pollution education, prevention, response and enforcement; foreign vessel inspections; and living marine resources protection).

The Transportation Security Administration (TSA). The TSA is responsible for security relating to civil aviation, maritime, and all other modes of transportation (including transportation facilities) and is the lead agency for security at airports, ports, and on the nation's railroads, highways, and public transit systems. The TSA National Explosives Detection Canine Program (NEDCP) exists to deter and detect the introduction of explosive devices into the transportation system. TSA-certified explosives detection canine teams are stationed at each of the nation's largest airports and are used daily to search aircraft and terminals, to check out suspect bags or cargo, and to deter terrorist activities.

The Office of Inspector General (OIG). The OIG's mission is to protect the integrity of Department of Health and Human Services (HHS) programs, as well as the health and welfare of program beneficiaries. The Office of Investigations (OI) is responsible for investigating a variety of crimes committed against over 300 departmental programs. A primary responsibility of a special agent for the OIG is to detect and investigate Medicare/Medicaid fraud, child support enforcement matters, internal investigations, and grant and contract fraud. Agents conduct interviews, serve search and arrest warrants, and use surveillance and undercover operations during their investigations. Agents also ensure the protection and safety of the secretary of the HHS.

The Federal Computer Incident Response Center (FedCIRC). FedCIRC, working with the United States Computer Emergency Readiness Team (US-CERT), is a collaboration of computer incident response, security, and law enforcement professionals working together to handle computer security incidents and to provide both proactive and reactive security services for the federal government. The primary purposes of the FedCIRC are to provide the means for federal agencies to work together to handle security incidents, share related information, solve common security problems, and to collaborate with the National Infrastructure Protection Center (NIPC) for the planning of future infrastructure protection strategies and dealing with criminal activities that pose a threat to the critical information infrastructure.

The Federal Bureau of Investigation (FBI). The FBI is the primary investigative agency of the federal government. Its special agents are responsible for investigating violations of more than 260 statutes and conducting sensitive national security investigations. Agents may conduct surveillance, monitor court-authorized wiretaps, examine business records, investigate white-collar crime, track the interstate movement of stolen property, collect evidence of espionage activities, or participate in sensitive undercover assignments. The FBI investigates organized crime, public corruption, financial crime, fraud against the government, bribery, copyright infringement, civil rights violations, bank robbery, extortion, kidnapping, air piracy, terrorism, espionage, interstate criminal activity, drug trafficking, and other violations of federal statutes.

The FBI also provides valuable services to law enforcement agencies throughout the country. The Identification Division is a central repository for fingerprint information, including the automated fingerprint identification system (AFIS), which greatly streamlines the matching of fingerprints with suspects. The National Crime Information Center (NCIC-2000) is a computerized, electronic data exchange network developed to complement computerized systems already in existence and those planned by local and state law enforcement agencies. The FBI Laboratory, the world's largest criminal laboratory, is available without cost to any city, county, state, or federal law enforcement agencies in the country. The Uniform Crime Reports (UCR) is a national clearinghouse for U.S. crime statistics.

The Federal Drug Enforcement Administration (DEA). DEA agents seek to stop the flow of drugs at their source, both domestic and foreign, and to assist state and local police in preventing illegal drugs from reaching local communities. Not only is the DEA the lead agency for domestic enforcement of federal drug laws, but it also has sole responsibility for coordinating and pursuing U.S. drug investigations abroad. DEA agents are involved in surveillance, undercover operations, raids, interviewing witnesses and suspects, searching for evidence, and seizing contraband. Positions within the DEA include special agent, intelligence research specialist, forensic chemist, diversion investigator, and attorney.

The U.S. Marshals. In 1789 Congress created the office of U.S. Marshals. Marshals are appointed by the president and are responsible for protecting the federal courts and ensuring the effective operation of the judicial system. Duties of U.S. marshals include (1) seizing property in both criminal and civil matters to satisfy judgments issued by a federal court, (2) providing physical security for U.S. courtrooms, (3) transporting federal prisoners, and (4) protecting government witnesses whose testimony might jeopardize their safety. They enjoy the widest jurisdiction of any federal law enforcement agency and are involved to some degree in nearly all federal law enforcement efforts. In addition, U.S. marshals pursue and arrest federal fugitives.

The Bureau of Prisons (BOP). The BOP is responsible for the care and custody of persons convicted of federal crimes and sentenced to federal penal institutions. The bureau operates a nationwide system of 114 maximum-, medium- and minimum-security institutions, 6 regional offices, a central office (headquarters), 2 staff training centers, and 28 community corrections offices. Community corrections offices oversee community corrections centers and home confinement programs. The bureau is responsible for the custody and care of more than 193,000 federal offenders, of which approximately 85 percent are confined in bureau-operated correctional institutions and detention centers. The rest are confined in privately operated prisons, detention centers, community corrections centers, and juvenile facilities, as well as some facilities operated by state or local governments.

The Bureau of Alcohol, Tobacco, Firearms and Explosives (ATF). The ATF is primarily a licensing and investigative agency involved in investigating violations of federal alcohol and tobacco tax regulations and violations of federal firearms and explosives laws. The Firearms Division enforces the Gun Control Act of 1968 and the Arms Export Control Act. Domestic and foreign investigations involve the development and use of informants; physical and electronic surveillance; and examination of records from importers/exporters, banks, couriers, and manufacturers. Agents conduct interviews, serve on joint task forces with other agencies, and obtain and execute search warrants.

Office of Justice Programs (OJP). The OJP is a conglomerate of bureaus, offices, and programs directed to provide federal leadership in developing the nation's capacity to prevent and control crime, improve the criminal and juvenile justice systems, increase knowledge about crime and related issues, and assist crime victims.

The five OJP bureaus include (1) the Bureau of Justice Assistance (BJA), which provides funding, training, and technical assistance to state and local governments to combat violent and drug-related crime and to help improve the criminal justice system; (2) the Bureau of Justice Statistics (BJS), the principal criminal justice statistical agency in the nation; (3) the National Institute of Justice (NIJ), the principal research and development agency in the Department of Justice, responsible for conducting demonstrations of innovative approaches to improve criminal justice, developing and testing new criminal justice technologies, evaluating the effectiveness of justice programs, and disseminating research findings to practitioners and policy makers; (4) the Office of Juvenile Justice and Delinquency Prevention (OJJDP), which provides federal leadership in preventing and controlling juvenile crime and improving the juvenile justice system at the state and local levels, in addition to administering the Missing and Exploited Children's program, four programs funded under the Victims of Child Abuse Act, and the Coordinating Council on Juvenile Justice and Delinquency Prevention; and (5) the Office for Victims of Crime (OVC), which provides federal leadership in assisting victims of crime and their families; administers two grant programs created by the Victims of Crime Act of 1984 (VOCA); and sponsors training for federal, state, and local criminal justice officials and other professionals to help improve their response to crime victims and their families.

OJP offices include (1) the Corrections Program Office (CPO), (2) the Drug Courts Program Office (DCPO), (3) the Violence Against Women Office (VAWO), (4) the Office of State and Local Domestic Preparedness Support (OSLDPS), (5) the Office of the Police Corps and Law Enforcement Education (OPCLEE), (6) the American Indian and Alaskan Native Affairs Office (AI/AN), and (7) the Executive Office for Weed and Seed (EOWS).

The Internal Revenue Service (IRS). The Internal Revenue Service, established in 1862, is the largest bureau of the Department of the Treasury. Its mission is to encourage the highest degree of voluntary compliance with the tax laws and regulations. IRS Criminal Investigation (CI) special agents are the premier financial investigators for the federal government and investigate potential criminal violations of the Internal Revenue Code and related financial crimes such as willful tax evasion, tax fraud, and the activities of gamblers and drug peddlers. IRS-CI special agents use accounting and law enforcement skills to investigate financial crimes and "follow the money." No matter what the source, all income earned, both legal and illegal, has the potential for becoming involved in crimes that fall within the investigative jurisdiction of the IRS.

The Federal Aviation Administration (FAA). The Federal Aviation Administration (FAA) is responsible for the safety of civil aviation. In 1970, President Nixon began a sky marshal program as part of the Customs Service. Following the 1985 hijacking of TWA Flight 847, this elite team of sharpshooters re-formed under the FAA.

Technically called Civil Aviation Security Specialists, federal air marshals fly on selected high-risk routes to deter hijacking attempts and thwart terrorist attacks with minimum endangerment of passengers and crew. Dressed in civilian clothes to maintain a low profile, air marshals board flights at random or in response to specific threats. They are authorized to carry firearms on planes and make arrests without warrants with the objective of using minimum force to achieve maximum security. They receive intensive, highly specialized law enforcement training, followed by recurrent training and recertification. This is an intensely stressful position requiring exceptional judgment. Having limited contact with family members during missions, agents can be deployed at any time and anywhere in the world. Agents must be comfortable working independently and be willing to travel extensively, as missions often involve long flights cross-country or overseas.

Bureau of Diplomatic Security. Part of the U.S. Department of State, these special agents investigate passport and visa fraud, conduct personnel security investigations, issue security clearances, and protect the secretary of state and foreign dignitaries. Overseas, they advise ambassadors on all security matters and manage a complex range of security programs designed to protect personnel, facilities, and information. They also train foreign civilian police and administer counterterrorism and counter-narcotics rewards programs. Their numbers are expected to grow rapidly as the threat of terrorism increases and the battle against it intensifies.

The U.S. Mint Police. Established in 1792, the U.S. Mint Police is one of the nation's oldest police forces. Mint Police are responsible for protecting the country's gold, silver, and coins located at Mint facilities in Fort Knox, Denver, San Francisco, West Point, Philadelphia, and Washington, DC: "In addition to guarding $100 billion in gold, silver and U.S. coins, Mint Police have also protected such unique holdings as the U.S. Constitution, Lincoln's Gettysburg Address and the crown jewels of King Stephen the Great of Hungary" (Bailer, 2006, p. 64).

Postal Inspectors. Postal inspectors protect the mail and recipients of mail by enforcing federal laws pertaining to mailing prohibited items such as explosives, obscene matter, and articles likely to injure or cause damage, including biological and chemical agents sent with intent to kill and terrorize, such as anthrax and cyanide. Any mail that may prove to be libelous, defamatory, or threatening can be excluded from being transported by the postal service. They also investigate any frauds perpetrated through the mail such as chain letters, gift enterprises, and similar schemes.

Bureau of Indian Affairs (BIA) Office of Tribal Justice.   From its earliest days, the United States has recognized the sovereign status of Native American tribes as "domestic dependent nations." Our Constitution recognizes Native American sovereignty and establishes Native American affairs as a unique area of federal concern. Consequently, Native American country has been allowed to develop and perpetuate its own justice system in line with Native American customs and laws. However, although some tribal governments have developed strong law enforcement programs, many others have encountered significant difficulty in doing so, with great numbers of Native American citizens receiving police, investigative, and detention services that lag far behind those existing in non–Native American territory. The BIA's Office of Law Enforcement Services (OLES) works in conjunction with the DOJ to train and certify the criminal investigators and uniformed officers needed to serve our nation's Native American population.

The U.S. Forest Service.   The Forest Service employs over 30,000 people. Rangers patrol federal lands, protect various cultural and natural resources, and investigate criminal activity. Crimes may involve anything from simple vandalism and theft of Forest Service property, such as chainsaws or solar panels, to timber theft, contract fraud, narcotics production on federal lands, theft of archeological artifacts, bombings, and personal assaults on Forest Service personnel.

National Park Service (NPS).   The NPS comprises 379 areas in nearly every state and U.S. possession, from the Hawaii Volcanoes National Park to the Statue of Liberty National Monument. NPS positions with law enforcement duties include the U.S. Park Police, Park Rangers, and Guard Force.

The primary duty of the U.S. Park Police is to protect lives. Park Police officers preserve the peace; prevent, detect, and investigate accidents and crimes; aid citizens in emergency situations; arrest violators; and often provide crowd control at large public gatherings. The Park Police force includes horse-mounted, motorcycle, helicopter, and canine units; a special equipment and tactics team; and investigations and security details.

Park Rangers supervise, manage, and perform work in the conservation and use of resources in national parks and other federally managed areas. Park Ranger duties include forest or structural fire control; protection of property; enforcement of laws and regulations; investigation of violations, complaints, trespass/encroachment, and accidents; search and rescue; and management of historical, cultural, and natural resources such as wildlife, forests, lakeshores, seashores, historic buildings, battlefields, archaeological properties, and recreation areas.

The uniformed guard force protects federal property and buildings. Guards may either serve at fixed posts or patrol assigned areas to prevent and protect them from hazards of fire, theft, accident, damage, and trespass. Most guards are located in the National Capitol Region, as a subunit of the Park Police, for which they work as permanent part-time employees. A few are located in other regions, and some have full-time positions.

The Military Services.   The armed forces also have law enforcement responsibilities. The uniformed divisions are known as the military police (Army), the shore patrol (Navy), and the security police (Marine Corps and Air Force). The military police are primarily concerned with the physical security of the various bases under their control. Within each operation, the security forces control criminal activity, court-martials, discipline, desertions, and the confinement of prisoners. Military law enforcement assignments such as the military police provide exceptional experience. Other non–law enforcement assignments, however, also provide proof that the individual can take orders, assume responsibility, and successfully accept challenges.

Even if you are not interested in the military as a career, it is a great background when looking for a law enforcement job. The military is particularly well suited for those who are younger and less certain as to what career direction to take. Any military experience is better than just throwing those years away, aimlessly wandering from job to job. Military experience is usually applicable directly to successful employment in law enforcement.

Federal Law Enforcement Training Center (FLETC). New recruits with most federal law enforcement agencies throughout the country receive their initial training at the Federal Law Enforcement Training Center (FLETC) in Glynco, Georgia. FLETC's mission is to serve as the federal government's leader for and provider of world-class law enforcement training and to prepare new and experienced law enforcement professionals to fulfill their responsibilities in a safe manner and at the highest level of proficiency. Of more than 250 programs taught each year, most of the 40,000-plus students that are trained annually receive basic instruction in rules and principles of law, investigation, detention, arrest, and search and seizure. Basic and advanced training also includes fingerprinting, photography, physical conditioning, interviewing skills, firearms use, radio communication procedures, high-speed pursuit and protection, undercover investigations, advanced computer crime detection, advanced fraud detection, and advanced marine law enforcement.

JURISDICTIONS COMPARED

Each agency level can have unique characteristics. Federal work may be considered more prestigious and dynamic by some and can have more attractive pay and benefits. However, it also usually has higher standards and often requires relocating, which can substantially interfere with today's common two-profession families and a desire for more stability. Because of the large number of people employed by the federal system, the bureaucracy can be frustrating, with a possibility of feeling lost or engulfed within the system. Age restrictions not applicable to other jurisdictions can apply at the federal level.

Employment with local law enforcement has its own appeal. The personal identity and control of police or sheriff's departments can allow officers to feel a closer connection with where they work. Smaller agencies may have fewer transfer or promotional opportunities, but may also permit officers to assume more responsibilities on the job.

> To find the greatest employment potential, consider agencies that have the greatest number of employees. More than half of all law enforcement positions are found in local police departments, and civilian opportunities exist at all three levels—local, state, and federal.

In general, the larger the agency, the greater the number of employment opportunities. In addition to more entry-level positions available, more jobs are available as transfers or promotions. For example, a small agency may have only one investigator, if that, with all of the officers expected to perform a greater variety of functions than officers in a large agency, where specialty positions exist. In a small agency the responding officer may process the crime scene, whereas in a larger department that officer may call specialized personnel to process the scene.

Smaller agencies also have fewer opportunities to advance in rank and few, if any, specialized positions in which to transfer. A smaller agency may provide the opportunity for an officer to become a detective but may not have specialty divisions commonly found in larger organizations, such as narcotics, traffic, crime lab, jail, internal affairs, K-9, and so on.

SALARIES

Simply put, government work will never share the nearly limitless compensation potential of private employment. This is not to say that law enforcement personnel are destined to be destitute. On the contrary, pay at the local, county, state, and federal levels is certainly comfortable. Considering the benefits associated with government work—pensions, medical coverage, vacation and sick time, and greater job security than that found in the private sector—a career in law enforcement is well compensated. Deferred compensation and generous retirement plans may allow for excellent early retirement. The advice here: start early and contribute the most you possibly can.

In many agencies, additional opportunities may make law enforcement employment more attractive. For example, most jurisdictions allow for some part-time work. This may include overtime work (usually paying more than the forty-hour-per-week pay scale) or moonlighting for local businesses doing security work, traffic control for special events, and so on. Although it is usually something other than money that motivates the law enforcement officer, salary is an important consideration. Different jurisdictions pay differently, and advancement offers pay incentives.

Local, County, and State Salaries

Salaries for police officers vary among agencies and differ depending upon the size of the agency, jurisdiction, and population served. In 2006 median annual earnings were $52,540 in state government, and $47,190 in local government (*OOH*). Police and sheriff's patrol officers had median annual earnings of $47,460 in May 2006, ranging from less than $27,310 to more than $72,450. Median annual earnings of police and detective supervisors were $69,310 ranging from less than $41,260 to more than $104,410. The median annual earnings of detectives and criminal investigators were $58,260, ranging from less than $34,480 to more than $92,590. Total earnings for local, state, and special police and detectives frequently exceed the stated salary due to overtime, which can be significant.

According to the International City-County Management Association's annual Police and Fire Personnel, Salaries, and Expenditures Survey, average salaries for sworn full-time positions in 2006 were:

	Minimum Annual Base Salary	Maximum Annual Base Salary
Police Chief	$78,547	$99,698
Deputy Chief	68,797	87,564
Police Captain	65,408	81,466
Police Lieutenant	59,940	72,454
Police Sergeant	53,734	63,564
Police Corporal	44,160	55,183

For the most current figures, check the Bureau of Labor Statistics (BLS) website: www.stats.bls.gov.

Federal Salaries

Because of the size and complexity of the federal system, pay statistics are intricate. The General Schedule (GS) pay scale includes law enforcement positions categorized according to such factors as level of responsibility, type of work, and qualifications required. According to the BLS: "Federal law provides special salary rates to federal employees in law enforcement. In 2007, FBI agents entered federal service as GS-10 employees on the pay scale at a base salary of $48,159, yet they earned about $60,199 a year with availability pay. They could advance to the GS-13 grade level in field nonsupervisory assignments at a base salary of $75,414, which was worth $94,268 with availability pay. FBI supervisory, management, and executive positions in grades GS-14 and GS-15 paid a base salary of about $89,115 and $104,826 a year, respectively, which amounted to $111,394 or $131,033 per year including availability pay."

More specific information about pay and benefits of any federal job, including law enforcement, is available on the website of the U.S. Office of Personnel Management at www.opm.gov.

Fringe Benefits

The benefits police officers receive are unique to their jurisdiction and based on negotiated collective bargaining or that jurisdiction's own compensation plan. New employees, especially, are surprised to learn how much in addition to their salary they will earn in total compensation. In addition to health insurance, life insurance, pension contributions, sick leave, and vacation time, most police officers receive additional benefits such as uniform and equipment allowance, training, and overtime.

With the continuing emphasis on education, many agencies offer tuition reimbursement for officers who further their schooling and pay incentives for those completing degrees. Additional pay for overtime, being on call, callouts, or special assignments can increase an officer's pay as well. Although many job applicants are eager just to get work, having a clear understanding of pay and benefits is an essential part of the job search process.

Promotions and Transfers

Most local and state law enforcement agencies are small, with about half employing fewer than ten officers (Reaves, p. 1). With so few officers, opportunities for promotion and transfers are limited.

> Promotions in law enforcement are limited. Most police officers retire at the employment level at which they were hired.

Promotions and transfers typically come from within a department. Not only does the administration know the individual, but the promotion bolsters morale by serving as recognition for that officer's work. Some agencies, however, see benefits to bringing in an outsider, particularly if no one from within the department is qualified or if internal problems require someone without prior ties to the department. Lateral and promotional opportunities outside one's department are occurring more often as the quest for the best candidates continues.

Like other professions, getting ahead in law enforcement requires time and commitment—sometimes combined with luck. Patience is a virtue for those wanting to advance. And some individuals want to remain in the position that motivated them to get into law enforcement, realizing they are happy where they are, with seniority allowing them to select their shift assignment and the first chance to schedule time off. Upward movement is not always the answer because some promotions come with increased responsibilities and related stress. As Stanek (2008) notes: "It can be discouraging to climb the ladder of success only to discover you don't like the view."

Many other employment opportunities exist in specialty positions within a department. Becoming a specialist in such areas as traffic enforcement, crash investigation/reconstruction, juvenile, narcotics enforcement, K-9 handling, or internal affairs may prevent officers from falling into a rut.

ADVANCED JOBS AND SPECIALIZATION

Although a majority of officers do, and possibly should, begin their careers as generalists, most upwardly mobile police professionals will specialize at some point. In larger agencies these specialties may be all they do, even as part of a full-time unit, or in smaller agencies such specialties may be in addition to their basic job.

Law enforcement continues to change and evolve. Many aspects of police work have become increasingly complex, providing even more opportunities to specialize. Although the basics of responding to calls or handling cases remain, the *how* and *with what* is changing at an ever-increasing rate. The Society of Police Futurists International (SPFI, 2007) surveyed members about what they predict to be the biggest challenging facing policing and criminal justice over the next two decades. Every response reflected social and technology changes that provide opportunities for increased skills, knowledge, and specialization. SPFI summarized the responses: "Four megatrends seem self-evident at this point: Moving toward a cashless society, a transmutation of culture to cyberspace, a blurring of war and crime and ubiquitous connectivity with everyone being able to communicate with anyone" (p.19). For the savvy job seeker or those keen on positioning themselves for advancement, these trends suggest the benefits of learning more about technology, enhancing one's computer skills, becoming better able to work within a global community and understanding social changes that continue to emerge at local, national, and international levels. Consider how these trends interplay with terrorism, cyber crime, immigration, and identity theft.

> A need exists for specialization within law enforcement. Although a majority of officers begin as generalists, those who wish to progress up the ladder of responsibility and salary will usually need to specialize.

This does not mean that the day of the generalist police officer is nearing an end. It is highly likely that patrol officers will continue as the backbone of any law enforcement agency. However, other opportunities abound in criminal justice. Many areas require special expertise in such diverse fields as training and firearms instruction, handwriting, and fingerprint identification, or forensic sciences such as chemical and microscopic analysis. Others areas require special units such as mounted, motorcycle, bicycle, harbor patrol, or K-9 units, or as part of special weapons and tactics (SWAT) or other emergency response teams.

Other specialists needed in the criminal justice system include psychologists, physicians, scientists, and accountants. The FBI, for example, specifically seeks people with very specialized training. Police officers with degrees in law, psychology, or medicine are of great value to their departments. A law degree, for instance, is an excellent education for any area of law enforcement, whether the person wants to use it in a courtroom or on the street. Expertise in such areas as drawing, photography, computers, firearms, flying, or even public relations can help any police professional on the move. Almost any specific area of interest can be successfully woven into a satisfying and advancing career.

Preparing for advancement may be as basic as obtaining a generalized advanced education to effectively interact with those of similar educational levels in other professions. It may be acknowledging the increasing cultural diversity of the United States and learning a foreign language or two. Or, it may be acquiring a degree in management, computer science, or public relations. It's your call.

To illustrate the wide variety of career options within law enforcement, following is a brief look at four specialty areas: juvenile officer, crime scene investigator (CSI), armed sky marshal, and humane law enforcement (HLE) officer.

The Juvenile Officer

For those who enjoy working with youths and families, the juvenile system provides very satisfying employment. With the growing amount of juvenile delinquency and serious, violent offenses committed by youths, the juvenile justice system is expanding at a phenomenal rate and should be a major employer of personnel in the years ahead.

Work in the juvenile justice system is very challenging, and the need for juvenile officers is growing.

The juvenile officer must operate within a system that handles a broad range of offenders and victims: "An extreme challenge facing the juvenile justice system is the one-pot approach to youths evident throughout history. The one-pot approach lumps children and youths who are abused and neglected, those who commit minor offenses and those who commit vicious, violent crimes into the same judicial 'pot.'" (Hess and Drowns, 2004, p. 72).

In many departments, juvenile work is considered a promotion after three to five years as a patrol officer. In addition, increasing numbers of departments have school resource officers (SROs) who work within local schools. In the accepted school resource officer model, SROs engage in three types of activities: law enforcement, teaching, and mentoring (Finn, 2006, p. 1). The emphasis devoted to each duty varies considerably from school to school. Finn (p. 2) reports: "Interest has grown in placing sworn law enforcement personnel in schools to improve school safety and relations between officers and young people." Finn's research found four main benefits of an SRO program: reducing the workload of patrol officers, improving the image of officers among juveniles, creating and maintaining better relationships with the schools, and enhancing the agency's reputation in the community.

In addition to jobs with police agencies, careers in juvenile justice include group home childcare workers and counselors, as well as intake officers and childcare workers in juvenile detention facilities or correctional facilities, such as boot camps, juvenile probation, and so on.

Those interested in working with juveniles might consider volunteering with a youth group to gain experience and to confirm that this is, indeed, an area of special interest.

Crime Scene Investigator (CSI)

A crime scene investigator (CSI) is a specialist in the organized scientific collection and processing of evidence. Popularized by recent television shows, this is an intriguing job to consider. The majority of people conducting crime scene work were promoted from law enforcement positions rather than entering into that position or as a civilian without prior police experience. Those who become CSIs without prior police experience have acquired substantial specialty skills, often of a scientific or technological forensic nature.

The plethora of criminal justice–type shows on television stimulates the public's intrigue with all things police, most recently the area of crime scene investigation. But this is another area where popular media does not necessarily equate to reality. Nelson (2008) explains that the job includes identifying, obtaining, and preserving evidence to help answer the questions only forensic evidence can and in a way that will ensure its admissibility in court: "Like any other police show, what we do doesn't much look like how they portray our jobs on a Hollywood set. Sitting at my microscope examining fingerprints for days or weeks at a time or sifting through the clutter at a filthy burglary scene all shift wouldn't make much of an hour-long drama." Nelson advises anyone considering this specialty work to go in with realistic expectations of what the job involves and how to get it, confirming no one walks in off the street and says, "I want a job like that on TV."

Mertens (p. 52) describes what happens when real-life CSI and Hollywood collide: "In today's world of TV and movie drama, every case is solved, a conclusion always reached and the 'smoking gun' consistently found, most times with very little effort. . . . The 'CSI' culture also includes costumes, sets and vehicles the real CSI teams don't even dream of." Fantino (2007, p. 26) calls this the "CSI effect," where "unrealistic portrayals of the science have translated to equally unrealistic expectations from not only the public but also other professions that operate within the justice system who now apparently believe in magic."

The increased interest in CSI can be seen in some colleges offering a degree in crime scene technology. In addition to general education requirements (including applied ethics), major course requirements include crime scene technology, photography, fingerprint classification, biological evidence, crime scene safety, and courtroom presentation of scientific evidence.

Armed Sky Marshal

Until the deadly September 11, 2001, airborne terrorist attacks on the World Trade Center and the Pentagon, most Americans had never heard of the federal air marshals: "The FAA has always been secretive about the air marshals, refusing to divulge their number, how they work or what they look like. The assault teams wear masks when giving rare public demonstrations" (Hawley, 2001). In the wake of the attacks, however, several congressional leaders and members of the Air Transportation Association, the trade organization for the U.S. airlines, have strongly urged expansion of the air marshal program, and it is likely this "shadowy force" will continue to be strengthened in the coming years.

Among other skills, sky marshals must be very comfortable with firearms. An FAA spokesperson states: "They have some of the highest, if not the highest, firearms qualifications in the federal government. They don't miss" (Hawley). Each agent spends at least three hours a week in shooting practice at their training base near Atlantic City, NJ, which includes a five-story simulated control tower, three outdoor shooting ranges with moving targets, and two retired airliners.

Humane Law Enforcement (HLE) Officer

The American Society for the Prevention of Cruelty to Animals (ASPCA), headquartered in New York City, staffs a Humane Law Enforcement (HLE) Department of fifteen uniformed and plainclothes officers, dedicated to investigating crimes against the city's animal population. As part of its original charter from the state of New York in 1866, the ASPCA was given the legal authority to investigate and make arrests for crimes against animals. For three seasons, cable TV's Animal Planet channel has aired *Animal Precinct,* an award-winning reality series that takes viewers on patrol with HLE agents.

Although not a requirement, many of the officers have backgrounds in law enforcement. For example, the vice president of the HLE Department was a twenty-seven-year veteran of the New York City Police Department prior to joining the ASPCA. Three of the current special agents are former NYPD officers, and another agent has held a variety of criminal justice positions, including federal police officer with the U.S. Veteran Affairs Department, park ranger, and private investigator. The ASPCA's website (www.aspca. org) suggests:

> When preparing for a career in Humane Law Enforcement, your choice of schooling is really up to you. Prior experience as police officer, park ranger, or peace officer may help make you a more attractive candidate. Many states offer specific training for humane law enforcement. In addition, classes in criminology and animal sciences will also complement a career in a humane law enforcement division.

In 2003, the HLE Department received approximately 45,000 complaints of suspected animal cruelty that resulted in the investigation of 3,809 cases and 277 arrests. Following the September 11, 2001, attacks on the World Trade Center, HLE agents and investigators rescued over 200 animals left homeless and/or injured by the event. In addition to investigating abuse and other animal-related issues, many humane officers perform community education services, taking their expertise into schools, talking with students about pet care, and answering their questions. Humane officers also train police officers in the skills needed to handle situations in the field where animals are involved, such as guard dogs at drug "labs." Animal control officers may accompany police officers on raids when an informant has warned of a guard dog in the house. Animal control may tranquilize or otherwise contain a threatening animal until police officers are able to complete their duties, making sure no one gets bitten in the process.

The Humane Society of the United States (HSUS), Investigative Services, works to expose animal fighting, the fur trade, greyhound racing, and the Norwegian whaling industry, among other issues. HSUS investigators handle national and international animal exploitation and abuse issues. Primary responsibilities include conducting (primarily undercover) field investigations, researching, analyzing, and providing input on strategy for proposed investigations. Investigators document acts of cruelty, neglect, and exploitation through still and video photography and write reports on the investigations. HSUS lists as qualifications a bachelor's degree and five or more years of experience in major undercover criminal investigations, with the ideal candidate having experience at a major metropolitan police force or federal agency. Frequent travel is required. Salary is in the mid- to high $40s with excellent benefits (www.hsus.org).

The HSUS and the Law Enforcement Training Institute (LETI) at the University of Missouri have collaborated to develop the National Cruelty Investigations School to train animal cruelty investigators at the federal, state, and local levels; humane society cruelty investigators; animal control officers; and police officers and sheriff's deputies responsible for the investigation of animal cruelty complaints.

Other Venues Requiring Law Enforcement

In addition to the more traditional police agencies, opportunities exist in more specialized environments. Many institutions, facilities, and industries are protected by their own police forces. Examples include college and university campus police and transportation/transit police for railroads and airports.

INTERNATIONAL JOBS

The vast majority of career areas have a new emphasis on international employment. Law enforcement is no exception. Many people are eager to travel, and if it can be part of their job, all the better.

International jobs are available in law enforcement, but obtaining them is not easy. Most overseas positions are classified jobs with special requirements such as security clearances and confidentiality. Because of such factors as jurisdiction, these jobs tend to be covert. Federal agencies such as the FBI, DEA, and Secret Service have agents around the world. Although it is not part of the criminal justice or law enforcement field, the Central Intelligence Agency (CIA) also offers opportunities for international travel. Again, travel can be a perk as well as a potential difficulty.

> As the field of law enforcement expands, so does the geographic availability of jobs. International job opportunities in law enforcement are slowly increasing, but obtaining them is still difficult.

In addition to the multitude of sworn positions, both domestic and abroad, you may also find a nonsworn position in a career field related to law enforcement.

NONSWORN CAREER OPTIONS RELATED TO LAW ENFORCEMENT

Some work traditionally performed by sworn personnel (those with full police powers) can be completed by nonsworn employees. These employees have no more authority than any other civilian, do not carry firearms, and can only make a citizen's arrest as any other civilian. Nonsworn personnel can serve in such areas as crime prevention, animal control, and work with youths and dispatching, thus freeing up sworn police officers for other work. Although some of these positions are filled by students attending law enforcement school or seeking employment to become an officer, not everyone wants to be first on the scene or work the shifts associated with police work.

> Civilians are increasingly common in various careers that support traditional law enforcement, including crime prevention specialists, animal control officers, and dispatchers.

Community Crime Prevention Specialists

The increased acceptance of community-oriented policing, a philosophy more than two decades old, has resulted in increased interest in and reliance on community crime prevention. Although some law enforcement agencies have sworn officers conduct such work, others assign civilians. Crime prevention specialists have the opportunity to work with the community in a positive effort *before* a crisis occurs, with the hope of *preventing* crime. Or, they may be the contact that lends valuable assistance after a crisis.

Crime prevention specialists educate the community about such issues as locks, lighting, alarms, and personal safety. They work with business owners and landlords to develop specific crime prevention strategies. This position offers an excellent opportunity to be creative because much of crime prevention involves developing programs, designing brochures, presenting speeches, and creating multimedia productions and local cable access programs.

Animal Control Officers

Animal control is one area within the realm of community service that can effectively serve as both an entry-level stepping stone to a job in law enforcement or as a specialty area that many find rewarding. For those with a special interest in animal welfare, this is an opportunity to get paid for doing what they love. In recent years, there has been a strong push to professionalize animal control and humane investigations. Although some jurisdictions have police officers or sheriff's deputies handle these tasks, others rely on nonsworn personnel to fulfill this role.

Dispatchers

Police, fire, and ambulance dispatchers, also called public safety dispatchers, monitor the location of emergency service personnel within their jurisdiction. The *OOH* states:

> These workers dispatch the appropriate type and number of units in response to calls for assistance. Dispatchers, or call takers, often are the first people the public contacts when emergency assistance is required. If certified for emergency medical services, the dispatcher may provide medical instruction to those on the scene of the emergency until the medical staff arrives.

> Police, fire, and ambulance dispatchers work in a variety of settings—a police station, a fire station, a hospital, or, increasingly, a centralized communications center. In some areas, one of the major departments serves as the communications center. In these situations, all emergency calls go to that department, where a dispatcher handles their calls and screens the others before transferring them to the appropriate service.

> The work of dispatchers can be very hectic when many calls come in at the same time. The job of public safety dispatchers is particularly stressful because a slow or an improper response to a call can result in serious injury or further harm. Also, callers who are anxious or afraid may become excited and be unable to provide needed information; some may even become abusive. (www.bls.gov/oco/ocos138.htm)

THE FIRE SERVICE

Many communities have a public safety department, encompassing both law enforcement and firefighting responsibilities.

> As with police work, a career in the fire service attracts many applicants seeking a position that combines challenging, action-oriented work, and excitement with the chance to perform an essential public service.

It can seem truly amazing that some people find such dangerous work to be so appealing. Lepore (2007) puts it this way:

> Very few people in the corporate world go to work in the morning wondering whether they'll be coming home at the end of their day. In the fire service, it is a reality every time a firefighter goes to the firehouse. Statistics show that firefighters have the most dangerous profession in the country. If this is the case, why do thousands line up to become one? Simply put, firefighters stand for all that is good in our society. Human instinct is to run away from fire for fear of being injured. Firefighters are the only ones who run toward a burning building in search of people in need of help. They are willing to risk their lives for complete strangers regardless of race, creed, color, or socioeconomic status (http://cms.firehouse.com/web/online/Fire-Service-Careers/What-is-a-Firefighter/8$52078)

Anyone considering firefighting needs to recognize the dangers involved. Firefighter deaths in recent years, as reported by "Firefighter Fatalities in the United States in 2006" (2007), were as follows: 92 firefighters died in the line of duty in 2006; 99 in 2005; 108 in 2004; 112 in 2003; 100 in 2002; and, in 2001, 449 firefighter fatalities occurred, 344 of which happened on September 11 while responding to the terrorist attacks on the World Trade Center in New York.

Risk notwithstanding, firefighting remains an appealing career for many. The U.S. Fire Administration includes under the category of "firefighter" the following:

> Career and volunteer firefighters; full-time public safety officers acting as firefighters; state, territory, and federal government fire service personnel, including wildland firefighters; and privately employed firefighters, including employees of contract fire departments and trained members of industrial fire brigades, whether full- or part-time. It also includes contract personnel working as firefighters or assigned to work in direct support of fire service organizations. The definition also includes prison inmates serving on firefighting crews; firefighters employed by other governmental agencies, such as the United States Department of Energy (DOE); military personnel performing assigned fire suppression activities; and civilian firefighters working at military installations (*Firefighter Fatalities*, 2007, pp.2-3).

Some communities have full-time, paid firefighters whereas others maintain a staff of volunteers, referred to as *paid-on-call,* because almost all "volunteer" departments provide some pay, and many also contribute to retirement plans. According to *OOH*: "In 2006, total paid employment in firefighting occupations was about 361,000. Firefighters held about 293,000 jobs, first-line supervisors/managers of firefighting and prevention workers held about 52,000, and fire inspectors and investigators held about 14,000 jobs. These employment figures include only paid career firefighters—they do not cover volunteer firefighters, who perform the same duties and may constitute the majority of firefighters in a residential area. According to the U.S. Fire Administration, about 71 percent of fire companies were staffed entirely by volunteer firefighters in 2005 (www.bls.gov/oco/ocos158.htm#emply). *OOH* describes the job like this:

> During duty hours, firefighters must be prepared to respond immediately to a fire or other emergency. Fighting fires is dangerous and complex and therefore requires organization and teamwork. At every emergency scene, firefighters perform specific duties assigned by a superior officer. At fires, they connect hose lines to hydrants and operate a pump to send water to high-pressure hoses. Some carry hoses, climb ladders, and enter burning buildings—using systematic and careful procedures—to put out fires. At times, they may need to use tools, like an ax, to make their way through doors, walls, and debris, sometimes with the aid of information about a building's floor plan. Some find and rescue occupants who are unable to safely leave the building without assistance. They also provide emergency medical attention, ventilate smoke-filled areas, and attempt to salvage the contents of buildings. Firefighters' duties may change several times while the company is in action. Sometimes they remain at the site of a disaster for days at a time, rescuing trapped survivors, and assisting with medical treatment. When they aren't responding to fires and other emergencies, firefighters clean and maintain equipment, study fire science and firefighting techniques, conduct practice drills and fire inspections, and participate in physical fitness activities. They also prepare written reports on fire incidents and review fire science literature to stay informed about technological developments and changing administrative practices and policies.

In addition to being physically fit, most firefighting jobs require a high school diploma, with community or technical education a plus for job seekers. All firefighters receive on-the-job training and continuing education. Among the various skills, training, and education firefighters receive, most become certified at some level of emergency medical response such as first responders or emergency medical technicians.

Firefighters assume a number of duties in various settings: "About 9 out of 10 firefighting workers were employed by local government. Some large cities have thousands of career firefighters, while many small towns have only a few. Most of the remainder worked in fire departments on federal and state installations, including airports. Private firefighting companies employ a small number of firefighters. In response to the expanding role of firefighters, some municipalities have combined fire prevention, public fire education, safety, and emergency medical services into a single organization commonly referred to as a public safety organization" (*OOH*).

Median annual earnings of firefighters were $41,190 in 2006, ranging from less than $20,660 to more than $66,140. Median annual earnings were $41,600 in local government, $41,070 in the federal government, and $37,000 in state governments. Median annual earnings of first-line supervisors/managers of firefighting and prevention workers were $62,900 in 2006, ranging from less than $36,820 to more than $97,820. First-line supervisors/managers of firefighting and prevention workers employed in local government earned a median income of about $64,070 a year. Median annual earnings of fire inspectors and investigators were $48,050 in 2006, ranging from less than $29,840 to more than $74,930. Fire inspectors and investigators employed in local government earned a median income of about $49,690 a year.

According to the International City-County Management Association, average salaries in 2006 for sworn full-time positions were as follows:

	Minimum Annual Base Salary	Maximum Annual Base Salary
Fire Chief	$73,435	$95,271
Deputy Chief	66,420	84,284
Assistant Fire Chief	61,887	78,914
Battalion Chief	62,199	78,611
Fire Captain	51,808	62,785
Fire Lieutenant	47,469	56,511
Fire Prevention/Code Inspector	45,951	58,349
Engineer	43,232	56,045

OOH adds:

> Firefighters who average more than a certain number of work hours per week are required to be paid overtime. The hours threshold is determined by the department. Firefighters often earn overtime for working extra shifts to maintain minimum staffing levels or during special emergencies. Firefighters benefits usually include medical and liability insurance, vacation and sick leave, and some paid holidays. Almost all fire departments provide protective clothing (helmets, boots, and coats) and breathing apparatus, and many also provide dress uniforms. Firefighters generally are covered by pension plans, often providing retirement at half pay after 25 years of service or if the individual is disabled in the line of duty.

The allure of firefighting can be realized by both career full-time firefighters and paid-on-call firefighters serving in addition to their full-time employment. And because of some similarity of work, desire for excitement and a desire to do even more as a member of the community, it is not uncommon for police officers to also serve as paid-on-call firefighters where they live when they are off-duty officers. In these cases the firefighting pension can make a very nice addition to their police pension.

EMERGENCY MEDICAL SERVICE (EMS)

Emergency medical service (EMS) personnel respond to a variety of incidents where people are in need of immediate medical attention, including automobile crashes, heart attacks, drownings, childbirths, and gunshot wounds.

Different agencies have different protocols for responding to medical emergencies. Sometimes the police are dispatched and arrive on the scene first, followed by the fire department's rescue squad, followed by an advanced life support paramedic ambulance. Sometimes just the police respond until the ambulance arrives; whereas in some communities only the fire department is dispatched, followed by the ambulance (unless there is a threat of violence or it's a crime scene; then police are always dispatched along with EMS units). And in some communities, police officers are also trained as paramedics.

The primary levels of emergency medical training are basic first aid, first responder, and emergency medical technician (EMT). A step beyond EMT basic is the EMT paramedic level. Each classification requires increasing hours of training and continuing education. Like firefighting, a person could work full time in any of these categories or volunteer. Most police and fire departments expect their personnel to have some level of emergency medical training, not only to help their response to calls, but also for preparation to assist other emergency response personnel who may become injured at the scene.

In addition to the less intense training (usually a week) for first responders, which many police and firefighters have, *OOH* describes the training usually provided:

> The EMT-Basic represents the first component of the emergency medical technician system. An EMT trained at this level is prepared to care for patients at the scene of an accident and while transporting patients by ambulance to the hospital under medical direction. The EMT-Basic has the emergency skills to assess a patient's condition and manage respiratory, cardiac, and trauma emergencies.
>
> The EMT-Intermediate has more advanced training. However, the specific tasks that those certified at this level are allowed to perform varies greatly from state to state.
>
> EMT-Paramedics provide the most extensive pre hospital care. In addition to carrying out the procedures of the other levels, paramedics may administer drugs orally and intravenously, interpret electrocardiograms (EKGs), perform endotracheal intubations, and use monitors and other complex equipment. However, like EMT-Intermediate, what paramedics are permitted to do varies by state.

EMTs and paramedics are usually dispatched by a 911 operator to the emergency, where they may work with police and firefighters following medical protocols and guidelines to provide appropriate emergency care. Emergency treatment is carried out under the medical direction of physicians.

Every state requires licensure for EMS responders with continuing education necessary to renew the license. Most employers require a high school diploma. Hours vary depending on whether the job is with a police or fire department, hospital, or ambulance service.

According to the *OOH*, earnings of EMTs and paramedics depend on the employer and geographic location as well as their training and experience. Median annual earnings of EMTs and paramedics were $27,070 in 2006, ranging from less than $17,300 to more than $45,280. Median annual earnings in the industries employing the largest numbers of EMTs and paramedics in 2006 were $23,250 in general medical and surgical hospitals and $20,350 in ambulance services.

Those in emergency medical services who are part of fire or police departments typically receive the same benefits as firefighters or police officers. For example, many are covered by pension plans that provide retirement at half pay after twenty or twenty-five years of service or if the worker is disabled in the line of duty.

EMERGENCY MANAGEMENT

Another emerging career opportunity is emergency management. Emergency managers are employed at all jurisdictional levels including the private sector. They plan and coordinate exercises to prepare for emergencies and disasters. An emergency is an event an agency can respond to using its own resources, whereas a disaster requires assistance from others. Federal legislation requires jurisdictions to have plans in place for hazardous materials events, and insurance carriers expect businesses to have strategies in place to both mitigate and respond to emergencies. Emergency managers coordinate all of this between government and private responders.

➤   Although emergency managers may be law enforcement or fire personnel, these positions can also be held by nonsworn civilian employees or community volunteers. In addition to the job of emergency management director or coordinator, larger jurisdictions may have such specialty positions as emergency plan reviewer, radiological specialists, and people committed to training and coordinating practice exercises.

➤   Pay varies with the size of the jurisdiction, scope of the job, and specific requirements of that agency. Private companies often have people within their organization responsible for their own planning and interface with government responders. Although no formal training is required, professional organizations can provide training and certifications. Since the September 11 terrorist attacks, an increasing number of educational opportunities have been offered by government and private organizations. Further, several colleges throughout the country are now offering two- and four-year degree programs in homeland security and related areas of studies, including Ph.D. programs.

➤   State organizations such as The New York State Emergency Management Association (www. nysema.org/) and the Utah Emergency Management Association (http://dhls.utah.gov/links/) provide information on this emerging field. Additional information is also available from the International Association of Emergency Managers, which lists its purpose as "promoting the goals of saving lives and protecting property during emergencies and disasters." The International Association of Emergency Managers (IAEM) lists on its website (www.iaem.com/index.htm) various resources, certification and career opportunities, and links to local emergency management organizations.

DISQUALIFIERS

Thus far the focus has been on exploring career options and setting the stage to develop a strategy to pursue your job aspirations. Before starting the job-seeking process you need to ask yourself whether there are any reasons you would not, or could not, get hired. If there is anything that will prevent you from being hired even before applying, this is the time to confront it and determine whether you can realistically continue the job search in this particular field. If not, it is unfair to employers and to you to present yourself as hirable when, in fact, you are not.

> Three categories of reasons may make a person unhirable, called *disqualifiers*: statutory bars, character concerns, and "nonfit issues."

Statutory Bars

Statutory bars are offenses that will prevent a person from being hired. Almost all states have laws prohibiting individuals with a felony or other crimes from being hired to perform jobs in which the public places their trust. For example, Minnesota law states: "No applicant may be appointed to the position of peace officer who has been convicted of . . . ." and then lists those specific crimes including any felony, theft, or narcotics offenses. Even youthful indiscretions may block a person from being hired years later. It is the applicant's responsibility to know what these bars are and backgrounds *will* be checked.

Character Concerns

Character concerns are events in your life that an employer perceives to be of sufficient concern such that they will not hire you. These could be convictions that would not, by themselves, bar you from being hired but reflect on your suitability for the job. A recent DWI may not be one of the statutory bars, but could be of concern to an employer, as might a series of traffic offenses. The popularity of such sites as MySpace and Facebook provides employers another means of determining character. What you post, what your friends post about you, and the photos that appear reflect your character and hirability. Nothing posted on the Internet is considered private, and employers can, and do, check.

Nonfit Issues

Whether an applicant appears desirable to a particular employer may depend not only on statutory bars or character issues, but also on whether those doing the hiring consider you "a fit" for the job. For example, failing to follow basic instructions provided for the application process may present you as a poor fit for a job that demands following direction. Inappropriate language, dress, or demeanor during the interview process might raise concerns. Showing a lack of interest, not being prepared, or being late for a scheduled interview could also cause the hiring authority to question whether you would be the right fit for them. As long as the reason is not a constitutionally protected one, employers have the right to not hire you for anything else that concerns them.

Although it can be disappointing, the more realistic you are about what you can be hired for, the better positioned you are to find the best fit. If there is something that will disqualify you from being hired, it does not mean you will never have a satisfying career; in fact, you may find something that suits you even more. The job search can be a very humbling experience because it will address things you cannot change, things you regret, and things you wish were not there. However, with a well-planned strategy, which includes realistically assessing what the right career for you is, positive results will prevail.

CONCLUSION

A multitude of options exist for those considering a career in law enforcement or related fields, including federal agencies, state agencies, county agencies, and local agencies. To find the greatest employment potential, consider agencies that have the greatest number of employees. Remember, more than half of all law enforcement positions are found in local police departments, and civilian opportunities exist at all three levels—local, state, and federal.

Keep in mind a need exists for specialization within the law enforcement field. Although a majority of officers begin as generalists, those who wish to progress up the ladder of responsibility and salary will usually need to specialize. Specialized training or expertise, whether in the form of advanced schooling, a law degree, a talent for drawing, or the ability to pilot an aircraft, can benefit any law enforcement professional seeking advancement. Also consider that as the field of law enforcement expands, so does the geographic availability of jobs. International job opportunities in law enforcement are slowly increasing, but obtaining them remains difficult. Globalization and technology continue to offer opportunities for specialization that will set you apart from the competition when apply for a job and promotion.

Civilians are becoming more common in the various careers that support traditional law enforcement, including crime prevention specialists, juvenile specialists, animal control officers, and dispatchers.

Other public safety careers that routinely interface with law enforcement include firefighting and emergency medical response. As with police work, a career in the fire service attracts many applicants seeking a position that combines challenging, action-oriented work, and excitement with the chance to perform an essential public service. Emergency medical technicians (EMTs) and paramedics respond to incidents where people need immediate medical attention, including automobile crashes, heart attacks, drownings, childbirths, and gunshot wounds.

AN INSIDER'S VIEW

IT'S NOT LIKE ON TV

Dennis L. Conroy, PhD

Former Director of the Employee Assistance Program
St. Paul (Minnesota) Police Department

It is crucial for those anticipating a career in law enforcement or private security to realize they will get a view of the world no one else has. They will do and see things that are boring, exciting and amusing. They will also do and see things that are painful, tragic and sometimes terrifying. Careers in law enforcement and private security can be rewarding, but the applicant must also remember there may very well be a "price to pay."

Very few, if any, people entering law enforcement know what they are getting into. *It's not like on television.* The endings aren't always successful, and officers don't always get respect. Those entering law enforcement look forward to becoming a police officer and intend to wear the uniform with pride. The lessons these new officers learn are often very difficult to accept and frequently result in alcoholism, physical problems, divorce and even suicide.

The first lesson new officers learn is that not everyone respects police officers simply because *they are police officers.* Officers soon learn that a large number of people they deal with do not even want them around most of the time. Some will call officers names like "Pig," lie to them, fight with them and even spit on them—just because they are officers. Officers subjected to such treatment discover they are not even permitted to respond except to defend themselves from the most grievous physical harm. Even in that response, they will frequently be challenged on the level of force used and will have to justify such actions later.

The next step in the discovery process occurs when officers learn they are *expected* not to respond when spit on. Being spit on is considered "part of the job." Officers learn that everyone else in the criminal justice system demands respect and inflicts sanctions on those refusing to comply. Can you imagine a defendant spitting on a prosecutor or a judge in a courtroom with impunity? But officers are prohibited from imposing their own sanctions.

New officers are usually shocked at the amount of pain and suffering in the world. Most police officers have grown up without exposure to situations requiring police intervention. They have not seen young children, or even babies, who have been beaten or killed simply for crying. They have not had to talk with and console an elderly couple whose house has been burglarized by teenage vandals, their world invaded and destroyed for no apparent reason. They have probably never had to console a rape victim and tell her that her "hell" may only be starting because if she wants to prosecute the offender she will have to relive the experience time and again and defend her own morality each time.

As new officers learn these lessons, they respond, they change. Officers learn that to work with these problems day after day, they must build a suit of armor to protect themselves. They build this armor by (1) becoming less personally involved and (2) not believing in anyone or anything. While such armor protects officers from work-related issues, it also changes them as individuals.

Many officers find they become cynical and isolated. They lose the capacity to believe in anything or anybody because they have seen or experienced so much disappointment in performing their duties. They see humanity at its worst and the system in almost constant failure. It becomes increasingly difficult to believe in successful outcomes. This cynicism is not only an "at work" attitude, but soon pervades every aspect of the officers' lives.

As officers become more and more cynical, they believe less and less in successful outcomes and begin to invest less and less in personal relationships. This can lead to isolation and loneliness. Officers in the end may have no one but themselves, and they are not sure that they can even believe in themselves.

If applicants know they are likely to experience change, this change can be monitored and, along with the law enforcement career, have a positive outcome. Officers will find rewards in the little things they can do to help individuals they come in contact with. They can brighten a small child's life with just a smile or brief "Hello." They can make an elderly couple feel a bit more secure by driving by and taking the time to wave, showing them that someone cares. As a result, the officers feel better knowing that they made even the smallest difference in the lives of those they have sworn to "protect and serve."

Dr. Dennis Conroy, *licensed psychologist, has recently retired after thirty-two years of service with the St. Paul (Minnesota) Police Department where he had such diverse assignments as patrol officer, juvenile officer, patrol supervisor, vice/narcotics investigator, director of the Professional Development Institute, director of the Field Training Program, and director of the Employee Assistance Program. His clinical experience spans more than twenty-five years and includes working with children, adolescents, and adults. Dr. Conroy has also taught upper-level college courses blending the fields of psychology and law enforcement, including Adolescent Psychology, Human Behavior in Law Enforcement, Police Stress, Peer Counseling in Law Enforcement, and The Psychology of Victims.*

 MIND STRETCHES

1.   What do most people think of as a "police job"? Where did you acquire the information on which you base your answer?

2.   Do you see law enforcement changing to respond to new challenges?

3.   Why might you *not* want to consider a job as a police officer "on the street"?

4.   Do "nonsworn" law enforcement positions, such as civilian crime prevention specialists, have career benefits not available to police officers? What negatives would you want to be aware of in considering a career such as a community service officer?

5.   What other vocational or avocational skills could blend well with a police career? Can you think of unique skills that could make a candidate for a job more attractive to a hiring agency?

6.   Why might someone interested in a career in policing fail to consider other jobs in the security or criminal justice fields?

7.   Can law enforcement continue as it has been in serving communities, or is some change inevitable? What change do you foresee, if any? What can you begin doing right now to meet the challenge?

8.   Why do you think the entertainment field is so obsessed with law enforcement? Do you think this obsession helps or hurts the profession? Why?

9.   What is your favorite television police show? Why? Do you think television and the movies have influenced your career choice?

10.   Are police salaries more or less than you had anticipated? Does salary affect your decision as to what field of employment you will eventually pursue? Why or why not?

REFERENCES

American Society for the Prevention of Cruelty to Animals. 2004, pp. 45–46. Available online at www.aspca.org.

Bailer, Bryn. "United States Mint Police." *Police*, December 2006, pp. 64–67.

Bostrom, Matthew D. "The Influence of Higher Education on Police Officer Work Habits." *The Police Chief*, October 2005, pp. 18–23.

Carlan, Philip. "Do Officers Value Their Degrees?" *Law and Order*, 2006, pp. 59–62.

Department of Homeland Security. Available online at www.dhs.gov.

Fantino, Julian. "Forensic Science: A Fundamental Perspective." *The Police Chief*, November 2007, pp. 26–28.

Finn, Peter. "School Resource Officer Programs: Finding the Funding, Reaping the Benefits." *FBI Law Enforcement Bulletin*, August 2006, pp. 1–7.

Firefighter Fatalities in the United States in 2006. U.S. Fire Administration, July 2007, www.usfa.dhs.gov/downloads/pdf/publications/ff_fat06.pdf.

Fox, Robert. "Stress Management—and the Stress-Proof Vest." *Law and Order*, February 2007, pp. 352–355.

Hawley, Chris. "Armed Sky Marshals May Increase." *Associated Press,* as reported on LATimes.com (*Los Angeles Times*), September 15, 2001.

Hess, Kären M. *Introduction to Law Enforcement and Criminal Justice*, 9th ed. Belmont, CA: Wadsworth Publishing Company, 2009.

Hess, Kären M., and Drowns, Robert W. *Juvenile Justice,* 4th ed. Belmont, CA: Wadsworth Publishing Company, 2004.

Hickman, Matthew J. *Tribal Law Enforcement, 2000.* Washington, DC: U.S. Department of Justice, Bureau of Justice Statistics Fact Sheet, January 2003. (NCJ 197936)

Hickman, Matthew J.; Hughes, Kristen A.; Strom, Kevin J.; and Ropero-Miller, Jeri D. *Medical Examiners and Coroners' Officers, 2004.* Washington, DC: Bureau of Justice Statistics Special Report, June 2007. (NCH 216756)

International Association of Chiefs of Police. *2008 International Association of Chiefs of Police Membership Directory.* Available online at www.theiacp.org.

Kelly, Patricia, and Martin, Rich. "Police Suicide is Real." *Law and Order*, March 2006, pp. 93–95.

Lepore, Paul. "What Is a Firefighter?" Updated June 14, 2007. Available online at http://cms.firehouse.com/web/online/Fire-Service-Careers/What-is-a-Firefighter/8$52078.

Mertens, Jennifer. "The Smoking Gun." *Law Enforcement Technology,* March 2006, pp. 52–61.

Morash, Merry, Haarr, Robin, and Kwak, Dae-Hoon. "Multilevel Influences on Police Stress." *Journal of Contemporary Criminal Justice*, February 2006, pp. 26–43.

Napier, Mark. "The Need for Higher Education." *Law and Order*, September 2005, pp. 86–94.

National Law Enforcement Officers. Memorial Fund (NLEOMF). Available online at www.nleomf.com

Nelson, Diane. Hennepin County (Minneapolis) Sheriff's Crime Lab Deputy. Inyrtbire2008.

Occupational Outlook Handbook, 2008–09 Edition. U.S. Department of Labor, Bureau of Labor Statistics. Washington, DC: U.S. Government Printing Office, 2008. Available online at http://stats.bls.gov/oco. Accessed October 20, 2008.

Reaves, Brian A. *Census of State and Local Law Enforcement Agencies, 2004.* Washington, DC: Bureau of Justice Statistics Bulletin, June 2007. (NCJ 212749)

Reaves, Brian A., and Bauer, Lynn M. *Federal Law Enforcement Officers, 2002.* Washington, DC: Bureau of Justice Statistics Bulletin, August 2003. (NCJ 199995)

Schanlaub, Russ. "Degree or No Degree." *Law and Order*, September 2005, pp. 76–82.

Scoville, Dean. "The Blue Mosaic." *Police*, February 2008, pp. 42–51.

Society of Police Futurists International (SPFI). "What Do You Think Will Be the Biggest Changes in Policing or Criminal Justice in the Next Decade? Next Two Decades?" *Police Futurist*, Summer 2007, pp. 19–21. Available Online at www.policefuturists.org/pdf/PFINewsletter2007Summer.pdf.

Stanek, Susan. Concordia University St. Paul criminal justice professor, Personal interview, 2008.

HELPFUL WEBSITES

Air Force Office of Special Investigations (AFOSI)
www.afpc.randolph.af.mil/osi

American Board of Medicolegal Death Investigators (ABMDI)
www.slu.edu/organizations/abmdi

American Federation of Police and Concerned Citizens
www.afp-cc.org/

American Society for the Prevention of Cruelty to Animals (ASPCA)
www.aspca.org

Association of Public Safety Communications Officials (dispatch)
www.apcointl.org

Bureau of Alcohol, Tobacco, Firearms and Explosives (ATF)
www.atf.gov

Bureau of Diplomatic Security (DS), U.S. Department of State
www.state.gov/m/ds/career

Bureau of Native American Affairs (BIA)
www.doi.gov/bureau-indian-affairs.html

Bureau of Justice Statistics (BJS)
www.ojp.usdoj.gov/bjs

Bureau of Labor Statistics (BLS), U.S. Department of Labor
www.bls.gov

Drug Enforcement Administration (DEA)
www.usdoj.gov/dea

Federal Air Marshals
www.faa.gov

Federal Bureau of Investigation (FBI)
www.fbi.gov

Federal Bureau of Prisons (BOP)
www.bop.gov

Federal Computer Incident Response Center (FedCIRC)
www.us-cert.gov/federal/

Federal Law Enforcement Training Center (FLETC)
http://fletc.gov

Humane Society of the United States (HSUS)
www.hsus.org

Internal Revenue Service (IRS)
http://jobs.irs.gov/opp_law_cisa.html

International Association of Chiefs of Police (IACP)
www.theiacp.org

International Association of Firefighters
www.iaff.org

International Union of Police Associations (IUPA)
www.iupa.org/

INTERPOL (International Law Enforcement)
www.usdoj.gov/usncb

National Association of Emergency
Medical Technicians (NAEMT)
www.naemt.org

National Association of Investigative Specialists (NAIS)
www.pimall.com/nais/dir.menu.html

National Association of Police Organizations (NAPO)
www.napo.org

National Cruelty Investigations School (Animal Cruelty)
www.missouri.edu/~letiwww/animal3.htm

National Fire Academy, U.S. Fire Administration
www.usfa.fema.gov/nfa

National Highway Transportation Safety
Administration (NHTSA)
www.nhtsa.dot.gov

National Law Enforcement Officers Memorial Fund
(NLEOMF)
www.nleomf.com

National Park Service
www.nps.gov

National Registry of Emergency Medical Technicians
(NREMT)
www.nremt.org

Occupational Outlook Handbook
www.bls.gov/oco

Office of Inspector General (OIG), Department of Health
and Human Services (HHS)
www.oig.hhs.gov

Office of Juvenile Justice and Delinquency Prevention (OJJDP)
http://ojjdp.ncjrs.org/

Office of Tribal Justice (OTJ), U.S. Department of Justice
www.usdoj.gov/otj

Transportation Security Administration (TSA)
www.tsa.gov

U.S. Citizenship and Immigration Services (USCIS)
www.dhs.gov/dhspublic/

U.S. Coast Guard (USCG)
www.uscg.mil

U.S. Customs and Border Protection (CBP)
www.cbp.gov

U.S. Department of Homeland Security (DHS)
www.dhs.gov

U.S. Department of Justice (DOJ)
www.usdoj.gov

U.S. Mint Police
www.usmint.gov/about_the_mint/mint_police

U.S. Forest Service
www.fs.fed.us/fsjobs

U.S. Office of Personnel Management (OPM)
www.opm.gov

U.S. Intelligence Community
www.intelligence.gov

U.S. Postal Inspector
www.usps.com/websites/depart/inspect

U.S. Marshals Service
www.usmarshals.gov

U.S. Secret Service
www.secretservice.gov

OTHER RESOURCES

www.officer.com

www.911hotjobs.com

www.lawenforcementjobs.com

http://rehiredbadge.com

www.policeemployment.com/

www.federaljobsearch.com

Applying for Federal Jobs—A Guide to Writing Successful Applications and Resumes for the Job You Want in Government.
   By Patricia B. Wood. May be ordered from: Workbooks, Inc., 9039 Sligo Creek Parkway, #316, Silver Springs, MD 20901
      Phone/FAX (301) 565-9467.

Promote Yourself! How to Use Your Knowledge, Skills and Abilities . . . and Advance in the Federal GovernmentBest Jobs for the 21st Century, 3rd ed.
   By Michael Farr and Laurence Shatkin. Indianapolis: JIST Publishing, Inc., © 2004. www.jist.com.

CHAPTER 3

CAREERS IN THE COURTS, CORRECTIONS, AND RELATED FIELDS

The pessimist complains about the wind; the optimist expects it to change; the realist adjusts the sails.

—William Arthur Ward

Do You Know:

➢ How a law degree may be useful to someone not seeking to become a lawyer?
➢ Besides lawyers, what other professionals work in our nation's courts?
➢ What purposes corrections serve in our criminal justice system?
➢ What the primary difference between adult corrections and juvenile corrections has traditionally been and whether this is still the case?
➢ What corrections officers do and how the future looks for those seeking this job?
➢ What the primary difference is between probation and parole?
➢ What the job outlook is for probation and parole officers?
➢ What impact home detention and electronic monitoring have on jobs in corrections?

INTRODUCTION

As seen in Chapter 2, an incredible variety of jobs are available within the law enforcement profession—everything from patrol officers to police surgeons—assuring a niche for almost every interest. Beyond that, the criminal justice field offers more than you may have considered. You may be destined for a job you have never considered or even knew existed—until now.

The criminal justice system is so complex it needs a tremendous number of participants. Although many of these jobs may not appear as glamorous as those frequently depicted on television, they are extremely important and provide exceptional opportunities.

This chapter presents numerous job opportunities within two components of the criminal justice system—the courts and corrections. It begins with a discussion of the judicial system in the United States and the critical role lawyers play. Also discussed are numerous other careers that might interest those wishing to become a part of the criminal justice system. The chapter then discusses corrections in the United States, including the adult and juvenile systems as well as careers at the local, state, and federal levels.

OPPORTUNITIES IN OUR JUDICIAL SYSTEM—THE COURTS

Before exploring the various jobs within the judicial system, briefly consider the nature of our legal system. It is highly complex and, by design, adversarial—an accuser versus an accused. Although this process has been criticized for being too complicated, full of loopholes and technicalities, one thing is certain: the system requires a lot of employees.

Lawyers

Most people think of lawyers when they think of jobs within the legal system. Attorneys work as advisors on legal matters and represent clients throughout the legal process. Many lawyers use their legal training to work in areas other than the actual practice of law; for example, an increasing number of law enforcement officers at various ranks have law degrees and may be licensed as lawyers.

Just as it is a fallacy that police officers routinely engage in high-speed pursuits and shoot-outs throughout their shifts, a lawyer's job is also often misunderstood. TV and the movies suggest that lawyers are always in court, when in fact, most lawyers never see the inside of a courtroom. Even trial lawyers spend much more time researching the law and preparing a case than actually arguing it before a judge and jury, the exception being government lawyers representing the prosecution or defense. Not every lawyer wants to be a trial lawyer, and many other options are available for those with law degrees.

Other misunderstandings relate to how lawyers do their jobs and their relationship with clients. First, lawyers are bound by their professional code of conduct to aggressively represent their clients to the fullest extent allowed, a duty which can make lawyers appear hostile and biased when, in fact, they are only doing their jobs. However, failure to aggressively represent a client could result in being sued for malpractice. Second, it may appear that a lawyer is endorsing a client's behavior by representing them; however, everyone has a right to representation. The defense lawyer's job is to ensure that clients' rights are not violated and to help them navigate a complicated legal system.

> A career option for those seeking active employment in our nation's courts is that of law. In fact, many already employed in the field of criminal justice are pursuing law degrees to help them achieve their professional goals, even if they do not include the traditional practice of law.

Although other criminal justice careers can be pursued with a high school diploma or community and technical college courses, getting admitted to law school and doing well involves considerably more. The *Occupational Outlook Handbook* (*OOH*) states:

> Although there is no recommended "prelaw" undergraduate major, prospective lawyers should develop proficiency in writing and speaking, reading, researching, analyzing, and thinking logically—skills needed to succeed both in law school and in the law. Regardless of major, a multidisciplinary background is recommended. Courses in English, foreign languages, public speaking, government, philosophy, history, economics, mathematics, and computer science, among others, are useful. Students interested in a particular aspect of law may find related courses helpful. For example, prospective patent lawyers need a strong background in engineering or science, and future tax lawyers must have extensive knowledge of accounting.

Acceptance by most law schools depends on the applicant's ability to demonstrate an aptitude for the study of law, usually through undergraduate grades, the Law School Admission Test (LSAT), the quality of the applicant's undergraduate school, any prior work experience, and sometimes, a personal interview. However, law schools vary in the weight they place on each of these and other factors.

To earn a law degree, otherwise known as a doctor of law or juris doctorate (JD), requires completing at least three years of intense study beyond a bachelor's degree. Realities of law school are that it takes a significant amount of time (three years if you go full-time and take summers off for internships/ clerkships; four years for part-time/night school) and a significant amount of money: "Tuition and costs at public and private law schools have skyrocketed since 1990. For in-state residents at public law schools, students are paying 267 percent more than in 1990, according to information compiled for the American Bar Association. For nonresidents, public law school costs have soared by 197 percent. Private tuition since 1990 has risen by 130 percent. Tuition in 2004 at public law schools for in-state residents averaged $11,860 and $21,905 for nonresidents, and at private schools, tuition was $26,952" (Jones, 2006).

Upon graduation from law school, most people then study for the bar exam to be licensed to practice, which is required in every state. Even those not intending to practice law usually study for and take the bar exam, both for the credibility of being licensed and to leave open the option to later practice law. Most states require continuing education to maintain licensure.

The *OOH* describes the variety of legal jobs:

Lawyers may specialize in a number of areas, such as bankruptcy, probate, international, elder or environmental law. Those specializing in environmental law, for example, may represent interest groups, waste disposal companies or construction firms in their dealings with the U.S. Environmental Protection Agency and other federal and state agencies. . . . Some lawyers specialize in the growing field of intellectual property, helping to protect clients' claims to copyrights, artwork under contract, product designs and computer programs. Other lawyers advise insurance companies about the legality of insurance transactions, guiding the company in writing insurance policies to conform to the law and to protect the companies from unwarranted claims. When claims are filed against insurance companies, these attorneys review the claims and represent the companies in court. . . .

Most lawyers are in private practice, concentrating on criminal or civil law. In criminal law, lawyers represent individuals who have been charged with crimes and argue their cases in courts of law. Attorneys dealing with civil law assist clients with litigation, wills, trusts, contracts, mortgages, titles, and leases. Other lawyers handle only public-interest cases—civil or criminal—concentrating on particular causes and choosing cases that might have an impact on the way law is applied. Lawyers are sometimes employed full time by a single client. If the client is a corporation, the lawyer is known as "house counsel" and usually advises the company concerning legal issues related to its business activities. These issues might involve patents, government regulations, contracts with other companies, property interests, or collective bargaining agreements with unions.

According to *OOH*, some 761,000 jobs were held by lawyers in 2006:

Approximately 27 percent of lawyers were self-employed, practicing either as partners in law firms or in solo practices. Most salaried lawyers held positions in government, in law firms or other corporations, or in nonprofit organizations. Most government-employed lawyers worked at the local level. In the federal government, lawyers worked for many different agencies but were concentrated in the Departments of Justice, Treasury, and Defense. Many salaried lawyers working outside of government were employed as house counsel by public utilities, banks, insurance companies, real estate agencies, manufacturing firms, and other business firms and nonprofit organizations. Some also had part-time independent practices, while others worked part time as lawyers and full time in another occupation. A relatively small number of trained attorneys work in law schools.

What attorney jobs pay depend on the specific job. There is no "average" salary, just as there is no "average" law job. Salaries are commensurate with the type of law practiced. On the top end, corporate and plaintiff's personal injury lawyers can make what many consider exorbitant incomes. On the other end of the spectrum, public service lawyers do not make nearly as much and have an income ceiling. Why people pursue a legal career and what they want to accomplish with their work will influence the kind of lawyering they will do and what salary they can expect to make.

OOH provides a snapshot of attorney salaries in 2006: "The median annual earnings of all wage-and-salaried lawyers were $102,470. Median annual earnings in the industries employing the largest numbers of lawyers is mentioned in the below tabular column."

Management of companies and enterprises	$128,610
Federal government	119,240
Legal services	108,100
Local government	78,810
State government	75,840

"Salaries of experienced attorneys vary widely according to the type, size and location of their employer. Lawyers who own their own practices usually earn less than those who are partners in law firms. Lawyers starting their own practice may need to work part time in other occupations to supplement their income until their practice is well established" (*OOH*).

Because the study of law applies to all aspects of society, and therefore to all career fields, law schools are marketing law degrees as having a more generic purpose than just for practicing law. Regardless of their field of work, employees with law degrees have a great deal to offer. This unique degree can be influential when applying for promotion or seeking other work. The *Occupational Outlook Handbook* (*OOH*) notes: "Some law school graduates use their law degrees in their current jobs as their employers discover it helpful to have people knowledgeable about the law on staff. Others simply enjoy the academic challenge of attaining this level of degree and continue in their present line of work."

For those considering law school, an excellent start is to attend an information session, which most schools offer. Talking to lawyers in various areas of employment is another good way to learn more about the process of applying to schools, what is involved as a student, and what the job prospects appear to be; and it is great networking as well.

There are many issues to consider. For example, some criminal justice agencies might view someone with a law degree as "overqualified" for a patrol position, whereas some colleges and universities (other than law schools) consider a juris doctorate more on par with a master's degree and not a "terminal degree" for tenure track positions. Many lawyers advance to become judges or other judicial workers.

Judges, Magistrates, and Other Judicial Workers

The *OOH* states:

> Judges, magistrates and other judicial workers apply the law and oversee the legal process in courts. They preside over cases concerning every aspect of society, from traffic offenses to disputes over the management of professional sports to issues concerning the rights of huge corporations. All judicial workers must

ensure that trials and hearings are conducted fairly and that the court safeguards the legal rights of all parties involved.

The most visible responsibility of judges is presiding over trials or hearings and listening as attorneys represent their clients. Judges rule on the admissibility of evidence and the methods of conducting testimony, and they may be called on to settle disputes between opposing attorneys. Also, they ensure that rules and procedures are followed, and if unusual circumstances arise for which standard procedures have not been established, judges interpret the law to determine how the trial will proceed.

Any judge or judicial officer gets their authority from the legislature having the power to grant it. Whether at the municipal, county, state, or federal level, judges are strictly empowered by state or federal mandate and must adhere to judicial standards of ethics and behavior. According to the *OOH*:

Judges, magistrates and other judicial workers held 51,000 jobs in 2006. Judges, magistrates and magistrate judges held 27,000 jobs, all in state and local governments. Administrative law judges, adjudicators, and hearing officers held 15,000 jobs, with 59 percent in state governments, 22 percent in the federal government, and 19 percent in local governments. Arbitrators, mediators and conciliators held another 8,500 jobs. Approximately 29 percent worked for state and local governments. The remainder worked for labor organizations, law offices, insurance carriers and other private companies and for organizations that specialize in providing dispute resolution services.

Generally speaking, escalating responsibilities correspond to higher salaries, although private practice lawyers always have the potential of making as much as their practice allows. The prestige and influence of being a judge has its own allure and is a position many attorneys either seek or wish to culminate their careers with.

Judges, magistrate judges, and magistrates had median annual earnings of $101,690 in 2006, ranging from less than $29,540 to more than $145,600. Median annual earnings in the industries employing the largest numbers of judges, magistrate judges, and magistrates in 2006 were $117,760 in state government and $74,630 in local government. Administrative law judges, adjudicators, and hearing officers earned a median of $72,600, and arbitrators, mediators, and conciliators earned a median of $49,490 (*OOH*).

In the federal court system, the chief justice of the U.S. Supreme Court earned $212,100 in 2006, and the associate justices earned $203,000. Federal court of appeals judges earned $175,100 a year, whereas district court judges had salaries of $165,200, as did judges in the Court of Federal Claims and the Court of International Trade. Federal judges with limited jurisdiction, such as magistrates and bankruptcy judges, had salaries of $151,984.

Many fascinating, lucrative, and very satisfying nonlawyer job opportunities also exist within our judicial system. In fact, most people are not aware of the multitude of other careers within the courts.

Other career alternatives for those wishing to work in a courtroom setting include legal secretaries, assistants or paralegals, court reporters, bailiffs, clerks, psychologists, social workers, case managers, and a variety of counseling positions.

Legal Secretaries, Assistants, and Paralegals

Positions that support attorneys are becoming increasingly popular for many reasons. Although legal secretaries, assistants, and paralegals enjoy being involved with the process, having confidential insight into the legal actions in which they are involved and may even attend court hearings, they are not burdened with the increased responsibilities and workload of lawyers.

According to the *OOH*: "While lawyers assume ultimate responsibility for legal work, they often delegate many of their tasks to paralegals. In fact, paralegals—also called legal assistants—are continuing to assume a growing range of tasks in legal offices and perform many of the same tasks as lawyers. Nevertheless, they are explicitly prohibited from carrying out duties considered to be the practice of law, such as setting legal fees, giving legal advice and presenting cases in court."

Preparing for and getting work as a legal assistant or paralegal varies depending mostly on what the employer wants since no certification or licensure is required. There are specialized training programs, two-year colleges, and four-year degree programs specifically for this area of work. Some firms and organizations will hire and train on the job with little or no previous experience. The National Association of Legal Assistants (NALA) offers professional certifications which can be earned after demonstrating specific competencies.

The *OOH* states: "Employment of paralegals and legal assistants is projected to grow 22 percent between 2006 and 2016, much faster than the average for all occupations. Employers are trying to reduce costs and increase the availability and efficiency of legal services by hiring paralegals to perform tasks once done by lawyers. Paralegals are performing a wider variety of duties, making them more useful to businesses."

The *OOH* further notes: "Earnings of paralegals and legal assistants vary greatly. Salaries depend on education, training, experience, the type and size of employer, and the geographic location of the job. In general, paralegals who work for large law firms or in large metropolitan areas earn more than those who work for smaller firms or in less populated regions. In 2006, full-time wage-and-salary paralegals and legal assistants had median annual earnings, including bonuses, of $43,040, ranging from less than $27,450 to more than $67,540. Median annual earnings in the industries employing the largest numbers of paralegals is mentioned in the below tabular column."

Federal government	$56,080
Management of companies and enterprises	52,220
Local government	42,170
Legal services	41,460
State government	38,020

Many in this field feel they get the opportunity to do almost as much as the lawyers—they investigate the facts of the case; research precedent case law; and help lawyers prepare for closings, hearings, trials and corporate meetings. Because they often interact with the clients and witnesses and are actively involved in working up the cases, there can be a great deal of job satisfaction. All states require a license to actually practice law; thus, legal assistants and paralegals must work under a supervising lawyer (*OOH*).

Court Reporters

You've seen them on TV or in the movies. As testimony and questioning swirls about the courtroom, the court reporter sits before a tiny typewriter, nearly motionless, except for flying fingers, which seem to be moving considerably slower than the words being spoken. Yet the entire proceeding is captured verbatim.

According to the *OOH:*

> Court reporters play a critical role not only in judicial proceedings, but at every meeting where the spoken word must be preserved as a written transcript. They are responsible for ensuring a complete, accurate and secure legal record.

> Although many court reporters record official proceedings in the courtroom, others work outside the courtroom. For example, they may take depositions for attorneys in offices and document proceedings of meetings, conventions, and other private activities. Still others capture the proceedings taking place in government agencies at all levels, from the U.S. Congress to state and local governing bodies (*OOH*).

In addition to preparing and protecting the legal record, many court reporters assist judges and trial attorneys in such ways as organizing and searching for information in the official record. Although some court reporters are court employees, others work for themselves or private companies to record various legal meetings such as depositions. According to the *OOH*:

> The amount of training required to become a court reporter varies with the type of reporting chosen. It usually takes less than a year to become a novice voice writer, although it takes at least two years to become proficient at realtime voice writing. Electronic reporters and transcribers learn their skills on the job. The average length of time it takes to become a realtime stenotypist is 33 months. Training is offered by about 130 postsecondary vocational and technical schools and colleges. The National Court Reporters Association (NCRA) has certified about 70 programs, all of which offer courses in stenotype computer-aided transcription and real-time reporting. Electronic court reporters use audio-capture technology and, therefore, usually learn their skills on the job. Students read manuals, review them with their trainers and observe skilled electronic transcribers perform procedures.

The *OOH* goes on to explain:

> In addition to possessing speed and accuracy, court reporters must have excellent listening skills and hearing, good English grammar and vocabulary, and punctuation skills. They must be aware of business practices and current events as well as the correct spelling of names of people, places and events that may be mentioned in a broadcast or in court proceedings. For those who work in courtrooms, an expert knowledge of legal terminology and criminal and appellate procedure is essential. Because capturing proceedings requires the use of computerized stenography or speech recognition equipment, court reporters must be knowledgeable about computer hardware and software applications. Voice writers must learn to listen and speak simultaneously and very quickly and quietly, while also identifying speakers and describing peripheral activities in the courtroom or deposition room. Certifications can help court reporters get jobs and advance in their careers. Several associations offer certifications for different types of reporters.

Court reporting is a specialty that many find rewarding because of the direct involvement in a variety of proceedings. Whether working overtime, picking up extra work on the side, or making it one's own business, opportunities make this a lucrative job choice. The *OOH* predicts job opportunities to be excellent for court reporters, with jobs growing at a rate of 25 percent between 2006 and 2016. Wage and salary court reporters had median annual earnings of $45,610 in 2006, ranging from less than $23,430 to more than $77,770. Median annual earnings were $45,080 for court reporters working in local government and $41,720 for those working in business support service (*OOH*).

Compensation and compensation methods for court reporters vary with the type of reporting job, the experience of the individual reporter, the level of certification achieved, and the region of the country. Official court reporters earn a salary and a per-page fee for transcripts. Many salaried court reporters supplement their income by doing freelance work, being paid by the job, and on a per-page fee.

Bailiffs

The *OOH* explains: "Bailiffs, also known as *marshals* or *court officers*, are law enforcement officers who maintain safety and order in courtrooms. Their duties, which vary by location, include enforcing courtroom rules, assisting judges, guarding juries from outside contact, delivering court documents and providing general security for courthouses." These positions go by different titles in different jurisdictions and have various classifications and pay rates.

Some positions are sworn police officers and deputies and some are nonsworn, unarmed personnel. What used to be a more sedate job has become increasingly important—and dangerous—with courtroom violence creating greater concerns and increased security measures. Individuals interested in these positions should speak with the agencies responsible for courtroom security to learn their specific requirements, including the U.S. Marshals Service at www.usmarshals.gov.

Median annual earnings of bailiffs were $34,210 in 2006, ranging from less than $18,390 to more than $58,270. Median annual earnings were $30,510 in local government.

Clerks

Court clerks fill many roles that assist the administration of justice. Although not as glamorous as being on the front line, this important job includes maintaining accurate records and ensuring that court schedules are made and kept. The system, whether criminal or civil, revolves around records and paperwork. Clerks are responsible for assuring that all records are properly generated while processing a case and maintained according to agency policy and procedure as well as statutory data retention laws. This may include filing indictments, information, and verdicts. The clerk may also accept and document filings and other legal submissions to ensure deadlines are met, providing records in accordance with data practices law and receiving fees and fines, court costs, forfeitures, and victim restitution. Although many of these positions are clerical, those who work their way up to be *the* clerk of court attain a prestigious, well-paying position.

Other "Helping" Professions Necessary to the Justice System

The number of jobs within criminal justice is quite astounding. Not all of these are what many associate with the criminal justice system. Although some are uniformed, armed law enforcement-related careers, other important jobs are considered more "helping," but are equally important. Psychologists, social workers, and case managers are involved with both the adult and juvenile systems. Chemical dependency and domestic abuse counselors work hand-in-hand with financial, marriage, and vocational counselors. The variety of jobs from prevention on the one end to treatment on the other offers a wide array of career options.

Because our legal system seeks to help people who become involved with it, including those being punished, almost every job in the helping professions *outside* the legal system can be found *within* the system. The *OOH* states:

> Social and human service assistant is a generic term for people with a wide array of job titles, including human service worker, case management aide, social work assistant, community support worker, mental health aid, community outreach worker, life skill counselor, or gerontology aide. . . . Social and human service assistants . . . assess clients' needs, establish their eligibility for benefits and services . . . and help to obtain them.

The *OOH* also reports:

> Social work is a profession for those with a strong desire to help improve people's lives. Social workers help people function the best way they can in their environment, deal with their relationships, and solve personal and family problems. . . . These problems may include inadequate housing, unemployment, serious illness, disability, or substance abuse. Social workers also assist families that have serious domestic conflicts, including those involving child or spousal abuse. . . .
>
> Most social workers specialize. Although some conduct research or are involved in planning or policy development, most social workers prefer an area of practice in which they interact with clients.
>
> *Child, family, and school social workers* provide social services and assistance to improve the social and psychological functioning of children and their families and to maximize the family well-being and academic functioning of children. Some social workers . . . help find foster homes for neglected, abandoned, or abused children. In schools, they address such problems as teenage pregnancy, misbehavior and truancy. They also advise teachers on how to cope with problem students. . . .
>
> *Mental health and substance abuse social workers* assess and treat individuals with mental illness, or substance abuse problems, including abuse of alcohol, tobacco or other drugs. Such services include individual and group therapy, outreach, crisis intervention, social rehabilitation and training in skills of everyday living. They may also help plan for supportive services to ease patients' return to the community. Mental health and substance abuse social workers are likely to work in hospitals, substance abuse treatment centers, individual and family services agencies, or local governments.

Median annual earnings of child, family, and school social workers were $37,480 in 2006, ranging from less than $24,480 to more than $62,530. Median annual earnings in the industries employing the largest numbers of child, family, and school social workers in 2006 were:

Elementary and secondary schools	$48,360
Local government	43,500
State government	39,000
Individual and family services	32,680
Other residential care facilities	32,590

Median annual earnings of medical and public health social workers were $43,040 in 2006, ranging from less than $27,280 to more than $64,070. Median annual earnings in the industries employing the largest numbers of medical and public health social workers in 2006 were:

General medical and surgical hospitals	$48,420
Home health care services	44,470
Local government	41,590
Nursing care facilities	38,550
Individual and family services	35,510

Median annual earnings of mental health and substance abuse social workers were $35,410 in 2006, ranging from less than $22,490 to more than $57,630. Median annual earnings in the industries employing the largest numbers of mental health and substance abuse social workers in 2006 were:

Local government	$39,550
Psychiatric and substance abuse hospitals	39,240
Individual and family services	34,920
Residential mental retardation, mental health, and substance abuse facilities	30,590
Outpatient mental health and substance abuse centers	34,290

Median annual earnings of all other social workers were $43,580 in 2006, ranging from less than $25,540 to more than $68,500. Median annual earnings in the industries employing the largest numbers of all other social workers in 2006 were:

Local government	$46,330
State government	45,070
Individual and family services	35,150

According to the *OOH*: "Employment of social workers is expected to increase by 22 percent during the 2006–16 decade, which is much faster than the average for all occupations. The growing elderly population and the aging baby boom generation will create greater demand for health and social services, resulting in rapid job growth among gerontology social workers. Employment of social workers in private social service agencies also will increase."

Counseling is another occupation projected to grow much faster than average through 2012. "Counselors assist people with personal, family, educational, mental health and career problems. Their duties vary greatly depending on their occupational specialty, which is determined by the setting in which they work and the population they serve" says the *OOH*.

"Job prospects vary greatly based on the occupational specialty. Prospects for rehabilitation counselors are excellent because many people are leaving the field or retiring. Furthermore, opportunities are very good in substance abuse and behavioral disorder counseling because relatively low wages and long hours make recruiting new entrants difficult. For school counselors, job prospects should be good because many people are leaving the occupation to retire; however, opportunities may be more favorable in rural and urban areas, rather than the suburbs, because it is often difficult to recruit people to these areas" (*OOH*).

According to the *OOH*: "Education requirements vary based on occupational specialty and state licensure and certification requirements. A master's degree is usually required to be licensed as a counselor. Some states require counselors in public employment to have a master's degree; others accept a bachelor's degree with appropriate counseling courses. Counselor education programs in colleges and universities are often found in departments of education or psychology." Different states have different licensing requirements that should be investigated.

The judicial system provides work for people of all levels of education, experience, and background. In fact, some people who were "on the wrong side" of the law earlier in their lives are now playing valuable roles in criminal justice. Some believe those who have been in trouble themselves, and possibly even served jail or prison time, can address the issues and concerns of those presently involved better than those who have merely read about it. Similarly, some exceptional chemical dependency and domestic abuse counselors have police records dating back to before they received treatment. Such experiences give them valuable insight for helping those currently needing treatment. So, whether you like to work with the young or the old, those accused of committing a crime or those victimized by it, the legal system has a place for you.

A Caution

Just as other criminal justice careers have risks, so too do jobs in the helping professions. Any work having direct interaction with those involved in the criminal justice system has the potential to provide great personal and professional satisfaction, but also has the potential to lead to stress and burnout.

A study by Evans et al. (2006, p. 80) states the reality of such positions: "Excessive job demands, limited latitude in decision-making and unhappiness about the place of the mental health social worker in modern services contribute to poor job satisfaction and burnout." Left unattended, stress can produce negative physical and emotional effects, even a desire to leave the profession that was once so attractive.

Everyone should manage both their physical and emotional health. Social worker Robb (2004) states: "If social workers fail to respect their own needs and limitations, they can just fall in on themselves. Lots of social workers, myself included, want to save the world. But, this drive must be tempered by realism." (That actually speaks to everyone in criminal justice.) As Nobel Peace Prize winner Emily Greene Balch (1867–1961) said in 1946: "Let us be patient with one another, And even patient with ourselves. We have a long, long way to go."

Consider next the third component of the criminal justice system, corrections.

OPPORTUNITIES IN CORRECTIONS

"One out of every 31 adults was either in prison or on probation or parole according to two new reports from the Bureau of Justice Statistics (summarized in the following paragraph). In total, 7.2 million or 3.2 percent of adults in the United States were part of the correctional system ("7.2 Million U.S. Adults Part of the Corrections System," 2007, p. 10). From a societal perspective, these numbers are troubling. From a careers perspective, however, this is nothing short of a windfall of job opportunities.

At year-end 2006 federal and state correctional authorities had jurisdiction over 1,570,861 prisoners, an increase of 2.8 percent since year-end 2005 (Sabol et al., 2007, p. 1). The federal system held 12.3 percent of these prisoners. During 2006, the prison population grew at a faster rate than in the previous five years (Sabol et al., p. 1). In addition, the number of adult men and women in the United States being supervised on probation or parole at the end of 2006 reached 5,035,225, up by 1.8 percent (Glaze and Bonczar, 2007, p. 1). Figure 3–1 illustrates this dramatic growth.

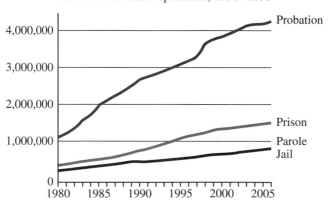

Adult Correctional Populations, 1980–2006

FIGURE 3–1   Adult Correctional Populations 1980–2006

SOURCE: U.S. Department of Justice Bureau of Justice Statistics, www.ojp.usdoj.gov/bjs/glance/corr2.htm.

Probation—court-ordered community supervision of convicted offenders by a probation agency. In many instances, the supervision requires adherence to specific rules of conduct while in the community.

Prison—confinement in a state or federal correctional facility to serve a sentence of more than one year, although in some jurisdictions the length of sentence which results in prison confinement is longer.

Jail—confinement in a local jail while pending trial, awaiting sentencing, serving a sentence that is usually less than one year, or awaiting transfer to other facilities after conviction.

Parole—community supervision after a period of incarceration. These data include only adults who are on active or inactive parole supervision or some other form of conditional release, including mandatory release, following a term of incarceration.

Purposes of Corrections

The title "corrections" reflects the desire to rehabilitate, or correct, antisocial behavior. Methods used to "correct" offenders exist a along a continuum of increasing severity, with counseling on one end and incarceration on the other. Corrections mirrors society's changing perspectives on how to deal with people who commit crimes. When society is more interested in rehabilitation, corrections is expected to respond with increased treatment programs both in and out of institutions. When a more conservative trend advocates "getting tough on crime," more lockup space is demanded. A primary purpose of corrections is to make society safer. Those who are incarcerated can do no harm.

> The purposes of corrections are to punish and to rehabilitate offenders while protecting the public and making our society safer.

The Purposes of Adult and Juvenile Corrections Compared. Like law enforcement and the courts, corrections is divided into an adult system and a juvenile system. Traditionally, the adult system has tended to be more punitive and punishment-oriented whereas the juvenile system has emphasized treatment and rehabilitation. Typical of state statutes regarding adult offenders is Chapter 609 of the *Minnesota Statutes,* which states that the purpose of the adult criminal code is:

> To protect the public safety and welfare by preventing the commission of crime through the deterring effect of the sentences authorized, the rehabilitation of those convicted, and their confinement when the public safety and interest requires.

In contrast, typical of state statutes regarding juveniles is Chapter 260 of the *Minnesota Statutes:*

> The purpose of the laws relating to children alleged or adjudicated to be delinquent is to promote the public safety and reduce juvenile delinquency by maintaining the integrity of the substantive law prohibiting certain behavior and by developing individual responsibility for lawful behavior. This purpose should be pursued through means that are fair and just, that recognize the unique characteristics and needs of children, and that give children access to opportunities for personal and social growth.

The trend of punishing adults and "treating" juveniles seems to be reversing itself to some extent. More emphasis is being placed on the *treatment* of adult offenders while, at the same time, more traditional penalties, such as incarceration and even manual labor, are being used more frequently as "treatment" for juvenile offenders. Nonetheless, some people prefer working with juveniles because the system remains more treatment-oriented, and our society retains the belief that youths are generally more capable than adults of redirecting their lives.

> The primary difference between adult corrections and juvenile corrections has traditionally been the *punishment* of adults and the *treatment* of juveniles, although this distinction has become somewhat blurred in recent years.

Is corrections as exciting as being in on the action-packed arrest? (Remember, that's only 20 percent of police work.) Maybe not. However, police work doesn't offer the long-range benefits of helping people change. Many police officers are frustrated by seeing only the misery caused by crime and not having a positive influence on people, as those who work in corrections often do, particularly those in probation and parole, as discussed shortly. First, let's look at the most prevalent professional in corrections—the corrections officer, or CO.

Corrections Officers (COs)

As noted by the *OOH:* "Correctional officers, also known as *detention officers*, are responsible for overseeing individuals who have been arrested and are awaiting trial or who have been convicted of a crime and sentenced to serve time in a jail, reformatory or penitentiary." Although corrections officers and detention officers both perform their functions behind bars, and their jobs are similar in some ways, their jobs are also different in critical ways. One major distinction is the different constitutional justifications for doing what they do. Individuals held in detention have not yet appeared before the court and, therefore, retain the presumption of innocence. Consequently, any punitive aspect of the correctional environment is not justified. The officer's duty regarding such individuals is to keep them secure until they can be brought before a judge.

The jail population changes constantly as some are released, some are convicted and transferred to prison, and new offenders are arrested and enter the system. Correctional officers in local jails admit and process about 12 million people a year, with about 700,000 offenders in jail at any given time. Correctional officers maintain security and inmate accountability to prevent disturbances, assaults, and escapes. According to the *OOH*:

> Correctional officers learn most of what they need to know for their work through on-the-job training. Qualifications vary by agency, but all agencies require a high school diploma or equivalent, and some also require some college education or full-time work experience. A high school diploma or graduation equivalency degree is required by all employers. The Federal Bureau of Prisons requires entry-level correctional officers to have at least a bachelor's degree; 3 years of full-time experience in a field providing counseling, assistance or supervision to individuals; or a combination of the two. Some state and local corrections agencies require some college credits, but law enforcement or military experience may be substituted to fulfill this requirement. . . .

> All institutions require correctional officers to be at least 18 to 21 years of age, be a U.S. citizen or permanent resident and have no felony convictions. . . .

> Correctional officers must be in good health. Candidates for employment generally are required to meet formal standards of physical fitness, eyesight and hearing. In addition, many jurisdictions use standard tests to determine applicant suitability to work in a correctional environment. Good judgment and the ability to think and act quickly are indispensable. Applicants are typically screened for drug abuse, subject to background checks and required to pass a written examination.

Like many other jobs in criminal justice, working in correctional institutions likely involves shift work including working nights, weekends, and holidays, with an element of danger always present. Also similar to other criminal justice jobs, stress can result from working in corrections. Thus, this job isn't for everyone. Deputy Warden Ross (2008) explains how it takes a unique combination of being able to maintain calm but spring to immediate action when necessary:

> Any correctional facility, no matter how big or how small, is like a self-contained city. Correctional officers can benefit from having many skills. Some skills such as first aid, self-defense and tactical response can be learned. Others such as good communication skills, keeping calm during intense circumstances and being a team player are often brought to the job as personality traits proven at prior jobs.

> I can't think of another job in the criminal justice system that requires such a keen sense of both how to respond in a crisis while knowing what to look for and to avoid the crisis in the first place. This job is not for anyone easily intimidated or bothered by the fact they, too, are locked within a facility whose inhabitants society has determined aren't safe.

It is a unique challenge to be employed in an environment that requires determined concentration and awareness of all your actions and even your dialogue. A prison is a "glass house" where a critical incident is always imminent. More times than not the officer's version of an incident is placed against dozens of inmate witnesses. The most successful officers are habitually firm but fair. The inmates' respect has to be earned through interaction, truthfulness, integrity and professionalism. You have to be quick to remember names, ID numbers and especially nicknames with identifiers for gang affiliation.

The most successful corrections employees are never complacent and keep lines of communication open with the inmates. A career in corrections requires honed and polished people skills and simply is not for the timid. Inmate leaders in population actually seek out the strongest officers with whom to communicate their concerns. They have a genuine need to live in a safe environment, and most want to do their time with no unnecessary trouble. Officers who carry a professional persona and are approachable, willing to assist with the inmates' concerns, will acquire valuable information. Such knowledge keeps the prison administration abreast of the condition or "pulse" of the camp. The successful prison hinges on strong front-line officers. They are the most critical link in the necessary daily routine to gather and analyze information.

TV reality shows have provided some insight into what it's like to work on the inside, but just like police work, there's more to it. It takes courage to be a corrections officer, and distinct skills to do it well. It's one thing to work the road and upset a motorist giving them a ticket. It's another to contribute to starting a riot. Those who aren't a fit for this work know it almost immediately; those who are can pursue a long and satisfying career in this special part of the criminal justice system.

Ross concludes: "More than 20 years in a corrections career has continued to provide me a chance to be a part of a progressive law enforcement field that offered quick advancement, highly evolved training and allowed first-hand interaction with the fascinating criminal element."

> Corrections officers comprise over half of all employees in corrections. Duties include maintaining the security and safety of those being held within the correctional facility, enforcing rules and regulations, and sometimes providing counseling to inmates. Present and predicted increases in inmate populations mean more corrections officers will be needed in the future.

The *OOH* states:

> Employment of correctional officers is expected to grow 16 percent between 2006 and 2016, faster than the average for all occupations. Increasing demand for correctional officers will stem from population growth and rising rates of incarceration. Mandatory sentencing guidelines calling for longer sentences and reduced parole for inmates are a primary reason for historically increasing incarceration rates. Some states are reconsidering mandatory sentencing guidelines because of budgetary constraints, court decisions and doubts about their effectiveness. Additionally, the Supreme Court recently ruled to make federal sentencing guidelines voluntary rather than mandatory, for judges. It is unclear how many states will change their sentencing policies and how long it will be before any changes affect the prison population. Nevertheless, these developments could moderate future increases in the prison population and cause employment of correctional officers to grow more slowly than they have in the past.

Median annual earnings of correctional officers and jailers were $35,760 in 2006, ranging from less than $23,600 to more than $58,580. Median annual earnings in the public sector were $47,750 in the federal government, $36,140 in state government, and $34,820 in local government. In the facilities support services industry, where the relatively small number of officers employed by privately operated prisons is classified, median annual earnings were $25,050 (*OOH*).

Median annual earnings of first-line supervisors/managers of correctional officers were $52,580 in 2006, ranging from less than $33,270 to more than $81,230. Median annual earnings were $51,500 in state government and \$52,940 in local government. According to the Federal Bureau of Prisons, the starting salary for federal correctional officers was \$28,862 a year. Starting federal salaries were slightly higher in areas where prevailing local pay levels were higher.

In addition to typical benefits, correctional officers employed in the public sector usually are provided with uniforms or a clothing allowance. Civil service systems or merit boards cover officers employed by the federal government and most state governments. Their retirement coverage entitles correctional officers to retire at age fifty after twenty years of service or at any age with twenty-five years of service (*OOH*).

A career in corrections, although demanding and challenging, can be extremely rewarding and an ideal fit for those wanting to make society safer. Furthermore, the trend toward new generation prisons and direct supervision gives correctional officers more involvement with inmates and more control over the populations they supervise, which translates into enhanced professionalism and greater job satisfaction. Once considered "just a guard," as professionalism in this career continues to be recognized and expected, so do opportunities to make a difference. Because most inmates will be released, the impact correctional officers have on those serving their time is significant.

Probation and Parole Officers

Careers in probation and parole are other options for those seeking employment in corrections. Like corrections officers, probation and parole officers counsel and monitor offenders, but they also evaluate the progress of offenders to determine whether they are abiding by what is expected of them by the courts and whether they will eventually be released from supervision.

> The primary difference between probation and parole is that probation is an alternative to incarceration, whereas parole is supervised release from incarceration before the expiration of the sentence. Both probation and parole officers have considerable interaction with offenders.

Although their work will find them meeting with offenders within the confines of jails and prisons, probation and parole work is considered "community corrections" as opposed to "institutional corrections," which is work with those who are confined. Probation is considered a supervisory status an offender is given rather than incarceration. Parole is an early release from prison, with any violation reports or requests for action going directly to the releasing authority (usually considered the department of corrections). Early release is often predicated on good behavior and may be influenced by such issues as institutional overcrowding.

The *OOH* notes: "Many people who are convicted of crimes are placed on probation instead of being sent to prison. People who have served time in prison are often released on parole. During probation and parole, offenders must stay out of trouble and meet various other requirements. Probation officers, parole officers and correctional treatment specialists work with and monitor offenders to prevent them from committing new crimes."

Probation officers, called community supervision officers in some states, supervise people placed on probation. *Correctional treatment specialists*, also known as case managers, counsel offenders and create rehabilitation plans for them to follow when they are no longer in prison or on parole. *Parole officers* perform many of the same duties as probation officers. The difference is that parole officers supervise offenders who have been released from prison, whereas probation officers work with those who are sentenced to probation instead of prison. *Pretrial services officers* conduct pretrial investigations, the findings of which help determine whether suspects should be released before their trial (*OOH*).

According to Arvidson (2008): "The work of a probation officer changes throughout every day. It's never the same thing twice, and a variety of skills are required. You have to know how to treat people with respect but not let them take advantage of you. A working knowledge of the Constitution, as well as of federal and state laws is a requirement, as is knowing the variety of policies and procedures within the organization you work for. You have to know how to appear in court and develop professional relationships with the judges and the police. Of course, our job like all others is becoming increasingly dependent on technology, so computer skills are necessary."

The job of a probation officer can be even more varied depending on special opportunities one may pursue. Arvidson explains: "I've been in community corrections for over 20 years. My present role working specifically with adult gang members is especially satisfying. I'm often out of the office interviewing clients, testifying in court or executing search and arrest warrants along with the police. I see my job as both helping keep the community safe and providing an opportunity for offenders to get their lives back together for those who want. For those who don't, I'm the one who holds them accountable."

In most states at least a four-year degree is required, and can often be in any area of study associated with the work (criminal justice, psychology, social work, etc.). Different agencies may prefer certain levels of experience or specific training or education. According to the *OOH*: "A typical agency has several levels of probation and parole officers and correctional treatment specialists, as well as supervisors. Advancement is primarily based on length of experience and performance. A graduate degree, such as a master's degree in criminal justice, social work or psychology, may be helpful for advancement."

Probation and parole officers are professionals with vital roles in our corrections system. The job outlook for those interested in becoming probation and/or parole officers is positive, as the entire area of corrections continues to expand.

The *OOH* states:

> Employment of probation officers and correctional treatment specialists is projected to grow as fast as the average for all occupations through 2016. Job opportunities are expected to be excellent. Employment of probation officers and correctional treatment specialists is projected to grow 11 percent between 2006 and 2016, as fast as the average for all occupations. … In addition to openings due to growth, many openings will be created by replacement needs, especially openings due to the large number of these workers who are expected to retire. This occupation is not attractive to some potential entrants due to relatively low earnings, heavy workloads, and high stress. For these reasons, job opportunities are expected to be excellent.

"Median annual earnings of probation officers and correctional treatment specialists in 2006 were $42,500, ranging from less than $28,000 to more than $71,160. Median annual earnings for probation officers and correctional treatment specialists employed in state government were $42,970; those employed in local government earned $43,100. Higher wages tend to be found in urban areas" (*OOH*).

The fact is, no one works in the criminal justice field to become wealthy, but job satisfaction and what one can do to contribute to community is the reward those finding a satisfying career in this area receive.

Juvenile Corrections

If you're interested in working with youths, the same positions needed in adult corrections can generally be found in the juvenile justice system. In fact, considering that the historical focus of juvenile justice have been treatment and rehabilitation, this area of corrections depends heavily on probation officers, counselors, case workers, social workers, educators, and those interested in providing "surrogate" families for troubled youths.

As Gondles (2004, p. 6) observes: "Kids today may be maturing physically earlier than before, but mentally they still require teaching, training, loving, skill-building and learning through years of maturity. Bodies may be growing faster, but no child is born with morals, with judgment or with remorse; they learn these and other emotions and controls."

In answering the question, "Why would anyone want to work in the business of juvenile corrections?" Frank Alarcon (2004, pp. 8–9) asserts:

> We have the wonderful opportunity to help change people's lives in positive ways. As we have embraced restorative principles and practices, we continue to improve public safety. We assist victims of juvenile crime, help communities strengthen families and neighborhoods, and give young people opportunities to reduce deficits and develop the skills necessary to make it in the real world. . . .
>
> Our work takes us to every nook and cranny of our communities—poor and affluent, rural and urban, diverse and homogeneous. We run small six-bed group homes and large 1,000-bed facilities. We see courtrooms and boardrooms and visit the YMCA and jail.

It is unfortunate, but true, that the roles of those working in adult corrections and the juvenile system are becoming more blurred as the level of sophistication increases at younger ages. Younger offenders being placed in adult facilities is causing challenges, as is the demand for separate secure facilities for only juveniles. The appeal of working with juveniles, who are often considered more amenable to treatment and capable of change than adults, is what draws people to this area.

Correctional Alternatives to Incarceration

Because of factors such as increasing jail and prison populations, decreasing funding, aging facilities with limited housing, and ever-changing societal demands and expectations, both the adult and juvenile systems are considering alternatives to incarceration. Some options are residential facilities such as halfway houses, prerelease centers, transition centers, work furlough and community work centers, community treatment centers, and restitution centers. These facilities employ a wide range of staff, including probation/parole officers, counselors, caseworkers, educators, health care workers, and numerous administrative, management, and support/clerical personnel. Nonresidential correctional alternatives, such as day reporting centers, require similar personnel. Other options include less costly but often very effective alternatives, such as bringing offenders, victims, and community members together to confront the issues and support change by the offender.

Another option that eases overcrowded jails and prisons is to allow offenders to remain in their own homes under house arrest.

Electronic Monitoring and House Arrest.   Used in conjunction with *electronic monitoring* (EM), house arrest or home detention offers an effective, inexpensive method of supervising probationers. A typical electronic monitoring system (EMS) consists of a bracelet worn on the offender's wrist or ankle. The bracelet contains a transmitter that emits a signal that is continuously monitored, enabling authorities to know the whereabouts of the offender at all times. The increasing use of home detention and electronic monitoring is creating new work opportunities for those who implement and manage these programs.

> As house arrest and electronic monitoring gain popularity and grow in use, new job opportunities are created for those who implement and manage such programs.

According to Arvidson:

> The trend in community corrections work is no longer in simply finding alternatives to incarcerating the offender. That only begins to address the issues of cost savings and offender re-integration. Community corrections agencies continue to refine their risk/needs assessment tools. The goal is to ensure that the most serious offenders are getting the closer attention they warrant. . . . Although it has been used by correctional agencies for over 20 years, electronic monitoring, specifically GPS (Global Positioning Satellite) based monitoring, is gaining tremendous ground as an implemented innovation. . . . Today's technology not only can determine that an offender is speeding on his way home from work, but can also send him a text page instructing him to slow down. That is just one example of how much the job has changed and will certainly continue to change. Twenty years ago you could cite the responsibilities of a PO and have a list of 10 or 12 things. With today's specialty caseloads, that list doesn't end.

Other Careers in Corrections

Although corrections officers make up the largest number of careers, many other careers are available, including administrative, clerical, educational, professional/technical, treatment-oriented, medical, religious, recreational, and maintenance/food service positions.

Furthermore, those facilities involved in prison labor must also staff personnel knowledgeable in the specific industry and the products being produced. Finally, as more correctional facilities are built, an increasing number of staff in *all* of these categories must be hired to keep the institutions operating effectively and constitutionally.

Ross explains two factors affecting corrections and resulting in even more jobs. The first factor is the increasing sophistication of the criminals themselves, which has enhanced the need for specialists within the system, such as specialized gang investigators, where little or no need existed in the past. These positions also require greater numbers of support staff. A second change is the openness of corrections, especially prisons, which was not the case decades ago when no one was allowed past the front gate. Therefore, a key member of the prison's executive staff must be trained as a public information officer who specializes in working with the media and public. "Making people aware of what our job is is definitely a good thing" (Ross, 2008).

DISQUALIFIERS

As noted, all jobs have disqualifiers—background issues or behaviors that can stand in the way of you being hired. Any number of factors could disqualify a candidate from a position in the judicial system or corrections. Whatever they may be, realistically consider and confront them.

Some factors such as disabilities covered by federal law should not prevent you from being considered, whereas others may disqualify you from certain duties. If you feel something is unfair, appropriately check it further.

If a job has statutory bars, as discussed in the previous chapter, it can be over before it starts. If a statutory bar exists, such as being convicted of a felony, check your state's laws. In a state where you can't be a police officer, prison guard, or social worker with a felony on your record, nothing will change the legislative mandate and you will need to realistically consider other careers. Some states do permit felony records to be expunged or pardoned, clearing the way for employment in certain criminal justice fields. Find out whether you have legal options to deal with a prior conviction. Even if an issue isn't a statutory bar to being hired, lying about *anything* during the process is grounds for immediate disqualification.

Even without statutory bars, many employers in criminal justice positions believe that past behavior is the best predictor of future behavior. Whether you agree with this philosophy or not, what you have done in the past, both positive and negative, will influence the hiring process for you. Events from your past that may disqualify you from employment in a given department include a DWI, especially a recent one, or a series of traffic tickets—behaviors that suggest you are unable to obey the law or otherwise lack good judgment, both of which are red flags to an employer. How you manage your personal life may also be considered. An inability to manage your finances, having to file for bankruptcy, or being the subject of multiple police calls because you can't get along with your neighbor can lead an employer to wonder if you'd be a good "fit" with the department.

If you have a clean record, keep it that way. If not, put as much time between any potential disqualifier incidents and your search for work, and reinforce your positive character by doing outstanding things to show you have learned and changed. Also make sure you present other positive features and facets that demonstrate you are "well rounded," such as volunteering, being involved in sports, having hobbies or other interests, and the like. When applying for criminal justice work, community service is always a plus, along with a lifestyle in line with the responsibilities you wish to be hired for.

CONCLUSION

The numbers speak for themselves. Career opportunities in all areas of the criminal justice system will continue to grow. For qualified applicants this is very promising. Many more jobs are within the system than most people realize.

Although social and political demands may change how society expects offenders to be handled, there is no denying the fact that the number of offenders to be dealt with continues to increase. Whether these people are in confinement or in the community, job opportunities of every sort provide exciting careers to make a difference.

AN INSIDER'S VIEW

LAWYERS WEAR MANY HATS: IS ONE RIGHT FOR YOU?

Marsh J. Halberg

Attorney at Law
Edina, Minnesota

The dilemma most students face, whether in college or law school, is trying to envision a job they will enjoy when they enter the workforce. Each of you knows that the "real world" is far different from that which you learn about in books.

When I was going to law school, the most common question people would ask me was what type of law I intended to practice. My standard answer at that time was, "I don't know. It could be anything except criminal law." Reflecting back on that, for the past 20 years over 90 percent of my practice has involved criminal law. I laugh at my poor prediction of what lay ahead for future employment!

What I discovered, upon looking more closely at the practice of law, was that a great number of lawyers spend their days sitting behind a desk and pushing papers, whether it be drafting corporate documents, preparing real estate papers or drafting wills. I recognized that I was very much a "people person" and that it would be a slow, agonizing death for me to sit behind a desk all day, staring at four walls. This meant that I wanted to practice in an area of law that involved interacting with people and getting out of the office. Criminal law, more than any other area, allows an attorney to interact with many different people daily and to also spend a great deal of time in the courtroom.

While corporate or commercial legal battles can drag on for many years, a criminal case is typically charged soon after the alleged crime occurs. The defendant has a right to a speedy trial, which may occur within several months after the case is charged. As such, criminal law involves a high-volume, fast-turnover type of workload.

Because of the high volume of criminal cases, most matters (over 95 percent) never go to trial. As such, the attorneys involved for both the prosecution and defense become professional negotiators, required to make quick decisions and move on to the next case. This is necessitated by the pure volume of cases in the system. We have all heard the saying, "It's not *what* you know but *who* you know." To a certain extent this is true in the state criminal court system. Because so many case negotiations occur, the practice of criminal law is very relationship-oriented. Attorneys work together over and over on a weekly, if not daily, basis negotiating, if not trying, cases. A level of confidence, respect and friendship develops between lawyers when that much contact occurs. As such, a relatively small band of criminal defense attorneys practice the lion's share of the criminal work.

Where I live, most of the municipal communities contract with private law firms to represent them on city prosecution matters because it is more cost-effective than hiring full-time government employees. The city attorneys prosecute all of the lesser crimes (i.e., everything short of felony cases). This might involve DWI, forgery, assault, prostitution and so on. The "big cases" (murder, robbery, etc.) are handled by a full-time county attorney's office.

The same private lawyers who handle the city prosecution matters on a contract basis are free to practice criminal defense work outside of the communities for which they prosecute. Therefore, it is very common to see an attorney being a prosecutor in a courtroom one morning and, that afternoon, being a defense attorney in a separate courtroom. This is an ethical and recognized course of practice. Frankly, it allows attorneys who are both prosecutors and defense attorneys to better serve both of their clients. That is, prosecutors know all of the defense tricks and vice versa. I think it also prevents attorneys from becoming too jaded by working on only one side of the fence. Specifically, attorneys see that police officers are not always right, nor are defendants always falsely accused. It gives the attorney a far better perspective of the tough job on both sides.

For 25 years I worked as a city prosecutor for a suburb of Minneapolis. Although the city is relatively small, we generate in excess of 10,000 charges per year. Many of the minor traffic matters are simply handled by the violator paying the fine and never going to court. Many cases, however, whether traffic charges or criminal charges, involve the defendants making a required court appearance. Another part-time prosecutor and I handle thousands of criminal prosecution files each year. I typically spent approximately 50 percent of every day in the courtroom. It was not uncommon, on a typical day, to work through in excess of 100 separate cases.

In the last several years I switched to the defense side for a change of pace. I tell my clients that much of what they are paying for are my relationships with others within the system—it is my ability to be a professional negotiator rather than Clarence Darrow in the courtroom. More deals are done over the water cooler than standing in front of the judge in the courtroom.

I would encourage you to do internships for various lawyers to get a better feel for what the practice of law is actually like before making the dive into law school.

Marsh J. Halberg *has been employed in the legal profession for over twenty-five years, during which he has served as an assistant county attorney, a city prosecutor, and a defense attorney. Having been a partner with the law firm of Thomsen & Nybeck, P.A., he has begun his own firm as founding partner of Halberg Criminal Defense in Edina, Minnesota.*

 MIND STRETCHES

1. How do you feel about lawyers?

2. If you were to become a criminal lawyer, would you rather be a prosecutor or a defense attorney?

3. Do you think judges should be elected public officials or appointed by members of local and state government?

4. What do most people think of when they think of a "correctional officer job"? Where did you acquire the information on which you base your answer?

5. What benefits would you find in a job in corrections that may not exist in a street police job?

6. What negatives would you want to be aware of in considering a job as a correctional officer?

7. Can you think of unique skills that could make a job candidate more attractive to a hiring agency?

8. Is there a danger in pursuing a specific job that "really excites" you, to the point you do not believe any other job would be worthwhile?

9.   What corrections jobs might become more necessary in the future? Less necessary?

10.   How do you predict corrections will change? Why?

REFERENCES

Alarcon, Francisco "Frank" J. "Juvenile Corrections: Why Would Anyone Want to Work in This Business?" *Corrections Today* (June 2004): 8–9.

Arvidson, Joe. Probation officer, Ramsey County, Minnesota. Personal interview, February 25, 2008.

Evans, Sherrill; Huxley, Peter; Gately, Claire; Webber, Martin; Mears, Alex; Pajak, Sarah; Medina, Jibby; Kendall, Tim; and Katona, Cornelius. "Mental Health, Burnout and Job Satisfaction among Mental Health Social Workers in England and Wales." *British Journal of Psychiatry*, Vol. 188, No.1 2006, pp. 75–80.

Glaze, Lauren E., and Thomas P. Bonczar. *Probation and Parole in the United States, 2006.* Washington, DC: Bureau of Justice Statistics Bulletin, December 2007. (NCJ 220218)

Gondles, James A., Jr. "Kids Are Kids, Not Adults." *Corrections Today* (June 2004): 6–7.

Jones, Leigh. "Law School Costs Outpace Associate Raises." *National Law Journal*, January 30, 2006.

Occupational Outlook Handbook, 2008–09 Edition. Bureau of Labor Statistics, U.S. Department of Labor. Washington, DC: U.S. Government Printing Office, December 18, 2007.

Robb, Matthew. "7 Habits of Highly Effective Social Workers." *Social Work Today,* Vol. 4, No. 3, March/April 2004, p. 24. Available online at www.socialworktoday.com/archive/swt_0304p24.htm.

Ross, Alan. Deputy Warden of Administration at Dooly State Prison in Georgia. Personal interview, 2008.

Sabol, William J., Heather Couture, and Paige M. Harrison. *Prisoners in 2006.* Washington, DC: Bureau of Justice Statistics Bulletin, December 2007. (NCJ 219416)

"7.2 Million U.S. Adults Part of the Corrections System." *Justice Bulletin* (December 2007): 10–11.

HELPFUL WEBSITES

American Bar Association (ABA)
www.abanet.org

International Corrections and Prisons Association
www.icpa.ca/

American Correctional Association (ACA)
www.corrections.com/aca

Law School Admission Council
www.lsac.org

American Jail Association (AJA)
www.corrections.com/aja/index.html

National Court Reporters Association
www.verbatimreporters.com

American Probation and Parole Association
e-mail: appa@csg.org

Standing Committee on Legal Assistants
www.abanet.org/legalassts

Federal Bureau of Prisons (BOP)
www.bop.gov

United States Court Reporters Association
www.uscra.org

OTHER RESOURCES

American Correctional Association Publications—Call (800) 222-5646, extension 1860
        Correctional Officer Resource Guide, 3rd ed.; Item #631-CC01; $29.95
        Correctional Law for the Correctional Officer, 3rd ed., by William C. Collins, JD; Item #630-CC01; $19.95
        Mental Health in Corrections: An Overview for Correctional Staff, by Wesley Sowers, MD, Kenneth Thompson,
            MD, and Stephen Mullins, MD; Item #210-CC01; $15.00
        Staff Supervision Made Easy, by Scott D. Hutton, PhD; Item #194-CC01; $19.95

CHAPTER 4

CAREERS IN PRIVATE SECURITY

Private security is the invisible empire of criminal justice.

—*Christopher A. Hertig*

Do You Know:

➢ What qualities employers seek in private security applicants?
➢ What promotions are available in private security?
➢ What are the differences between proprietary, contractual, and hybrid security?
➢ Why many law enforcement officers desire jobs as private security directors?
➢ Why cooperation between public law enforcement and private security is necessary and what are some examples of such cooperation?
➢ What areas of public justice are being affected by privatization?
➢ What trend is occurring in corrections?
➢ What typical entry-level, mid-level, and top-level positions exist in private security?
➢ What the outlook for jobs is in private security?

INTRODUCTION

Security. Since September 11, 2001, the word has taken on new meaning and unprecedented importance to most, if not all, Americans. Its significance was captured in the creation of an entirely new government agency—the Department of Homeland Security:

> Many do not stop to realize that private security professionals in business places, at public gathering sites, and in corporate environments are truly first responders to every conceivable calamity from crime to natural disasters. . . . Most people tend to think of public fire, law enforcement and emergency response personnel as first responders, but private security practitioners are often the first responders in their business or corporate environments. They played a key role during the initial moments after the September 11, 2001, terrorist attacks and were instrumental in getting many people safely out of the buildings. They were first responders; they were already on the scene at the time of the attacks, and unfortunately, in some instances, they were also first victims. (Cooke and Hahn, 2006, p. 16)

A trend well underway a decade before the terrorist attacks of 9/11, private security *is* big business and a protective presence that continues to grow every year. An estimated 85 percent of the country's critical infrastructure is protected by private security (*Building Private Security/Public Policing Partnerships to Respond to Terrorism and Public Disorder*, 2004, p. 1). The American Society for Industrial Security (ASIS) notes: "Security is one of the fastest-growing professional careers worldwide. A career in the security field provides a multitude of opportunities. These opportunities range from entry-level security officer positions to investigators specializing in specific areas and managers and directors of security at major corporations and organizations around the world. The demand for heightened security is being increased by theft of information, workplace violence, terrorism and economic crime" ("Career Opportunities in Security," n.d.).

According to the ASIS: "The security industry in the U.S. is a $100 billion a year business and growing. Opportunities exist at all levels within the security industry. All businesses, no matter how small, have security concerns such as fraud, theft, computer hacking, economic espionage or workplace violence. All organizations need to protect themselves from activities that disrupt their normal operations."

As one of the fastest-growing professional careers worldwide, the security field provides a multitude of opportunities, ranging from entry-level security officer positions to investigators specializing in specific areas and managers and directors of security at major corporations and organizations around the world. The demand for heightened security is increased by theft of information, workplace violence, terrorism, and white-collar crime.

A further sign of the maturing nature of corporate security is that Boyden Global Executive Search saw a market need for a formalized chief security officer (CSO) job description. The ASIS International Guidelines Commission is now in the process of helping to develop that description as a guide for companies looking to fill the top security position.

This chapter begins with a comparison of the private security officer and the public law enforcement officer. It then examines the relationship between these two fields; the criticality of cooperation between them, particularly in post-9/11 homeland security efforts; and the expanding privatization of public justice. This is followed by an up-close look at career opportunities within the security profession, including salaries and the potential for growth in this field.

PRIVATE SECURITY: AN OVERVIEW

Because private security is profit-oriented, opportunities exist that are not available in the public sector. With corporate America recognizing that security and loss prevention are as critical to a successful business as management and marketing, an increasing number of very appealing job opportunities are developing, some with pay opportunities and benefits government cannot provide. The stereotype of the retiree sitting at a guard desk overnight for minimum wage is no longer an accurate portrayal of what has become a profession in every sense of the word. Like law enforcement and corrections, much of what happens in this profession is not common knowledge. Consequently, many people considering employment in private security may find themselves relying on inaccurate data. Unless you know someone in the field, you probably obtained information about security work where most people do: the media, which may lead you to believe security work consists primarily of solving crimes the police cannot or will not deal with, perhaps using exotic, if not downright illegal means. Television shows about private detectives frequently do two injustices to the profession. First, they unrealistically glamorize it. Second, they fail to explain that it is a lucrative and necessary business..

The law enforcement officer's job is limited in what they can do. It is just one aspect of the criminal justice system. The role of the police is to investigate *crimes*. But what about facts surrounding a civil, noncriminal negligence case such as a car accident, which falls short of criminal activity but which might spawn significant litigation? Even if it *is* a police matter, police do not always put as much emphasis on obtaining evidence as a defense attorney might like—evidence that could help exonerate the accused. Furthermore, the police have little interest in personal matters such as infidelity investigations or even workers' compensation violations. These are excellent opportunities for the private investigator. Private contract and business disagreements are not jobs of the police. These are also excellent opportunities for the private investigator.

When you consider that the private sector may provide more advancement potential and more overall control of one's professional and personal life, it is easy to see why many law enforcement officers set eventual goals to become private security directors.

Although many individuals who have enjoyed a successful career in law enforcement will enjoy a "second career" in private security, many people successfully use work in the private sector as a stepping-stone into the public sector in order to become a police or corrections officer. Law enforcement is a popular career, and these jobs can be difficult to come by. Having worked in security at any level says a number of things about an applicant for any other position in the criminal justice system:

➤   The applicant has been successfully employed.

➤   The applicant has worked in a position of trust and responsibility.

➤   Unusual hours do not present a problem.

➤   The uniform does not create a power-hungry person.

➤   The applicant can remain calm under stressful circumstances.

Those seeking careers in private security may also wish to consider public security positions as well as those of "special deputies," code enforcement officers, and others with limited law enforcement authority. With increased respect and acceptance by others in the criminal justice system, private sector jobs are becoming more blended than in the past. Many government agencies hire special deputies or part-time police officers who possess law enforcement authority while on duty. These special deputies perform many of the same functions carried out by private security personnel but do so for the government. For example, these officers may work special civic events like parades or other community events. Or they may work at concerts and conventions requiring this level of security, or seasonal work in communities that have increased people in town during vacation season. These officers fill a need by allowing regularly assigned officers to continue performing their jobs. Depending on the hiring authority, some of these positions are considered part-time positions, whereas others are more volunteer, not unlike paid on-call firefighters.

Special deputies are also found in the federal government. For example, the U.S. Marshals assign special deputy marshals to courthouse security as the need arises, either because there is not enough work to justify people full-time, or because there is too much work for the full-time personnel. Similarly, county sheriffs may use part-time personnel for bailiff duty, court security, and even prisoner transport details. Such deputies are often contract employees who possess law enforcement authority only while on duty and only at their assigned venue.

In fact, almost every branch of local, state, and federal government employs people who are not sworn officers or armed to do security work. Examples include police and sheriff reserve officers as well as animal control and code enforcement officers. They may wear a uniform closely resembling any other officer, or it may be modified so as to be noticeably different, or may be purely civilian attire.

Most employers seek security applicants with high school diplomas and some experience in the military police or in state or local-level police work. Other important qualities include good character references, good health, good personal habits, and no police record. A valid driver's license may also be required.

Salaries in private security vary greatly, ranging from around $17,000 a year for unarmed contract security officers to $150,000 or more a year for corporate security managers working for large public companies.

Fringe Benefits

Most security professionals receive benefits from their employers, although various surveys indicate different percentages of employees are receiving certain benefits. Nonetheless, most security employees receive paid vacation time, paid holidays, health care coverage, life insurance, dental insurance, sick leave, a 401(k) plan, and a long-term disability plan. Other benefits frequently provided include tuition reimbursement, childcare support, a pension plan, personal time off, vision insurance, short-term disability, cellular/airtime usage, trade show/convention expenses, and association memberships.

In addition to these benefits, nearly half of security employees receive performance bonuses and many are offered stock options or stock purchase plans and allowed to participate in a profit sharing plan.

Promotions

Like law enforcement, security careers can meet a stumbling block not as prevalent in other careers. Promotions can come few and far between—if at all. The problem is that jobs in the security field tend to be at one end of the spectrum or the other. At the entry level, security jobs can be minimum-wage jobs, with minimal raises. Middle management positions are usually few in number. The money is in top management jobs, either for a corporation or for one's own business. At these levels there is literally no upward limit.

As in law enforcement, promotions in private security may be scarcer than in other professions, particularly into middle management where positions are limited.

Levinson (2006) offers several suggestions for getting promoted: "The time and money you invest to achieve certain security certifications can pay off later in higher salary and better employment possibilities." Many certifications can be found, among other places, on the www.asisonline.org website that include Certified Protection Professional, Professional Certified Investigator, and Physical Security Professional. Levinson also recommends reading: "Whether or not you're interested in certification, there are a variety of options for advancing your skills and experience. If you don't have the money for expensive training, self-study could be the way to go. . . . You may want to consider specializing in a certain security niche. There are many different security specializations out there, and you can't possibly become an expert at them all."

Disqualifiers

Keep in mind criminal history and other issues that can disqualify you from being hired, as some jobs are more restrictive than others. It is your responsibility to know what, if any, convictions will bar you from employment and to understand other issues that cause employers concern.

Political Trends

Politics influence the job market. Just as politics can restrict tax dollars available to hire more public police officers, thus stimulating the market for private sector security-related jobs, national and international politics can cause shifts in the job market. Unquestionably the world politics since September 11, 2001, have contributed to increased security here and abroad. In fact, since the last edition of this book was published, an entire new realm of travel-related security work at airports and elsewhere has evolved. Both public and private sectors have needed to reevaluate the importance and staffing of security-related divisions, creating many new and previously underconsidered or not-even-considered jobs. This includes front-line security, risk management, and emergency response. These areas are among those with the best job outlook and highest growth potential for future career opportunity and development.

PUBLIC VERSUS PRIVATE OFFICERS

Because public policing and private security are closely related, and because people employed in one field often become involved at some time in the other, we will start by looking at how the two fields differ.

A primary difference between public policing and private security, as the names imply, is who you work for. Who pays your salary? Individuals in public policing are paid with tax dollars and, consequently, are accountable to the tax-paying citizens, whether on a local, county, state, or federal level. They are under constant scrutiny by both the public and the politicians charged with overseeing expenditures of public funds, and their incomes are heavily influenced by the tax dollars allocated to policing. Private security positions, in contrast, are funded by business, industry, or any entity in the private sector needing protection beyond what public law enforcement provides.

Another basic difference between public policing and private security is the essential goals of each. Public law enforcement has traditionally been quite reactive, operating as a service to the jurisdiction that pays for it (although the move toward community policing is leading officers to take a more proactive approach to jurisdictional issues). Ideally, public police serve everyone within the jurisdiction equally, without a profit motive. People call, and the police are expected to respond. Private security is proactive, seeking to prevent problems and limit losses for a particular private employer. Whether a private security operation is *proprietary* (the security officers are actual employees of the company) or *contractual* (the security officers are hired from an independent security company), the private security profession is profit-oriented and serves the employer paying for such service. The current trend is *hybrid security,* which combines contractual and proprietary security.

Proprietary security officers are actual employees of the company for which they work. Contractual security officers work for an independent security company and are assigned to guard a company without its own internal security staff. The trend is toward using hybrid security, combining both proprietary and contractual security services.

A third basic difference between public and private policing is the statutory power involved. Public police officers are an arm of the government and act with its full authority, including the authority of arrest. Although police powers of arrest are awesome, public officers may be denied access to private facilities that are accessible to those facilities' security officers. Without a warrant, public police could well be denied access to an industrial facility that relies on its own security department to deal with such concerns as industrial espionage.

Private security officers have no more power than that of private citizens. However, as citizens, they can carry weapons, conduct investigations, defend property, and make arrests. And they may, in fact, *appear* to have more authority than regular citizens as a result of wearing a uniform, carrying a weapon, and having the approval and support of the organization to defend the property.

Differences between public police and private security officers include:
1. Where the paycheck comes from (public tax dollars versus private sector budgets)
2. Whether the response is reactive or proactive
3. The statutory power involved

Frequently, public policing and private security have been viewed as being competitors. Additionally, some people in public law enforcement have looked down on security officers, calling them "wannabes"; that is, individuals who really want to be police officers but didn't make it. But these attitudes have changed—private security as a profession has come of age.

Employment in the private sector can provide more advancement potential and greater control over one's professional and personal life, explaining why many law enforcement officers desire jobs as private security directors.

PUBLIC/PRIVATE COOPERATION

Private security has become a major player in safeguarding Americans and their property. As our increasing elderly and business populations are likely to continue their inhabitation of high-rise condos and office buildings, their reliance on private security will also increase. The traditional police officer patrolling public roads or a beat officer on foot cannot practically be expected to patrol such structures. Unlike public police officers, private security officers can and do patrol specific buildings, even specific floors or rooms within buildings. It can be anticipated that the fields of public law enforcement and private security may tend to blend together as society recognizes the need for each and as these professions themselves learn how they can best work together—for the benefit of all.

 Private security is making a substantial contribution in safeguarding Americans and their property. Private security can also be harnessed to combat major criminal activity and terrorism. Terrorist groups often rob banks, shoplift, commit credit card fraud, and engage in other theft offenses as "fund-raisers." Private security officers are in a position to help uncover serious terrorist threats. Protection officers are on the front lines in the fight against crime, often feeding intelligence and preliminary investigative information to public law enforcement entities. In many cases, security officers at retail stores, shopping centers, colleges, health care facilities, and parks apprehend criminals and turn them over to police. In the wake of the 2001 terrorist attacks, states have been directed to organize their own homeland security efforts and take steps to assess and enhance the security of their local resources: "Today's police departments are under monumental pressure to perform, keep crime rates low, and do it all with fewer resources. Agencies can accomplish this seemingly impossible mandate by forming supportive partnerships with private security providers" (Youngs, 2004).

Another reason for cooperation is that individuals often move from one field to the other. Some individuals use private security as a stepping-stone into public policing. Likewise, some individuals in public policing enter private security, sometimes as a consultant, sometimes after retiring from public policing, sometimes as a part-time job while working as a public police officer, and sometimes as a highly paid corporate security director. As Samuels (2003, p. 8) notes: "One retired FBI agent, an expert in counterintelligence, now works for a detective agency specializing in employee background checks. A former director of a state police agency now runs the security division for a major bank." According to ASIS (www.asisonline.org): "ASIS International is comprised of more than 33,000 security management professionals worldwide. Many hold senior security positions with major corporations, and they often have military and/or law enforcement backgrounds including work with the CIA, ATF and FBI."

> Cooperation between public law enforcement and private security can benefit both sides and is an important step toward enhanced safety for all.

Examples of cooperation between the public and private sector include combined efforts at the sites of natural disasters, common initiatives in controlling and securing large public events, and cooperation in preventing and handling neighborhood crime.

PRIVATIZATION OF PUBLIC JUSTICE

The privatization trend has extended to more than just police officers. It is working its way into other areas of the justice system as well.

> The trend toward private justice can also be found in corrections and juvenile justice.

Private Corrections

Privatization in corrections dates back as early as 1607 when private parties transported felons to America (Feeler, 1991, p. 3). Because corrections has mostly operated, literally, behind closed doors, it is difficult to know how many jobs are required, or that many are actually not government jobs. Approximately 7 percent of the 1.5 million prisoners in the United States were held in privately operated prisons by midyear 2006, a 10 percent increase over the previous year (Sabol et al., 2007).

The privatization of corrections has been controversial, especially for public labor unions. In a nutshell, critics fear the quality of inmate care is compromised when private facilities focus on generating profit, and raise concerns about the degree of control government has over the nation's criminals if they are housed in privately operated facilities or involve too many civilian employees. A less expensive effective alternative has proven more elusive than some assumed it would be, but since the early 1600s private vendors have been a part of the system in one way or another.

A proponent of prison privatization, Segal (2005) states: "The major charge against privatization is that by reducing costs, quality and security are sacrificed. Yet, there is clear and significant evidence that private facilities provide at least the level of service that government-run facilities do. Private correctional facilities have fared well against government-run facilities in almost all measures of quality." Segal contends that research has not shown a decrease in quality; in fact: "there is clear and significant evidence that private prisons actually improve quality."

On the other hand, a report by McDonald and Carlson (2005, p. vii) states the cost of running a prison would be the same whether run privately or by the government. There are enough differences between the ways public and private prisons have operated and what they offer that study results have not reached a clear conclusion (Clear et al., 2009, p. 255).

The same conclusion is drawn by Gaes (2008), reporting on four studies of prisons, three public prisons, and one private prison. The researchers concluded that cost comparisons are deceivingly complex and that a uniform method of comparing publicly and privately operated prisons on the basis of audits should be developed. The researchers found that the research groups used different approaches to overhead costs, leading to different findings. However, almost everyone agrees on one aspect of corrections: it is expensive.

> The privatization of corrections has been increasing since the 1980s.

Job seekers interested in corrections should look beyond the traditional government-only employers. For example, Corrections Corporation of American (CCA) designs, builds, and manages prisons, jails, and detention facilities and provides inmate residential and prisoner transportation services in partnership with government. CCA advertises for such positions as correctional officer, facility controller, nurse, doctor, psychologist, maintenance worker, human resources manager, dental assistant, library aid, academic instructor, accounting clerk, case manager, mailroom clerk, mental health specialist, addictions treatment counselor, receptionist, and chaplain.

Privatization is not limited to institutional corrections: "There is also movement toward privatization in community corrections, including offender assessment, drug testing and treatment, electronic monitoring, halfway house management, and probation field services" (Schmalleger and Smykla, 2006, p. 529). The motivation is the same as with prisons; government's limited resources just cannot provide all that society expects. And sometimes traditional government either does not have the kinds of facilities or employment classifications needed for juvenile or other community corrections programs. Family, outreach, school, faith-based, or neighborhood programs may be a better fit for private resources than public. The debate over who will provide these services continues, but the fact remains that people are needed to provide them regardless of who actually employs them.

PRIVATE SECURITY—UP CLOSE

The continuously evolving complexity of our society is necessitating specially trained private security officers in all phases of life. Businesses need individuals who can effectively use a variety of electronic surveillance equipment. They rely on private suppliers of search dogs and strike/civil disobedience response teams. The increase of identity theft and other computer crimes make technology skills highly desirable in the security field.

Technology has changed things, but not entirely. Certain businesses still need twenty-four-hour surveillance, either by a camera or a person. Sports and entertainment celebrities, as well as wealthy businesspeople and politicians, may employ security personnel as bodyguards. Margaret Ray gained notoriety for stalking late-night TV host David Letterman because of her delusion they were romantically linked. She camped on his tennis court, stole his car, and broke into his home a number of times, including when he was there. Her mental illness, culminating with her suicide, reflects the threat potential that can require additional security.

The public's fascination, even obsession, with celebrities has provided greater opportunities in private security. Britney Spears, Jodie Foster, and Sheryl Crow are among those having been plagued by stalkers. Madonna's bodyguard shot her stalker, Robert Hoskins, who had allegedly threatened to "slice her throat from ear to ear" if she did not marry him. Even the media can present a risk, as evidenced in the 1997 fatal car crash in which Princess Diana was killed while being pursued by photographers.

One need not be famous to be a target of kidnapping and extortion. Executive protection, including protecting the executive's family and home, is becoming a lucrative specialty business. Those whose political position or work incites emotion can also be at risk. Larry Flynt was shot and paralyzed by someone offended by contents of his pornographic magazine; medical personnel who perform abortions have been targets of shootings and bombings; and Alan Berg, a controversial radio talk show host, was shot and killed in his driveway, presumably for the political positions he took on his show.

An ASIS survey of security professionals found them handling a variety of specific responsibilities, including physical security; loss and crime prevention; fraud and economic crime investigation; information security; background investigations; fire and life safety; business continuity, contingency planning, and disaster management; executive protection; human resources–related functions; general management and administrative functions; and computer/Internet/network security.

With the enhanced function of private security has come the opportunity for specialization. As the private security profession has expanded, so have the kinds of jobs available. ASIS lists the following as security specialties with career opportunities (www.asisonline.org):

Corporate Security	High-Rise Facilities Security	Risk Assessment
Cyber Security	IT Security	Strategic Intelligence
Executive Protection	Loss Prevention	Terrorism (including agro-terrorism)
Financial Services Security	Physical Security	Workplace Violence & Legal Liability
Government Security	Private Security Management	
Health Care Security		

Regardless of the specific security discipline or specialty, opportunities in the private sector are often categorized as entry-level, mid-level, and top-level positions. *Note:* Unless attributed to another source, job descriptions and statistics for entry-level, mid-level, and top-level positions are adapted from the *Occupational Outlook Handbook*.

Entry-Level Positions

Security officers' responsibilities vary with the size, type and location of the employer. In department stores, they protect people, records, merchandise, money and equipment. They often work with undercover store detectives to prevent theft and help apprehend shoplifting suspects. Some shopping centers and theaters have officers patrolling their parking lots to deter car thefts and robberies. In office buildings, banks and hospitals, security officers maintain order and protect the institution's customers, staff and property. At air, sea and rail terminals and other transportation facilities, they protect people, freight, property and equipment. They may screen passengers and visitors for weapons and explosives, ensure that nothing is stolen while a vehicle is being loaded or unloaded, and watch for fires and criminals.

Officers working in public buildings such as museums or art galleries protect paintings and exhibits by inspecting people and packages entering and leaving the building. In factories, laboratories, government buildings, data processing centers and military bases, security officers protect information, products, computer codes and defense secrets and check the credentials of people and vehicles entering and leaving the premises. Officers working at universities, parks and sports stadiums perform crowd control, supervise parking and seating, and direct traffic.

Typical entry-level jobs include private security officers and private patrol officers. Private security officers control access to private property; protect against loss through theft, vandalism, or fire; enforce rules; maintain order; and lower risks of all kinds. Private patrol officers, similar to patrol units of the public police force, move from one location to another, on foot or in a vehicle, protecting property and preventing losses.

Most security officers wear a uniform and/or identification; however, some are in plain clothes with or without a name tag. Some carry weapons but must be trained and must carry them within the law. Insurance premiums are especially high for officers carrying weapons or using K9's. Officers may be stationed at one point; walk or drive their rounds; or monitor electronic surveillance equipment. Hours vary and may include nights, holidays and weekends.

Employment of security officers is expected to grow by 17 percent between 2006 and 2016, faster than the average for all occupations. This occupation will have a very large number of new jobs arise, about 175,000 over the projections decade. Concern about crime, vandalism and terrorism continues to increase the need for security. Demand also will grow as security firms increasingly perform duties—such as providing security at public events and in residential neighborhoods—formerly handled by police.

Employment in 2006. Security officers held over 1 million jobs in 2006, more than half of which were in investigation and security services, including guard and armored car services. These organizations provide security on a contract basis, assigning their guards to buildings and other sites as needed. Most other security officers were employed directly by educational services, hospitals, food services and drinking places, traveler accommodations (hotels), department stores, manufacturing firms, lessors of real estate (residential and nonresidential buildings), and governments. These jobs are found throughout the country, most commonly in metropolitan areas.

The casino industry has prompted another demand for security personnel. Gaming surveillance officers work primarily in gambling industries; traveler accommodations, which includes casino hotels and local government in states and on Indian reservations where gambling is legal. These security personnel possess no more authority than any other private security officer, although jurisdictional issues may arise at casinos on Indian land.

Earnings. According to the latest hourly figures available (Anderson, 2004), the average hourly salary ranges for entry-level positions were:

	Low End	*High End*
Security Officers		
Contract—Unarmed	$10/hour	$14/hour
Proprietary—Unarmed	$13/hour	$17/hour
Contract—Armed	$17/hour	$19/hour
Proprietary—Armed	$15/hour	$21/hour
Console Operators		
Contract	$12/hour	$15/hour
Proprietary	$12/hour	$15/hour

The median annual wage and salary earnings of security officers in 2006 were $21,530 in 2006, ranging from less than $15,030 to more than $35,840. Median annual earnings in the industries employing the largest numbers of security officers were:

General medical and surgical hospitals	$26,610
Elementary and secondary schools	26,290
Local government	24,950
Investigation, guard, and armored car services	20,280

Gaming surveillance officers and gaming investigators had median annual wage and salary earnings of $27,130 in 2006, ranging from less than $18,720 to more than $45,940.

Employment Requirements. Many employers of unarmed security officers have no specific educational requirements. However, for armed officers, employers usually prefer high school graduates or those with an equivalent certification.

Private security is joining the trend of other fields that stress the importance of achieving certain basic professional requirements. Employers with proprietary forces usually set their own standards for security officers. Contractual security companies often are regulated by state law. Nearly every state now has licensing or registration requirements for officers who work for contract security agencies. Some states have a residency requirement, and many states have regulations concerning autos and uniforms. Individuals who wish to provide security services on their own may need to be licensed by their state. Requirements vary, so it is important to check on your local situation.

An increasing number of states are making ongoing training a legal requirement for retention of licensure. Officers may receive training in protection, public relations, report writing, crisis deterrence, first aid and specialized training relevant to their particular assignment.

Job Outlook. Private sector security is clearly a critical protective resource today, and the job outlook for those choosing this career path is positive. Job prospects for security officers should be excellent because of growing demand for these workers and the need to replace experienced workers who leave the occupation. In addition to full-time job opportunities, the limited training requirements and flexible hours attract many people seeking part-time or second jobs. However, competition is expected for higher paying positions that require longer periods of training; these positions usually are found at facilities that require a high level of security, such as nuclear power plants or weapons installations. Job prospects for gaming surveillance officers should be good, but they will be better for those with experience in the gaming industry.

Mid-Level Positions

Almost any additional duties or expertise required can put workers into another level of private employment, for example, private investigators, armed couriers, armored transportation personnel, alarm company workers or those consulting in various areas of safety and security. More stringent entry requirements, background checks and specific skills can result in better pay and opportunities.

Private detectives and investigators assist individuals, businesses and attorneys find and analyze information. They connect small clues to solve mysteries or to uncover facts about legal, financial, or personal matters. Private detectives and investigators offer many services, including executive, corporate and celebrity protection; pre-employment verification and individual background profiles. Some investigate computer crimes, such as identity theft, harassing e-mails, and illegal downloading of copyrighted material. They also assist in criminal and civil liability cases, insurance claims and fraud, child custody and protection cases, missing persons cases, and premarital screening. They are sometimes hired to investigate individuals to prove or disprove infidelity.

Mid-level jobs in private security include private investigators, detectives, armed couriers, central alarm respondents, and consultants.

Specialization. Private detectives and investigators often specialize. Those who focus on intellectual property theft, for example, investigate and document acts of piracy, help clients stop illegal activity, and provide intelligence for prosecution and civil action. Other investigators specialize in developing financial profiles and asset searches. Their reports reflect information gathered through interviews, investigation and surveillance, and research, including review of public documents.

Computer forensic investigators specialize in recovering, analyzing and presenting data from computers for use in investigations or as evidence. They determine the details of intrusions into computer systems, recover data from encrypted or erased files, and recover e-mails and deleted passwords.

Legal investigators help prepare criminal defenses, locate witnesses, serve legal documents, interview police and prospective witnesses, and gather and review evidence. Legal investigators also may collect information on the parties to the litigation, take photographs, testify in court, and assemble evidence and reports for trials. They often work for law firms or lawyers.

Corporate investigators conduct internal and external investigations for companies. Internal investigations may include drug use in the workplace, expense accounts abused or employees' theft of merchandise or information. External investigations may include criminal schemes from outside the corporation, such as fraudulent billing by a supplier.

Financial investigators may develop confidential financial profiles of individuals or companies that are prospective parties to large financial transactions. These investigators often are certified public accountants (CPAs) who work closely with investment bankers and other accountants. They might also search for assets to recover damages awarded by a court in fraud or theft cases.

Detectives who work for retail stores or hotels are responsible for controlling losses and protecting assets. *Store detectives*, also known as *loss prevention agents*, safeguard the assets of retail stores by apprehending anyone attempting to steal merchandise or destroy store property. They prevent theft by shoplifters, vendor representatives, delivery personnel and store employees.

They also conduct periodic inspections of stock areas, dressing rooms and restrooms, and sometimes assist in opening and closing the store. They may prepare loss prevention and security reports for management and testify in court against people they apprehend. *Hotel detectives* protect guests from theft of their belongings and preserve order in hotel restaurants and bars. They also may keep undesirable individuals, such as known thieves, off the premises.

Employment in 2006. Private detectives and investigators held about 52,000 jobs in 2006. Approximately 30 percent were self-employed, including many for whom investigative work was a second job. Around 34 percent of jobs were in investigation and security services, including private detective agencies, while another 9 percent were in department or other general merchandise stores. The rest worked mostly in state and local government, legal services firms, employment services companies, insurance agencies and credit mediation establishments, including banks and other depository institutions.

Earnings. The most recent hourly salaries available (Anderson, 2004) report the following ranges for investigators:

Contract	$31/hour	$56/hour
Proprietary	$24/hour	$31/hour

Median annual earnings of salaried private detectives and investigators were $33,750 in 2006, ranging from less than $19,720 to more than $64,380. Earnings of private detectives and investigators vary greatly by employer, specialty, and geographic area.

Employment Requirements. There are no formal education requirements for most private detective and investigator jobs, although many have college degrees. Courses in criminal justice and police science are helpful to aspiring private detectives and investigators. Although related experience is usually required, some people enter the occupation directly after graduation from college, generally with an associate or bachelor's degree in criminal justice or police science. The 2006 educational attainment for private detectives and investigators, in percent, was as follows:

High school graduate or equivalent	18%
Some college, no degree	26
Associate's degree	8
Bachelor's degree	34
Master's degree	13
Professional degree or PhD	3

Most corporate investigators must have a bachelor's degree, preferably in a business-related field. Some corporate investigators have a master's degree in business administration or a law degree; others are CPAs.

The majority of states and the District of Columbia require private detectives and investigators to be licensed. Licensing requirements vary, however. Seven states—Alabama, Alaska, Colorado, Idaho, Mississippi, Missouri and South Dakota—have no statewide licensing requirements, some states have few requirements, and many others have stringent regulations. For example, the Bureau of Security and Investigative Services of the California Department of Consumer Affairs requires private investigators to be 18 years of age or older; have a combination of education in police science, criminal law, or justice and experience equaling 3 years (6,000 hours); pass a criminal history background check by the California Department of Justice and the FBI (in most states, convicted felons cannot be issued a license); and receive a qualifying score on a 2-hour written examination covering laws and regulations. Detectives and investigators in all states who carry handguns must meet additional requirements for a firearms permit. It can be a criminal offense to work as a private detective without the required license, or to be licensed in one state and work in another.

Top-Level Positions

Top jobs in security include loss prevention specialists, security directors, risk managers, and chief security officers (CSOs). Top jobs in security include managing a private security company or heading up security for a private concern.

Security positions at the upper end of management put these opportunities in another class of employment similar to other business leadership positions. In fact, major corporations consider their security executives as critical as any other executives with similar corporate pay and such benefits as cars, stock investment plans, and very attractive vacation and retirement plans. Additional school, knowledge, ability, and leadership experience is expected for these positions.

> In some organizations, *computer security specialists* may plan, coordinate and implement the organization's information security. These professionals educate users about computer security, install security software, monitor networks for security breaches, respond to cyber attacks, and, in some cases, gather data and evidence to be used in prosecuting cyber crime. Computer security specialists' responsibilities have increased in recent years as cyber attacks become more common. This and other growing specialty occupations reflect an increasing emphasis on client-server applications, the expansion of Internet and intranet applications and the demand for more end-user support.

Boyd et al. (2004, p. 5) state: "A common theme among members of the Society of Police Futurists International is the fear that the law enforcement profession will never 'catch up' with the necessary computer-based investigative skills to keep pace with criminals who use computer technology." This speaks volumes about opportunities in this area.

Because competition for prime security positions is increasing, applicants should strive to increase their marketability by gaining knowledge of the field through education and other types of experiences. According to ASIS (*Career Opportunities in Security*, p. 2): "Students seeking careers in security should pursue course work in security, computer science, electronics, business management, law, police science, personnel and information management."

In addition, some individuals may want to be certified by the ASIS through their *Certified Protection Professional (CPP)* program. This program, organized in 1977, is designed to recognize individuals meeting specific criteria of professional protection knowledge and conduct. To be eligible to take the examination, candidates must either have ten years of experience with no degree, eight years of experience and an associate's degree, five years of experience and a bachelor's degree, four years of experience and a master's degree, or three years of experience and a doctoral degree. At least half of the experience must be in "responsible charge" of a security function. The examination takes a full day, with the morning devoted to general security knowledge and the afternoon devoted to a choice of four specialty tests selected from a wide variety of areas.

Earnings. As with other work, different levels of pay increase with responsibility. And, jobs with higher responsibility often require more experience, specialty experience, and education. But it can be worth it. The highest paid security professionals manage multiple facilities for publicly owned global enterprises and work in the fields of information technology, manufacturing, and retail. According to the most recent data available, the 2002 annual average salary of security managers, as related to several factors were (Anderson, 2004):

NUMBER OF LOCATIONS		SIZE OF SECURITY BUDGET MANAGED		CERTIFICATION AND EDUCATION	
One location (building or facility)	$65,700	$500,000 and under	Low $60,000	CPP designation	$98,332
Two or more locations within one state	$75,300	$1,000,001 to $2,500,000	$89,049	No CPP certification	$80,485
Two or more locations in more than one state	$95,800	More than $2,500,000	$126,116	Master's degree	$102,600
Two or more locations in more than one country	$132,500			Four-year degree	$89,954
				No degree	$74,100

Moran (2007, p. 67) reports: "The average compensation of security professionals in the United States rose to $117,000 for 2007 from $87,900 the year prior—a stunning 33 percent increase. The median compensation—a more representative number—rose only 6 percent to $91,000 from $86,000. And base salaries increased a mere 4 percent from a median $79,500 to a median $83,000. The increases are partially due to the number of security professionals holding stock options." In addition, performance bonuses were awarded to 54 percent of the respondents. Moran (p. 72) also reports that more than half of the respondents held a professional security certification and reported compensation 18 percent higher than those with no certification.

When considering potential salaries in the private sector, changing economic times must be factored in. Although some private sector jobs will pay less than public positions, the increased awareness and reliance on private sector protection means the salaries may not be as limited as in the public arena.

THE OUTLOOK FOR EMPLOYMENT IN PRIVATE SECURITY

Given the enhanced state of alert within the United States following 9/11, it seems safe to say the demand for security forces will most certainly remain high in the foreseeable future. The CERT® Coordination Center (2004) asserts:

> The need to address security within organizations is growing in the public awareness. Customers are demanding it as concerns about privacy and identify theft rise. Business partners, suppliers, and vendors are starting to require it from one another, particularly when providing mutual network access. There is a wide range of current and pending US national and international legislation that calls for organizations to exercise due diligence and demonstrate an acceptable standard of due care in how they manage their computing infrastructures and the information that such networks and systems create, transmit, and store, particularly when connected to the Internet.

Another area of growth is contract security and investigations, as more companies outsource these positions in an effort to improve cost-effectiveness.

> The private security field is expected to grow more rapidly through 2008 than the average for all occupations, requiring the hiring of many employees to meet the increasing security needs.

CONCLUSION

Private security is a critical protective resource in our nation today. The private security field is expected to grow rapidly through the year 2008, requiring the hiring of a large number of employees to meet the increasing security needs. A security job can serve as a stepping-stone to other employment or a chance to obtain supplemental income as a second job or while attending school. Whether you seek employment in private security as a chance to acquire valuable training to help gain future employment in law enforcement or because the security field has exceptional future potential, private security can provide satisfying work.

AN INSIDER'S VIEW

CAREER OPPORTUNITIES IN PRIVATE SECURITY

Robert B. Iannone

Certified Protection Professional
President, Iannone Security Management, Inc.

Preparing yourself for employment in any field should include achieving competency through pursuing three factors: (1) training, (2) education and (3) experience. Training includes attending security seminars, conferences and on-the-job training. Education refers to achieving a college degree in the security field or a related field. Gaining experience, of course, requires working in your chosen field. These elements apply no matter what field you pursue.

In private security, formal education can be obtained from the numerous colleges and universities throughout the United States that offer associate of arts degrees, bachelor's degrees and graduate degrees in security. Core courses in these curricula may include such subjects as Introduction to Security, Physical Security, Information Security, Information Technology, Ethics, Legal Aspects of Security, and Security Management and Administration. A degree in a related field might include a curriculum in business or management.

Following graduation, experience can be achieved by obtaining an entry-level position. To help prospective security applicants obtain the entry-level experience necessary, colleges and universities may offer a core security internship. Internships allow students to be employed in industry and perform actual security-related functions while earning credits toward graduation. In many instances, employers have retained interns following graduation.

Security-related training can be gained through professional security organizations such as the American Society for Industrial Security (ASIS), the International Security Conference (ISC), Research Security Administrators (RSA) and the National Classification Management Society (NCMS). Additional information pertaining to these organizations may be obtained by viewing their web sites on the Internet. Security-related training courses offered through the ASIS, ISC, RSA and NCMS include virtually all aspects of the security profession. In addition, numerous periodicals published by security organizations such as the ASIS and ISC address a variety of security-related subjects. Full advantage of the services offered by professional security organizations can be gained through becoming a member. Services offered through membership range from newsletters, periodicals and announcements to sponsored seminars and conferences. There is no membership to ISC and RSA; however, there are mailing lists.

Employment opportunities in the security field have increased in recent years. Some factors causing this increase include (1) the doubling of personnel working in the field over the past 30 years, (2) a current shortage of qualified personnel, (3) technological advances, (4) higher salaries, (5) a shift from the law enforcement image and (6) the availability of two-year, four-year and graduate degrees. Employment opportunities available in the security industry include government service (military and civilian), banking/finance, retail, health care, airport/airline, campus, lodging, computer, aerospace and the security services.

Although employment opportunities in the aerospace industry have decreased in recent years, the security services industry has increased significantly. The security services include providers of security-related hardware such as intrusion detection systems and devices, access control systems and devices, closed-circuit television, fire detection systems and devices, lock and key control, physical barriers and identification systems. Other security service providers include suppliers of contract security officers. With the increase in the use of personal computers, there are also suppliers of computer software for a variety of applications such as wireless technology, data management and material accountability systems.

Salaries in the security field vary, depending on the industry. In addition, salaries vary within specific industries depending on such factors as training, education and experience. Salaries also differ between geographic areas and policy-making and non–policy-making positions.

In summary, career development begins with each individual; therefore, individuals who prepare themselves by acquiring job-specific training, formal education and field-related experience will obtain the best positions. In addition, regardless of the security discipline, they will be assured of higher salaries.

Robert B. Iannone, *CPP, is the president of Iannone Security Management, Incorporated, located in Fountain Valley, California. He has over thirty years' experience as a security practitioner, manager, author, consultant, expert witness, lecturer, educator, and advisor to security book publishers. Mr. Iannone is a life member of the American Society for Industrial Security since 1966, and has been conferred a Lifetime Certified Protection Professional (CPP). He also serves as a member of the Board of Directors, Research Security Administrators.*

A consultant since 1989, he provides objective, independent studies and surveys of a security organization's personnel, systems, and equipment. He also provides consulting and expert witness services to the legal profession. For more than two decades, Mr. Iannone has been an adjunct professor of security-related courses at the California State University, San Marco; California State University, Long Beach; and Golden West College, Huntington Beach, California. He holds a Bachelor of Science degree in Criminal Justice (Security Management) from California State University, Long Beach, and a Master of Science degree in Management from the University of LaVerne. He has been married forty-two years to Theresa; they have one married daughter and one grandson. His hobbies include spectator sports and working with personal computers.

MIND STRETCHES

1.   Why do you think the entertainment field is obsessed with depicting private security? Do you think this obsession helps or hurts the profession? Why?

2.   Do you personally know any security officers? Are they like the private investigators depicted on television?

3.   What is your favorite private detective show? Why?

4.   Do you think television and the movies have influenced your career choice?

5.   Do you think security work will become more specialized or more generalized in the future? Why? How will your job goals be affected?

6.   What stereotype do you think private security officers have? Why? Is it justified?

7.   Why do you think the trend to license professions exists? Do you think it is helpful?

8.   Are security salaries more or less than you had anticipated? Does salary affect your decision as to what field of employment you will eventually pursue? Why or why not?

9.   How do you predict the field of private security will change? Why?

REFERENCES

American Society for Industrial Security (ASIS). Available online at www.asisonline.org.

Anderson, Teresa. "The Key to Earnings." *Security Management Online,* January 2004. Available online at www.securitymanagement .com/library/001549.html.

Boyd, Sandy, Alberto Melis, and Richard Meyers. "Preparing for the Challenges Ahead: Practical Applications of Futures Research." *FBI Law Enforcement Bulletin*, January 2004.

Building Private Security/Public Policing Partnerships to Respond to Terrorism and Public Disorder (National Policy Summit). Washington, DC: U.S. Department of Justice, 2004. Available online at www.theiacp.org/documents/pdfs/Publications/ ACFAB5D.pdf

"Career Opportunities in Security." Alexandria, VA: American Society for Industrial Security, n. d. Available online at www. asisonline.org/careercenter/careers2005.pdf.

CERT® Coordination Center. "Governing for Enterprise Security." May 28, 2004. Available online at www.cert.org/.

Clear, Todd R., George F. Cole, and Michael D. Reisig. *American Corrections*. New York: McGraw-Hill, 2009.

Cooke, Leonard G., and Lisa R. Hahn. "The Missing Link in Homeland Security." *The Police Chief* (November 2006): 16–21.

Feeler, Malcolm M. "The Privatization of Prisons in Historical Perspective." *Criminal Justice Research Bulletin*, 6, no. 2 (1991): 3.

Gaes, Gerry. "Cost, Performance Studies Look at Prison Privatization." *NIJ Journal* (March 2008): 32–36.

Levinson, Karl. "Security Career Advancement: 'Cracking' into the Security Industry in Just 92 Easy Steps." July 12, 2006, Looking Glass Systems. Available online at www.microsoft.com/technet/community/columns/secmvp/sv0706.mspx.

McDonald, Douglas and Carlson, Kenneth. *Contracting for Imprisonment in the Federal Prison System: Cost and Performance of the Privately Operated Taft Correctional Institution.* Washington, DC: U.S. Department of Justice, unpublished report, November 2005. (Document No. 211990) Available online at www.ncjrs.gov/pdffiles1/nij/grants/211990.pdf.

Occupational Outlook Handbook, 2008–09 Edition. Bureau of Labor Statistics, U.S. Department of Labor. Washington, DC: U.S. Government Printing Office, 2008.

Moran, Mike. "What Are You Worth?" *Security Management* (August 2007): 67–73.

"Privatization Can Save Money in Prison Construction, Study Says." *Criminal Justice Newsletter* (May 25, 2001): 3–4.

Sabol, W. B., T. D. Minton, and P. M. Harrison. *Prison and Jail Inmates at Midyear 2006*. Washington, DC: Bureau of Justice Statistics, 2007.

Samuels, Joseph, Jr. "Building Partnerships between Private-Sector Security and Public-Sector Police." *The Police Chief*, September 2003, p.8.

Schmalleger, Frank, and John O. Smykla. *Corrections in the 21st Century*, 3rd ed. New York: McGraw-Hill, 2006.

Segal, Geoffrey. "Significant Evidence that Prison Privatization Improves Quality: Private Prisons Produce Cost Savings, Provide Better or Equal Service." Testimony before the Commission on Safety and Abuse in America's Prisons, November 2, 2005. Available online at www.reason.org/commentaries/segal_20051102.shtml.

Youngs, Al. "The Future of Public/Private Partnerships." *FBI Law Enforcement Bulletin* (January 2004): 7–11.

HELPFUL WEBSITES

American Society for Industrial Security (ASIS)
www.asisonline.org

CERT® Coordination Center
www.cert.org

National Association of Legal Investigators (NALI)
www.nalionline.org

Security Magazine
www.securitymagazine.com

Security, Police and Fire Professionals of America (SPFPA)
www.spfpa.org

CHAPTER 5

ON CHOOSING A CAREER:
KNOWING THE JOB AND YOURSELF

Life is to be lived. If you have to support yourself, you had bloody well better find some way that is going to be interesting. And you don't do that by sitting around wondering about yourself.

—*Katharine Hepburn*

Do You Know:

➤ Why job satisfaction is so important?
➤ The best way to avoid job dissatisfaction?
➤ What the four steps are of the career development process?
➤ What specific requirements and limitations you should consider when choosing a career?
➤ How your background could prevent employment in the criminal justice or security fields?
➤ What an *inventurer* is? If you are one?
➤ What five essential parts of a dream job must be considered before it can become a reality?
➤ The importance of taking risks?

INTRODUCTION

Previous chapters discussed some realities of careers in criminal justice and security. As you consider these professions, understand what they are—and what they are *not*. Also, take a serious inventory of your abilities and interests to determine if your career goals are realistic.

In this chapter you'll combine knowledge about your chosen field with an honest look at yourself, to make certain you are, indeed, on a road that will take you where you want to go. How often would drive your car without a thought of where you want to go? Yet many people launch themselves toward a career with very limited forethought—or with unrealistic dreams. Many job seekers have dreams—dreams of a successful career and a carefree, pleasurable lifestyle. However, as Leider and Shapiro (2002, pp. 100–101) state:

> The "perfect job" isn't really about enjoyment. Instead, it's one that mirrors perfectly the person who holds it. And people do find, or invent, or create these jobs. They do it by working a process . . . that links who you are with what you do. The process involves developing a clarity about your talents, passions, and values— looking inside yourself to discover what you do best, what you like to do best, and the type of working environment that supports what you care about most. And then combining all three to develop a clear vision of the kind of work that links who you are with what you do. . . .

> The perfect job isn't a standard of living—it's a state of mind and state of being. In the perfect job, you're applying the talents you enjoy most to an interest you're passionate about, in an environment that fits who you are and what you value.

The romanticized dream of a successful career becomes even more problematic when it involves the fields within criminal justice. Many people are intrigued by such employment because they want to be like the TV undercover police officer or private investigator they watch week after week. You must enter your career search with a much more open mind. Realistically, what *is* the job you are seeking?

SELECTING AND DEVELOPING A CAREER

Carelessly pursuing a career can be costly. First, selecting a career is extremely important because the vast majority of your waking hours will be spent working—why spend so much time being unhappy and unfulfilled? Perhaps even worse is that job frustrations may manifest themselves in unpleasant, if not dangerous, ways. People who dislike their work show it. For people employed by the criminal justice system, job dissatisfaction can seriously affect job performance. At best, they may appear as unfeeling individuals, expressing little concern for anyone, including victims. At worst, inappropriate physical force, even brutality, may be evidence of something going on "inside." Such behavior can result in nationwide antipolice publicity, as seen in the beating of Rodney King.

> Career dissatisfaction can lead to unhappiness, negativity, and cynicism in the individual and to a decrease in productivity and morale for the unit in which the individual works. The impact may be felt by coworkers and may affect their work attitudes as well.

The best ways to prevent career dissatisfaction are to research the field carefully before applying for employment, ask questions of those already in the field, and carefully evaluate the positive and negative aspects of the occupation *as they apply to your values and expectations.* Rather than jumping into a career you know little about, including how well suited to it *you* are, look objectively at the whole picture. Consider the job. Consider yourself. Is it a "match"? Or is it the frustrating pursuit of a fantasy? There is a story about a woman who loved everything about being an engine mechanic—except getting dirty. Absolutely nothing could prevent her from leaving work each night grimy and greasy, and it was causing her to consider a career change. The simple fact was that an inherent part of her work was to get dirty. Determining whether getting dirty was worth it was an issue that had to be addressed.

Similarly, facts about working in criminal justice and private security must be faced. The relatively mediocre pay, difficult hours, odd days off, public's perception of the job, limited opportunity for promotions and inherent danger are issues that may make the job unacceptable to some. For other job seekers, this field remains attractive for reasons that go far beyond the motivations for other fields of work: the desire to play a helping role in society, to have an exciting career, or to have a job with significant power over others (good or bad). Take a realistic look at these issues now, examining why you want to work in this field and your true expectations.

> The best way to avoid career dissatisfaction is to thoroughly research the field of interest and to carefully and realistically address issues concerning the nature of the work, the hours, the pay—any and all positives *and* negatives. Go in with your eyes wide open, free from unrealistic expectations.

Although this text is specifically directed at helping develop your own job-seeking strategy, there is much more to the process than merely learning to write a résumé. If you are not heading in the right direction, your work will not be fulfilling.

Career coaches and counselors help people develop the ability to examine their motivations, a skill that applies to people seeking to enter a certain career as well as those considering a departure. Nathan and Hill (2006, p. 1) view career counseling as a process that enables clients to become more aware of their own resources in order to lead a more satisfying life as well as to "take into account the interdependence of career and non-career considerations" (p. 3). They cite the approach advocated by Parsons (1909) nearly a century ago:

> In the wise choice of vocation, there are three factors:
> 1. A clear understanding of yourself
> 2. A knowledge of the requirements and prospects in different lines of work
> 3. True reasoning on the relations of these two groups of facts

In Figure 5–1, Krannich (2005, p. 91) illustrates how the first two factors are critical to career development (see steps 1 and 2 in the figure). The next section of this book focuses on steps 3 and 4.

Krannich identifies the four steps of the career development process as (1) self-assessment, (2) career exploration, (3) job-search skill development, and (4) implementation of the job-search steps.

Indeed, many Americans become encumbered by an ideal of the perfect job. But as Leider and Shapiro (2002, p. 100) note: "Every job has its good parts and its bad parts. It's hard to imagine any kind of work that would be enjoyable 100 percent of the time. Even sports heroes and movie stars have their bad days."

The Career Development Process

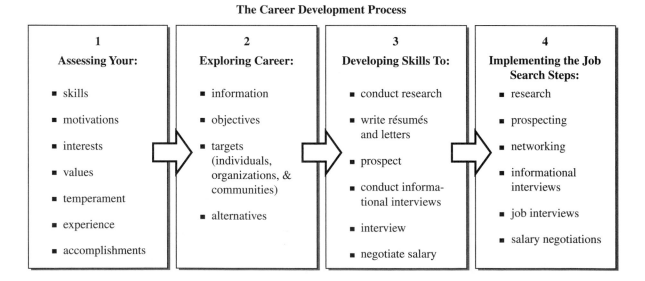

FIGURE 5–1   The Career Development Process

SOURCE: Ronald L. Krannich. *Change Your Job, Change Your Life,* 9th ed. Manassas Park, VA: Impact Publications, 2005, p. 91. Reprinted by permission.

Unrealistic expectations of work may be a natural evolution of American society. Post-Depression work, followed by post–World War II work, really did help satisfy the American dream. The economy was strong and growing; opportunities were everywhere, and work itself provided much to so many. Even as people expected more and more, the workplace was able to keep up . . . at least for awhile. Increasing salaries, benefits, and new types of jobs seemed limitless. But they weren't. And as time passed, jobs became more scarce, upward mobility more challenging, and the seemingly "unlimited potential" noticeably more limited.

The world of work, including why people seek the jobs they do, has come back to where it arguably began: to provide for our more basic needs. Personal, perhaps selfish, needs take precedence over the broader things that work provides. How satisfying a job can be is only one aspect of a job's benefits. Now the important question that needs to be asked is whether a job provides the leisure time for individuals to achieve their goals beyond just being successful on the job.

Charting Your Future Course

It's difficult to consider the future without becoming philosophical. No one knows what the future will bring, so all you can do is speculate about what might occur. Of course, you can make some good guesses based on what has occurred in the past combined with what is happening right now.

Here's what is known for sure: Technology demands that successful job candidates have certain skill levels, and work affects your life to the degree that careful thought must be invested in future job considerations. The future of *your* work will be dictated by the decisions you make about it. Even if you make no decision and let yourself drift about the job market, you have, indeed, made that decision.

Not only is the rapid development of technology influencing the working world, so too are the reasons people pursue certain jobs. Job seeking *does* influence feelings about yourself and those around you. You must have a balance of interests and activities, a sense of identity, a realistic sense of your capabilities, and reasonable goals for your life. It is also important to feel in control of your destiny. By examining yourself and your goals, together with a realistic idea of what expectations are truly important to you, you place yourself in control of your future.

One way to find out your true career interests *before* committing to a particular line of work is to volunteer with a potential employer, request a ride-along, or interview some officers or other employees. Visit agencies you think you'd like to work for and see what a typical workday is like. Local colleges and universities can often supply the names of recent graduates working in your field. Call them to find out what they are doing and how they like it.

Career Coaches and Counselors

A variety of tools exist to help you better understand your own aptitudes and interests. You are encouraged to take interest inventories and aptitude tests to help highlight career areas that might satisfy your many needs. There may even be job options you have never heard about or considered. A great place to start is the counseling department at your school or career counselors in the private sector.

Bolles (2008, pp. 379–384) offers advice on selecting a coach or counselor, by collecting three names of career counselors in your geographical area. Starting places include your friends, the Yellow Pages (under such headings as "Aptitude and Employment Testing" or "Career and Vocational Counseling"), local schools, and community organizations, where you may receive recommendations on qualified counselors: "Once you have three names, you need to go do some comparison shopping. You want to talk with all three of them face-to-face, and decide which of the three (if any) you want to hook up with" (Bolles, p. 382). In searching for a good career counselor, Bolles (p. 383) suggests asking the following questions:

➤ What is involved in your program?

➤ Who will be in the counseling with me? And how long has this person been counseling?

➤ What is your success rate?

➤ What is the cost of your services?

➤ Is there a contract up front? If so, may I see it please, and take it home with me?

Bolles (p. 384) contends: "As you look over your notes, you will realize there is no definitive way for you to determine a career counselor's expertise. It's something you'll have to *smell out,* as you go along." He also cautions: "If they [the career counselors] give you the feeling that everything will be done for you, by them . . . rather than asserting that you are going to have to do almost all of the work, with their basically assuming the role of coach, give them 15 bad points." For more information about career counselors or a list of certified counselors in your area, contact one of the agencies listed at the end of this chapter.

Finally, don't overlook the resources readily at hand who already know you well: family and friends. Ask their opinions about what they think you'd be good at and whether they can see you in the work you're considering.

The steps to understanding yourself and your career goals have a beginning but never an end! Here's the beginning.

BRAINSTORMING POSSIBILITIES

Even if you are fairly certain about what you want to do with your life, it is worthwhile to consider other alternatives. These may be similar jobs, or they may be different altogether. Choices are what life is about, so start developing some.

 Of all the exercises you will complete, this will be one of the easiest. Sit down with a clear mind and list in your journal the most appealing jobs. Don't analyze what you think you will or will not be qualified for. Simply write down the jobs that intrigue you.

➤ Do any general patterns emerge?

➤ Are the jobs you listed more in the service fields? The academic fields?

➤ Do the jobs stress physical skills? Mental ability? Both equally?

➤ Do they stress working with people or alone? Indoors or outdoors?

➤ Why do you think you picked these jobs?

JUST THE FACTS

Having generated some career choices, next determine the facts about these alternatives.

In deciding which career is best suited to you and your needs, consider age requirements, physical requirements, educational requirements, background limitations, and experience requirements.

Age

A common question asked is, "Am I too old" to consider law enforcement or criminal justice as a career? Frankly, a better question is, "Am I too *young*?" Criminal justice hiring can be both fickle and cyclical, with hiring authorities more interested, at times, in young people they can "mold" and, at other times, favoring older candidates with more experience and maturity. More than ever, maturity is playing a very important part in who gets hired. Increased public scrutiny, increased liability concerns, and the departure from the traditional paramilitary perspective make people with more life experience more attractive to employers. All that is recommended is people who are realistic about age desirability for various jobs.

Some jobs are better suited for young adults; others are ideal for retirees. Some positions, including certain law enforcement and security jobs, have age limitations. For example, most states require that police officer recruits be at least twenty-one years old. Although the majority of policing jobs do not have an upward age limit for applicants, the federal system usually will not accept applicants older than thirty-five years old. Even though the majority of criminal justice jobs do not have an upward age limit, federal agencies and others may. It is important to learn about any restrictions prior to applying.

Corrections and private security are open to an even greater variety of ages. On one hand, either field is exceptional for entry-level people seeking experience to help them eventually obtain police officer jobs. On the other hand, corrections and security work can be great fields in their own right or ideal jobs for retired police officers or others.

Physical Requirements

The jobs you are interested in likely have physical requirements. Most agencies or companies set minimum vision and hearing requirements. One young man went through law school to be an FBI agent, only to learn later that his vision disqualified him from even taking the entrance test. Check with the agencies to find out the requirements.

Most agencies want proportionate height and weight, even if they do not follow a specific chart. If you need to lose weight, start an exercise program now, preferably one you can continue throughout your career. An increasing number of agencies are requiring physical "stress tests" to assess candidates' vascular health. You can prepare for this by participating in a regular exercise program.

Most departments or companies will ask if you have any physical or health restrictions that will interfere with job performance. Be realistic with yourself and honest with the employer. Although occasional back pain may not be a problem, an inability to lift heavy items might cause a problem. Various medical conditions will not necessarily eliminate you either. For instance, controllable diabetes should not be a problem for most jobs. Again, be honest with yourself and the employer regarding any health problems you have.

Education

Different states have different requirements regarding required schooling. Similarly, different employers have different standards. Employers in either the private or public sectors may require at least a high school diploma or general equivalency diploma (GED). Some states, Minnesota for example, require at least two years of college. Some agencies, particularly in the federal system, may require graduate credits or even a graduate degree, such as a law degree.

The more knowledge you have, the better. This can include specialized training such as first-aid courses, first-responder courses, CPR, and the like. Knowing a foreign language, knowing how to sign to hearing-impaired people, or having skills in photography—any specialized knowledge is likely to be a plus in pursuing your career, and you'll make more money.

America is becoming a better educated society. What was once considered a luxury, education is now a necessity, at least for most jobs having the potential to be considered desirable. Whether seeking initial employment or a promotion, education is a good investment in oneself and could prove to be the differentiator between you and the competition: "The more education you have, the greater your career options will be. Data consistently show that, on average, college graduates earn more money, experience less unemployment, and have a wider variety of career options than other workers do. Between 2004 and 2014, almost 14 million job openings are projected to be filled by workers who have a bachelor's or higher degree and who are entering an occupation for the first time. Some occupations will offer more openings and bigger paychecks than others will" (*Occupational Outlook Quarterly*, 2006).

The *Occupational Outlook Quarterly* (*OOQ*) states: "More people are going to college now than ever before, in part because of the advantages that a college degree confers. College-educated workers' higher earnings and lower unemployment are good reasons to go to college, and these benefits are also evidence of the demand for college graduates. Higher earnings show that employers are willing to pay more to have college graduates work for them. And lower unemployment means college graduates are more likely to find a job when they want one."

The FBI's web page notes that the agency is interested in people with the following backgrounds: law, accounting, foreign language, and "generalist." Many believe getting a degree in a field besides criminal justice might "set them apart" from other applicants, since they will eventually learn what they need to know about being an officer by attending a police academy. It is further noted that a recent trend regarding hiring practices of the FBI and some other federal law enforcement agencies is to *not* hire students directly out of college, but rather to seek college graduates with two or three years of local law enforcement experience.

Background

Most private security companies, corrections facilities, and certainly all law enforcement agencies will thoroughly investigate applicants' backgrounds. You should know what facts about your past will and will not affect your employment potential. As previously discussed, most police departments and security agencies will not accept applicants with a felony conviction on their adult record. Depending on the nature of the crime, a misdemeanor may not automatically eliminate you. Be prepared to honestly explain the situation to the employer.

Although it will be difficult to deal with any criminal record, it may be easier to explain an error in judgment when you were younger than a conviction when you were twenty-eight. Unfortunately, some students make serious errors in judgment while studying to become police or security officers—errors that ruin their chances at a career in criminal justice. Act responsibly.

Traffic records, like lesser criminal records, may or may not be a hindrance. Although they generally won't be grounds for automatic elimination from the application process, they will be strikes against you. Be honest about the circumstances. Many applicants make the mistake of saying they have no traffic record when, in fact, they do. It is easier to explain why you got a ticket ten years ago than why you lied on your application. *Lying is justification to eliminate an applicant.* A traffic record may not be.

Juvenile records may also be a factor. Although the record may be sealed, an agency may likely find out about it during a background check. When police do a neighborhood check during the course of a background check, a neighbor may recall an incident involving the applicant and the police.

Illicit drug use is also considered. Experimental drug use within a year or so of applying may be cause for disqualification. Current illegal drug use will most certainly eliminate you from the candidate pool.

Other situations need to be thought out honestly. Past counseling, or even institutionalization, may not be sufficient grounds for eliminating you from the running, but lying about it would be. Some agencies may be more likely to consider applicants who helped themselves by going through Alcoholics Anonymous or other self-help programs.

Most police departments and security agencies will not accept applicants with a felony conviction on their adult record. A misdemeanor may not automatically eliminate you. Traffic records, like lesser criminal records, may or may not be a hindrance. Past counseling, or even institutionalization, may not be sufficient grounds for eliminating you from the running, but lying about it would be. *Always be honest* about such background circumstances.

Experience

Some agencies require previous experience in a related field. You should be aware of these requirements before applying for positions in these agencies. But remember, employers will be interested not only in direct experience (work similar to what you are applying for) but also "indirect" experience or *life experience.* Have you had some variety in your life, personally and professionally? Were you willing to take an entry-level job to work your way through school? Have you had jobs interacting with the public? Have you been enthusiastic enough to travel? Involved enough to participate in school activities and organizations? In other words, do you have experiences in life that contribute to your uniqueness that will stand out from the competition? Experience is not just having held a job in that particular field; rather, it's the background you bring as an individual. Something that sets you apart may be the one ability the employer is looking for, or be reason for them to remember you favorably.

Develop a Positive Attitude

Seeking employment and promotion can become frustrating. Be certain your attitude is not contributing to this frustration. Attitude can be your best friend or worst enemy; the fact is, either you control it or it will control you. It has been said that attitude is what controls your altitude. If you are harboring unresolved anger, are frustrated, or lack confidence, it shows. Those speaking with you may not know what they are picking up on, but are likely to pick up on something.

Nathan and Hill (2006, p. 70) list several attitudes and beliefs that are often unconsciously held and may be self-defeating:

- I don't need anyone's help.
- I can't live on less than I earn now.
- Somewhere there's the perfect job.
- Nobody will take me seriously.
- Life is so unfair to me.
- I won't be good enough.
- I do well enough, Mum/Dad will love me.
- It's so competitive, I'd never get in.
- It's too late.
- I'm too old/young/overqualified/underqualified.

- "X" will sort it all out for me.
- It's undignified to have to promote yourself.
- There's no point planning ahead when there's so much change afoot.
- Everybody else is better off than me.
- It's safer not to try than to risk failure.
- I'll fail.
- I can't change anything—I don't have any power.
- If I wait long enough, things will change.
- I can't help the way I am—it's just the way I'm made.

(Reprinted by permission of Sage Publications, Inc.)

WHAT DO YOU WANT FROM A CAREER?

A career is different from a job. A job is a short-term means to an end: money. High school and college students have jobs during the summer and people get jobs between careers to pay their bills. A career is more long-term, with more serious implications. Too many people find their jobs dull, laborious, and repetitive. Most people are afraid to make changes—to take risks—and yet this is what is needed to be happy. One who risks nothing usually gains nothing.

Many people are trapped in jobs they dislike—even hate. This trapped feeling may be hard for younger job seekers to understand, especially those who are single. But as you get older, changing jobs becomes less attractive. The benefits associated with seniority—acquired sick time, vacation time, and preferential scheduling—can make it difficult to consider leaving an "old" job.

A primary reason people find themselves in a rut is that they fell into it. The deeper the rut, the easier it is to feel trapped. Rather than allowing yourself to fall into the job rut and become trapped, plan what you want out of life and then go after it. Nathan and Hill describe several "career drivers" to consider:

- Material rewards—seeking possession, wealth and a high standard of living

- Power and influence—seeking to be in control of people and resources

- Search for meaning—seeking to do things believed to be valuable for their own sake

- Expertise—seeking a high level of accomplishment in a specialized field

- Creativity—seeking to innovate and be identified with original input

➤ Affiliation—seeking nourishing relationships with others at work

➤ Autonomy—seeking to be independent and make key decisions for oneself

➤ Status—seeking to be recognized, admired, and respected by the community at large

➤ Security—seeking a solid and predictable future

> (Reproduced from Robert Nathan and Linda Hill, *Career Counseling,* pp. 78–79, copyright © 2006 by Sage Publications. Reprinted by permission of Sage Publications, Inc.)

Take an introspective look at yourself and apply the information learned to answer this question: "Will this job allow me to get what I want from life?" By answering honestly, you are being an "inventurer, one of those special breed of people who take charge and create your own challenges to get yourself moving" (Hagberg and Leider, 1988, p. 4). Hagberg and Leider explain:

> You are an inventurer if you are willing to take a long look at yourself and consider new options, venture inward, and explore. You are an inventurer if you see life as a series of changes, changes as growth experiences, and growth as positive. You are inventuring on life's *excursions* and learning about yourself as a result. You may feel lonely at times, and get discouraged for a while. But you are willing to risk some disappointments and take some knocks in your quest because you are committed to a balanced lifestyle and to more than just making a living. You are part of a unique group of people who want to make a living at work. If you have these qualities, you are an inventurer.
>
> Inventurers are people who choose to take a fresh look in the mirror to renew and perhaps recycle their lifestyle and careers. Some inventurers, seemingly snug in life and career patterns, are exploring their "greener pasture" . . . in search of their own personal Declaration of Independence: the pursuit of happiness. Other inventurers are planning second careers or early retirements. Some are underemployed and seeking careers more integrated with their abilities and lifestyle. They are female and male, old and young, and in between. (pp. 3–4).

According to Hagberg and Leider (p. 9): "These inventurers prove what wise teachers have said for ages: *'The knowledge is right in us—all we have to do is clear our minds and open ourselves to see the obvious.'"*

Inventurers are people who take charge and create their own challenges to get themselves moving. They are willing to take a long look at themselves and consider new options, venture inward, and explore. They see life as a series of changes, changes as growth experiences, and growth as positive.

One important step is looking at what you love to do: "Discovering your creative passion, the work you love, not only brings greater personal fulfillment but also gives you a leg up in the new economy. Mere interest in a career may have been enough when you could settle into a job and stay there for years. Today, you need the sustained motivation that comes from having a real passion for your work, and that requires a self-defined sense of purpose" (Boldt, 2004, pp. xxviii–xxix).

Boldt (p. 12) states: "Since you probably spend more waking hours working than doing anything else, your work must be something that you can be proud of, be creative in, and enjoy—if you are to have a happy and fulfilling life." Boldt (pp. 13–14) also adds: "People who are truly dedicated to their work—Buckminster Fuller, Albert Schweitzer, Mahatma Gandhi, Mother Teresa, and Pablo Picasso were excellent examples—continue to thrive on into old age."

You might want to keep a "values journal" to help identify what is personally important and what is not. Write down how you spend your time. What problems do you encounter? What makes you happy, angry, sad, up, down? After keeping the journal for a while, review it, looking for patterns to such issues as the following:

➢   How do I, on an average day, generally spend my time?

➢   What are five or ten things that really interest me?

➢   What conflicts or problems do I have? Which ones have I created for myself, and which ones have stemmed from outside factors?

➢   What short-range and long-range goals can I identify?

➢   What, ultimately, do I want to accomplish?

Also consider the "human equation" to answer the question, "How important is time with family and friends?" An involved family life may not be compatible with a career requiring sixty-hour workweeks, a lot of traveling, and hectic scheduling. Consider also where you want to live. Is climate important to you?

At this point in your self-inquiry, look at yourself and the world around you in relatively general terms. As you develop a sense of what is important to you, apply these ideas to the specific job choices that came out of the earlier brainstorming exercise. Ask yourself: Are my needs compatible with that particular job? Don't fool yourself. No one is watching to make certain you are honest. You will have only yourself to blame by kidding yourself. Begin to apply some of your answers to the previous questions to the overall requirements of the jobs listed at the start of this chapter. Can you get what you need from the jobs that interest you? Consider the following:

➢   Am I old enough? Mature enough?

➢   Do I have a background that will prohibit me from any certain work?

➢   Am I healthy enough for such work?

➢   Does the job coincide with my personal values?

➢   Do I have the skills for this work?

➢   Will I be able to achieve my long-term goals (e.g., financial, promotional) through such work?

➢   Can my family goals be achieved with this job (considering such issues as travel and time commitments)?

Bolles (pp. 325–352) encourages people to pursue their "ideal" jobs by creating a visual depiction of the essential parts of that work through an exercise he calls "the flower exercise":

> In order to hunt for your ideal job, or even something close to your ideal job, you must have a picture of it, in your head. The clearer the picture, the easier it will be to hunt for it. . . . We have chosen a "Flower" as the model for that picture. . . . Skills are at the center of the Flower, even as they are at the center of your mission, career, or job. They are listed in order of priority. Surrounding them are six petals . . .

- Geography
- Interests (Fields of Fascination)
- People Environments
- Values, Purposes, and Goals
- Working Conditions
- Salary & Level of Responsibility

Consider each of these "essential parts" for your "ideal work" and record your responses:

> **Geography**—Where would you most like to live and work, if you had a choice? In what kind of setting do you see yourself working? "Setting" means both physical location and invisible places your heart, mind, and soul most often yearn to be—values and the like.

> **Interests**—What are your favorite subjects? If you were stuck on a desert island with a person who had the capacity to speak on only a few subjects, what would you pray those subjects were? What kinds of tasks, using what kinds of skills, do you see yourself doing? With what kind of style?

> **People Environments**—The people you are surrounded by have great importance in job satisfaction. Dr. John Holland describes six principal people environments among which, he theorizes, everyone has three preferred groups (your "Holland Code"):
> > *Realistic (R):* people who like nature, or athletics, or tools and machinery
> > *Investigative (I):* people who are very curious, liking to investigate or analyze things
> > *Artistic (A):* people who are very artistic, imaginative, and innovative
> > *Social (S):* people who are bent on trying to help, teach, or serve people
> > *Enterprising (E):* people who like to start up projects or organizations, and/or influence or persuade people
> > *Conventional (C):* people who like detailed work, and like to complete tasks or projects

> **Values, Purposes, and Goals**—What guides you through every day, every task, every encounter with another person? What qualities do you want people to remember you for? What goals do you hope to accomplish in your life?

> **Working Conditions**—Under what circumstances do you accomplish your most effective work? Degree of supervision? Autonomy? Discretion? Pressure to meet deadlines? Public eye? Desk job or out in the field? Loud, crazy, and chaotic? Quiet, calm, and orderly?

> **Salary and Level of Responsibility**—What kind of salary or other types of compensation do you want to have? What rewards do you hope your work will bring you?

You might also consider taking an occupational preference test such as "Discovery II" to see how your interests and preferences match up with different occupations. Such tests are programmed so that computers can match your answers with answers given by representatives of different occupations. The computer compares your answers and indicates which occupational fields best match your interests.

Essential parts for your ideal work, besides skills, are geography; interests; people environments; values, purposes, and goals; working conditions; and salary and level of responsibility. These parts must be considered for your dream job to become a reality.

MOVING TOWARD YOUR CAREER GOAL

Perhaps some jobs you considered in the brainstorming exercise were eliminated after thinking about what you need from a career to be fulfilled in life. Perhaps you are still considering whether the career field or a specific career is right for you.

Be honest in considering a career because, as stressed, the very nature of the work in many areas of criminal justice and security is disruptive to what many consider a "normal work routine." Scheduling; having days off in the middle of the week; working nights, holidays, and weekends; seeing people at their worst; having your professionalism and honesty challenged in court—all are realities of the criminal justice and security fields. Also be aware of the areas on which the various levels of government are spending their resources. If you know you want to work in corrections but are unsure about where the majority of jobs are or how the payrolls compare, research the current available data.

In the final equation, do your goals, needs, and desires balance with the realities of the job? Only you can make this determination. For example, if you were to enroll in an introductory course in law enforcement, where do you fit among the three groups of "typical" students enrolled in such classes?

➢   Students who have known since they were very young that they were destined to be police officers

➢   Students who are considering the career, but have yet to make the commitment

➢   Students who are fascinated by the subject, not the career

If you have the chance to take an introductory course in law enforcement, corrections, private security, or criminal justice, consider doing it. It's one good way to better understand what the careers involve and if they are right for you. Some students who have always wanted to go into law enforcement become troubled when they learn more about the field and begin to question whether or not it is right for them. This is an appropriate benefit of exposure to new knowledge and experiences, for it is far better to learn such things *before* you (and the agency that hires you) have spent the time and resources needed to complete the police academy. Although many students end up feeling alone following this discovery, they are not. These fields are not for everyone.

Acquire What You Need

As you continue to assess whether your career goals are compatible with your needs and interests, you will also learn what else is required to get into the field. If you need college, register; if you need a physical fitness regime, begin one; and if you need experience, get it.

As mentioned earlier, do some investigative research by visiting agencies and interviewing those working in the field(s) you are considering. Volunteer and get involved in short-term experiences with potential employers—step into the shoes and walk around in them for a while to make sure they fit *before* you commit to buying them. Plodding along an uncharted path will get you, at best, nowhere, and at worst, somewhere you don't want to be. *Now* is the time to develop your own realistic, exciting career map.

Internships

Internships are an excellent way to discover if a specific area of criminal justice is a good fit for you. An internship is an opportunity to receive supervised, practical, on-the-job training in a specific area. Many law enforcement agencies and correctional institutions offer internships, usually without pay, for those interested in learning about a specific area of employment while acquiring skills that make them more employable in that area. Internships are the focus of discussion in Chapter 6.

ALTERNATIVES

Look around and contemplate the almost infinite number of jobs that make up the criminal justice system and its related fields. It is truly amazing. Even if one job is not for you, another will be. Don't be afraid to change your mind, to take some risks. For many people, taking risks is more frightening than facing a gun. Facing a gun lasts only an instant—a wrong career choice lasts much longer!

Our culture does not encourage risk taking. Even during the 1960s and 1970s, when a different cultural climate prevailed, a conservative work ethic encouraged people to be complacent. A successful career was often defined as a long career with one employer.

Thereafter a shift toward looking for a more satisfying career began, which meant exploring work options and being open to changing employers and jobs. Even employers found benefits to hiring someone who had worked elsewhere. Rather than someone asking, "Why did you change jobs?" employees began wondering why someone didn't.

Today, change has become a fact of life in the world of work. Regardless of whether you ever want to change jobs, it is likely you will have to at some point. Change *is* intimidating, but stagnation is even more frightening.

Risk taking is important because it exposes you to challenges and prevents you from getting stuck in a rut. Ruts lead to stagnation, which leads to job dissatisfaction and other adverse effects.

A certain amount of risk taking is important because it exposes you to challenges, keeps you flexible, and prevents personal and professional stagnation, which can lead to job dissatisfaction and burnout, which in turn affect one's personal life. Laurence J. Peter, an educator who espoused the "Peter Principle" ("In a hierarchy every employee tends to rise to his level of incompetence."), is also credited for the phrase, "A rut is a grave with the ends knocked out." Although ruts are predictable and therefore comfortable, who wants to live in a grave? Further, in criminal justice the boredom that accompanies a rut can make a person complacent. Losing one's edge can result in being unsafe.

TO RISK OR NOT TO RISK—THAT IS THE QUESTION

Like everything else, risk carries with it a certain amount of . . . well, risk. Change is all well and good, but there isn't always a happy result. Particularly now, when job security isn't guaranteed, maintaining a job that meets your needs may prove to be every bit as important, if not more so, as leaving for the sake of leaving, or changing just for the sake of change. Although staying in a job that makes you miserable and negatively affects all other aspects of your life makes no sense, leaving a secure job "just because" may not either.

In the first place, "dream jobs" often do not live up to the fantasy. A friend recently shared that his newly acquired dream job, one he'd worked all his career to achieve, was now ruining his life because of the associated demands and stress. A colleague who quit a seventeen-year successful job to take a "calculated risk" with a start-up venture found himself out of the new job after only three months because of the precarious financial times. In addition, it is wise to stay with a job for at least a minimum length of time to give yourself a chance to acclimate to a new environment and to avoid being thought of as a "job hopper."

Who Moved My Cheese? An Amazing Way to Deal with Change in Your Work and in Your Life, by Dr. Spencer Johnson, is a best-seller about how people respond and react to change. You are encouraged to get this book and read it now, and reread it from time to time. It's straightforward and whimsical but sends a powerful message: Whether you intend to change or not, you will find yourself confronting change, and so your strategy for dealing with it becomes as important as other life strategies you develop.

Is change always worth it? That depends. Is change always an option? Absolutely! And it's nice to have options.

GET GOING!

An effective exercise for motivating yourself to change is the "last day of my life" test. Bolles suggests that you consider the statement "Before I die, I want to . . ." and then list the things you would like to do before you die. Or write on the topic: "On the last day of my life, what must I have done or been so that my life will have been satisfying to me?"

 As the concluding exercise in this chapter, take time to write your feelings on one of these two topics.

Picking Daisies

If I had my life to live all over again, I would pick more Daisies.
If I had my life to live over, I would try to make more mistakes next time.
I would be sillier than I have been this trip.
I would relax. I would limber up.

I know very few things I would take seriously. I would be crazier;
I would be less hygienic; I would take more chances;
I would take more trips, I would climb more mountains, Swim more rivers, and watch more sunsets.
I would burn more gasoline. I would eat more ice cream and less meals.

I would have more actual troubles, and fewer imaginary ones. You see, I am one of those people who lives prophylactically and sensibly and sanely, hour after hour, day after day.
Oh, I have had my mad moments, and if I had it to do all over again,
I would have more of them; in fact, I'd try to have nothing else,
just moments, one after another, instead of living so many years ahead.

I have been one of those people who never go anywhere without a thermometer, a hot-water bottle, a gargle, a raincoat and a parachute.
If I had it to live all over again I would go places and travel lighter than I have.
If I had my life to live over again, I would start barefoot earlier in the spring, and stay that way later in the fall. I would play hookey more, I would ride on more merry-go-rounds. I'd pick more Daisies.

(Reproduced from *Mindstyles/Lifestyles,* by Nathaniel Lande, published by Price Stern Sloan, Inc., Los Angeles, California. Copyright 1976 by Price Stern Sloan, Inc. Reprinted by permission.)

IT'S JUST A JOB . . .

Work and careers are unquestionably important. But it is critical to bear in mind that this is only *part* of the balance that makes up anyone's life. Exploring careers should be an ongoing process that focuses on the questions: What am I doing now, and what do I want to do in the future? Figure 5.2 helps you navigate the process of determining which career area(s) to consider, taking into account the "big picture" of what you want for your life, not just your work. No law says you must stay in the same job or career forever. In fact, it's a crime when people do so to the detriment of themselves and their families, who then become casualties of the effects of work. And yet many people elect to stay in a job that is, quite literally, killing them.

This may sound extreme to a young person looking toward a career that can be as exciting as criminal justice. But things change, and so do priorities. It always pays to look ahead while assessing what's going on at the moment. Be prepared for change. It's going to happen. Control it, rather than letting it control you.

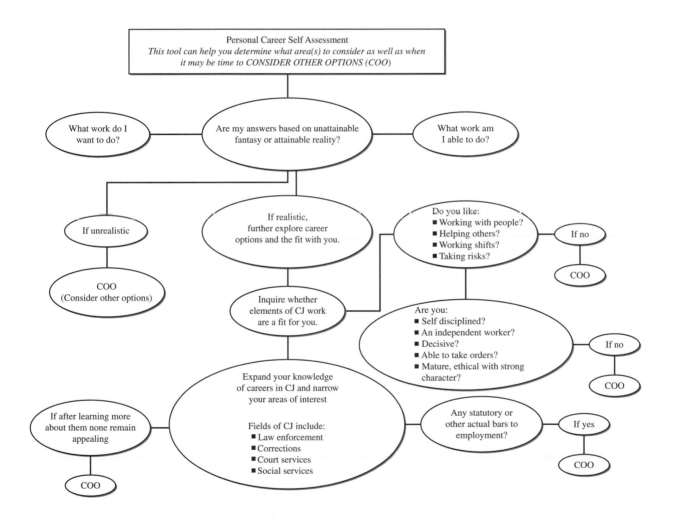

FIGURE 5–2   Personal Career Self Assessment (*continued*)

FIGURE 5–2   *(continued)*

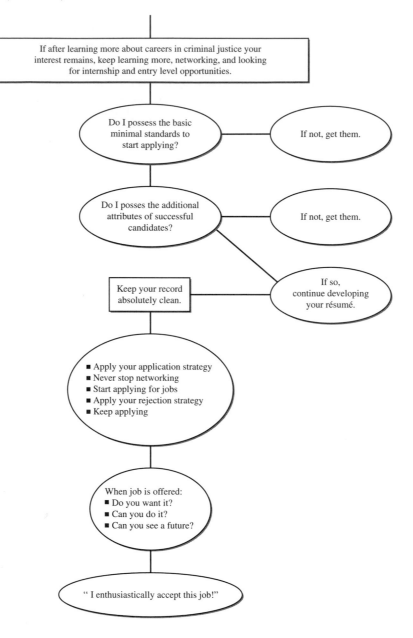

CONCLUSION

It is important to think carefully about what career you'd like to pursue *before* jumping into it. A hasty decision, or one based on rumor or television portrayals, will likely lead to disappointment and dissatisfaction. The four steps that comprise the career development process are (1) self-assessment, (2) career exploration, (3) job-search skill development, and (4) implementation of the job-search steps. The first two steps are very important. In deciding which career is best suited to you and your needs, you *must* assess yourself and how your abilities and needs compare to the demands of the job.

Risk taking is important because it exposes you to challenges and prevents you from getting stuck in a rut, which could lead to stagnation and job dissatisfaction. Become an *inventurer,* someone who takes charge and creates their own challenges to get themselves moving. Be willing to take a long look at yourself and consider new options. Venture inward and explore. See life as a series of changes, changes as growth experiences, and growth as positive.

AN INSIDER'S VIEW

PRIVATE SECURITY AND THE NUCLEAR OPTION

David A. Axt

Security Manager
Prairie Island Nuclear Generating Plant

I first learned about nuclear security while on leave from the U.S. Marine Corps in 1983. A local newspaper featured a contract security company that provided security for a Department of Energy (DOE) nuclear weapons complex. The article included a photo of a balaclava clad Special Response Team (SRT) standing with their submachine guns in front of their helicopter. Knowing I would soon be leaving the Corps, I set my sights on applying for and joining this SRT. Although technically I would be a civilian, I would still wear the same uniform and carry the same weapons I used in the Corps, which might serve as a good transition from military to civilian life.

After leaving the Marine Corps in 1984, I got the job at the 300 square mile DOE facility. My new employer was under contract with the DOE. I started working at a vehicle checkpoint processing visitors and vehicles before becoming a security police officer (SPO) at a DOE nuclear reactor facility. Four months later, I was eligible to try out for the SRT. The basic SRT qualification course consisted of intense physical training, small-unit tactics, live-fire hostage rescue, close-quarters-battle, helicopter insertion, repelling, land navigation and suspect pursuit. Our instructors, who came from some of the most elite military counterterrorist organizations in the U.S., provided cutting-edge training and equipped us with state-of-the-art weapons and equipment. After successfully completing SRT training, I applied for and was selected as a SRT Team Sniper. A year later, I applied for and was promoted to SRT Team Leader, where I led my own small unit of SRT members.

The on-duty SRT units had to remain ready to respond to any threatened facility and provide tactical backup to the security police officers stationed at each facility. When we were not patrolling, team leaders conducted "team training" to hone individual and team skills, all the while remaining within our required response timelines. Periodically, SRT members would role-play as "terrorists" for force-on-force drills. This training and drill experience reinforced the importance of how vital it is to thoroughly "think like a terrorist" before ever thinking about security countermeasures.

After an unfortunate SRT training accident injured my back, my doctor strongly suggested I cease jumping out of helicopters and pursue a desk job. So I applied for and accepted a position as a Quality Assurance (QA) Auditor with the same DOE contract security organization. With the QA department, I was trained and certified as a Lead Auditor. And with my SRT experience, I became the team lead for internal audits of the SRT. As a QA auditor, I essentially compared what we were doing with what we were supposed to be doing and wrote reports and recommendations.

Soon after joining the QA department, my security company's contract with the DOE was up for "re-bid" for another five-year contract. To ensure my company provided a detailed, accurate response, they recruited current employees to temporarily serve on the proposal writing team. With lots of experience writing QA audit reports and with my security operations and SRT experience, I was selected to serve on this team. Here, I gained valuable experience in the *business* of contract security, project management and contract security proposal writing.

A few months after returning to my QA auditing position, I learned about a corporate security job opportunity with another contract security company. I put together a resume and cover letter and followed up with several phone calls until I got an interview. This was a big step that involved uprooting my family and moving to Oakland, California. But career wise, it was definitely a positive move. I interviewed and got the job of Corporate Security Coordinator. It involved assisting the security director with overseeing contract security organizations at various commercial nuclear power plants. Periodically, I would help write proposals for new contracts.

Soon after joining the new contract security company, one of our commercial nuclear power plant clients was scheduled for a Nuclear Regulatory Commission (NRC) Force-on-Force inspection. For these inspections, the NRC evaluated the security force's ability to respond to and repel various simulated terrorist attacks and attempted radiological sabotage. Because of my previous experience, my manager recommended I help our client facility prepare for their NRC inspection. After a successful NRC inspection, several other commercial nuclear power plants contacted me for assistance. Soon, I found myself establishing and managing my own consulting subdivision, the Special Service Group. In some cases, I wrote consulting proposals and made sales presentations, competing for the consulting contracts. It was the ideal opportunity to capitalize on my basic security, SRT, security auditing and proposal writing skills. But with success came frequent travel.

After five years of traveling, I learned about a corporate security position with one of my electric utility companies in the upper Midwest. Since I was already known to the client—as a nuclear security consultant—I was offered a position as a Corporate Security Coordinator. My duties entailed oversight of various security programs at the company's two nuclear power plants. My background and consulting experience helped me assist with the plants' tactical training and force-on-force drill programs.

Post 9/11, my job became increasingly challenging as the threat became less theoretical and more defined, and the likelihood of a terrorist attack increased exponentially. I spent the next few years assessing and implementing new NRC security requirements. As intelligence agencies learned more about Al Qaida tactics and their interest in nuclear power plants, we tweaked our posture further.

Like clockwork, five years later, I was ready to change gears. I applied for and accepted a security manager position at one of my company's nuclear power plants, which is where I work today. Here, I am responsible for the overall physical security program, the training and drill programs and a 9.5M operating budget. With a staff of 14 and about 100 contract security force members, this was a very big change compared to my previous corporate security positions. Like any new manager, I have to resist getting too involved in those things I enjoy and which make up the majority of my experience: tactics, protective strategy and force-on-force drills. Instead, I deal with personnel issues daily, endless meetings and budget tracking, and of course, the daily crisis which requires immediate attention and decision-making. As the security manager, however, I occasionally serve as the Security Group Leader for one of the plant's incident command posts, as well as Security Liaison for law enforcement's on-site Incident Command Post. It may not be as fun or exhilarating as my days on the SRT, but dealing with threats from a strategic, management level can have its exciting moments.

For anyone interested in private or nuclear security, corporate security or consulting, I offer the following tips.

➢   First and foremost, finish your four-year college degree before venturing into law enforcement or private security. Trust me.

➢   Join the American Society for Industrial Security (ASIS) as soon as you qualify. Student memberships are available. Then network.

➢   Learn to type and to use basic computer software and email. In this age of "information overload" an inability to use standard business software and communicate efficiently and effectively in writing is a silent, subtle career killer.

➤ Never be afraid to start at the bottom.

➤ For interviews, dress conservatively and leave the earrings at home.

➤ Once you've got your foot in the door, find a mentor and be like a sponge.

➤ Apply for and take every internal company training course available.

➤ Be prepared and be willing to move or travel. For many companies, this is a must.

➤ If you have had trouble with the law (e.g., DWI, assault), BE HONEST when filling out your application. If you omit anything, it WILL BE discovered and you WILL BE deemed "untrustworthy and unreliable" and will be immediately rejected. If you are honest, you will at least have a chance.

➤ Do everything in your power to stay with a company for at least five years. If you change jobs too frequently, a potential employer may view you as a "job hopper."

David A. Axt *has been employed in the nuclear security profession for twenty-three years. Past positions include security police officer, special response team (SRT) sniper and team leader, and quality assurance auditor for Wackenhut Security Services at the DOE Savannah River Site, Nuclear Weapons Complex; corporate security coordinator, and Special Services Group manager, American Protective Services, Inc; corporate security coordinator, Northern States Power Company; and security manager, Prairie Island Nuclear Generating Plant, Xcel Energy.*

Mr. Axt holds a Master of Science degree in Security & Crime Risk Management from the University of Leicester, Leicester England. He is also a graduate of the Executive Development Program, University of Minnesota, Carlson School of Management.

  MIND STRETCHES

1. What is your strategy for identifying a career path? Do you know anyone who has just "floated along," letting the current carry them? Are they happy? Why or why not?

2. Do you think American workers are cynical? Why?

3. How important is job security to you? Can you see it changing in five years? Ten years?

4. How important is money to you? Will you be satisfied with an officer's pay? Can you see this need changing for you?

5. Have you ever worked nights, holidays, or weekends? What can you imagine would be good about such a schedule? Bad?

6. What prevents people from accepting change? What keeps people from taking risks? Why do you think many people stick with a less-than-satisfactory job?

7. What five jobs within the criminal justice field interest you? Why? What jobs in the field do not appeal to you? Why?

8.   What elements of your personal history might be negative factors in pursuing your career goals? How can you deal with these at the interview?

9.   Why do you think more people don't take an active role in their career choices?

10.   What are the five most important things you will consider when selecting a job? Are these under your control?

REFERENCES

Boldt, Laurence G. *How to Find the Work You Love,* 2nd ed. New York: Penguin Group, 2004.

Bolles, Richard Nelson. *What Color Is Your Parachute? A Practical Manual for Job-Hunters & Career-Changers.* Berkeley, CA: Ten Speed Press, 2008.

Hagberg, Janet, and Richard Leider. *The Inventurers: Excursions in Life and Career Renewal.* Reading, MA: Addison-Wesley Publishing Company, 1988.

Krannich, Ronald L. *Change Your Job, Change Your Life,* 9th ed. Manassas Park, VA: Impact Publications, 2005.

Lande, Nathaniel. "Picking Daisies." *Mindstyles/Lifestyles.* Los Angeles: Price Stern Sloan, Inc., 1976.

Leider, Richard J., and David A. Shapiro. *Repacking Your Bags: Lighten Your Load for the Rest of Your Life,* 2nd ed. San Francisco: Berrett-Koehler Publishers, Inc., 2002.

Nathan, Robert, and Linda Hill. *Career Counseling*, 2nd ed.. Newbury Park, CA: Sage Publications, 2006.

Occupational Outlook Quarterly, Fall 2006. Available online at www.bls.gov/opub/ooq/2006/fall/art03.htm.

Parsons, F. *Choosing a Vocation.* Boston, MA: Houghton-Mifflin, 1909.

ADDITIONAL CONTACTS AND SOURCES OF INFORMATION

National Board of Certified Counselors (NBCC)
3 Terrace Way, Suite D
Greensboro, NC 27403
(910) 547-0607
www.nbcc.org

National Career Development Association (NCDA)
5999 Stevenson Avenue
Alexandria, VA 22304
(703) 823-9800
www.ncda.org

CHAPTER 6

INTERNSHIPS: TESTING THE WATERS

*People are always blaming their circumstances for what they are. I don't believe in
circumstances. The people who get on in this world are the people who get up and look
for the circumstances they want, and if they can't find them—make them.*

—*George Bernard Shaw*

Do You Know:

- ➤ The difference between a passive intern and an active intern?
- ➤ What the two general types of internships are and how they differ?
- ➤ Where internship opportunities may be located?
- ➤ How much lead time may be needed to arrange for an internship?
- ➤ What service learning involves?
- ➤ How much employers want interns to talk, listen, or participate in work activities?
- ➤ How to make the most of an internship opportunity?
- ➤ What to do if an internship does not work out?

INTRODUCTION

Dictionary.com defines *internship* as "A student or a recent graduate undergoing supervised practical
training" and "to train or serve as an intern." Rubinstein (2002) further explains: "An internship is a trial
run. It's a chance for you to explore a particular career field without making a long-term commitment.
Whether you love it or hate it, your internship will put you one step closer to determining what you might
want to do once you graduate from college." With Google promptly serving up well over three million hits
on the term, internships are certainly an aspect of job searching *and* professional development worthy of
understanding and taking advantage of.

Many college students are concerned about how important their major is to obtaining employment.
However, Asher (2008) asserts: "Any major prepares most students for most jobs. Internships are far more
important than a specific major."

In *The Internship Bible,* Oldman and Hamadeh (2005, p. xiii) suggest: "It's now accepted wisdom that if
you don't do internships, you're at a competitive disadvantage when it comes to launching a career . . . that
more than 87 percent of U.S. college seniors graduating in spring 2002 had completed at least one internship
by graduation, and over 70 percent had done two or more." There are certain things employers expect to see
on résumés, if for no other reason than that the majority of applicants possess them. It is very possible that

internships are becoming one of these *expectations*. Even if they aren't, it might just be what differentiates you from the other applicants.

Internships are an excellent way to discover if a specific area of criminal justice is a good fit for you. An internship is an opportunity to receive supervised, practical, on-the-job training in a specific area. Many law enforcement agencies and correctional institutions offer internships, usually without pay, for those interested in learning about a specific area of employment while acquiring skills that make them more employable in that area. Often, individuals who complete an internship with a specific police department are hired by that department after their formal education is complete. Or, conversely, the intern or the department may find that the fit is not good, and both are spared a difficult situation.

In this chapter you will explore the concept of internships—where they are rooted in history, the general kinds of interns and internships, how to find internship opportunities, what is expected of you as an intern, how to make the most of an internship and what to do if a good internship goes bad, being evaluated as an intern, and participating in internships even after you land a job. The chapter concludes with a recap of the dos and don'ts of internships.

NOTHING NEW HERE!

The idea of interning is not new. In fact, the concept has a rich history rooted in apprenticeships dating back thousands of years before Christ: "The Babylonian Code of Hammurabi, written in 2100 B.C., contains a provision requiring artisans to teach their handicrafts to their sons. Similarly, records of ancient Greece, Egypt, and Rome show that the young learned their trade under the supervision of skilled workers" (Oldman and Hamadeh, p. 393). Some famous apprentices in history (and where they apprenticed) were (p. 393):

> Benedict Arnold, famous "traitor" and military leader (apothecary's shop)
> Benjamin Franklin, scientist and politician (printer's shop of brother James, 1718–1723)
> Samuel Gompers, labor leader (shoemaker, 1860)
> Alexander Hamilton, Secretary of the Treasury and author of the Federalist Papers (merchant on St. Croix)
> Thomas Hardy, author (architect, 1856)
> Andrew Johnson, 17th President of the United States (tailor in Raleigh, NC, 1820–1826)
> Alfred Nobel, Swedish philanthropist, originator of the Nobel prizes (Swedish ship designer, 1860)
> Paul Revere, courier and political activist (gold and silversmith shop, 1753)
> Mark Twain, author and journalist (printer's shop, 1846, and riverboat, 1857)
> Martin Van Buren, 8th President of the United States (NY law offices of Francis Silvester, 1796–1801)

ON INTERNS AND INTERNSHIPS

In *Internships for Dummies,* Donovan and Garnett (2001, p. 18) describe two general kinds of interns: passive and active. Passive interns are those who "wait for opportunities to come to them . . . wait until an internship falls into their lap," whereas active interns take responsibility for their own internship—for their own work and learning and, ultimately, for their own future. Table 6–1 compares the skills of passive and active interns.

> Passive interns *wait* for things to happen *to* them. Active interns *make* things happen *for* themselves.

Just as there are two basic types of interns, so too are there two types of internships. One is a *survey internship;* the other is a *practical internship.* Although intended for different people at different times of their careers, both become exceptionally important.

TABLE 6–1   Comparing Passive and Active Interns

Skill	Passive Interns	Active Interns
Assessing needs and goals	Only casually think about their needs and goals if they do it at all.	Systematically reflect on their needs and goals for an internship.
Searching for internships	Wait for opportunities to come their way or only come up with a few leads through the obvious sources.	Explore a range of leads using a range of sources (not just the obvious ones) and compare those leads to their needs and goals.
Getting the internship	Submit one or two applications, wait for a response and take the first offer if they get one.	Submit a number of applications for internships that meet their needs and goals, follow up with prospective employers, don't automatically jump at the first offer and negotiate terms if feasible.
Orienting yourself to the workplace	Wait for a formal orientation and go through the motions during the orientation. If no orientation occurs, passive interns let the opportunity drop.	Take the initiative to get the most out of any organized orientation, but if none is arranged, they actively orient themselves and work to get an organized orientation.
Handling problems	Wait until problems occur during the internship and wait for the work supervisor, school intern advisor or someone else to solve these problems.	Anticipate the kinds of problems that might occur and work to avoid these problems. Actively seek appropriate help before a situation gets out of control.
Doing the work	Wait until assigned a task, fail to get essential information for completing that task and fail to keep supervisors informed of progress (or problems).	Energetically seek assignments, probe to get essential information about them and actively keep supervisors informed of progress and problems before they get out of hand.
Evaluating own performance	Wait until the end-of-the-internship evaluation to find out what they are doing well and poorly. If no formal evaluation exists, they write off this opportunity for feedback.	Conscientiously (but tactfully) seek informal feedback each week or with each task. They learn what the formal evaluations are and prepare for them.
Networking	Wait until coworkers or others contact them. If contact occurs, passive interns let the other person carry the relationship. If contact doesn't happen, they miss these chances to network.	Systematically and conscientiously contact other people to share experiences and to obtain advice about the immediate job and career. Active interns keep up their end of the professional relationship by helping mentors and others where possible.
Linking to a job or career	Sit back to see what happens at the end of the internship. If nothing happens, back to square one!	Conscientiously work toward parlaying their internship into full-time jobs or other opportunities by performing well during the internship, building a professional network and developing knowledge and skills for the next step.

SOURCE: Adapted from Craig P. Donovan and Jim Garnett. *Internships for Dummies.* New York: Wiley and Sons, 2001, pp. 19–20. Used with permission.

The survey internship is a relatively short-term experience during which the intern, most often a student, is permitted to observe work being done and ask questions pertinent to the profession and requisite tasks. It is a passive experience, as the intern does not actually participate in any work activities but merely watches them being done. Nonetheless, this kind of internship provides an excellent opportunity to learn about a job through observation and inquiry.

In criminal justice, a survey internship involves visiting the various divisions of a particular agency to observe others completing their jobs. For example, a student might sit in the dispatch center and see how incoming calls are handled and personnel dispatched. Later the student may observe jail operations, watch evidence technicians, sit with the administrative division, and even take a ride-along with a patrol unit. The result of such an experience is to see firsthand what really occurs in such an agency and how it differs from any preconceived notions the student may have.

The practical internship differs from the survey experience because, as the name implies, actual experience is the goal. The practical internship allows students to learn through hands-on involvement. These experiences tend to be longer than survey internships and can last months or more.

Practical internships in criminal justice can involve any number of activities, from entry-level tasks to actually working side-by-side with officers or other personnel. These experiences are not just for people exploring a career path or new to the field. It is not uncommon for more senior practitioners to participate in a practical internship with another agency that does things differently or specializes in something their home agency does not. It is also a way to cross-train employees and keep superiors in touch with the daily functions of their subordinates.

Survey internships are passive, observation-based experiences best suited to people in the initial stages of career exploration. Practical internships are active, hands-on experiences intended primarily for people developing their experience (either as students or practitioners) in a particular area.

LOCATING INTERNSHIP OPPORTUNITIES

Much of what this book recommends regarding seeking employment in criminal justice can directly apply to internships as well, with some adjustments. Although internships may be advertised, they are usually not advertised the way actual jobs are; that is, it is most unusual to see an internship opportunity in the newspaper. They are, however, posted, but you need a strategy to know where to find the postings.

 List as many resources as you can to obtain information on where to find out about internships.

Books are available that compile tens of thousands of internship sites along with general information about them. Princeton Review's *The Internship Bible* claims to offer "100,000 opportunities to launch your career," and *Peterson's Internships* provides almost 50,000 paid and unpaid internships. A quick Internet search provides a wealth of resources such as www.studentjobs.gov/ offered by the U.S. Office of Personnel Management and listings of thousands of jobs for students along with helpful hints and ways to post your résumé online for these jobs. Specific agencies will appear on a general search too, such as the Metropolitan Washington D.C. Police Department at http://dcpolice.jobs/internships.aspx.

School-Related Internships

Many, if not most, schools have relationships with agencies that provide internships. Some programs are formally structured, with internships taking the format of actual courses for which the student receives credit. Other programs offer rather informal or unstructured internship opportunities where students receive no credit but are afforded an invaluable "inside look" at a career they are considering.

> A logical place to begin seeking internship opportunities is through school contacts.

Some school-coordinated internships are optional, most likely providing elective credits, whereas other internships are required. An example of this is a criminal justice and law enforcement school that requires students to complete 115 hours of interning at a social service agency, the primary purpose being to learn about resources available to criminal justice practitioners. Zapor (2008) says: "An internship experience is required of our criminal justice students because it provides the invaluable real-life experience of seeing how their education is applied to the field as well as being an education itself being there. It's also a great thing to include on their resumes. I consider interning for students a chance for them to apply what they've learned and learn more to apply later, either back in class or at another job. We can teach much in the classroom, but not everything. Interning gives students the best of both worlds."

In addition to speaking with a counselor, teacher, or program director, be sure you know when agencies may have recruiters on campus to engage potential interns. These people are often asked to speak to classes, attend criminal justice/law enforcement club meetings, and staff display tables at job fairs. If these individuals offer you their card or provide their contact information, *keep it and follow up*. And never forget networking with other students who may currently be interning, working, or otherwise know of opportunities. It *always* pays to ask.

Credit versus Compensation

Some interns receive college credit and some actually get paid. And some are fortunate enough to get both. In some instances it can be the student's choice. Be clear what a particular internship offers and realize that interns are seldom afforded the opportunity to negotiate placement terms.

Locating Internships Online

With agency websites now the norm rather than the exception, the Internet has enhanced the ability to locate internship (as well as employment) opportunities at departments, quite literally, anywhere on earth. For example, the International Association of Chiefs of Police (IACP) home page (www.theiacp.org) offers an FAQ (frequently asked questions) link, which brings up a list of common queries, including: "Does the IACP accept interns?" The answer: "Yes. IACP seeks undergraduate and graduate students with a background in criminal justice, law enforcement, communications, public administration, or a related field for potential internship positions. See the Jobs Database for 'Jobs at IACP Headquarters.' "

Another example: Someone interested in a career in law enforcement at the federal level could go to the FLETC website (www.fletc.gov), search for "intern," and receive multiple results, one of which describes FLETC's college intern program. (When searching online, use "intern" instead of "internship" to maximize the number of results.)

> The Internet provides an almost limitless resource for locating internships in criminal justice.

START EARLY! STAY ORGANIZED!

Internships, especially in the criminal justice field, require that you begin your search well before you are actually interested in beginning. As O'Connor (2008) asserts: "The best internships . . . require long-range planning, sometimes at least a year or more in advance." Many agencies require some sort of background check, so give yourself plenty of lead time when exploring internship options.

> Plan your internship well in advance.

Because many people will be looking for a limited number of internships, keep a notebook of contacts, just as you should as part of your job-seeking strategy, so you have a ready networking list to use now and in the future. In addition to the obvious benefits of internships, the process of seeking such an experience is great, too, because of the similarities to job seeking. It is all about developing a strategy to achieve what you want . . . and part of that strategy is to recognize the necessary time constraints.

 Begin compiling a list of the types of work you are interested in. These can be general positions, such as probation officer, police officer, corrections officer, forensics, investigation, armed sky marshal.

 Next, consider which jurisdictional level(s) are most appealing to you right now (federal, state, local) and explore the reasons you feel this way.

PRESENTING YOURSELF

This chapter on internships appears before the chapters dealing with presenting yourself because often people apply for internships before considering their overall job search strategy. But make no mistake, applying for an internship is no different than applying for any other job: "First impressions are critical in your internship and job search. An employer will decide in the first 7 seconds if they want to know more about you or not. This means that all of your communication (including face to face, phone, resume, cover letter and email) must be professional and error-free. Be prepared; be ready; be sure to have someone proof read your work!" (Sukut, 2008).

SERVICE LEARNING

"Service learning" is gaining popularity in college programs. This concept integrates community service work with the objectives of a particular course, providing an even richer educational experience. According to Hendricks (2008): "Service learning is a form of experiential learning that requires students to participate in service projects, or unpaid internships, while they apply knowledge and skills to meet real community needs. The key is to understand that service projects must, in some way, be connected to an intentional course objective and outcome and must, in some way, meet a real need in the 'community.'" Hendricks goes on to explain:

> A course in Community Policing may integrate a service project with the curriculum in a number of different ways. For example, as students are discussing and learning about the various factors that influence public perception of law enforcement, they are instructed to develop a survey that they use to compile data and

information on local perceptions of law enforcement. Once the data is collected and analyzed, the same group of students uses the data to present their findings to local law enforcement agencies. In this example, the students are learning valuable tools and skills to determine and understand public perception while providing a needed service by working to educate local law enforcement agencies of the current public perception of law enforcement.

The most effective learning is *applied* learning, and service learning embraces this ideal.

WHAT IS EXPECTED OF YOU?

An intern is basically considered an entry-level member of the organization. This does not mean you are entitled to the same benefits as bona fide employees, but you are expected to behave similarly. In addition, it is probable the experience is linked to a school program with which you are involved. Thus, you are playing two roles: that of someone with whom you are interning and that of a student.

If you have not previously interacted with the profession you are interning with, you will not likely know the culture, the jargon, or the behavior expected (other than being polite and other commonsense factors). So *ask*. Before the internship even occurs, you should ask what manner of dress is appropriate. If you are doing a ride-along, ask the person you are with to tell you what to do. Do not just go running after them into a call. If they do not verbally express their expectations, ask, "Should I come with you or wait here?"

Among the reasons you don't want to interfere is because any criminal justice internship involves exposure to situations most people never consider, and certainly things you do not yet know about (that's why you are interning, after all). For starters, there is the issue of safety. You will be exposed to new, potentially dangerous situations where you may not necessarily know how to react. This may occur on an emergency police call, working in a correctional facility, or interacting with people on probation. The professionals know what to do; you don't. And they will not expect you to. Furthermore, pretending you do could be hazardous to your internship in any number of ways.

You could become a witness just by being present at an incident. You may even be asked to write down your observations or what you heard. You absolutely do *not* want to interfere with an investigation by touching anything, disturbing evidence, or engaging in conversations. If another agency representative makes an assumption and asks you to do something, assert that you are an intern and identify the person you are accompanying. If a witness or suspect asks you a question, immediately defer to the person with whom you are interning. If anyone says anything to you, report it. Violations of these basic tenets are grounds for immediate termination of your internship and could cause the loss of a criminal case, even if due to an unintentional indiscretion.

If employers have one solid recommendation for most interns, it's two fairly simple words, followed by some encouragement. The words are *quietly listen*. The encouragement is, when asked to, participate. Similar to our recommendations later in this book on how to keep a job once you get it, you want to be very careful of your behavior and speech. One student couldn't keep quiet long enough to make it through her first ride-along before the officer returned her to the police station and simply said, "Get out." By the time she reached the station door the commander had already been advised she was no longer welcome as an intern. Her fault was not talking too much (although an irritation, to be sure); it was behaving inappropriately. The details are not important because there are plenty of similar stories: being a know-it-all, telling officers how to do their job, being critical of the agency or profession, getting in the way, behaving immaturely, wearing inappropriate clothing or anything else that would equate to "this person is not right for this internship or profession."

Employers expect interns to *quietly listen* and to *participate only when asked*. Above all, interns are expected to *behave appropriately*.

Clark (2004, pp. 13–15) offers the following intern dos and don'ts:

Don't

➢ Be late or abuse your breaks.

➢ Make personal phone calls.

➢ Play on the computer.

➢ Dress inappropriately.

➢ Disrespect other people's workspaces.

➢ Be a complainer or a slacker.

➢ Be a know-it-all.

➢ Be afraid to ask questions or speak up at the right time.

Do

➢ Be an active and enthusiastic learner.

➢ Give your internship some time to develop before concluding there are problems.

➢ Actively seek out opportunities to create your own projects.

➢ Go the extra mile at tmes to demonstrate your willingness to pitch in and be a team player.

➢ Share your career aspirations with supervisors, coworkers, and those you encounter outside the workplace.

➢ Build your own workplace portfolio (things said about you, projects you've worked on).

MAKING THE MOST OF THE EXPERIENCE

Whether a survey or practical internship, for credit or not, you want to make the most of the experience. Not only do you want to gain as much information as possible, but you want to take full advantage of the networking opportunities to develop contacts that may serve your future job-search efforts. You will be meeting people actively engaged in the profession of interest, many of whom may be potential points of contact when you are ready to seek employment. Furthermore, if you participate in an internship long enough, some individuals will likely readily allow you to list them as a reference. You may even find a mentor, someone who will be supportive of and helpful to you throughout your job-seeking efforts, or even your career.

Oldman and Hamadeh, in *The Internship Bible* (pp. xii–xiv), remind us that things are just beginning when an internship is obtained. They provide ten suggestions to help make the most of an internship [From *The Princeton Review: The Internship Bible,* 2004, ed. by Mark Oldman, copyright © 2004 by Princeton Review Publishing, LLC. Used by permission of Princeton Review, a division of Random House, Inc.]:

➤ **Chart Your Course:** Before starting an internship, create a checklist. List the skills you hope to learn, people you want to meet, types of projects you'd like to work on, ideas you have about the company, etc. As the internship progresses, check off items on the list to ensure that you're making the most of your experience.

➤ **Expect Some Busywork:** All internships—and most jobs for that matter—involve some menial tasks like photocopying, faxing, and filing. Although your internship will hopefully involve substantive work beyond busywork, don't expect to be running the show. No one likes an intern with unrealistic expectations or delusions of grandeur.

➤ **Use Your "Intern-al Access":** Because interns tend to be viewed by employees as young, energetic visitors, they often have access to meetings and areas of the company that young employees don't. Make the most of this access to learn about the inner workings of the company and the people who work there.

➤ **Bond with Your Fellow Interns:** Be sure to meet and share ideas with the other interns at your company—even ones who are not in your particular department. Your fellow interns can be a powerful source of information about the company, letting you know, for example, which departments are hot and which are not.

➤ **Say Hello to Higher-Ups:** When passing executives in the hallway, don't hesitate to introduce yourself and chat with them about the company. Most interns are too intimidated to say hello to higher-ups, so by taking the initiative, you'll stand out as motivated and engaged.

➤ **Volunteer for Extra Assignments:** During slow periods, be sure to track down your supervisor and volunteer for extra assignments—something few interns bother to do. The more initiative and enthusiasm you show, the more responsibility you'll get.

➤ **Participate in "Extracurriculars":** If your company offers interns access to field trips, brown-bag luncheons with executives, barbecues, tickets to sporting events or other traditional internship "extracurriculars," by all means participate. Some interns' most memorable and rewarding experiences occur outside the direct scope of employment.

➤ **Be Nice to Everyone:** Many interns don't realize that gaining the respect of assistants, mail-room workers, and other support staff can be as important as winning the appreciation of executives. When it comes time to be considered for a full-time position, how you treat support staff can make the difference in whether you get a job offer.

➤ **Get a Rec:** While your work is still fresh in the minds of your supervisor, make sure to ask him or her for a detailed letter of recommendation. Even if you have no immediate need for a recommendation, it is useful to have already secured one when searching for a job or applying to graduate school.

➤ **Stay in Touch:** After your internship ends, keep in touch with coworkers with periodic calls or e-mails. This is an easy way to get company updates and keep your name fresh in the minds of employees when hiring decisions are made.

The "10 Commandments" of internships include:
➤ Chart Your Course
➤ Expect Some Busywork
➤ Use Your "Intern-al Access"
➤ Bond with Your Fellow Interns
➤ Say "Hello" to Higher-Ups
➤ Volunteer for Extra Assignments
➤ Participate in "Extracurriculars"
➤ Be Nice to Everyone
➤ Get a Recommendation
➤ Stay in Touch

 As the first "commandment" directs, create a checklist for your internship, if only hypothetical. In thinking about the type of agency or department you would like to explore job opportunities with (via an internship), list the skills you would be expected to gain proficiency in, the people you want to meet, and the types of assignments or projects you would like to work on.

It is generally helpful, when embarking on a new experience, to know a little of what to expect. On his website, Dr. O'Connor familiarizes students with the world of interning by providing a list of what a criminal justice internship *is* and what it is *not*:

A criminal justice internship IS:

- An opportunity to get real exposure to a variety of agencies in the local criminal justice community
- A chance to meet professionals in the field who can advocate for your future employment
- An opportunity to explore a specific profession prior to committing yourself to it in a full-time capacity
- An appointment as a representative and ambassador of [your academic institution]
- A privilege
- An opportunity to broaden your educational experience with some real practical experience
- A huge responsibility—the vast majority of which falls upon the student
- Unpaid (usually)
- To be set up far in advance of starting, usually five to ten weeks before the internship semester begins
- To be completed by individuals who have declared criminal justice as their major and are of junior or senior standing
- To be granted at the complete and mutual discretion of the internship coordinator and the participating agency
- For students who have demonstrated adequate academic performance, and are in good academic standing with the department, any faculty committees, and the college/university

A criminal justice internship is NOT:

- To be taken for granted
- A filler because you can't find a class that you like
- Something to do because you can't think of anything else to do

- A "fast-track" to guaranteed post-graduation employment
- A blow-off course
- A right as a student (see "privilege" above)
- Required
- A guaranteed "A"—students are assessed as stringently as in most other courses in the department
- To be done at an agency or business where you already work, or have worked in the past
- For students who have any type of criminal history in their past (or present)—this would include outstanding traffic violations and other minor infractions that have turned into warrants

Some may think the worst thing to have happen with an internship is to select one that doesn't produce the anticipated results, whether that is a good grade, a strong letter of recommendation, or a solid job offer. *Wrong*. The worst thing is to leave on a bad note—one that could haunt you during your future job-seeking efforts.

WHEN GOOD INTERNSHIPS GO BAD

No one thing is ever right for everyone, including internships. Reasons we have heard to explain why a particular placement did not work for someone include:

➢   There just was so little to do, it seemed like a waste of time.

➢   Expectations weren't made clear, so I didn't know what to do.

➢   The placement turned out to be of no interest to me whatsoever.

➢   The hours negatively affected things at home, work, or school.

➢   I saw unethical, even illegal, behavior, and worse, was told to ignore it.

➢   I was placed in situations for which I had no training and that sometimes proved dangerous.

Although an entry-level internship may not be the most exciting, you are expected to complete it, barring any extreme circumstances. Just as "job hopping" does not look good on a résumé, neither does failing to finish an internship. Yes, criminal justice work can be monotonous at times, so there is something to be said for being able to fulfill a dull, even tedious, internship. There are times in any job, and criminal justice is no exception, that you will be directed to complete tasks you may not particularly like. Remember: Experiences lead to other, often better, experiences. Especially if you have little or no previous experience, you want to prove you have what it takes to survive the monotony on the bottom rung and to progress into something even better. This is exactly what the job world is like.

Anytime an internship placement does not work, regardless of why, you must speak to someone about it. If it is a school- or work-related internship (in other words, completing it as part of your school program or a part of another job), immediately discuss it with your academic advisor or job supervisor. Even though you may then be directed to discuss the issue with a supervisor at the internship site, always begin with your own supervisor.

It is crucial for you to listen carefully to your internal responses to the internship experience. Many students ignore their reactions or discount their "gut feelings," writing off negative responses as merely a sign of their inexperience or a need to develop a tougher hide. Some students decide, in error, that the agency they interned with is not truly representative of the field as a whole—that they just got stuck with a particularly boring department, the clientele was unusually rude, the personnel were atypically unfriendly, and that work in other agencies must be more exciting and more tolerable. If the internship does not measure up to your expectations, don't automatically assume you just happened to have a bad experience. Although every department is different, and maybe the personalities involved during your internship didn't quite mesh optimally, it could also be that the field was not the fit needed in your career. Be realistic.

Although not common, there are occasions when an internship truly is "no good." In these exceptions, such as when personal safety is at issue, or illegal or unethical behavior is occurring and you are told to "look the other way," it is definitely better that you honorably terminate the internship than to be terminated in any other way. It is a great sign of maturity to recognize what is not right and take proactive and decisive measures. You will be much further ahead when asked why you left an internship early if you can explain what occurred and the steps that went into your decision than to have to explain that you just quit going or, worse, were asked not to return.

What If You Are Told to "Get Out"?

Having an internship terminated is not just something you walk away from. It follows you. If the experience was part of a school program, it will be documented for background investigators to see for years to come. People know people, and people talk. Under no circumstances do you want to be talked about, except in a positive light.

If you think such a bad experience is easily concealed by simply "not mentioning it" to prospective employers, know that you will be asked about internships during your application process. If you lie, you will have quite possibly terminated any success at future job-seeking efforts in the field.

If, for whatever reason, an internship does not work out, there is only one option: *Learn from it and be honest.*

BEING EVALUATED

Most schools and agencies with formal internship programs have some means of evaluating the intern. According to Donovan and Garnett (p. 203): "Even if you don't get regular, ongoing feedback, you will almost certainly have a formal intern evaluation. Because you're a proactive intern, try to talk about your final evaluation as early as possible. How will it be done? When? What information will be used? From what sources will this information come?"

Although specific evaluation procedures and forms vary among organizations, many are completed by the intern's immediate supervisor and include the following elements (Donovan and Garnett, pp. 203–206):

➢   Name of the intern, date of internship, and approximate number of hours worked

➢   Summary of intern's specific job duties and responsibilities

➢   Description of specific accomplishments and/or improvements made by intern while under supervision

➢ An evaluation of the intern's traits, usually on a scale of 1 to 5 or 1 to 10, with a low score being negative or unfavorable and a high score being positive or favorable (e.g., 1 is poor; 3 is average; 5 is outstanding):

Dependability	Pride in work	Verbal communication skills
Creativity	Speed	Written communication skills
Initiative	Accuracy	Professional skills
Professional appearance	Interest in job	Judgment skills
Self-confidence	Ability to learn	Contributes to the organization
Emotional maturity	Ability to organize	Understands procedures
Emotional stability	Ability to work with others	Follows procedures
Promptness	Ability to work alone	Accepts and makes use of criticism
Resourcefulness	Ability to work under pressure	Promise of future success

➢ What specific actions can you suggest to help interns improve their future performance?

Interns are often allowed to add comments to their evaluations and are usually required to sign them, confirming they have seen and discussed the evaluation with the supervisor who prepared it.

INTERNSHIPS THROUGHOUT YOUR CAREER

As you struggle and sweat to land that first job in criminal justice, it may seem hard to believe that, once "in," anyone would even consider leaving—but they do. We have observed professional five-year cycles that can lead people to want to do something different. After five years, give or take a year, you will know your job inside-out, and that is when people start to get tired of it, even burned out. This is one factor to keep in mind when considering what size agency you want to work for. The variety of positions increases with agency size, and it is typically much easier to transfer within a large agency than in a smaller one. However, even personnel in large departments may eventually get "stuck" and need a drastic change of scenery to find career satisfaction.

Interning when you already have a job serves similar purposes to interning before you get a job. These experiences help you learn. Many professionals pursue a practical internship to learn more about the work they do from people doing different or specialized work. For example, a colleague, already a successful police detective, completed several internships with different agencies that handle certain types of investigations differently than his. Similarly, professionals considering transferring or doing something altogether different may intern to learn whether it is work they would like to do.

A word of caution: Do not assume that having an internship is always the best thing to have on your résumé. Internships are especially good for younger applicants with no experience in the field. Internships also provide something to add to a résumé when one has little else to include. But to quit another job altogether just because it isn't in a criminal justice–related field may be a mistake. For example, a thirty-something law enforcement student was prepared to quit his ten-year well-paying position with an insurance company to take an entry-level nonsworn parking enforcement position "to get his foot in the door." Although that particular department did use animal control and parking enforcement personnel as a pool from which to consider applicants, after discussing this move, he rethought the benefits. He had an excellent work record in a responsible position. This, combined with the other attributes he had in his résumé, made having his "foot in the door" not as critical as maintaining a stable work history, and he didn't have to take a massive pay cut. He had things going in his favor the younger, inexperienced applicants didn't, and he decided it was best to keep it that way. This isn't to say some departments do not rely on their entry-level personnel pool, which is why this is one more reason to learn about the agency to which you are applying.

A RECAP—THE DOS AND DON'TS OF INTERNSHIPS

Mistakes often happen because people simply have not taken time to think about what they would do *if* circumstances arose that had not been considered. It is a little like peer pressure in that if people think ahead of time how they would respond to situations, they may well not find themselves there in the first place, or at least handle them better. Here are some thoughts to help prepare you for those "what ifs" that have happened to others.

Do

➢   Explore internship options well ahead of when you want to intern.

➢   Apply for internships just as you would any other position (see chapters on résumés, cover letters, follow-up and thank-you letters, etc.).

➢   Maintain a clean record that will reflect positively on you when applying for an internship, especially one in criminal justice that may well require a background check.

➢   Arrive on time, know who to report to, do what you're told, and leave when instructed to ("I finished my work, so I just left" is not acceptable on-the-job behavior).

➢   Dress professionally, and ask ahead of time about the appropriate dress code. Even if casual, dress smartly to make your best impression. You are better off overdressing the first day than finding yourself embarrassingly underdressed.

➢   Ask if you should go along on calls or exit the vehicle on stops. Do not assume that because you are riding along, you get to go everywhere and do everything. Never assume; always *ask*.

➢   Be prepared to make at least mental notes in the event something out of the ordinary is encountered. You may have become a witness to a significant event. The prepared intern will have a small notebook, pen, and money for coffee or lunch stops.

➢   Speak up if you observe inappropriate actions by the person you are with or someone else. And under no circumstances go along with something illegal or unethical or be part of a cover-up, even if told to do so. You do not want to end your career before it has even begun.

➢   If appropriate, ask for a general letter confirming your successfull participation in an internship. What would make it not appropriate to ask? Perhaps you only rode along for an hour or a day, or things did not go well. Then you are better off to let it go.

➢   Relax, enjoy the experience, and leave on a good note. Thank-you's to the person or people you were with shows class and maturity, and a thank-you and good words to the supervisor of the person who accommodated you will be greatly appreciated—and remembered.

Don't

➢   Start looking for an internship too late.

➢   Submit a handwritten application or one that includes typos or grammatical errors.

➢   Keep getting traffic tickets or get yourself into trouble that would reflect poorly on you when being considered for an internship, *particularly* in the criminal justice field.

➢   Assume you know what to wear on the first day, and certainly don't show up in something altogether inappropriate.

➢   Be unfit. You should appear able to do the work you are interested in learning about.

➢   Be a know-it-all (remember, you are there to learn, not to teach senior personnel!).

➢   Do anything in excess, including talking (imagine what that's like for a patrol officer used to working alone).

➢   Assume it is permissible to jump out of your seat every time the person you are assigned to does (ask beforehand when you should accompany them).

➢   Talk to people you have no business talking to (victims, witnesses, suspects).

➢   Assume anyone else present knows who you are (when appropriate, introduce yourself, or answer at a hectic scene when someone challenges, "Who are you?").

➢   Assume you are invisible to all that is going on around you (you may have to provide a report on what you observed).

➢   Forget your manners when you arrive.

➢   Show up late or leave early—ever. If it is unavoidable, call.

➢   Do anything that would reflect poorly on the agency you are assigned to or the program you are from.

➢   Cover up any misdeeds you observe, even if asked to by anyone.

➢   Tell the person you are with how they should do their job, what kind of equipment they should be using, or why anything they are doing is not correct (even if it is).

➢   Be critical of others in that profession.

➤   Be too passive. (Ask questions and show interest, but do so appropriately.)

➤   Leave on a negative note, no matter how the experience went.

Having successfully completed an internship, it is wise to ask for a "to whom it may concern" letter from someone at the agency. This letter will serve to document the experience, as well as explain you did a good job. Especially for younger people without a great deal of work history, letters like this contribute greatly to an application packet for future employment.

CONCLUSION

Internships are about people learning from others. They are among the most basic forms of active learning and should be taken advantage of whenever possible. Similarly, there is a resurgence of mentoring, with many employers assigning a more experienced mentor to new hires for the sole purpose of helping the new person learn faster and more effectively in the workplace. There is no question that internships offer many benefits, both for the person entering a career area as well as for those already employed in the field. Whether required, as in the medical profession, or as part of professional development at any level, interning returns greatly on the time invested.

As you continue to develop yourself for employment in the career of your choice, continue to ask yourself whether you are the kind of person you would want to hire. Interning makes a strong statement; that is, it shows that you have participated in the work outside of the school environment and that you are able to plan, behave appropriately, exercise your desire to learn, and get along with people. Combined with your academic education, interning and service learning will help you present yourself as a very viable job candidate.

AN INSIDER'S VIEW

AN INTERNSHIP TRILOGY:

From three who benefitted from their internship experiences

Internships help not only confirm whether a specific career path is right for you, they also can be a determining factor in employers' hiring decisions. Because internships are so important, this trilogy is included.

Sgt. Darren Juntunen, Minnesota State Patrol

Internship: Two months with the Minnesota State Patrol

In many colleges and universities internships are required. I voluntarily pursued mine for several reasons. There was no pay involved. In fact, considering the time I spent I could have been working, food and gas for the two hours travel time each way, it cost me money. I worked rotating shifts, doing whatever I could to gain as much experience as I could. Having always thought I wanted to be a State Trooper since I was a child, this was my opportunity to confirm it was the right job for me.

I prepared for my internship by making sure all my college courses and electives would apply to this field of work. Even if not required, I chose classes that would help me on the job. I also kept in mind that everything I did, including the classes I took and my internship, would influence those doing the hiring when I eventually applied for work.

The internship with the Minnesota State Patrol was a competitive process that included a written application, an interview and recommendations from instructors.

My internship with the State Patrol is one I will always remember. I gained so much in the short two months that reaffirmed my decision to work for the Minnesota State Patrol. By working closely with experienced troopers, I observed these professionals in action and eventually began to develop my own working style.

Helpful hints from my experience I share with students participating in internships include: Take your time. Get to know those you are working with. Be respectful, and don't overstep your bounds. Don't get me wrong; you need to appear confident, but don't make suggestions on how to do the job to people who have been doing it for years. Don't be a know-it-all or come across the way you think others think you should; after all, you're there to learn.

I made lasting friendships during my interning. I have also had interns ride with me. Some were very eager to learn, asked questions, and did not overstep their level of experience. On the other hand, I have had interns who immediately started playing with the in-squad camera or computer, not realizing they were there to watch, not do. Some were as bold as to tell me what vehicles to stop and how I should be doing my job.

My best advice, having been on both sides, is to be patient, absorb all you can and offer assistance when appropriate. When you're fresh out of school, you need all the experience you can get to add to your resume. Without a doubt, my internship played a big part in me reaching my goal of becoming a Minnesota State Trooper.

An internship can be a valuable part of your education. I have had interns with me who have seen and endured some parts of the job they just couldn't handle, deciding not to seek a job in law enforcement. Others decided they needed more maturity before pursuing a job of this nature. This is your time to see firsthand if this is what you want to do for the majority of your life. Find something you love to do, do it well, and everything else will fall into place.

****

Officer Jason Weber, Owatonna Police Department, Minnesota

Internship: 3 months with the Springfield (MO) Police Department and 6 months with the Greene County (MO) Sheriff's Department

I was entering my junior year of college when I finally thought I had figured out what I wanted to do with my life. I wanted to be a police officer. I knew I needed to find an opportunity to become involved with a police agency that would give me a true understanding of how a police department works and what officers do. Because I was new to the area, my college advisor was an excellent resource and helped me attain internships with the Springfield Police Department and the Greene County Sheriff's Department, both in Missouri.

With the Springfield Police Department I worked very hard and asked A LOT of questions. Even if I didn't think I would like an opportunity, I never turned it down. I was fortunate enough to be asked to work with the Investigations Division.

Knowing they were doing me a favor by allowing me to actually help on cases, I made sure I was always respectful, and no matter what they asked, I did it as well as I could. This included making sure I was always on time and never abused the community recognition that goes along with being employed with a police department, even "just" as an intern. My reputation at the police department followed me to the sheriff's office because officers talk, and they knew I "was OK" even before I got there—that's how important your actions are. I was honored to work on their annual report, something the department had been without for quite some time.

I applied what I'd learned in school to the job, all the while affirming this was the line of work I wanted to pursue. I also learned how important school was for my future. Police academies teach you a method to complete a task. College provided opportunities to process issues while expanding my view of the world.

A classmate of mine discovered from his internship experience the job just wasn't what he thought it was. He changed his goals and has become very successful in another career altogether. For both of us, interning blended what we thought the job was with classroom theory and on the job reality. Interning also provides valuable feedback from professionals doing the work to help you better prepare yourself.

My advice is to make sure the internship you are interested in will best suit you. Talk with your college advisor to find out what you'll be doing at specific internship sites and how that will, or won't, help you. Taking the time to research agencies should eliminate those agencies that are only looking for a free janitor or something else you really aren't interested in doing.

My interning contributed to the pleasant reality that when I graduated I was offered three job opportunities. By successfully completing my internships I showed these departments my passion for the job. My internship experience also helped me better know what job I wanted and helped me pick the one that best served me rather than taking the first one that presented itself. My goal was to do my best while interning, and in return my interning certainly helped me develop my career.

****

Eric Clinton, Senior at Concordia University St. Paul, Criminal Justice major

Internship: 420 hours (one semester) at Hennepin County Powderhorn Partners community social service outreach center in south Minneapolis.

The experience I gained from my internship at this county service was both educational and life changing. Helping people has always been one of my passions and why I pursued college. I have always been interested in working in corrections, specifically probation, so this was my chance to learn more about it beyond just school. One of my goals was to learn more about whether I wanted to work with juveniles or adults. By explaining this during my interview I was allowed to do something no other intern had. I would mainly work under the supervision of the juvenile probation officer but also get to work with a probation officer working with adults. So my first lesson was to be assertive during interviews and explain your goals.

Among things I learned I could never have learned in the classroom was that working with juveniles is much more complicated than working with the adults. I learned how growing up affects kids, how family relationships come into play, how much some parents want to be involved while others don't, and how school and work play a part while juveniles are involved in the criminal justice system. I learned that much of working with kids is being a counselor. When you work with adults they know more about reality and understand what they have to do to get their lives back together. Adult probation officers are there basically to monitor and help guide them with their efforts to get back into society.

Internships for students in college are one of the most important opportunities to learn firsthand what careers are about and how you fit in. Not only do they provide education, but an internship provides experience that puts you ahead of other job seekers interested in the same work you are. Real world experience is the key to getting a job. Just because you have a degree doesn't mean you have the skills necessary for the job you want. Picking a good internship will give you an advantage when you begin applying for work. In fact, applying for internships gives you experience with the job-seeking process itself. Employers want to hire people who have experience along with a degree. Experience gives you the self-confidence you need when you're applying for jobs and getting ready for that BIG interview.

Another important aspect to interning is networking. The more people you know, the better your chances for finding a great job. Get to know the people you work with because they always know other people who can help you in the future.

My advice for students starting an internship is to be prepared, which is a good life lesson itself. Start looking early and get advice from your teachers and advisors where to look for internships. Give yourself plenty of time to prepare for your internship. Pick several you're really interested in and contact them. When it's time for you to interview, it's best to practice questions by having friends or family interview you. Make sure you are dressed appropriately. When I showed up to my interview I had a very nice collared shirt on, but I made the mistake of wearing jeans with it. My interviewer wasn't totally upset but suggested that I not wear jeans to future interviews; and she was right. Make sure you don't wear any type of perfumes or colognes. There's nothing more annoying to some people then smelling twenty different fragrances in your place of work.

Then when you start your internship make sure you have all the necessary materials you're going to need, including paper, pens and a good calendar. Don't be too quiet. Introduce yourself and give firm handshakes. It's important to make good first impressions to the people you're going to work with. With any luck, and your hard work, if you don't get a job at that site, your experience and reputation will help you get another.

MIND STRETCHES

1. In what ways would an internship help you in your criminal justice job search?

2. If you were an employer, what kind(s) of interning completed by a prospective officer would impress you the most? Why?

3. What do you think would be the most difficult part of interning in criminal justice, and what could you do to plan for it?

4. Once you secure an internship, what things could you do to make it a success before you even begin?

5. What are some reasons an internship might not be a good fit for someone? What should be done in such cases?

6. Recognizing that an internship provides many opportunities to network, how would you go about taking full advantage of this?

7. How would you deal with a problem during an internship?

8. Brainstorm a list of how a good criminal justice internship could go "bad."

9. Create a "top 10" list of attributes that make for a good criminal justice intern.

10. In what ways do you think a criminal justice internship is similar to and different from a "job" in the same field?

REFERENCES

Asher, Donal. "Does Your Major Matter?" MSN Encarta, March 2008.

Clark, Joel F. "Making the Most of Your Internship Experience," in *Peterson's Internships: Find the Right Internship for You*, ed. Tera A. Oram. The Thompson Corporation, 2004.

Donovan, Craig P., and Jim Garnett. *Internships for Dummies.* New York: John Wiley & Sons, 2001.

Hendricks, Carter. Professor, Hopkinsville Community College, Kentucky. Direct correspondence for this text, June 2008.

O'Connor, Thomas R. Available online at www.apsu.edu/oconnort/4860/default.htm (last updated October 28, 2008).

Oldman, Mark, and Samer Hamadeh. *The Internship Bible.* New York: Random House, Inc. and Princeton Review Publishing, 2005.

Rubinstein, Ellen. *Scoring a Great Internship (Students Helping Students).* New York: Natavi Guides, Inc., 2002.

Sukut, Diana. Concordia University St. Paul, Director of Career Services. Personal interview, 2008.

Zapor, Carolyn. Concordia University St. Paul, Sociology Department. Personal interview, 2008.

SECTION TWO

MEETING THE CHALLENGE: PREPARING

Even if you are on the right track, you'll still get run over if you just sit there.

—Will Rogers

Most people don't plan to fail—they fail to plan.

—Anonymous

Before everything else, getting ready is the secret of success.

—Henry Ford

For every officer who is hired, there are 250 applicants who are not. The secret to accomplishing your dream comes down to one objective—preparation.

—Larry R. Frerkes

The normal process in seeking a job is to find where job openings exist, apply, submit a résumé, undergo various kinds of testing, be interviewed, and be hired! This section does not follow that order. Rather, it asks you to continue doing what you began in Chapter 5—looking at your own qualities, experiences, and preferences and seeing how they fit with what criminal justice agencies and security departments are looking for. It also suggests ways to overcome any shortcomings you might find when considering yourself in relation to the job requirements. This should be done *before* you actually begin looking for specific jobs. This section is written as though you were already actively engaged in testing and interviewing.

You'll begin by looking at the physical requirements of these fields and what tests you might have to pass (Chapter 7). One of the most important attributes of successful candidates is physical fitness—which doesn't happen overnight. Next, you'll look at the educational and psychological requirements that might be considered and how they might be tested (Chapter 8).

This is followed by a discussion of the "beneficial attributes" of successful candidates in these fields, that is, who is most likely to be hired (Chapter 9), giving you a chance to realistically assess what attributes *you* have and how you might fare. The next chapter discusses how you can assemble the information collected about yourself thus far into that all-important document—your résumé (Chapter 10). This section concludes with a critical part of the job-hunting process—being prepared for rejection (Chapter 11). Each rejection must be seen as a learning situation, a chance to become better at presenting yourself and as being one step closer to that job you *will* eventually get.

These chapters should be reread at appropriate times during your actual job hunt. For example, if you are scheduled for a physical fitness test, reread Chapter 7. If you don't make it to the testing stage, reread Chapter 11. When ready, move on to Section Three, which presents specific job-seeking strategies to enhance your chances of getting a job in your chosen field.

CHAPTER 7

PHYSICAL FITNESS AND TESTING

It's easier to maintain your health than to regain it.

—Dr. Ken Cooper

Do You Know:

➢ Why physical fitness is crucial for police, corrections, or security officers?
➢ Why it is difficult for people in these fields to stay in shape?
➢ What five parameters are generally considered in evaluating physical fitness?
➢ What four things most physical fitness tests seek to measure?
➢ What three areas are of critical importance during the medical examination and what other tests might be conducted?
➢ What impact the ADA has had on medical examinations and inquiries about disabilities?
➢ How fitness and stress interrelate?
➢ How personality and stress interrelate?
➢ Why proper nutrition is important?
➢ Whether an unhealthy lifestyle is linked to premature death?

INTRODUCTION

An essential criterion for obtaining a job in criminal justice, security, and related areas is physical fitness. The importance of having fit personnel goes without saying—the work is physically and emotionally taxing, and the job demands that those who pursue employment in these fields enter such work in shape and *remain* in shape.

This chapter examines how fitness is defined; the importance of fitness to those seeking employment in criminal justice; the nature of fitness testing and medical examinations; how you can assess your own fitness levels and design a program to improve and maintain your personal fitness; and the interplay between physical fitness and stress, nutrition, and lifestyle.

WHAT IS FITNESS?

Dictionary.com defines *fitness* as: "Good health or physical condition, especially as the result of exercise and proper nutrition." The Illinois Law Enforcement Training and Standards Board states: "Physical fitness is a health status pertaining to the individual officer having the physiological readiness to perform maximum physical effort when required. Physical fitness consists of three areas:

➤ Aerobic capacity or cardiovascular endurance pertaining to the heart and vascular system's capacity to transport oxygen. . . .

➤ Strength pertains to the ability of muscles to generate force. . . .

➤ Flexibility pertains to the range of motion of the joints and muscles."

The term *fitness* has rightfully earned a place in the daily lexicon of Americans; unfortunately, probably because it is too often ignored. As work hours have expanded, and with many desk jobs involving little or no physical component, less time and energy remains at the end of the day for participation in activities that contribute to healthy lifestyles. Combining this with fast food that often accompanies fast-paced lives, it is little wonder fitness is now something most American chase after rather than maintain.

WHY IS FITNESS IMPORTANT AND FOR WHOM?

Aerobic capacity or cardiovascular endurance is a key area for heart disease. Low *strength* levels have a bearing on upper torso and lower back disorders. Lack of lower back *flexibility* is a major risk area for lower back disorders:

> These three fitness areas have also been shown to be predicative of job performance ratings, sick time, and number of commendations of police officers. Data also shows that the fitness level is predicative of *trainability* and academy performance. Physical fitness can be an important area for minimizing *liability*. The unfit officer is less able to respond fully to strenuous physical activity. Consequently, the *risk of not performing physical duties* is increased. (Illinois Law Enforcement Standards and Training Board)

Collingwood et al. (2003, p. 49) add: "The public's expectation of a responding officer in a situation requiring physical effort, especially in a use of force situation, is the ability to provide the requisite service. They expect and deserve a fit officer because in a situation with injury and life and death consequences having those physical capabilities can minimize those threats." According to Grossi (2007, p. 26): "The FBI believes physical fitness is such an important part of an officer's lifestyle regimen that its National Academy at Quantico, Virginia, has made CJ 340 'Fitness in Law Enforcement' the only required course for all police students attending."

There's no arguing law enforcement and fire personnel should be fit. But what about those working in the related fields; how important is fitness for them? The answer: very important. Although the majority of the cites in this chapter refer to police and fire personnel, fitness is important to everyone working in any criminal justice or related field:

> It's important for people considering the criminal justice field to understand it's not just police officers and firefighters who need to prepare themselves physically for their work. Besides the obvious benefits of fitness for everyone, there is much more to any kind of criminal justice work than just sitting at a desk. It may include becoming involved with searching for a client or having a usually passive situation turn ugly. Remember, these clients are the ones that law enforcement and corrections officers interacted with in a manner to insure their own safety, as should anyone representing the system. When training social service workers and others about staying safe on the job, I remind them basic fitness can't be ignored. Their safety may depend on it. (Stiehm, 2008)

Fitness can become a legal issue, too. The people and property you are paid to protect will depend on your being able to do your job. If unable to, you could be sued. In *Parker v. District of Columbia* (1988), the jury awarded $425,046 to a man shot by a police officer who was arresting him. As part of the case, the court noted: "Officer Hayes simply was not in adequate physical shape. This condition posed a foreseeable risk of harm to others." Oldham (2001, p. 77) notes: "Recent studies indicate officers who are in good physical condition are involved in far fewer uses of force than other, less fit officers."

> Your future in criminal justice or security, your very life, and the lives of the civilians you've sworn to protect, depend on your physical fitness.

As noted, these professions, although appearing to be full of exciting chases and confrontations, are more likely to consist of extended periods of idle waiting, punctuated by immediate demands for extreme activity. Strandberg (2002, p. 38) states: "Law enforcement isn't a high activity job, unless you're in the bike patrol unit. It is essentially sedentary—sitting in a patrol car or riding a desk. The job does call for bursts of activity when there is action, so it's important for officers to be in tip-top condition or going from inactivity to full sprints will be too much to handle." Collingwood et al. (p. 44) bring the need for fitness into focus:

> The images are burned into our memories: Hundreds of New York/New Jersey Port Authority Police, New York City Police and Fire Department of New York Officers performing heroic tasks. Carrying people out of the towers, assisting the injured and eventually running for their lives when the collapse of the buildings began. Not one of those officers woke up on September 11, 2001, thinking that today would be the day he would be called on to exhibit levels of fitness beyond anything most of them had ever previously needed on the job.

Fitness is an obligation officers owe not only the public but also one another: "Everyone in uniform has an ethical obligation to everyone else in uniform to be fit enough to back them up" (Sanow, 2008, p. 6).

> The very nature of police and security jobs can contribute a great deal to officers being out of shape. The often-sedentary duties, such as driving a car or sitting at a desk, and the need to eat quick meals on the go—often fast food high in calories and fat—all contribute to the deterioration of physical fitness.

PHYSICAL FITNESS TESTING

Most candidates undergo some sort of physical fitness testing. Although specific fitness standards may vary from agency to agency, a typical well-balanced, comprehensive testing program will include five general parameters:

➤ Cardiorespiratory endurance or aerobic capacity (commonly measured by a 1.5-mile run)

➤ Abdominal and lower back strength (measured by sit-ups)

➤ Muscular strength and endurance (measured by push-ups)

➤ Flexibility (measured by a controlled sit-and-reach test)

➤ Body composition (percentage of body fat) or body mass index (BMI)

> Physical fitness is often evaluated using five general parameters: cardiorespiratory endurance or aerobic capacity, abdominal and lower back strength, muscular strength and endurance, flexibility, and body composition or BMI.

An example of fitness expectations is that set by the U.S. Marshals Service: "Deputy U.S. Marshals must be physically able to safely and efficiently perform the full range of duties of the position. Any medical or physical condition which affects this ability is disqualifying." The specific requirements for the job may be found at www.usmarshals.gov/careers/faq.html#What_are_the_fitness_standards. Table 7–1 shows the U.S. Marshals Service Fitness Standards for male and female applicants in the 20–29 and 30–39 age brackets.

TABLE 7–1   U.S. Marshals Service Fitness Standards for Male and Female Applicants in the 20–29 and 30–39 Age Brackets

You must score Minimum or higher in all sections of the fitness test in order to pass.

Men's Applicant Fitness Standards

Men's Fitness Category 20–29				
	% Body Fat	Sit and Reach	Push-Ups	Sit-Ups	1.5-Mile Run
Superior	< 5.3	> 22.9	> 61	> 54	< 8.14
Excellent	5.3–9.4	20.5–22.9	47–61	47–54	8:14–10:16
Good	9.5–14.1	18.5–20.4	37–46	42–46	10:17–11:41
Fair	14.2–17.4	16.5–18.4	29–36	38–41	11:42–12:51
Minimum	15.9	17.5	33	40	12:18
Poor	17.5–22.4	14.4–16.4	22–28	33–37	12:52–14:13
Very Poor	22.4	< 14.4	< 22	< 33	> 14:13

Men's Fitness Category 30–39				
	% Body Fat	Sit and Reach	Push-Ups	Sit-Ups	1.5-Mile Run
Superior	< 9.2	> 21.9	> 51	> 50	< 8:45
Excellent	9.2–13.9	19.5–21.9	39–51	43–50	8:45–10:47
Good	14.0–17.5	17.5–19.4	30–38	39–42	10:48–12:20
Fair	17.6–20.5	15.5–17.4	24–29	35–38	12:21–13:36
Minimum	19.0	16.5	27	36	12:51
Poor	20.6–24.2	13.0–15.4	17–23	30–34	13:37–14:52
Very Poor	> 24.2	< 13.0	< 17	< 30	> 14:52

Women's Applicant Fitness Standards

Women's Fitness Category 20–29				
	% Body Fat	Sit and Reach	Push-Ups	Sit-Ups	1.5-Mile Run
Superior	< 10.9	> 24.4	—	> 50	< 10:48
Excellent	10.9–17.1	22.5–24.4	> 24	44–50	10:48–12:51
Good	17.2–20.6	20.5–22.4	20–24	38–43	12:52–14:24
Fair	20.7–23.7	19.3–20.4	14–19	32–37	14:25–15:26
Minimum	22.1	20.0	16	35	14:55
Poor	23.8–27.7	17.0–19.2	9–13	27–31	15:27–16:33
Very Poor	> 27.7	< 17.0	< 9	< 27	> 16:33

	Women's Fitness Category 30–39				
	% Body Fat	**Sit and Reach**	**Push-Ups**	**Sit-Ups**	**1.5-Mile Run**
Superior	< 13.5	> 23.9	—	> 41	< 11:50
Excellent	13.5–18.0	21.5–23.9	> 22	35–41	11:50–13:43
Good	18.1–21.6	20.0–21.4	18–22	29–34	13:44–15:08
Fair	21.7–24.9	18.3–19.9	12–17	25–28	15:09–15:57
Minimum	23.1	19.0	14	27	15:26
Poor	25.0–29.3	16.5–18.2	7–11	20–24	15:58–17:14
Very Poor	> 29.3	< 16.5	< 7	< 20	> 17:14

Another example is the "POWER (Peace Officer Wellness Evaluation Report) test" used by the Illinois Law Enforcement Training and Standards Board consisting of four areas:

1. Sit-and-Reach Test

This measures the flexibility of the lower back and upper leg area, important for performing police tasks involving range of motion and also important in minimizing lower back problems. The test involves stretching out to touch the toes or beyond with extended arms from the sitting position. *The score is in the inches reached on a yardstick.*

2. 1-Minute Sit-Up Test

This measures the muscular endurance of the abdominal muscles, important for performing police tasks involving use of force and also important for maintaining good posture and minimizing lower back problems. *The score is in the number of bent leg sit-ups performed in one minute.*

3. 1 Repetition Maximum Bench Press

This is a maximum weight pushed from the bench press position and measures the amount of force the upper body can generate, important for performing police tasks requiring upper body strength. *The score is a ratio of weight pushed divided by body weight.*

4. 1.5-Mile Run

This timed run measures the heart and vascular system's capability to transport oxygen, important for performing police tasks involving stamina and endurance and minimizing the risk of cardiovascular problems. *The score is in minutes and seconds.*

What Are the Standards?

➤   The actual performance requirement for each test is based on norms for a national population sample.

➤   The applicant must pass every test.

➤   The required performance to pass each test is based on age (decade) and sex.

To Prepare for the Power Test

For the Sit-and-Reach Test Two exercises are recommended (1) **Sit and Reach**. Sit on the ground with legs straight. Slowly extend forward at the waist and extend the fingertips

POWER CHART

Test	MALES				FEMALES			
	20–29	30–39	40–49	50–59	20–29	30–39	40–49	50–59
Sit and Reach	16.0	15.0	13.8	12.8	18.8	17.8	16.8	16.3
1 Minute Sit-Up	37	34	28	23	31	24	19	13
Maximum Bench Press Ratio	.98	.87	.79	.70	.58	.52	.49	.43
1.5 Mile Run	13.46	14.31	15.24	16.21	16.21	16.52	17.53	18.44

SOURCE: From Peggy Wilkins Krainik, "Chicago's Fit Officers Count Their Benefits," in *Law and Order*, Feb. 2003, p. 55. Reprinted by permission of Hendon Publishing.

toward the toes (keeping legs straight). Hold for ten seconds. Do five repetitions. (2) **Towel Stretch.** Sit on the ground with the legs straight. Wrap a towel around the feet, holding each end with each hand. Lean forward and pull gently on the towel, extending the torso toward the toes.

For the Sit-Up Test The progressive routine is to do as many bent leg sit-ups (hands behind the head) as possible in one minute. At least three times a week, do three sets (three groups of the number of repetitions one did in one minute).

Week	Activity	Distance	Time	Frequency
1	Walk	1 Mile	20'-17'	5/Week
2	Walk	1.5 Miles	29'-25'	5/Week
3	Walk	2 Miles	35'-32'	5/Week
4	Walk	2 Miles	30'-28'	5/Week
5	Walk/Jog	2 Miles	27'	5/Week
6	Walk/Jog	2 Miles	26'	5/Week
7	Walk/Jog	2 Miles	25'	5/Week
8	Walk/Jog	2 Miles	24'	4/Week
9	Jog	2 Miles	23'	4/Week
10	Jog	2 Miles	22'	4/Week
11	Jog	2 Miles	21'	4/Week
12	Jog	2 Miles	20'	4/Week

Regarding body composition, the trend is to look at the amount of body fat rather than weight as compared to height. The generally accepted percentage of fat for males is 14 to 16 percent of total body weight; for females, between 23 and 26 percent of body weight. A body mass index (BMI) is used to determine obesity and will be explained in more detail later in the chapter.

Another approach used by departments is having candidates perform "events," such as a Back Yard Pursuit, a Stretcher Carry, a Body Drag, and a 300-Yard Sprint. In some agencies, multiple events are combined to form an obstacle course, through which candidates must maneuver within a set time limit. Ebling (2002, p. 3) describes one such course used at the FBI National Academy:

> The Yellow Brick Road is the final test of the Fitness Challenge. Its wooded trails, 3 walls, 6 ropes, and 26 obstacles make it the ultimate challenge for everyone. Students either must run out to or back from the Yellow Brick Road for a total of 6.1 miles. . . .
>
> Once at the site, students face a bear trap, barbed wire, and numerous hills that wind through rough terrain. . . . Climbing over walls, running across creeks, jumping through simulated windows, and scaling sheer rock faces with the help of ropes present physically demanding tasks for the runners. . . .
>
> Next comes the most well-known obstacle—the cargo net made famous in the motion picture *The Silence of the Lambs*. Flipping over the top of the net, approximately 10 to 12 feet above the ground, offers a tough but exhilarating test for everyone. After accomplishing this, . . . [students continue] the last three-quarters of a mile, which includes a combat crawl under barbed wire in muddy water, to the finish line.

A wide variety of physical fitness tests may be administered, but they are all likely to measure the same things: endurance, agility, flexibility, and strength.

Be aware that "one-size" training programs are unrealistic: "A corrections officer may need to have a better grip strength for altercations with prisoners, whereas a SWAT member will need stronger trunk muscles to compensate for the body armor and/or ruck sack he will carry" (Moore, 2006, p. 13). Your training should be tailored to the requirements of the job you are seeking.

Most police departments, correctional institutions, or businesses hiring security personnel require that job applicants have a medical examination as well as a physical test of some sort to be certain potential employees are physically fit.

THE MEDICAL EXAMINATION

Three areas of critical importance during the medical examination are vision, hearing, and the condition of the cardiovascular respiratory system.

The vision test may include a test for color blindness. Most agencies will accept applicants who have *corrected* vision and hearing problems, that is, those who wear a hearing aid and/or eye glasses or contact lenses or who have had laser eye surgery. If you think you may have problems in any of these areas, get checked out before applying for a position.

The cardiovascular and respiratory systems play critical roles in fitness and so are tested. The medical exam may also include tests for determining blood pressure, smoking status, drug use, blood sugar level (for diabetes), and the ratio of total cholesterol to HDL cholesterol (to identify cardiovascular risk factors). If a physician finds that you have a functional or organic disorder, the recommendation may be made to disqualify you.

The use of medical examinations in hiring is governed by the Americans with Disabilities Act (ADA): "During the application/interview process, the ADA bars employers' disability-related inquiries (i.e., those that are likely to elicit information about disabilities)" (Colbridge, 2001, p. 25). In addition:

> Medical examinations are prohibited during the application/interview stage. Tests for illegal drug use are not considered medical examinations under the ADA, so employers may test applicants for current illegal drug

use. However, the EEOC has ruled that tests for alcohol use are medical in nature, and violate the ADA at this stage of the employment process.

Two other kinds of tests may also be given at this stage. Physical agility tests that demonstrate the ability to do actual or simulated job-related tasks . . . are permissible if given to all applicants. . . . Employers may also require that applicants take physical fitness tests that measure their ability to do physical tasks such as running and lifting, so long as all applicants must do so. Neither test is considered a medical examination under the ADA unless applicants' physiological or psychological responses to the tests are measured. (Colbridge, p. 26)

Colbridge (p. 27) further explains: "Once employers have judged applicants based upon their non-disability related qualifications during the application/interview stage, found them qualified, and made bona fide job offers to them, the ADA permits employers to face the issue of disabilities. Employers may now inquire about disabilities, require medical examinations, and condition their employment offers on the results of these medical examinations."

> The Americans with Disabilities Act (ADA) prohibits medical examinations or inquiries regarding mental or physical problems or disabilities *before* a conditional offer of employment has been made.

In other words, the employer makes the candidate a job offer provided the candidate passes the medical examination.

SELF-ASSESSMENT

It is important to know how physically fit you are. Just because you feel good does not necessarily mean you are "in shape." The FBI's publication *Physical Fitness for Law Enforcement Officers* (n.d.) recommends the following:

➤ Feel your arms, shoulders, stomach, buttocks, and legs. Are your muscles well-toned or are you soft and flabby?

➤ Give yourself the pinch test. Take hold of the skin just above your belt. Are your fingers separated by more than one-half inch?

This publication describes cardiovascular, balance, flexibility, agility, strength, and power tests to assess your physical fitness. Their descriptions follow.

Cardiovascular Tests

Cureton's Breath-Holding Test. One simple way to test your respiratory capacity is to step onto and off a chair, bench, or stool (approximately seventeen inches high) for a period of one minute and then see how long you can hold your breath. You should be able to hold it for at least thirty seconds. If you can't, it indicates your cardiovascular function has deteriorated below a desirable level.

Kasch Pulse Recovery Test (3 min.). This test can be performed at almost any age. Only the infirm or the extremely unfit would find it too strenuous. You should not smoke for one hour or eat for two hours before taking the test. Also, rest for five minutes before taking the test.

EQUIPMENT
12-inch bench or stool
Clock or watch with a sweep second hand

PROCEDURE

a. Start stepping onto and off the bench when sweep second hand is at 11.
b. Step 24 times per minute, total 72.
c. Duration is three minutes.
d. Stop stepping when sweep second hand is again at 11, after three revolutions, and sit down.
e. Start counting the pulse rate when sweep second hand reaches 12 on the clock, using either the artery located inside the wrist or the carotid artery in the throat. Count every 10 seconds and record for one minute.
f. Total the six pulse counts for one minute and compare with the following scale:

Classification	0–1 Minute Pulse Rate after Exercise
Excellent	71–78
Very Good	79–83
Average	84–99
Below Average	100–107
Poor	108–118

Cooper's 12-Minute Walk/Run Test. Find a place where you can run/walk a measured distance of up to two miles. A quarter-mile track at a local school would be ideal; however, a nearby park, field, or quiet stretch of road can be used. The test is quite simple—see how much of the two miles you can comfortably cover in twelve minutes. Try to run the entire time at a pace you can maintain without excessive strain. If your breath becomes short, walk until it returns to normal, then run again. Keep going for a full twelve minutes; then check your performance on the following scale:

Fitness Category (under age 30)	Distance Covered in 12 Minutes (in miles)
Very Poor	less than 1.0
Poor	1.00–1.24
Fair	1.25–1.49
Good	1.50–1.74
Excellent	1.75 +

(*Note:* People over age 30 should not take this test until they have had a complete medical examination and have completed approximately six weeks in a "starter physical fitness program.")

Balance Test

Stand on your toes, heels together, eyes closed, and your arms stretched forward at shoulder level. Maintain this position for twenty seconds without shifting your feet or opening your eyes.

Flexibility Tests

Trunk Flexion. Keeping your legs together and your knees locked, bend at the waist and touch the floor with your fingers.

Trunk Extension. Lie flat on your stomach, face down, fingers laced behind your neck, and your feet anchored to the floor. Now raise your chin until it is eighteen inches off the floor. (*Note*: Average for male students at the University of Illinois is twelve and one-half inches.)

Agility Test

Squat Thrusts. Standing, drop down to squatting position, palms flat against the floor, arms straight. Next, with weight supported on the hands, kick backward so that your legs are extended fully. Immediately kick forward to the squatting position and stand up. You should be able to perform four in eight seconds.

Strength Tests

Pull-Ups. Hang from a bar, hands slightly wider than shoulders, palms turned away, arms fully extended. Pull up until your chin is over the bar. Lower yourself until your arms are fully extended and repeat. You should be able to perform four pull-ups.

Push-Ups. From the front leaning rest position, hands slightly wider than the shoulders with fingers pointed straight ahead, lower your body until your chest barely touches the floor. Push up to the front leaning rest position, keeping your body straight. Standards from the Institute for Aerobics Research for push-ups done in one minute are:

> 60 and up, superior;
> 50–59, excellent;
> 35–49, good;
> 25–34, average;
> 18–24, below average; and
> 17 or less, poor.

Sit-Ups. Lie on your back with your hands behind your neck, with your legs straight and free. Flex the trunk and sit up, and then return to the starting position. Standards from the Institute for Aerobics Research for sit-ups done in one minute are:

> 49 and up, superior;
> 46–48, excellent;
> 42–45, good;
> 40–41, average;
> 33–39, below average; and
> 32 or less, poor.

Power Tests

Standing Broad Jump. From a standing position, jump as far forward as you can, landing on both feet. Do not take a running start. The length of your jump should equal your height.

Vertical Jump. Stand facing a wall, feet and chin touching the wall, arms extended over your head. Using chalk, mark the height of your hands on the wall. Now jump up and touch the wall as high as you can with one hand. (Again, use chalk.) Note the difference between the two marks on the wall. You should be able to perform a vertical jump of eighteen inches or more.

Even if you successfully pass all these tests, be sure you remain in good physical shape. Your lifestyle may be such that you do not require a formal physical fitness program. Many people active in sports such as swimming, tennis, jogging, or running do not need to do much more to keep in shape. If, however, you have a relatively sedentary lifestyle, you may want to start a basic physical fitness program.

A BASIC PHYSICAL FITNESS PROGRAM

An exercise program should start gradually and then build up. Oldham (p. 76) suggests: "Walking is one of the easiest and most beneficial of all cardiovascular exercises. Recent studies have found little difference between walking and running." You should exercise at least three times a week. As you progress into your fitness program, you can increase the number of weekly workouts. Numerous books and articles outline fitness programs. Find one that suits you.

Tips

The following tips on exercising might be considered:

➢ Exercise to music.

➢ Vary your exercises to give yourself some variety.

➢ Drink water during your breaks.

➢ Plan your program to easily fit your daily routine. Exercise at the same time each day.

➢ Start small and work up to a full regime, gradually to reduce your chance of injury.

➢ Record your efforts.

➢ Do not expect immediate benefits. It takes regular, long-term effort.

➢ Wait ten minutes after your cool-down to take a warm shower. *A hot or cold shower can dangerously affect your blood pressure.*

➢ If you stop exercising for a while—even a week or two—start at a lower level and gradually work your way up again.

(*Note:* Never pursue an exercise program without consulting with your physician.)

Sticking to Your Fitness Program

We are creatures of habit. And if your previous habit has been to skip the bike ride in favor of watching highlights of the Tour de France from the comfort of your sofa, you may find it difficult to stick to a fitness program. Creating a new habit, no matter how beneficial to you, takes a sustained effort. The key to long-term success with an exercise routine is to stay motivated.

The Challenge of Maintaining Fitness

It is a given that you will be expected to be fit when you apply for certain criminal justice careers (any of the first-responder positions, to be sure), and you may have no problem ramping up your activity level for a short while to prepare for your fitness tests. The real challenge comes after you've been hired, put in a few years, and maybe put on a few pounds: "Spending hours in a patrol car or sitting on surveillance, eating fast food when there's time to grab a bite and sleeping at odd hours, can pack on the pounds" (Moore, p. 12).

Davis, an internationally recognized authority on the subject of fitness standards and employment opportunity issues, has developed job-related physical performance and medical standards for a number of law enforcement agencies. In addition to consulting for a number of criminal justice organizations, including the DEA, U.S. Secret Service, IACP, and the FBI, Davis has also conducted in-depth studies of the physical performance requirements for SWAT, K-9, and industrial security positions. He (2002, p. 35) contends:

> Considerable effort is expended in the training academy environment enhancing the fitness level of cadets. I'm certain that the annual effort expended to provide a modicum of fitness costs taxpayers millions of dollars. The better model is to hire people who present for employment ready to perform the essential function of the job. Then, rather than having to rehabilitate people who should have been ready for employment in the first place, effort is better spent in training that is focused on other law enforcement topics. The current model creates, at best, only a temporary change in the fitness condition. Peer pressure is one of the cultural forces that retards organizations from implementing change. Hiring individuals who have no penchant for fitness perpetuates a practice of mediocrity. As we know, so much of what we attempt to accomplish in the academy is undermined once the officer leaves the sanctity of the training environment.

When you select a career in criminal justice, you must accept physical fitness as part of your cache of skills that, like firearms use and defensive tactics, will deteriorate if not actively maintained. Strandberg (p. 42) notes:

> Police academies are doing a good job of setting the table for lifelong fitness. In the past, the academies only tested the fitness of recruits, but now are trying to train them to look at fitness not as a short-term "help me pass the test" goal but rather a lifelong goal. Classes at the academy are now more about the benefits of a healthy lifestyle, sensible fitness programs, good nutrition and all the elements of being fit.

As Barnett points out: "A lot of studies show that fitness decreases sick days, cardiovascular disease and more, so in the long run it will help with health care costs. Also, there is nothing better to relieve stress than working out" (Strandberg, p. 40).

FITNESS AND STRESS

Careers in criminal justice and security can be highly stressful—and so can seeking employment in these fields: "Police commit suicide at up to three times the national average and are eight times more likely to kill themselves than to become a victim of a homicide. They divorce at double the national average, and up to 25 percent have alcohol-abuse problems. By profession, police officers are at high risk for stress disorders" (Fox, 2007, p. 352). The same can be said for other careers in the criminal justice system and in the security profession.

Zhao et al. (2002, pp. 43–44) state: "[A] careful monitoring of stress is particularly important for the police profession, widely considered to be among the most stressful occupations due to the range of discretion allowed to officers in oftentimes critical circumstances." Atkinson-Tovar (2003, p. 119) adds: "Constantly, officers are asked to take on more and more responsibilities and become increasingly more efficient at the performance of their jobs. The increased complication comes with the factor of exposure to traumatic events during the course of a day." An important part of being physically and mentally fit is managing stress.

> Physically fit bodies are better able to cope with stress, and stress is abundant in the professions of criminal justice and private security. Keep fit to ward off stress.

Some personality types tend to be more susceptible to stress, particularly those identified as *Type A*, a concept developed in the late 1950s by two cardiologists who noted similar behavior traits among their heart attack patients. People described as having Type A personalities "generally try to do too many things at once, are often preoccupied with what they are going to do next, and tend to have few interests outside their work" (Rosch, 2004). They are commonly perceived as competitive, ambitious, impatient, aggressive, preoccupied with work, unable to sit and relax, and constantly aware of the time, seeming always to operate with a sense of urgency. If you are a Type A personality, which many people drawn to criminal justice and security are, be aware of these risks. Exercise and relaxation techniques can help reduce them.

> People with Type A personalities are more susceptible to stress and are at increased risk for heart disease. It is vital for such people to learn and use exercise and relaxation techniques.

Reese (2001, pp. 15–17) posits "six keys to stress-free living" that can help protect against the negative stress everyone experiences as part of living in our fast-moving, complex society: challenge, choice, change, courage, control, and commitment: "The first key to consider is that of challenge. Law enforcement officers are drawn to the occupation because of the challenges it presents to them daily." Some of the occupational challenges inherent in criminal justice professions include shift work, a paramilitary structure, court rulings perceived as too lenient on offenders or too restrictive on methods of criminal suppression and investigation, and anxiety over the responsibility to protect others (Reese, p. 16). *Challenge* also means accepting setbacks as something to be overcome.

The second key to controlling stress is *choice*: "While we may blame others for our current occupation, position, financial status, and more, we are actually the product of the choices we have made in life. Among the many choices we make every day, our attitudes are most important. . . . Among our many choices are: . . . the type of job we seek, the job we finally accept, how we see ourselves in that job, whether or not to seek a promotion, seeking a transfer, getting bitter or getting better" (Reese, p. 16).

The third key, *change,* is a paradox because of its constancy. Change can cause significant stress, but it is imperative that you treat change as something to be adapted to. As U.S. author and marketing executive Bruce Barton stated: "When you're through changing, you're through."

Courage, the fourth of Reese's keys to stress-free living, is doing what you believe in, even if it means taking the unpopular or difficult path. For those in criminal justice, courage might mean reporting a fellow officer's unethical behavior or working with juvenile delinquents to get their lives back on track.

Control means taking charge of your life, being confident in your ability to direct your own life rather than letting it be directed by outside forces. And *commitment* means being actively involved and caring about your family, friends, job, hobbies, and the like. It also includes being committed to personal fitness: "Choosing to be healthy is the best weapon against the negative influences of stress. Once a commitment is made to fight back against the negative factors of stress, life becomes healthier and more enjoyable" (Harpold and Feemster, 2002, p. 6).

FITNESS AND NUTRITION

The U.S. Army's total fitness program emphasizes nutrition. Among the concepts it stresses are the following:

➢   Drink six to eight glasses of water a day.

➢   Avoid too much sugar.

➢   Avoid too much sodium (salt).

➢   Include fiber in your daily diet.

➢   Cut down on protein and fats.

Scoville (2002, p. 52) suggests:

> Treat deep-fried foods and cheese eats with the same contempt you'd normally reserve for a violent third-strike offender: Lock 'em up and throw away the key. If you're starving and the only eating establishment in sight is a Stop 'n Rob, skip the beef jerky and grab a nutrition bar. . . . Try to eat like you do at home (unless you eat like a pig there, too). Skip the "glutton specials" and stop "super sizing." Eat normal-sized meals, as portions are an important consideration.

Obesity

Recall the heightened incidence of heart disease and diabetes among those in the law enforcement profession. Obesity is an important risk factor in these diseases and contributes to the shortened life span of affected individuals. High blood pressure, common among police officers, is also related to obesity. Unfortunately, many police officers and those in related professions are obese.

> Proper nutrition is an important part of fitness and avoiding obesity, which is believed to increase the risk of certain diseases and to shorten the life span.

FITNESS AND LIFESTYLE

As discussed, fitness, to be truly effective and beneficial, must be incorporated into the way you live every day—your lifestyle. The Centers for Disease Control and Prevention (CDC) have long promoted an active lifestyle as one of the best ways to prevent a host of diseases and reduce the risk of premature death, and their web site home page (www.cdc.gov) provides numerous links for finding information on healthy lifestyles. Marcus et al. (2006, p.27–39) report: "Sedentary behavior has been identified as one of the leading preventable causes of death, and an inverse linear relationship exists between volume of physical activity behavior and all-cause mortality." These researchers suggest lifestyle physical activity is a better overall method to achieving long-term health than is structured, class-based activity, but they also stress that physical activity of any nature is better than the sedentary alternative.

In the United States, many deaths each year are attributed to chronic diseases brought about by unhealthy lifestyles.

Fitness also involves more than just exercising, eating right, and maintaining a proper weight. Lifestyle habits such as getting seven to eight hours of sleep each night and avoiding cigarettes, drugs, and alcohol can significantly enhance longevity.

Smoking, Alcohol, and Other Drugs

These substances are harmful to your health and your career. Keep in mind that an increasing number of both public and private agencies are limiting candidates to those who are nonsmokers. So if you smoke, quit. If you use illegal controlled substances, stop. And if you drink alcoholic beverages, do so in moderation. Other people's lives, not to mention your own, depend on you having a clear head and quick reflexes. Increasingly, companies are conducting random drug tests on current and prospective employees.

BENEFITS OF BEING PHYSICALLY FIT

Grossi (p. 26) reports: "Many studies reveal that fit cops are not only more productive, but use force less often, live a lot longer and are more likely to survive a high risk (or deadly) encounter."

Other benefits of being physically fit, many of which would be advantageous to the job seeker, are:

- ➢ More personal energy.
- ➢ Increased ability to handle job-related stress.
- ➢ Less depression, hypochondria, and anxiety.
- ➢ Fewer aches, pains, and other physical complaints.
- ➢ More efficient digestion.
- ➢ Stronger bones.
- ➢ Slowing of the aging process.
- ➢ A better self-image and more self-confidence.
- ➢ A more attractive body.
- ➢ More restful sleep.
- ➢ Better concentration at work.

Common sense supports studies showing that healthy employees in any occupation, but especially in criminal justice and related fields, are simply better employees, as job effectiveness and overall health are maintained along with fitness.

CONCLUSION

Your future in criminal justice or security, your life, and the lives of the civilians you're sworn to protect depend on your physical fitness. Being out of shape can even become a legal issue. Fortunately, fitness is one area you *can* control. Once you get in shape, *stay there*. This may not be easy because the very nature of criminal justice and security jobs can contribute a great deal to being out of shape. However, physically fit bodies are better able to cope with stress, and stress is abundant in the professions of criminal justice and private security.

Everyone has made decisions they later wish they had not. It is what we are doing now that makes a difference. Some decisions may be countermanded by what we have done with them. For example, paying off debt shows an ability to be accountable to oneself. Fitness is different, in that "what you see is what you get," at least at interview time. For the most part, preparing yourself by getting into shape for the job-seeking process gives you the opportunity to present yourself in the best possible light. This is a significant opportunity, particularly in professions that understandably demand fitness.

AN INSIDER'S VIEW

FITNESS: THE MOST IMPORTANT WEAPON YOU WILL EVER CARRY

Ron J. Nierenhausen

Sergeant, Patrol Division
Elk River (Minnesota) Police Department

The most overlooked and grossly neglected aspect of an officer's arsenal is their fitness. We concentrate on firearms, defensive tactics, procedure, policy and equipment yet fail to focus on the most important weapon you will ever carry—fitness. During my 16 years in law enforcement I have staunchly opined that without a proper fitness regimen an officer's performance will be greatly hampered. A sound mind and body equals sound and safe decisions. One cannot be successful without the other.

But fitness does not just pertain to people on the job; it's as important to those seeking employment in any area of criminal justice. How you present yourself and how you plan to maintain your fitness level are important attributes to any hiring authority.

Officers typically have two excuses for not adopting a personal fitness plan, the first being lack of time. Understanding the rigors of law enforcement—schedules, shifts, court appearances, etc., it is feasible to see why so many simply push a fitness plan to the bottom of the list. Although other commitments are important, so is the commitment to fitness. You may be able to keep up with the hectic schedule for awhile, but eventually it will wear you down to the point of serious risk. It has been well established in the medical community that fitness affects all aspects of life. The healthier you are, the better your ability to fight off disease, ailments and fatigue, along with enhanced injury recovery.

The second excuse used is lack of instruction or knowledge. I find this ironic since those who choose a life in law enforcement are inherently curious individuals. We spend countless hours searching for "bad guys" and investigating crimes yet refuse to do a small amount of research on fitness. A trip to the local bookstore will reveal volumes of "How To" books on fitness and exercise lining the shelves. You may even ask other officers in your department for help since they may be the best resource of all. They can be tremendous mentors if you are new or a support system if you have experience yet lack the continued desire.

Image is another aspect of fitness in law enforcement that must be addressed. The better you present yourself to the public, the more receptive they will be. It would be difficult to listen to a doctor's advice on health if they were unkempt, overweight and, most importantly, unprofessional. The same holds true for police officers. Your first impression may set the tone for the entire call. If a citizen feels you look the part, then they'll assume you fit it also. During hazardous situations an offender will size you up before making a move, and if you look unbeatable they will assume you are unbeatable. Either way you go home at the end of the shift in one piece.

Durability is key to the success of an officer's career. By incorporating a fitness plan into your daily life you will be more apt to sustain the rigors of the schedule. Working overnights and double-backs while wearing 40 pounds of gear can take its toll. Not to mention dealing with offenders. As we age our bodies tend not to recover as well or as quickly as when we were young. Being fit won't stop you from aging but will help your body maintain a higher level of durability and resilience.

Finally, self-esteem must be addressed. The more fit you are, the better you will feel about yourself. I have seen many officers who just don't care anymore. That's a terrible mindset to be in, since much of what we do is mindset itself. We need to adopt a warrior attitude from the aspect of "never lose, never back down." We are a symbol, and that symbol must be proud at all times.

The benefits of a well-planned, well-attended fitness program will help you during your job application efforts, carry you through the rough times and give you the added energy needed to handle the rigors of criminal justice employment. So much is discussed about the benefits that I cannot list them all in this short submission. I can only reaffirm what you already know. Criminal justice and fitness go hand-in-hand and should be viewed as "the most important weapon you will ever carry."

Ron J. Nierenhausen *is a patrol sergeant with the Elk River (Minnesota) Police Department, having worked there for sixteen years. In addition to supervising patrol officers, he is also a SWAT team member, honor guard member, fitness instructor, firearms instructor, and Field Training Coordinator. Sgt. Nierenhausen holds a BA in Criminal Justice from St. Cloud (Minnesota) State University and an MA in Human Services from Concordia (Minnesota) University. He is a graduate of Northwestern University (Illinois) School of Police Staff and Command and holds certificates in Police Fitness Instruction from both Northwestern University and Cooper Aerobic Institute (Dallas, TX). Sgt. Nierenhausen instructs both officers and city employees on fitness and helps coordinate the city wellness program. Ron is married to his wife, Kathy, and has one stepdaughter, Ashley.*

MIND STRETCHES

1.   How would you judge your current level of physical fitness?

2.   Are you currently working out? What is your fitness program?

3.   Why do you imagine the stereotype of the overweight, donut-eating cop exists?

4.   How do law enforcement and security careers tend to prevent fitness?

5.   Is being overweight and out of shape possibly part of the "macho" image of being a cop or security guard? If so, is this changing?

6.   What does an out-of-shape officer communicate to the public by appearance alone?

7.   Why do you think so few Americans exercise regularly?

8.   Recognizing that perhaps working the night shift would make keeping in shape difficult, in what creative ways could an officer working such a shift exercise?

9.   Are criminal justice and private security more stressful than other careers? Why or why not?

10.   How would you define *physically fit?*

REFERENCES

Atkinson-Tovar, Lynn. "The Impact of Repeated Exposure to Trauma." *Law and Order,* September 2003, pp. 118–123.

Colbridge, Thomas D. "The Americans with Disabilities Act: A Practical Guide for Police Departments." *FBI Law Enforcement Bulletin,* January 2001, pp. 23–32.

Collingwood, Thomas, Robert J. Hoffman, and Jay Smith. "The Need for Physical Fitness." *Law and Order,* June 2003, pp. 44–50.

Davis, Paul O. "A New Approach to an Age-Old Problem: Officer Fitness and Readiness." *The Law Enforcement Trainer,* July/August 2002, pp. 33–37.

Ebling, Patti. "Physical Fitness in Law Enforcement: Follow the Yellow Brick Road." *FBI Law Enforcement Bulletin,* October 2002, pp. 1–5.

Fox, Robert. "Stress Management . . . and the Stress-Proof Vest." *Law and Order*, February 2007, pp. 352–355.

Grossi, Dave. "Tactical Wellness." *Law Officer Magazine*, October 2007, pp. 26–27.

Harpold, Joseph A., and Samuel L. Feemster. "Negative Influences of Police Stress." *FBI Law Enforcement Bulletin,* September 2002, pp. 1–7.

Illinois Law Enforcement Training and Standards Board. Available online at www.ptb.state.il.us/pdf/POWER.pdf.

Marcus, Bess H.; Williams, David M.; Dubbert, Patricia M.; Sallis. James F.; King, Abby C.; Yancey, Antronette K.; Franklin, Barry A.; Buchner, David; Daniels, Stephen R.; and Claytor, Randal P. "Physical Activity Intervention Studies: What We Know and What We Need to Know: A Scientific Statement from the American Heart Association Council on Nutrition, Physical Activity, and Metabolism (Subcommittee on Physical Activity); Council on Cardiovascular Disease in the Young; and the Interdisciplinary Working Group on Quality of Care and Outcomes Research." Circulation (*Journal of the American Heart Association*), Vol. 114, No.24, 2006, pp. 2739–2752.

Moore, Carole. "Fit for Duty." *Law Enforcement Technology*, September 2006, pp. 10–18.

Oldham, Scott. "Physical Fitness Training for Law Enforcement Officers." *Law and Order*, June 2001, pp. 75–77.

Physical Fitness for Law Enforcement Officers. Washington, DC: Federal Bureau of Investigation, U.S. Department of Justice, n. d.

"POWER (Peace Officer Wellness Evaluation Report) Test." Illinois Law Enforcement Training and Standards Board. Available online at www.ptb.state.il.us/pdf/POWER.pdf.

Reese, James T. "6 Keys to Stress-Free Living." *The Associate*, January/February 2001, pp. 14–17.

Rosch, Paul J. "Type A and Coronary Disease: Separating Fact from Fiction. An Interview with Ray H. Rosenman." New York: American Institute of Stress, June 2004. Available online at www.stress.org/interview-TypeA_CoronaryDisease.htm?AIS=6dd0f575076c266a3349d71525d183d7. Accessed November 4, 2008.

Sanow, Ed. "Fitness: An Ethical Obligation." *Law and Order,* March 2008, p. 6.

Scoville, Dean. "Code 7." *Police,* July 2002, pp. 46–52.

Stiehm, Matthew. Law Enforcement Program Director, Leech Lake Tribal College, Minnesota. Personal interview, 2008.

Strandberg, Keith W. "Fitness after the Academy." *Law Enforcement Technology,* November 2002, pp. 38–43.

U.S. Marshals Service. Available online at www.usmarshals.gov/careers/basic_training.htm.

Zhao, Jihong "Solomon", Ni He, and Nicholas Lovrich. "Predicting Five Dimensions of Police Officer Stress: Looking More Deeply into Organizational Settings for Sources of Police Stress." *Police Quarterly,* March 2002, pp. 43–62.

CHAPTER 8

OTHER FORMS OF TESTING

Experience is not what happens to you; it is what you do with what happens to you.

—*Aldous Huxley*

Do You Know:

➤ What test anxiety is and how common it is?
➤ How you can improve your test-taking performance?
➤ What areas of general knowledge on which you might be tested?
➤ What other kinds of knowledge on which you might be tested?
➤ What the most common kinds of tests are and what you should know about each?
➤ What assessment centers are and what purpose they serve?
➤ What psychological tests measure and if you can prepare for such tests?
➤ What integrity tests try to determine?
➤ What polygraph tests try to determine, how accurate they are, and what law governs their use in preemployment screening?

INTRODUCTION

The tests used in the hiring process may include the following:

➤ Knowledge

➤ Psychological

➤ Polygraph

This chapter reviews areas commonly tested to help you understand what the tests are and what purpose they serve. You will not be given "suggested" answers. In fact, for some tests, preparing for or trying to "out-psych" them can be a mistake. It's important to know what to expect and what aspects of the testing you can prepare for. Before considering the specific areas, however, take a few minutes to look at a very common phenomenon: *test anxiety.*

TEST ANXIETY

Test anxiety is a general uneasiness or dread characterized by heightened self-awareness and perceived helplessness that frequently leads to diminished performance on tests. It includes the psychological, physiological, and behavioral responses to stimuli associated with the experience of testing. Test anxiety is a reality for most people. Recognize its existence and take control. How? By being as prepared as possible. The fewer surprises a test-taker encounters, the less anxiety is felt.

Test anxiety is the worry, concern, and stress commonly associated with any circumstance in which individuals find themselves being evaluated. It is a reality for most people.

It is possible for applicants to prepare for entrance exams and, consequently, improve their scores by practicing. Many books are available that provide hundreds of practice questions typical of those found in written tests. For example, http://policetests.com is a website offering exam guides for a wide variety of criminal justice careers, including police, corrections, probation, 911 dispatchers, treasury enforcement agents, and border patrols. Arco publishes several general intelligence study references to help you prepare for the written tests used by many criminal justice agencies and departments. Specific books are listed at the end of the chapter to help officer applicants prepare for such exams. Whichever aspect of criminal justice is of interest to you, through practice and repetition you can improve your testing success. And as you gain confidence in your test-taking abilities, you will also likely notice a decrease in test anxiety.

Test performance can be improved through practice and repetition. The more practice you have with such written tests, the better you are likely to do.

In addition to being as prepared as possible, the following will help reduce test anxiety:

➢   Get a good night's sleep before the test.

➢   Eat.

➢   Take at least two pens, two #2 pencils, and a large eraser.

➢   Know exactly where the test will be given and how to get there. (You might make a practice run to the site.)

➢   Arrive with time to spare so parking or other hassles do not make you anxious.

Harr (2008) explains:

> Everyone has different ability levels when it comes to test taking. Remember, there can be only one person scoring first, but that doesn't mean they will or won't be considered the best in the group. Testing is just one phase of any assessment process. Nothing negatively impacts anyone in a testing situation as much as worry, most of which is self-imposed. You prepare the best you can, practice and control what factors you can. From there you practice self-talk, by reassuring yourself you've done your best and that's all you can expect of yourself. Staying up all night before a test to keep studying, fretting about how you will do or worrying about what you might be asked that you don't know will only ensure one thing: that you'll do less well than if you prepare, practice and control what you can.

TESTING KNOWLEDGE

It is hard to imagine that only a few years ago a person could become a law enforcement officer by merely responding to an advertisement. In fact, many fine officers today applied for their jobs rather spontaneously one day and were handed a gun and badge the next. Even today, many security jobs, some involving immense responsibility, require little, if any, knowledge by the applicant.

As appealing as this may sound at this stage of your job search, it is easy to see the many problems associated with what is quickly becoming a practice of the past. As these fields strive to become recognized professions and respond to the increasing demands and potential liability created by our complex society, employment agencies must take their hiring practices much more seriously. Whether the job for which you are applying requires certification or licensure or just requires applicants to be responsible individuals, almost all employers will want to assess what the applicant knows and the likelihood of success.

General Knowledge

Some tests are designed to assess certain basic levels of ability in areas such as math, English, grammar, and composition. Because communication skills are vitally important, employers want assurance that the people they are considering hiring (for any level job) can express themselves well. Many large departments, particularly those sensitive to diversity, focus more on general knowledge, such as reading comprehension, vocabulary, analogies, and general math. Computer literacy and keyboarding skills are also becoming more critical.

General knowledge commonly tested includes reading comprehension, vocabulary, analogies, basic reading, writing, and arithmetic. Computer literacy is also becoming more important.

Although different tests can be used to examine these basic areas, they will all look at the same basic abilities. Ask yourself if you possess the necessary reading, writing, and math skills required of any employee (usually a college freshman level). If you are not at this level, immediately start a plan to improve your skills. Many community colleges have a policy of open admission. As part of the process, the student is tested in reading, writing, and math skills. Colleges also offer remedial courses for the underprepared student.

Once on the job, lack of basic reading, writing, and math skills can't be hidden long from an employer. To avoid wasting everyone's time, many job applications include some basic questions to let the hiring agency know if you have these basic academic abilities. An increasing number of application forms have a section that requires a brief essay to test your writing, spelling, grammar, and organizational abilities.

For example, the Minnesota Police Corps requires applicants to submit a personal essay and be prepared to write three short essays during testing:

Part VI. Personal Statement and Essays

Attach a personal statement to this application. Word limit: 500–700 words.

Tell us something about yourself. Why do you think you would be a great candidate for the Police Corps? What do you consider your greatest strength and why? What do you consider your greatest weakness and why? If you feel that you have faced difficult circumstances in your life, please write about how you have overcome these obstacles.

Although you are not required to write about any specific topic, an essay that shows growth, maturity, leadership, courage, and commitment could be particularly helpful to your application. We are looking for a demonstrated interest in law enforcement and dedication to public service. (**5 points**)

Be prepared to write several essays when you are called in for testing.

You will be required to write a short (200–300 word) essay on each of the following topics. Your written statements should be concise and should reflect your true feelings and beliefs. Please give some thought to each topic ahead of time. Your writing must be legible. Illegible answers will not be graded and you will lose those points.

- Why are you applying to the Police Corps? (**5 points**)
- What do you see as the primary challenges confronting children growing up today in the communities of Minnesota? What role do you see for the police in addressing those challenges? (**5 points**)
- List three books that have influenced your thinking or contributed to your development. Briefly explain how and why. (**5 points**)

The essays are evaluated by the following standards:

➢ A clear main idea that fulfills the assignment.

➢ Adequate, specific support.

➢ Organized into logical paragraphs with coherent transitions.

➢ A concise style.

➢ Appropriate word choice.

➢ Sentences that are complete, varied, and effective.

➢ Standard grammar: correct use of pronouns, adjectives, adverbs, negation, articles, and subject/verb agreement.

➢ Mechanically correct spelling, abbreviations, numbers, capitalization, and punctuation.

Because writing is a skill you will need for the rest of your life, regardless of your professional pursuits, do not overlook this all-important area. Take advantage of classes during your education, and if you have already completed a degree-seeking program, do not hesitate to return to school to become an adequate writer. There is no getting around it—you must be able to write well. Even if you somehow obtain a job without having adequate writing skills, this is an area you will be evaluated on during your probationary period when you will write constantly.

If you need remedial help in any area, get it now. Many opportunities exist to help improve yourself. Often the only thing stopping someone from improving themselves is that they feel too embarrassed to ask for help. The help you need may be in a review book available from a library or bookstore, or you may want to enroll in a class at a community college or in an adult learning program.

Specific Knowledge

Applicants may be required to know specific information for certain jobs. In states requiring certification or licensure, successful completion of requisite levels of training or education will be evidence of such knowledge. Certainly such required knowledge will indicate the areas of specific knowledge you will be expected to know. Such areas might include practical applications and techniques, criminal justice systems, civil and criminal law, community policing, victims and victims' rights, and leading and communication. Other states may require a comprehensive licensing exam. For example, in Minnesota, which requires a minimum of two years of college to be eligible to be licensed as a police officer, areas of required knowledge (the Peace Officer Standards and Training Learning Objectives) include:

➢ Administration of justice
➢ Criminal investigation
➢ Criminal procedure
➢ Cultural awareness
➢ Defensive tactics

➢ Firearms
➢ Human behavior
➢ Juvenile justice
➢ Patrol functions
➢ Police operations and procedures

➢ Report writing
➢ Statutes
➢ Testifying in court
➢ Traffic law enforcement

Other areas that might be tested include emergency motor vehicle operation, evidence collection, first aid, gang education and prevention, interviewing, ethics, and leadership. Less specific knowledge is required to be a private investigator in Minnesota, but in addition to passing a strict background investigation, a minimum of three years' experience in security work is required.

Even if the areas of specific knowledge are not set forth clearly, you should be able to foresee what may be asked during an oral interview. Basic statutes that apply to public or private officers would be likely questions. Often, such questions are intertwined with the "What would you do if . . . ?" question. This allows employers to test not only specific knowledge, but the application while using problem-solving techniques and communications skills.

Applicants should expect to be tested on some specific knowledge in areas pertaining to the field, such as relevant statutes and procedures.

It's your responsibility to be prepared to the best of your ability. If you do not know what you might be tested on, it does no harm to call ahead to ask. The worst that could happen is that they won't say. But it is much more likely you could be told, putting you a giant step ahead of applicants who don't know what will be on the test.

It's also a good idea to learn as much as possible about the department or agency you are applying to as well as the community in which it is located. If it is a law enforcement position, try to arrange for a ride-along, thus providing an opportunity to ask questions about the department. If it is a corrections position, arrange to visit the institution if possible. If it is a private security position, visit the facility and talk with a security officer. With the Internet, the availability of information about a department and the community it serves has never been greater. Do some research on the neighborhood demographics, or the type of business or industry the private company you are applying to is involved in. Being able to speak intelligently about the setting the company, agency, or institution operates in will set you apart from other candidates.

Although online information is valuable, remember this work is all about people. Walk around town and talk with some business owners and citizens. Not only are you likely to acquire some exceptional information, but it shows how serious you are in wanting the job.

Learn what you can and review what you think will be asked. Remember, no one can know everything. Sometimes you will be able to immediately give the exact answer, maybe even amazing yourself, sometimes you may give a wrong answer, or sometimes you may draw a complete mental blank. You are likely to experience all these reactions at one time or another during testing; all may be expected to some degree. Before you discount your performance, remember those testing you were in your seat once, too, and so are likely to be more understanding than you may give them credit for.

Keep in mind the purpose of the testing process. If the only thing employers wanted were accurate answers, they would replace their employees with computers. Employers want someone who can think and act human. Part of being human is to not know it all and yet to keep functioning. Even if totally stumped, to hang your head and mutter, "I have absolutely no idea," is never the best option. One person applying for an entry-level dispatcher position had no experience in the field, and so the various scenario questions asking him to prioritize calls and how calls would be handled proved quite challenging. There was no logical way answers could be "made up," but his answer of, "I don't know the answer to that yet, but I can't wait to learn how to handle that scenario as effectively as possible!" was good enough to get the job.

Some tests might even include an off-the-wall question just to see how you respond. In all probability, you will look a lot better admitting you are nervous and forgot, or don't know the answer (but know where to find it), than to fake it. In short:

➢ Be as prepared as you can be.

➢ Seek remedial help if necessary.

➢ Know as much as you can.

➢ Know how to find what you don't know.

➢ Don't make up answers or pretend to know more than you really do.

➢ Don't be afraid to admit what you don't know.

➢ If you draw a blank or realize later you gave a wrong answer, consider following up in writing to let them know you recognize you missed it but that you now know the answer.

Memory and Observation Tests

Many police departments use tests to determine applicants' ability to recall information. For example, pictures of several suspects may be flashed on a screen and personal information given about each of the individuals, such as names, ages, criminal activity, etc. The test then continues by flashing a picture on the screen and requiring the applicant to recall all the information about the subject, or recall a nickname, or match a crime with a face. Will you be able to remember everything? Probably not. But they'll want to know you have some recall ability.

STRATEGIES FOR TAKING TESTS

No matter whether the tests cover general information, specific knowledge, memory and observation skills, or a combination of these, the successful candidate knows how to approach the specific type of test given.

> The most common tests are multiple choice, true/false, and essay, and each type of test has its own guidelines and strategies to follow.

Landsberger (2004) offers practical advice for approaching such tests.

Tips for Better Test Taking[1]

Successful test taking avoids carelessness. In general:

- **Read the directions carefully.**
  This may be obvious, but it will help you avoid careless errors. If there is time, quickly look through the test for an overview.

- **Answer questions in a strategic order:**
  1. **First easy questions**—to build confidence, score points, and mentally orient yourself to vocabulary, concepts, etc. It may help you make associations with more difficult questions.
  2. **Then difficult questions**—or those with the most point value.

  With objective tests, first eliminate those answers you know to be wrong, or are likely to be wrong, don't seem to fit, or where two options are so similar as to be both incorrect.

  With essay/subjective questions, broadly outline your answer and sequence the order of your points.

- **Review:**
  Resist the urge to leave as soon as you have completed all the items.

  Review your test to make sure that you have answered all questions, not mis-marked the answer sheet, or made some other simple mistake.

  Proofread your writing for spelling, grammar, punctuation, decimal points, etc.

  Do not "second-guess" yourself and change your original answers. Research has indicated that your first hunch is more likely to be correct. You should only change answers to questions if you originally misread them or if you have encountered information elsewhere in the test that indicates with certainty that your first choice is incorrect.

Multiple-Choice Tests

Multiple-choice questions usually include a phrase or stem followed by three to five options:

Test Strategies:
- Read the directions carefully.
- Know if each question has one or more correct options.
- Know if you are penalized for guessing.
- Answer easy questions first.

---

[1]Joseph Landsberger, author and developer of website Study Guides and Strategies, www.studygs.net/#tests, St. Paul, MN, 2004 . Reprinted by permission.

Answering options

Improve your odds, think critically:

Cover the options, read the stem, and try to answer—Select the option that most closely matches your answer.

Read the stem with each option—Treat each option as a true/false question, and choose the "most true."

Strategies to answer difficult questions:

- **Eliminate options you know to be incorrect.**
- **Question options that grammatically don't fit with the stem.**
- **Question options that are totally unfamiliar to you.**
- **Question options that contain negative or absolute words**—Try substituting a qualified term for the absolute one, like *frequently* for *always* or *typical* for *every*, to see if you can eliminate it.
- **"All of the above"**—If you know two of three options seem correct, "all of the above" is a strong possibility.
- **Number answers**—Toss out the high and low and consider the middle range numbers.
- **"Look alike options"**—Probably one is correct; choose the best but eliminate choices that mean basically the same thing, and thus cancel each other out.
- **Echo options**—If two options are opposite each other, chances are one of them is correct.
- **Favor options that contain qualifiers**—The result is longer, more inclusive items that better fill the role of the answer.
- **If two alternatives seem correct**—Compare them for differences, then refer to the stem to find your best answer.

Guessing:

- **Always guess when there is no penalty** for guessing or you can eliminate options.
- **Don't guess if you are penalized** for guessing and if you have no basis for your choice.
- **Don't change your answers** unless you are sure of the correction.
- **Use hints from questions you know** to answer questions you do not.

True/False Tests

Every part of a true sentence must be true—If any part of the sentence is false, the whole sentence is false despite many other true statements.

Pay close attention to negatives, qualifiers, absolutes, and long strings of statements.

Negatives can be confusing.

If the question contains negatives, as in *no, not, cannot,* drop the negative and read what remains. Decide whether that sentence is true or false.

If it is true, its opposite, or negative, is usually false.

Qualifiers are words that restrict or open up general statements.

Words like *sometimes, often, frequently, ordinarily,* and *generally* open up the possibilities of making accurate statements. They make more modest claims, are more likely to reflect reality, and usually indicate true answers.

Absolute words restrict possibilities.

"No, never, none, always, every, entirely, only" imply the statement must be true 100 percent of the time and usually indicate false answers.

Long sentences often include groups of words set off by punctuation.

Pay attention to the truth of each of these phrases. If one is false, it usually indicates a false answer.

Guessing:

Often true/false tests contain more true answers than false answers. You have a more than 50 percent chance of being right with true. However, this is not always the case.

Essay Exams

Organization and neatness have merit.

Before writing out the exam:

Set up a time schedule to answer each question and to review/edit all questions

- If six questions are to be answered in sixty minutes, allow yourself only seven minutes for each.
- If questions are weighted, prioritize that into your time allocation for each question.
- When the time is up for one question, stop writing, leave space, and begin the next question. The incomplete answers can be completed during the review time.
- Six incomplete answers will usually receive more credit than three complete ones.

Read through the questions once and note if you have any choice in answering questions

- Pay attention to how the question is phrased, or to the directives, or words such as *compare*, *contrast*, and *criticize*, etc.
- **Answers will come to mind immediately for some questions.**
   Write down their key words, listings, etc. as they are fresh in your mind; otherwise these ideas may be blocked (or be unavailable) when the times come to write the later questions. This will reduce "clutching" or panic (anxiety, actually fear which disrupts thoughts).

Before attempting to answer a question, put it in your own words

- Now compare your version with the original.
   Do they mean the same thing? If they don't, you've misread the question. You'll be surprised how often they don't agree.

Think before you write:

Make a brief outline for each question

Number the items in the order you will discuss them

- **Get right to the point.**
   State your main point in the first sentence.
   Use your first paragraph to provide an overview of your essay. Use the rest of your essay to discuss these points in more detail.
   Back up your points with specific information, examples, or quotations from your readings.
   - Teachers are influenced by compactness, completeness, and clarity of an organized answer.
   - Writing in the hope that the right answer will somehow turn up is time consuming and usually futile.
   - To know a little and to present that little well is, by and large, superior to knowing much and presenting it poorly.

Writing and answering:

Begin with a strong first sentence that states the main idea of your essay.
   Continue this first paragraph by presenting key points.

Develop your argument.

- **Begin each paragraph** with a key point from the introduction.
- **Develop each point** in a complete paragraph.
- **Use transitions**, or enumerate, to connect your points.
- **Hold to your time** allocation and organization.
- **Avoid very definite statements** when possible; a qualified statement connotes a philosophic attitude, the mark of an educated person.
- **Qualify the answer when in doubt.** It is better to say "toward the end of the nineteenth century" than to say "in 1894" when you can't remember whether it's 1884 or 1894. In many cases, the approximate time is all that is wanted; unfortunately 1894, though approximate, may be incorrect, and will usually be marked accordingly.

Summarize in your last paragraph

Restate your central idea and indicate why it is important.

Review:
    Complete questions left incomplete, but allow time to review all questions.
    Review, edit, and correct misspellings, incomplete words and sentences, miswritten dates and numbers.

Not enough time?
    Outline your answers.

Harr reminds people who are interviewing or taking tests about the importance of being your best. Research proves that rest and good nutrition before a test increases performance, as does reducing anxiety you can control.

ASSESSMENT CENTERS

Assessment center testing is gaining popularity, but is not a new concept. The technique involves placing candidates in a situation where they role-play the position they are seeking. The International Association of Chiefs of Police (IACP) website (www.theiacp.org) states:

> The assessment center process is a powerful technique.... Observing candidates' behavior in simulations of on-the-job challenges offers in-depth information concerning candidate strengths and weaknesses. In an assessment center, each candidate participates in a series of exercises that simulate actual situations from the target job. The performance of candidates is evaluated by expert assessors, providing information unattainable from written tests, interviews or any other source. . . . Because of their accurate simulation of the job and its duties. Assessment centers have proven highly defensible as a selection strategy. Our assessment centers are comprehensive, and a variety of assessment methods are available to meet every selection need from entry level to top executive.

> Assessment centers are processes that identify a candidate's strengths and weaknesses to evaluate how well that candidate is likely to perform on the job. Situational tests are a common part of such assessment centers.

PSYCHOLOGICAL TESTING

Psychological testing is a cause of anxiety for applicants because so much of it is out of their control. What should I say? How should I answer? What are they looking for? Psychological testing is an immense and complex subject about which hundreds of texts have been written. So what do you need to know? First of all, these tests should not and probably could not be prepared for through such traditional means as memorization. It is better to understand what these tests are meant to do, how they are administered, and what they can show.

Purposes of Psychological Testing

Although psychological testing is a relatively new practice, no doubt you have taken some form of psychological test, probably at some point in your school career: "Psychological testing has become a crucial element in the police officer recruiting process since the President's Commission on Law Enforcement and the Administration of Justice (1967) aggressively promoted the necessity of psychologically screening police applicants' emotional stability" (Ho, 2001, p. 319). Holzman and Kirschner (2003, p. 85) assert: "In the area of law enforcement psychological evaluations have proven invaluable as one of the necessary pre-employment activities for prospective officers. Due to the nature of law enforcement work, psychological evaluations serve a unique role by being able to identify potential officers who may not adjust successfully."

As Rostow and Davis (2002, p. 101) explain: "All police executives are aware that they are responsible for the misbehavior of officers and may be brought to court under 42 USC 1983. . . . In general, the failure to properly select an officer is a form of negligent hiring." Bercaw (2002, p. 134) adds:

> Departments want to make sure the applicant is not emotionally unbalanced—paranoid schizophrenics and psychopaths need not apply. Beyond that, the department needs to know something about the applicant's motivations for wanting to become an officer, what his personal strengths and weaknesses are, and what the likelihood the applicant will successfully complete the academy's training program or remain in law enforcement is.
>
> Additionally, how does the applicant manage stress, frustration, and anger? Is the applicant a team player? Does the applicant exhibit good judgment and have integrity? Would this individual actually be in harm's way as a weapons carrying officer? Can this person assert authority in such a manner that doesn't escalate situations, which are already potentially volatile? Does the applicant have a support system?

Ho (p. 334) states: "All else being equal, . . . applicants were almost 8.4 times more likely to be recruited by the police department if they had a positive recommendation by psychologists relative to those applicants who were not recommended by psychologists."

Most people would agree that law enforcement officers should be mentally and emotionally stable. But defining and assessing what this consists of is a complex, challenging task.

> Most psychological tests measure differences between individuals or between the reactions of the same individual on different occasions. Preparing for such tests is very different from preparing for more traditional knowledge-based tests, but you can prepare for them.

Conroy (2008), a former police officer and currently practicing clinical psychologist, offers the following advice concerning psychological tests administered to police/security candidates:

> To prepare for a psychological evaluation, applicants must begin to get psychologically "fit" several months before the examination. Preparation for a psychological evaluation cannot be rushed. Applicants must begin preparation early enough so they can make changes to assure that they are as psychologically healthy as possible. This includes looking at relationships, mature behavior and ways to deal with tension.
>
> Frequently applicants take psychological evaluations just after finishing school. Their lives have been hectic. They have not taken time to relax for months. They are wound tighter than a $2.00 watch. This stress affects their entire being. It determines how they see the world. It is crucial for applicants to take time to relax before a psychological examination. This requires more than a 15-minute process the day before the evaluation. Some practical suggestions after you have taken time for yourself are as follows:
> - Don't fight with your wife or husband, boyfriend or girlfriend or parents the night before the evaluation.
> - Get plenty of sleep the night before. Make sure you are at your best.
> - Get up early the morning of the evaluation so you have time for yourself. Take a walk and relax.
> - Leave early for the evaluation. Get there with about 15 minutes to spare. Take time to relax when you get there. Read the paper or something.
> - During the exam, be honest. You have honestly worked toward entering this profession for a long time. Don't change now. Copy from the person next to you only if you are absolutely sure you want his or her personality and are willing to bet your career on it.

Testing Methods

Methods vary greatly from test to test. Personality tests are of two main types: objective and projective. Objective personality tests, such as the California Personality Inventory (CPI) and Inwald Personality Inventory (IPI), ask objective true/false or multiple-choice questions. These questions are then grouped into scales to measure different aspects of personality. Projective tests involve ambiguous stimuli that the subject must interpret by "projecting" into the interpretation aspects of his or her own personality. Common projective tests are the Rorschach Inkblot Test and the Thematic Apperception Test (TAT).

Psychological and Other Tests

In attempting to anticipate how an applicant might perform on the job, evaluators look at both the past (grades, job references, traffic and police records, etc.) and the present. Psychological tests are tools employers use to learn about the applicant's present state of mind, what is important to that person, and how that person is likely to respond to certain stimuli. An applicant's answers form patterns that are evaluated to determine a psychological profile of the applicant. Tests frequently given include:

➤ Minnesota Multiphasic Personality Inventory-2 (MMPI-2)
➤ Myers-Briggs Type Indicator™ (MBTI)
➤ Inwald Personality Inventory (IWI)
➤ Behavioral Personal Assessment Device (B-PAD)
➤ California Psychological Inventory (CPI)
➤ Watson-Glaser Critical Thinking Appraisal (WGCTA)

➤ Strong Interest Inventory (SII)
➤ Thematic Apperception Test (TAT)
➤ Rorschach Inkblot Test
➤ Wonderlic Basic Skills Test (WBST)
➤ Personality Assessment Inventory
➤ 16PF

The *Minnesota Multiphasic Personality Inventory-2* (MMPI-2) is used primarily for emotional stability screening and frequently for entry-level psychological screening. This self-report questionnaire is the most widely used paper-and-pencil personality test being used (in all fields). Respondents are asked to indicate "true," "false," or "cannot say" to 567 statements covering a variety of psychological characteristics such as health, social, political, sexual, and religious values; attitudes about family, education, and occupation; emotional moods; and typical neurotic or psychotic displays such as obsessive-compulsive behavior, phobias, hallucinations, and delusions.

Conroy asserts the MMPI is virtually impossible to study for. Its validity scales have cross-indexed questions and, in most cases, applicants who try to "fool" the test "fool" themselves out of a job instead. The MMPI has numerous sufficiently similar items so that it is difficult to lie consistently. The best advice here, again, is to tell the truth. One candidate tried to beat the MMPI and was denied a federal job. When the same candidate took the test again a year later and told the truth, he got the job.

The *Myers-Briggs Type Indicator*™ (MBTI) is a widely used measure of people's disposition and preferences. Millions of people in a wide variety of occupations have taken the Myers-Briggs. The test describes sixteen easily understood personality types based on individuals' stated preferences on four indices:

➤ Extroversion-Introversion
➤ Sensing-Intuition

➤ Thinking-Feeling
➤ Judgment-Perception

The *Inwald Personality Inventory* (IPI) is a 310-question test in which an applicant has to respond to a statement as either "true" or "false," based on experience, attitude, or feeling toward the content of the statement. Designed specifically for police departments, the IPI's purpose is to screen out psychologically unsuitable law enforcement candidates. As Ho (p. 325) notes: "The IPI is designed to measure 26 behavioral characteristics, such as job difficulties or hyperactivity, which are presumably relevant to police-related functioning. . . . [Researchers] have proclaimed that the practical values of the IPI psychological measurement are critical to predict applicants' job performances as police officers in the future."

The *Behavioral Personal Assessment Device* (B-PAD) is one of the most progressive testing instruments in police recruiting and is used to measure problem-solving ability, judgment under pressure, decisiveness, diplomacy and interpersonal skills. Presented in video format, the test has applicants view numerous video screens and respond as if he or she was the officer at the scene. B-PAD was designed to assess an applicant's ability to effectively evaluate a variety of situations typically encountered by police officers. Other B-PAD video formats are available to test applicants for fire, EMS, corrections, and communications dispatcher positions.

The *California Psychological Inventory* (CPI) is a 434-item objective inventory including twenty scales that measure a broad array of individual difference variables and personality characteristics, including social expertise and interpersonal style; maturity, normative orientation, and values; achievement orientation; and personal interest styles. Thirteen Special Purpose Scales are derived to report on Creative Temperament, Managerial Potential, and Tough-Mindedness.

The *Watson-Glaser Critical Thinking Appraisal* (WGCTA) is an assessment tool designed to measure an individual's critical-thinking skills and has five subtests: (1) Inference, (2) Recognition of Assumptions, (3) Deduction, (4) Interpretation, and (5) Evaluation of Arguments. The test has eighty items, including problems, statements, arguments, and interpretations of data like those encountered daily at work and in the classroom, and is to be completed within sixty minutes. The short form is comprised of forty items to be completed in forty-five minutes.

The *Strong Interest Inventory* (SII) is based on the idea that individuals are more satisfied and productive when they work in jobs or at tasks that they find interesting and when they work with people whose interests are similar to their own. The SII contains 317 items that measure individual interests in a wide range of occupations, occupational activities, hobbies, leisure activities, and types of people. It compares a person's interests with the interests of people happily employed in a wide variety of occupations. It measures interests, not aptitude or intelligence.

The *Thematic Apperception Test* (TAT) is a projective instrument similar in context to the Rorschach Test but with no quantitative scoring technique. The test includes thirty-one picture cards with specific subsets for men and women. The purpose of the TAT is to provide insight into an applicant's self-image, perception of interpersonal relationships, relative strengths, and various needs by inducing thoughts, attitudes, and feelings about a subject depicted on the picture cards. The picture cards are used to stimulate stories or descriptions about relationships or social situations and can help identify dominant drives, emotions, sentiments, conflicts, and complexes.

The *Rorschach Inkblot Test* consists of ten inkblot patterns of various shades and colors. The applicant is shown a pattern and asked what it might be. This test helps evaluate basic personality structure and detect possible psychopathology. Because reading is not required for administration, this test can overcome language barriers.

The *Wonderlic Basic Skills Test* (WBST) is a ninety-five-item paper-and-pencil test that can be taken individually or in groups. This test predicts success in learning situations and is a very accurate estimate of intelligence that serves as a quick assessment of cognitive skills or as a screening device to determine the need for more detailed evaluations. It can be used to benchmark prospective employees' basic skills as defined by the U.S. Department of Labor in the *Dictionary of Occupational Titles*.

The *Personality Assessment Inventory* (PAI) is a 344-item instrument that takes fifty to sixty minutes to administer. Each item is rated on a four-point scale ranging from false, somewhat true, to very true. The PAI consists of twenty-two nonoverlapping full scales covering the constructs most relevant to a broad-based assessment of mental disorders: 4 validity scales, 11 clinical scales, 5 treatment scales, and 2 interpersonal scales. To facilitate interpretation and cover the full range of complex clinical constructs, ten full scales contain conceptually derived subscales.

The *16 Personality Factors* (16PF) questionnaire is used by organizations and human resource professionals to assesses the sixteen personality factors of warmth, reasoning, emotional stability, dominance, liveliness, rule-consciousness, social boldness, sensitivity, vigilance, abstractedness, privateness, apprehension, openness to change, self-reliance, perfectionism, and tension. Five additional global factors are also measured: extraversion, anxiety, tough-mindedness, independence, and self-control.

EMPLOYMENT PERSONALITY TESTS

Criminal justice and security employers continue to learn from the corporate world, which persists in recognizing the importance of personality traits that can be tested for: "Personality assessments offer rich portraits of how employees under stress, and under normal…conditions, deal with conflicts, solve problems, and arrive at results" (Hart and Sheldon, 2007, p. 12). When examining these personality tests results, employers are assessing your ability to connect and communicate clearly with others (Hart and Sheldon).

With all the Internet has to offer, you can learn more about almost any test given, and even find practice tests. If tests are available, practice tests can give you a strong edge over your competition. Most employers will tell you what tests they use, so it may be as simple as asking. Many of these "tests" are not really tests at all, but rather "questionnaires, classifiers, and various indictors that rely on the test taker being truthful about his or her personality…. your personality is what comes to the surface when you are under a lot of stress and the 'real you' emerges" (Hart and Sheldon, p. 115). Taking time to research what you can about these tests and practicing, or at least being familiar with them, helps you manage that stress.

Integrity Tests

One psychological test commonly used by employers is the paper-and-pencil honesty questionnaire. The first test of this type was developed in 1951 by John E. Reid and was called the Reid Report. Since then, various other ways have been devised to test applicants' integrity, which is defined as adherence to moral and ethical principles, soundness of moral character, and honesty (Dictionary.com, 2008). Barrett (2001, p. 3), commenting on preemployment integrity testing, notes:

> Two other terms have come into usage more recently, "employee reliability" . . . and "counter-productive behavior." . . . These two terms reflect the broadening of the meaning of honesty and integrity from the relatively narrow conceptualization of theft, lying, and cheating that first defined the overt integrity tests

of the early 1980s, through to a range of behaviors, attitudes, and dispositions that were considered "not conducive to efficient and effective work practices" or counter-productive to organizational "health."

Barrett (p. 6) asserts: "The most obvious way to assess the integrity and honesty of an individual is to interview them and ask questions that seem relevant to the evaluation of the job applicant's character and integrity." He adds:

> If considering using an interview to assess an applicant's honesty and counter-productive attitudes, it is prudent to use a formal structured technique such as the Reid Integrity Interview from Reid Associates Inc. This is a highly structured interview procedure for job applicants. The purpose of the interview is to develop factual information about the applicant's past behavioral patterns and outlook. The following areas are assessed during the interview: employment history, theft and related activities, work-related alcohol use, violations of company policy, use of illicit drugs, and past criminal behavior. In a recent study reported by Reid Associates, although not yet published, the information developed from Integrity Interviews conducted on police candidates was compared to the information acquired from more traditional background "checking." According to Reid Associates, the congruence between the information acquired from the Integrity Interview and that from traditional checks was 100%, with over one third of the interviews exceeding the information content of the background checks.

Integrity tests are psychological tests commonly used by employers to determine trustworthiness. The test asks questions about the candidate's ethics, criminal record, recent drug use, and work history.

POLYGRAPH TESTING

Modern polygraph tests evolved from the first "lie detector" invented in 1892. The polygraph collects physiological data from at least three systems in the human body and measures changes associated with being dishonest.

➤ Relative blood pressure and pulse rate (cardiovascular activity)

➤ Galvanic skin resistance (GSR), or perspiration (sweat gland activity)

➤ Stomach and chest breathing patterns (respiratory activity)

Use of the polygraph in preemployment is so controversial that it has become strictly regulated through the Employee Polygraph Protection Act (EPPA), signed into law by President Reagan in 1988. The American Polygraph Association (APA) notes that the EPPA "prohibits most private employers from using polygraph testing to screen applicants for employment." However, it does not affect public employers such as police agencies or other governmental institutions.

Thus, although using the polygraph during preemployment is prohibited in most fields and some states have extended this prohibition to police agencies, it is not prohibited in most law enforcement agencies or for many private security jobs.

Polygraph tests are used to determine a candidate's honesty and, according to most field practitioners, are generally very accurate. Use of the polygraph during preemployment screening is not prohibited in government jobs, including law enforcement. Not all employers or states use this form of testing.

The primary use of the polygraph is to substantiate the information gathered during the background investigation.

BACKGROUND CHECKS

Another common hurdle most candidates must pass is the background check, also referred to as preemployment screening or background investigation. The background check typically includes contacting past employers and references listed on the candidate's application form. It may also include a check on credit history, driving record, academic background, criminal record, and the possession of any and all required professional licenses. An area generally scrutinized closely is the applicant's work history: "The greatest predictor of future behavior is past behavior. If the applicant has an established pattern of poor work history, it is unlikely to improve" (Nelson, 2000, p. 87). However, a change in the course of one's life speaks to the ability to change, also a positive attribute.

When completing background information for the hiring process, be as thorough and complete as you can because the investigator will be as well.

ON BEING DISHONEST

Candidates for all jobs in criminal justice and security should anticipate a rigorous background check conducted by investigators trained in this specialty area. As odd as it may seem to even include, it is worth repeating: *Do not lie*. For reasons that should be obvious to anyone considering a career in criminal justice, honesty and integrity are required attributes. And don't try to hide anything. Today's background investigators will find it. They know who to ask, what to ask, and how to look for any indications of problem behaviors that might later cause someone to allege the hiring agency "should have known" the potential risks posed by an employee. Furthermore, in addition to whatever it was you were hiding, you will now be viewed as dishonest, a trait no agency wishes to deal with. Also bear in mind that most background investigators will want to know where else you have applied. If you have been dishonest during the application process in the past, it will follow you.

Although you may be able to change your level of physical fitness, you cannot change your background. You can improve it, definitely a positive attribute, but you cannot hide it. In addition to certain actions that will statutorily prohibit people from entering professions, some past acts will at least be of concern to potential employers. You will have the opportunity to address these issues, and maybe even turn some indiscretions around to your advantage (proving how you addressed a problem and have learned and improved as a result), but be assured lying in any manner about your background will be a legitimate reason for disqualification.

CONCLUSION

The testing process is another opportunity to prove to a prospective employer that you are the one to hire. Present yourself as you are. If you do not feel you would test well now, improve yourself by developing a rigorous plan to increase your fitness level, your knowledge, and your writing skills. Also, take some practice tests. Be realistic about who you are and what you can do and be honest with yourself. Because work greatly influences all aspects of your life, you do not want to pursue any career that will be a dead end. View the testing phase of the application process as a positive experience for both yourself and the employer in determining if there is a match. If not, it is best for everyone to learn this while there is time for you to find a different niche in the world of work.

AN INSIDER'S VIEW

PREPARING TO DO YOUR BEST

Dennis L. Conroy, PhD

Former Director of the Employee Assistance Program
St. Paul (Minnesota) Police Department Sergeant (Ret.)

In preparing for tests to become a police or security officer, it is crucial that you properly prepare for the various tests. There are likely to be tests in the areas of knowledge, physical fitness, psychological preparedness and perhaps even a polygraph.

You can study for knowledge tests. You must be able to not only understand the police/security function, but to articulate that function, specify ways in which that function can be fulfilled and how you will fit into the system to fulfill the function. In other words, expect more than just a multiple-choice or true/false test of knowledge. You must be able to state what police/security officers do (protect and serve), how that can best be accomplished (specific methods of protecting and serving) and what role you see for yourself in that system (how you see yourself functioning as a police or security officer).

Tests of physical fitness require significant preparation. There will often be tests of stamina (cardiovascular fitness), strength (muscle tone) and agility (mobility). Almost any fitness center has programs to help prepare for such tests. It is best to find the specifics of the department you are applying for and train to meet those standards.

Studying for a psychological test is much like studying for a urine test. There is important preparation, but it cannot be done the night before the exam, or even a week before.

You must begin to prepare for the psychological exam at least several months before the actual test itself. You must present yourself as psychologically fit to do police or security work, and such preparation takes time. It should be more a reaffirmation process than change. You should not be afraid of psychological examinations. Just be honest. If the assessment indicates that you may not be suitable for police work or security work, it is just as often indicating that police or security work will not be good for you.

Dr. Dennis Conroy, *licensed psychologist, has recently retired after thirty plus years of service with the St. Paul (Minnesota) Police Department. During his career, he had such diverse assignments as patrol officer, juvenile officer, patrol supervisor, vice/narcotics investigator, director of the Professional Development Institute, director of the Field Training Program, and director of the Employee Assistance Program. His clinical experience spans more than twenty years and includes working with children, adolescents, and adults. Dr. Conroy has also taught upper-level college courses blending the fields of psychology and law enforcement, including Adolescent Psychology, Human Behavior in Law Enforcement, Police Stress, Peer Counseling in Law Enforcement, and The Psychology of Victims.*

MIND STRETCHES

1.   Does your field require proof of certain levels of knowledge? How will you prepare for this?

2.   What do you anticipate a battery of psychological tests will say about you? Are there factors in your life that need to be attended to before pursuing your chosen career?

3.   How do you feel about taking a polygraph examination? Are there skeletons in your closet that you need to confront honestly?

4.   As part of your job-search strategy, have you taken into account what you can and cannot prepare yourself for?

5.   What areas of the hiring process do you have such limited control over that you can't prepare for them? Is there any area of the hiring process that you have absolutely no control over, or is there always something you can do to give yourself an edge over the competition?

6.   Is what you have done in the past a realistic indicator of how you will perform in the future?

7.   Have you ever taken a psychological test? If so, how did you feel: positive, neutral, or negative? If negative, what can you do to reduce these feelings?

8.   If you suffer from test anxiety, what can you do to reduce it?

9.   How well do you write? How can you know for sure?

REFERENCES

American Polygraph Association (APA). Available online at www.polygraph.org.

Barrett, Paul. *Pre-Employment Integrity Testing: Current Methods, Problems, and Solutions.* Paper presented at British Computer Society: Information Security Specialist Group, March 29–30, 2001, Milton Hill, Oxford. Available online at www.pbarrett.net/presentations/integrity_doc.pdf.

Bercaw, George H. "Psychological Assessment." *Law and Order*, July 2002, pp. 132–136.

Conroy, Dennis L. Former Director of the Employee Assistance Program, St. Paul (Minnesota) Police Department. Information provided specifically for this text, July 2008.

Dictionary.com. Lexico Publishing Group, 2008.

Harr, Diane. Educator and Faculty Development Coordinator for the Chaska School District, Minnesota. Information provided specifically for this text, May 2008.

Hart, Anne, and George Sheldon. *Employment Personality Tests Decoded.* Franklin Lakes, New Jersey: Career Press, 2007.

Ho, Taiping. "The Interrelationships of Psychological Testing, Psychologists' Recommendations, and Police Departments' Recruitment Decisions." *Police Quarterly*, September 2001, pp. 318–342.

Holzman, Arnold, and Mark Kirschner. "Pre-Employment Psychological Evaluations." *Law and Order*, September 2003, pp. 85–87.

International Association of Chiefs of Police. Available online at www.theiacp.org.

Landsberger, Joseph. Author and developer of *Study Guides and Strategies* website. St. Paul, MN, 2004. Available online at www.studygs.net/#tests.

Nelson, Kurt R. "A Tale of Two Cities: A Comparison of Background Investigations.*" Law and Order*, May 2000, pp. 85–88.

Rostow, Cary, and Robert Davis. "Psychological Screening." *Law and Order*, May 2002, pp. 101–106.

RECOMMENDED TEST PREPARATION BOOKS

ARCO Law Enforcement Exams, 4th ed.
by Eve P. Steinberg. ARCO, © 2000.

ARCO 24 Hours to the Law Enforcement Exams
by John Gosney.
Peterson's, © 2001

Guide to the Police Exams
by John E. Douglas.
Kaplan, © 2000

How to Prepare for the Police Officer Examination, 6th ed.
by Donald J. Schroeder and Frank A. Lombardo.
Barron's, © 2001

Police Exam Preparation Book, 2nd ed.
by Norman Hall. Adams Media Corporation, © 2003

Police Officer, 16th ed.
by Fred M. Rafilson.
ARCO, © 2003

Police Officer Exam, 2nd ed.
by Michael Spano.
LearningExpress, © 2003

Police Officer Examination Preparation Guide
by Larry F. Jetmore.
Cliff's Notes, © 1994

CHAPTER 9

ATTRIBUTES OF SUCCESSFUL CANDIDATES

It's not your aptitude, it's your attitude that determines your altitude.

—*Anonymous*

Do You Know:

➢ If a lack of law-related experiences seriously hurts your chances of obtaining employment in the fields of criminal justice or private security?
➢ What your past predicts?
➢ What past employment says about you?
➢ What the benefits are of volunteering?
➢ Where you might look to gain some work-related experience in criminal justice or security?
➢ If military experience is beneficial or detrimental to one seeking a job as a police, corrections, or security officer?
➢ What advanced education says about an applicant?
➢ The importance of communication skills?
➢ What the benefits are of internships?
➢ How you should handle past mistakes when applying for a new job?
➢ What role ethics plays in law enforcement and security?

INTRODUCTION

 Imagine yourself as an employer responsible for selecting the best candidate from a number of applicants. What criteria would you use to make this decision, which is sure to have important consequences? What positive attributes or characteristics would you, as an employer, look for? List these in your journal.

 What negative attributes would influence you not to hire a candidate? Again, write them down in your journal.

Employers are not just selecting employees; they are selecting people who will often directly influence other people's lives and who will also be representing their department or agency.

Police officers routinely deal with the most private business of the public for whom they work. Officers bandage wounds, intervene in disputes, guard property, search homes and offices, and educate children. Officers may bring victims back to life or have to watch them die. They uphold the law, which not only benefits the public, but also holds the guilty responsible by drawing them into the criminal justice system in a way that will alter those defendants' lives forever. Being a police officer is an awesome responsibility.

Correctional officers perform a vital function in guarding those sentenced to any of the variety of corrections facilities throughout our country. They deal with our nation's offenders daily and have the power to make positive changes in inmates' lives. Correctional officers are also tasked with protecting society from these offenders by making sure those they are guarding do not escape. Some correctional positions involve counseling inmates whereas others consist of an armed position in a watchtower.

Security officers also have great responsibility. Most security directors have complete access to every part of a company's assets—its secrets, its property, its cash—all are literally under the protection of the security manager and the security officers. Other professionals in criminal justice and public safety fields are equally entrusted with important issues. Whether social workers, psychologists, or others in the helping professions, all employees in criminal justice are truly professionals.

Do not overlook the other professions included in this text that also require appealing résumés. Firefighters and emergency medics deal with people in their homes and workplaces when they are most vulnerable, and emergency managers have not only individuals but entire communities relying on them.

What criteria are used when hiring criminal justice and security personnel? These criteria range from how you present yourself to who you really are.

HOW DO YOU APPEAR ON PAPER?

Impressions are important. Initial contacts, résumés, and follow-ups are critical. Employers will look at both what you have done and how you have done it. If you are determined to get the job, take control of your future by establishing a solid background of knowledge and experience. Many opportunities are available to acquire those attributes employers seek in candidates.

PERSONAL ATTRIBUTES

What kind of background will help you get that entry-level job? Recognize that employers are often as interested in non-law-related experience and attributes as they are in law-related ones.

Most employers are more interested in the type of a person you are than in what you know about law enforcement, corrections, or security work, especially for entry-level positions. A more general background helps anyone broaden their perspective of the world. Those doing the hiring want to know how you can relate your past experience to law enforcement, even if all you've done is flip burgers. Did you deal with the public? Did you have to solve problems? Did you do public relations? Did you have to communicate with people? These things will help the candidate get the job even if there has been no police experience.

Many candidates have difficulty recognizing the positive traits implied by past jobs. For example, the student who has worked for the same grocery store for three years but is now managing it while the owner is away, making the bank deposits, handling stock and supply issues, opening and closing—these tasks demonstrate not only responsibility and the capacity to work independently without supervision but also the respect in which he or she is held by the employer. Similarly, some students are embarrassed by their experience as bartenders and are reluctant to mention this part of their work history to a prospective employer. However, such students are failing to recognize that these jobs require the ability to handle unruly customers and demonstrate the applicant's ability to handle aggression and respond well under pressure—some of the same traits required of law enforcement officers, correctional officers, and security professionals.

A lack of law-related experience by no means disqualifies you as a candidate for work in criminal justice or security. In fact, most employers are more interested in the type of a person you are than in what you know about law enforcement, corrections, or security work.

Perry et al. (2003, p. 31) contend: "The factors that can be responsible for an officer's ultimate success or failure at a department can be identified most helpfully at the pre-employment stage." Indeed, as Mahoney (2001, p. 194) observes:

> For recruitment to be successful, law enforcement agencies must parse out those critical characteristics that cannot be trained from those characteristics that can. Then they must focus employment-screening procedures on accurately and reliably measuring those "cannot train" features. Two attributes often linked to successful performance in rapidly changing high-risk situations [such as those found in police work] are fluid intelligence and the ability to stay task-focused under stress.

Law enforcement agencies also screen recruits for a variety of other characteristics linked to successful performance as an officer, including "general cognitive ability; the ability to reason in novel, unfamiliar situations; the ability to apply knowledge and skills acquired through formal training to current problems; the effects of distractibility on memory; the capacity to focus attention under stress; and the ability to read the emotions of others through voice tone and body language" (Mahoney, p. 194). This final attribute, the ability to "read" a suspect, is what Pinizzotto et al. (2004, pp. 5–6) call *intuitive policing*:

> Since the first law enforcement officers accepted the responsibility of protecting their communities, accurately recognizing which individuals pose a threat to the safety and security of those jurisdictions has challenged all who belong to the profession. . . .

Intuitive policing represents a decision-making process that officers use frequently . . . [whereby] officers observe actions and behaviors exhibited by criminals that send danger signals to them that they react to before becoming consciously aware of these warnings. Such "gut feelings" or "intuitions" have saved many lives, not only those of innocent citizens but officers as well.

Results of various studies indicate show that the most powerful predictor of job success across a range of occupations is cognitive ability: "The ability to exercise sound judgment is particularly important in the field of law enforcement, as the problems faced by officers on the job are often challenging and ambiguous" (Perry et al., p. 31). In addition: "Officers' success and their safety depend in large measure on their ability to assert themselves and to take action that is appropriate to the circumstances at hand" (p. 33). Furthermore (p. 37):

> Although many dimensions are important to consider in hiring law enforcement officers, it is most crucial, according to our research, that departments employ individuals who meet their standards in the areas of problem-solving, assertiveness, motivation level, and openness to feedback.

Other desirable officer applicant characteristics include maturity, openness, flexibility, cheerfulness, judgment, congeniality, the ability to handle social situations, the ability to deal with people at their worst, and tolerance for other opinions. These same characteristics are vital if you're considering a career in corrections or private security. These traits are not genetic; they're learned. The more general life experiences you have, the better your chance of acquiring these traits. Broad experience also helps you better understand human behavior, a valuable attribute.

Other important attributes are ego strength and anger control. Ego strength is essential and comes from having good self-esteem and a good self-valuing system. Anger control is especially important because of the nature of the work. An empathetic attitude toward those who come to your attention because they are violating the law or a company policy is highly desirable. True professionals do not take client behaviors personally. They keep emotion out of decisions that affect others' lives through intellectualization—that is, they think before they act. In addition to having the preceding characteristics, successful candidates have also performed well in the past.

A good predictor of how candidates will perform in the future is how they performed in the past.

Experiences that can reflect positively on a candidate include:

- ➢ Past general employment
- ➢ Volunteer community experience
- ➢ Work-related experience
- ➢ Military service
- ➢ Education and continuing education
- ➢ Communication skills and experience

- ➢ Computer, keyboarding, and word processing skills
- ➢ Interning
- ➢ Hobbies
- ➢ Sports

Past General Employment

Although some employers may be looking for specific experience, those hiring entry-level personnel are usually more interested in a person's general background. Past employment says a lot about a person. The simple fact that a person was successfully employed says that someone wanted to hire that person and that they were responsible enough to stay on the job. Keeping a job says that the person could operate on a schedule, complete assigned tasks, not take advantage of the basic trust placed in all employees, and get along with others.

It might also be said that the more remote a person's past jobs were from the position being applied for, the more favorable the experience would be viewed. Many employers would rather hire entry-level personnel and train them from the start. Also, more general backgrounds provide a broader view of the world and opportunities to have developed varied experiences.

Don't worry if the only work experience you have is flipping burgers or stocking shelves. It says you chose to work. The more and varied experiences you have, the better you'll look—at least on paper. What previous jobs say about you is important enough that career counselors frequently advise students, particularly younger ones, that it will enhance their ability to be hired if they get a responsible job for a few years. Employers, especially those in such critical fields as criminal justice and security, would prefer not to be the first employer a person has.

> Past employment, regardless of the setting, says a lot about a person, such as the person was responsible enough to stay on the job, could operate on a schedule, complete assigned tasks, not take advantage of the basic trust placed in all employees, and get along with others.

Volunteer Community Service

Volunteering speaks highly of the way we view our neighbors, reaching out to help when needed. Those who give of themselves make the statement, "I am willing to help." Because a fundamental role of criminal justice and security professionals is interacting with and helping people, any volunteer community service will reflect positively.

Many people looking for work, especially younger people, are frustrated that most employers want some experience. The dilemma: How do you get a job without experience? How do you get experience without a job? Volunteering in any way in your community is an exceptional opportunity to gain experience. Furthermore, the trend in modern professional law enforcement is to emphasize community policing. Many police agencies want to know you are able to work in the community in something other than an enforcement capacity and that you genuinely want to be a contributing community member. For example, an interviewer might ask prospective candidates, "What do you do for your community?"

> Volunteering is an exceptional opportunity to gain experience and reflects positively by telling a prospective employer you are willing to help your community.

Work-Related Experience

Although experience not directly related to your career goals has many benefits associated with it, you may be eager to become involved in your chosen field. Opportunities for such experiences are abundant and provide a strong base from which to seek employment. Explorer posts, for example, provide opportunities to combine social and learning experiences. Similar to Boy Scouts and Girl Scouts, law enforcement explorer groups have a great deal of fun while learning about the profession. Generally sponsored by a community law enforcement agency, explorers learn such skills as shooting, first aid, defensive tactics, and crime scene investigation. Good-hearted competition helps to hone these valuable skills.

Police reserve units also serve several valuable functions. Not only do such units provide backup to the paid officers in such situations as crowd control and crime scene searches, but it is yet another chance to gain experience in the field while serving the community. Participating in a reserve unit says you can work as part of a team and not abuse this association.

Volunteer and paid-on-call fire departments offer another opportunity to do more than get your feet wet (literally). Firefighting, recognized as an extraordinarily dangerous activity, demands the same attributes required of police, corrections, and security officers: a cool head, the ability to work on a team, and the ability to confront dangerous obstacles. Because police officers may answer fire calls, too, it helps to know how to respond.

Other agencies have opportunities that provide valuable experience. For example, some sheriffs' departments have special rescue squads, water patrol units, and even mounted posses—all staffed by volunteers. Some departments have opportunities available for qualified individuals to provide patrol services to supplement their paid officers. In addition, some colleges have security departments staffed by students, another excellent opportunity to acquire experience in private "policing."

Work-related experience may be gained by becoming involved in an explorer post, police reserve unit, volunteer fire department, special rescue squad, water patrol unit, or mounted posse.

Note: Do not strive exclusively for work-related experience. If the only experiences you have include police reserves, police explorers, playing in the police band, and volunteering with the police holiday food drive, you will be viewed as a candidate with a shallow experience from which to draw. Many employers will place greater emphasis on the non-police-related experiences candidates have made for themselves.

Military Service

Military service has many advantages for people considering work in security and criminal justice. First, military service provides an opportunity to enter an admirable field of work with absolutely no previous experience. It allows you to gain valuable experience while enhancing your reputation and developing maturity—not to mention drawing a paycheck. Military service is a great chance to spend some time serving your country, even if you are unsure of your final career goals. Rather than wasting the time after high school or college by drifting, you could demonstrate your ability to develop in a professional field by joining the service.

Employers recognize that law enforcement, corrections, and security are paramilitary and that successful military service is a very good indication of potential success in such civilian service. If you know early on that you seek involvement in security or criminal justice, getting into a military policing unit can give you valuable experience.

A significant benefit employers recognize from military experience is discipline because, right or wrong, some think today's young people lack discipline. Military training makes a strong statement to the hiring authority. Some employers assert that individuals having military experience combined with advanced education make excellent officers.

Military experience can benefit those seeking employment in police, corrections, or security work because it develops discipline and allows the individual to mature. However, military training may also be a detriment because civilian policing strives for a more humanistic, less authoritarian approach and reversing the military training may be difficult.

Education

Education is important—especially today. The first edition of this text stated that some agencies required college, but for most it was something to simply consider. Now education is often the deciding factor in who gets hired or promoted. Education can separate the have's from the have-not's in the world of work, both in getting a job and getting promoted.

The facts support why schooling is a good investment: "How did the U.S. become the world's largest economy? A key part of the answer is education. Some 85% of adult Americans have at least a high school degree today, up from just 25% in 1940. Similarly, 28% have a college degree, a fivefold gain over this period. Today's U.S. workforce is the most educated in the world" (*BusinessWeek*, 2005). If you haven't pursued college, chances are those you're competing against have.

If you still aren't convinced, look at the numbers: "New information from the U.S. Census Bureau reinforces the value of a college education: workers 18 and over with a bachelor's degree earn an average of $51,206 a year, while those with a high school diploma earn $27,915. Workers with an advanced degree make an average of $74,602, and those without a high school diploma average $18,734" (U.S. Dept, of Commerce, 2005). Concurring, Meyers (2006, p. D1) states: "While there's no question that the cost of college has soared, the incomes of college graduates are still staying well ahead of those who don't have four-year degrees. How far ahead? Lifetime incomes of college grads in today's dollars average nearly $300,000 more than high school graduates over a 40-year career."

The focus remains on how well our schools are preparing young adults for life in the working world. To examine this issue, in 1990 the U.S. Department of Labor formed a committee known as the Secretary's Commission on Achieving Necessary Skills, or SCANS, with the goal of encouraging a high-performance economy characterized by high-skill, high-wage employment. The Commission's first report, issued in 1991 and titled "What Work Requires of Schools," identified the need for schools to help students develop a foundation of basic academic skills, thinking skills, and personal qualities necessary to achieve competency in the workplace, as shown in Figure 9–1. More than a decade later, these fundamental skills and competencies remain the focus of SCANS, as stated on their website: "Although the commission completed its work in 1992, its findings and recommendations continue to be a valuable source of information for individuals and organizations involved in education and workforce development."

Over twenty-five years ago the National Advisory Committee on Criminal Justice Standards and Goals warned: "There are few professions today that do not require a college degree. Police, in their quest for greater professionalism, should take notice." In response to conflicting data regarding the value of higher education to officer performance, Polk and Armstrong (2001, p. 97) state:

> Although the literature review revealed that there are inconclusive findings in prior studies about whether or not increased education caused an increase in the ability of law enforcement officers to perform their duties, this study showed no ambiguity in finding agencies are responding as if there are benefits if employees are more educated. . . .

> The study demonstrated conclusively . . . that those persons who hold higher levels of education, regardless of what other traits or personality characteristics they may possess, are more likely to hold higher rank and progress more quickly through their career path.

Because work has taken on a different look over the decades, so, too, have workers, students, and education. For example: "A significant portion of those enrolled in Minnesota schools are so-called 'non-traditional students'—37 percent of students are twenty-five and older and 17 percent thirty-five and older, according to the Minnesota Office of Higher Education. What do these adult learners go on to do? Anything other grads do—careers in business, industry, education, public service, high-tech, and beyond" (Bissen, 2006, p. 144). Clearly, "student" doesn't mean what it once did, and neither does retirement. For example, New Ulm Police Chief Weinkauf returned to graduate school as part of his "retirement plan" to transition from a thirty-year career in law enforcement to pursue his new dream of becoming a college

---

WORKPLACE KNOW-HOW

The know-how identified by SCANS is made up of five competencies and a three-part foundation of skills and personal qualities that are needed for solid job performance. These include:

COMPETENCIES—effective workers can productively use:

➢ **Resources**—allocating time, money, materials, space, and staff;
➢ **Interpersonal Skills**—working on teams, teaching others, serving customers, leading, negotiating, and working well with people from culturally diverse backgrounds;
➢ **Information**—acquiring and evaluating data, organizing and maintaining files, interpreting and communicating, and using computers to process information;
➢ **Systems**—understanding social, organizational, and technological systems, monitoring and correcting performance, and designing or improving systems;
➢ **Technology**—selecting equipment and tools, applying technology to specific tasks, and maintaining and troubleshooting technologies.

THE FOUNDATION—competence requires:

➢ **Basic Skills**—reading, writing, arithmetic and mathematics, speaking, and listening;
➢ **Thinking Skills**—thinking creatively, making decisions, solving problems, seeing things in the mind's eye, knowing how to learn, and reasoning;
➢ **Personal Qualities**—individual responsibility, self-esteem, sociability, self-management, and integrity.

FIGURE 9–1 SCANS Skills

SOURCE: The Secretary's Commission on Achieving Necessary Skills. "What Work Requires of Schools: A SCANS Report for America 2000." Washington, DC: U.S. Department of Labor, June 1991, p. iii. Accessed online at http://wdr.doleta.gov/SCANS/whatwork/whatwork.pdf.

professor, saying: "Retire? Why would I want to retire when there is so much more living to do, satisfying work to pursue and contributions to make? I've learned the value of being a life-long learner, maybe even more so when I went back to school at age 54. I never plan to stop learning, and my new career goal is to help others feel this way about education as well."

Weekend, evening, and online classes continue to make education more accessible to everyone, especially those who thought they couldn't return to school once their commitments included family, work, and the odd working hours that go along with jobs discussed in this book. Do not assume "different" means "less"; on the contrary, new approaches can be even better for adult learners. Online education allows access to programs people may never be able to drive to or attend face-to-face because of personal and work conflicts. Wise consumers of education explore various options, speak to students who have experienced that particular program, consider whether the school is regionally accredited, and if there is a philosophy of education that will fit for them.

Education says something about those who obtain it. It says the person can identify, pursue, and accomplish important goals; shows patience, drive, and self-determination; and shows the ability to commit to both short- and long-range goals. It also says those seeking education are interested in both themselves and the world in which they live. Education does make you view the world differently. Education expands horizons, helping you better understand the differences that make our diverse society not a threat, but a challenge.

> Advanced education is valuable to anyone seeking employment in criminal justice or private security not only because of the actual knowledge gained but also because of what pursuing such education says about you to a prospective employer—that you can identify, pursue, and accomplish important goals; that you have patience, drive, and self-determination; that you possess the ability to commit to both short- and long-range goals and that you are interested in both yourself and the world in which you live.

An increasing number of agencies require either a college degree or some college credits. Legal barriers no longer stand in the way of police departments requiring college education. In *Davis v. Dallas* (1986), a U.S. Court of Appeals upheld a requirement by the city of Dallas that entry-level police recruits have completed forty-five college credits with a C average.

You should keep a personal training log or journal documenting any training or educational programs in which you participate. Such a journal may be useful in preparing your résumé or in answering any questions prospective employers may ask about your training and/or education.

Continuing Education. Educators and learners now emphasize lifelong learning rather than just obtaining a degree. As with other professions, law enforcement and other careers in criminal justice are requiring their personnel keep up-to-date with the latest practices and technology through continuing education. Getting that diploma may be a great first step to the career of your dreams, but be prepared to continue learning throughout your careers.

Can You Be Overeducated? In all honesty, the answer might be "yes," at least in some employers' eyes—particularly for employers who may have achieved their position in the more traditional way of coming "up through the ranks" and at a time when higher education was considered less important for officers' career development than it is today. They may not regard advanced education as a necessary or desirable attribute. Some might see it as an outright threat to them. Although it is not as much a problem as it might have been once, candidates with a master's degree, for example, will want to be prepared to answer any similar questions to "Why did you pursue your education at the graduate level?" Those holding law degrees, PhDs, or other doctoral-level degrees will undoubtedly be asked about this, especially those applying for an entry-level position. You will have no difficulty pointing out the benefits the degree will have for the department if you are hired, but hiring authorities may have a legitimate concern whether you will be bored at the job you are applying for. Even if not asked directly, you will want to address this because they are probably, albeit silently, wondering about it.

Communication Skills and Experience

Communication skills are critical for public and private officers, for they communicate orally and in writing every day. Effective communication skills play an important part in getting the job, getting promoted, and, of course, doing the job.

Writing skills are especially important because once something is in writing, it is *permanent*; so are spoken words preserved in writing. Any written document becomes a testament to what was asserted; in the legal world it can become the means by which officers refresh their memories or even serve as evidence itself. It also says a great deal about the person doing the writing. Either by a chief striving to determine the best candidate or a jury wondering who to believe, how people write speaks volumes about how they are perceived. It can mean the difference between getting a job or not; or getting a conviction or not. Writing skills *are* that important. If you feel yours are lacking, improve by studying on your own or taking a class, but don't assume you can fake it. You can't.

Communication skills—oral and written—are critically important for public and private officers and may determine how far you will advance in your career.

Computer, Keyboarding, and Word-Processing Skills

The first edition of this book didn't address keyboarding or computer skills. It suggested readers might be thinking, "I'm not applying for a secretarial job. Why do I need to know how to keyboard?" Today, the majority of our readers can readily answer that question. For those who don't know why, take a class to gain basic computer skills now. If you don't, you'll find yourselves in the "no" pile of applicants.

A caution regarding the accuracy of spelling in reports and an overreliance on computer spell-check functions: Although spell-checkers are great, they do not guarantee error-free reports. Consider the following examples—all of which would get past a spell-check:

➢   He was arrested for a mister meaner.

➢   She was an admitted drug attic.

➢   The series of homicides is most likely the work of a cereal killer.

Interning

A great way to break into the real world of work while still learning is through interning. Internships were discussed in depth as the focus of Chapter 6 but are worth mentioning again, as many criminal justice programs across the nation are implementing internship programs and courses to help prepare their students for future careers.

Interning is seldom a requirement for a job and typically serves less experienced job seekers better than those who already have a responsible position, even if it is not in a criminal justice–related field. However, more and more agencies use their interns as a pool from which to consider actual job applicants. If an agency draws solely from its entry-level agency pool of candidates, then you may want to consider an internship. Research into the agency will help you decide whether interning will be of benefit.

Internships provide a unique opportunity to look into a field to determine if it's the right profession for you while allowing you to gain some valuable experience.

Hobbies and Sports: A Life Outside of Work

Appealing candidates for criminal justice jobs have come a long way from when military experience meant a good candidate was able to shoot and take orders. Today's candidates are expected to have balanced lives, including work, home, and self. Too much of anything isn't good, so chronic workaholics are not viewed favorably; people with balanced lives are.

Stable relationships with family and friends, community involvement, and fun, yes fun, all help paint a picture of healthy, happy people who make good employees. Being able to answer the question, "What do you like to do to relax or have fun?" shouldn't be one that catches you off-guard or result in the response, "Umm, I guess I don't really do anything for fun."

What you do with family and friends, and by yourself, also says something about you. Whether team sports or personal fitness, church or community activities, interest groups, or collecting on your own, employers know the benefits of a balanced life. If you really don't have anything you can tell about how you have fun and relax, now is the time to not only ask why you don't, but to develop some interests.

PAINTING A PICTURE

Consider your job application, in all respects, as a painting—a unique painting. It is not going to be like that of anyone else. Yours will be made up of the experiences developed for yourself and will have aspects others do not. You will have strengths where others have weaknesses, and there will be areas where you are building skills and improving. There may even be areas you have to clarify or explain to the person viewing it. Yet everything you have done and are doing will contribute to this picture that is uniquely you.

 What experiences do you have that make a statement, and what do they say about you? Write them in your journal.

MAKING THE BEST OF BAD SITUATIONS

How many people can honestly say they have absolutely no blemishes on their records? If you're like most people, you learn more by making mistakes than by doing it right the first time. Did you really believe your mother when she said the stove was hot? Honestly? Or did you have to see for yourself?

Dale Carnegie, famous for his courses on personal and business self-improvement, said: "When fate hands us a lemon, let's try to make lemonade." However you say it, if you have made a mistake—which everyone has—it does not mean you have forfeited your future in security or criminal justice. Granted, some mistakes will bar you from certain positions in these fields. For example, no state will permit you to be a police officer if you have a felony on your record. They may, however, allow a misdemeanor or traffic offense.

Know in advance how you will deal with past mistakes, and accept that they do not automatically make you an outcast from society or from your chosen profession. Most professions accept mistakes, but they do not accept people who cannot change their ways, nor do they accept dishonesty. Lying on an application says nothing less than that you can't be trusted; it may even be a crime.

How do you deal with blemishes such as traffic citations or misdemeanor criminal charges? Approach them up front and honestly. Since the best defense is often a good offense, you will usually want to confront these issues head-on. It looks better if you bring them up rather than having the employer find out about them during the background check. If they dredge up one questionable issue from your past, they may wonder what else may be hidden.

Once you have admitted you made a mistake (or two, or three), take it one step further. Share what you learned from the experience. If you have a less-than-perfect traffic record or a shoplifting charge from your youth, it would sound better to explain how that experience influenced you to want to become a police officer or a security officer. Consider how a hiring board would react when told you were so influenced by the professionalism shown by the police officer who gave you that ticket that you wanted to become a police officer and positively influence others in the same way. What about a DWI conviction? Rather than eliminating you from the running, it could result in your taking subsequent steps to get your life together. To admit any shortcoming and prove you took advantage of an opportunity to grow and change does not make you an undesirable person; it makes you exceptional.

Imagine, for example, that you had a questionable driving record and were in competition with one other applicant. Other than the driving record, you have identical attributes. Would the hiring board use your driving record to decide against you? Or maybe even for you? They might if you accept that you are what you are. Present yourself in the best light—honestly. Although you might have made some admittedly questionable decisions in the past, you want them to fully understand that that was then and you learned from it. To do otherwise makes you look, at best, on the defensive and, at worst, a liar.

Judge for yourself—which sounds best in response to an interviewer's question: "How is your driving record?"

> **Candidate #1.** Fine. (If this is true, great. But it will take about ten seconds to verify this on the computer. If you lied, you're out.)

> **Candidate #2.** Well, I've had a few tickets. But I was only a kid, and the cops in my town had it in for me because of that. I think they just had to meet their quotas and it was easier to do by picking on us kids.

> **Candidate #3.** As a matter of fact, I got some traffic tickets when I was a teenager. I can't say I didn't deserve them because I did. I learned about obeying traffic regulations the hard way— having to work summer jobs to pay for the tickets and the increased car insurance premiums. But it taught me a valuable lesson. I was accountable for my actions. It wasn't the fault of the officers who gave me the tickets or my parents for not picking up the tab. It was my own fault. It worked for me. This is one reason I want to be a police officer—to help others learn.

You get the picture. Consider another situation, this time with candidates responding to an interviewer's question: "Have you ever been intoxicated?"

> **Candidate #1.** No. I would never do something like that. (Again, if this is true, great. But if the background investigation proves you to be a liar, you are out.)

Candidate #2. Well, I did drink underage a couple times, once to excess. It was a mistake. I told my parents and I paid the consequences and had to earn back the respect of my parents. I learned a valuable lesson about peer pressure and who is in control of my life.

Although some mistakes will bar you from certain positions in these fields, most employers accept mistakes if you are open and up front about them during the preemployment interview, share what you learned from the experience and express honestly how you have changed your ways.

This is not to suggest you will be able to justify or "explain away" every indiscretion in your background. For example, a pattern of alcohol-related problems or financial difficulties are sure to concern those considering your application. Having chronic problems or an abundance of unresolved issues may well eliminate you from consideration. You must be realistic in this area, particularly if it continues happening as you apply for positions.

ETHICS

Ethics has become a requisite for every profession. This is certainly the case for criminal justice and related professions that have the power and temptations they do. You can anticipate having to deal with this issue. In fact, ethics is a favorite topic of interview boards, so carefully consider your values and what you believe ethical behavior is: "Ethics concerns right and wrong, moral duty and responsibility, and personal character" (Meese and Ortmeier, 2004, p. 62). It's having learned right from wrong and what's appropriate in certain circumstances, both social and professional. There's no question people in criminal justice and related fields are, and should be, held to a higher standard because of their circumstances. It's what the public expects, and what employers should demand.

Albanese (2008, p. xiv) says: "The most important life skill of all is often never taught; how to make decisions in the face of conflicting demands." But this is exactly what is expected of professionals working in a demanding, often conflicting, circumstances. Albanese defines critical thinking as "the ability to evaluate viewpoints, facts, and behaviors objectively to assess the presentation of information or methods of argumentation to establish the true worth or merit of an act or course of conduct." This definition is fundamental to ethical behavior because it's what enables people to know what's right and wrong.

An excellent strategy to prepare for the probability of being asked about ethics is to read any of the books dealing with criminal justice ethics.

The ethics of police, corrections, and security officers play a large role in whether these fields are viewed as true professions. In fact, ethics is a favorite topic of interview boards, so you should thoughtfully consider your values and what you consider ethical behavior.

The International Association of Chiefs of Police (IACP) has also developed a Police Code of Conduct that covers primary responsibilities of a police officer, performance of the duties of a police officer, discretion, use of force, confidentiality, integrity, cooperation with other officers and agencies, personal/professional capabilities, and private life. (See Appendix A for the entire IACP Police Code of Conduct.) The security profession has also developed a similar code of ethics, presented in Appendix B. The IACP has recommended a Law Enforcement Oath of Honor as a symbolic statement to ethical behavior (www.theiacp.org):

On my honor,
I will never betray my profession,
my integrity, my character,
or the public trust.
I will always have
the courage to hold myself
and others accountable for our actions.
I will always uphold the laws of my country,
my community and the agency I serve.

To develop and maintain a professional reputation, codes of ethics have been adopted in both law enforcement and private security. The Law Enforcement Code of Ethics is shown in Figure 9–2.

As a law enforcement officer, my fundamental duty is to serve the community; to safeguard lives and property; to protect the innocent against deception, the weak against oppression or intimidation, and the peaceful against violence or disorder; and to respect the constitutional rights of all to liberty, equality and justice.

I will keep my private life unsullied as an example to all and will behave in a manner that does not bring discredit to me or my agency. I will maintain courageous calm in the face of danger, scorn or ridicule; develop self-restraint; and be constantly mindful of the welfare of others. Honest in thought and deed both in my personal and official life, I will be exemplary in obeying the law and the regulations of my department. Whatever I see or hear of a confidential nature or that is confided to me in my official capacity will be kept ever secret unless revelation is necessary in the performance of my duty.

I will never act officiously or permit personal feelings, prejudices, political beliefs, aspirations, animosities or friendships to influence my decisions. With no compromise for crime and with relentless prosecution of criminals, I will enforce the law courteously and appropriately without fear or favor, malice or ill will, never employing unnecessary force or violence and never accepting gratuities.

I recognize the badge of my office as a symbol of public faith, and I accept it as a public trust to be held so long as I am true to the ethics of the police service. I will never engage in acts of corruption or bribery, nor will I condone such acts by other police officers. I will cooperate with all legally authorized agencies and their representatives in the pursuit of justice.

I know that I alone am responsible for my own standard of professional performance and will take every reasonable opportunity to enhance and improve my level of knowledge and competence.

I will constantly strive to achieve these objectives and ideals, dedicating myself before God to my chosen profession . . . law enforcement.

FIGURE 9–2 Law Enforcement Code of Ethics

SOURCE: Reprinted with permission from the International Association of Chiefs of Police, Alexandria, Virginia. Further reproduction without express written permission from IACP is strictly prohibited.

Values

To a potential employer, a person's values say a great deal about who they are and what kind of employee they will prove to be. Values are more than just having ethics or a positive background. Values define what is important to an individual. In fact, many consider one's values the best overall statement of who they really are. For example, the core values of the Minnesota State Patrol, which their cadets learn, are the essence of this organization. They provide a strong basis for the group and for the individual.

The mission of the Minnesota State Patrol is
working together to ensure a safe environment
on Minnesota's roadways.

The Minnesota State Patrol has adopted
the following core values as part of its training curriculum:

Core Values

Respect
Integrity
Courage
Honor

As an organization has basic values, written or unwritten, so does every individual. The picture you paint of yourself will reflect the values you hold to be important. Obviously, your values will make an impression on a prospective employer.

CONCLUSION

Your life is like a painting, continuously worked on. It will be developed, refined, altered, and improved. It is never completed. Although the canvas may occasionally be set aside briefly, the paint is never completely dried—unless allowed. At every phase of your life, you will appear to others as you have developed yourself. How will you appear to prospective employers? What can you add to your "life's painting" to be as appealing as possible? If you need more substance to your picture, get it. You have the control and the opportunity. Do you have the ambition and foresight?

AN INSIDER'S VIEW

GETTING YOUR FOOT IN THE DOOR

Michael P. Stein

Former Chief of Police
Escondido (California) Police Department

In California it is estimated that only one applicant out of 100 successfully competes for a police officer position, from the initial application to the final interview. As overwhelming as those odds are, some strategies can help you be that one in 100.

As departments go to community policing, the requirements for police officers are changing from the traditional enforcement role to one of community activism and facilitation. Police agencies are looking for candidates with experience in problem solving and working with various community elements. The successful candidate is one who has work experience with community agencies that aim to solve problems for the community good. Think about volunteering at your local Boys' and Girls' Clubs, your local school district or any other social agency in the community. This will give you hands-on experience in working with others and being a "team player."

It is never too early to begin planning to compete for that police officer position. When I was finishing high school, I knew that I wanted to join the police profession, but really didn't know how to go about it. After four years in the military, I was able to compete with just a high-school diploma. This is no longer the case. Now an applicant will be competing with many who are currently working toward a degree at the community college level and many others who may have a bachelor's degree.

Our department has recognized the need for better-educated applicants, even at the high-school level. In cooperation with the local high-school district, we have started a program called the "Code 3 Academy," where police officers present classes, lectures, field trips and physical training to students interested in preparing for a law enforcement career. Students learn based on what is being taught at local police academies. English classes include studies in report writing, computer keyboarding, powers of observation and exercises in written and verbal communication with their peer group and members of other cultures. The program gives students an opportunity to form a mentorship with police professionals who can assist them in their future law enforcement career goals. Another opportunity for high-school students is to join their local police department's Explorer Program. This gives the student the ability to see what police work is really about.

Any position that gets your foot in the door of a police agency is beneficial. Does your local department need volunteers? Does it have a police auxiliary or a reserve program? Establishing this type of personal relationship with a local department is one key thing you can do to increase the odds of being selected.

Once a year, our department holds a special recruitment for police officer trainee positions, when any of our active reserve officers can compete. The number then falls from one in 100 to something like one in 15 for a position. In the last 35 years, 49 of our reserve officers have been selected as police officer trainees with our department, and many others have been hired by other law enforcement agencies.

Does your local police academy allow you to attend without a department affiliation? In California a student can put himself/herself through any police academy in the state. Once you have your certificate of graduation from an academy, you then compete with only other academy graduates, not the at-large public. All departments are looking for experienced or previously trained candidates, and this is a real advantage as you compete for a position.

When applying for a police officer position, ask if any other positions are currently being recruited for in the department, such as community service officer, traffic control officer, dispatcher, etc. These are positions where the competition must not be as stringent as for a police officer, but, if hired, this gives you an opportunity to show your work ethic to the department as you compete later for a police officer position. In our department, nine former community service officers now serve as police officers.

Does the agency that you aspire to join serve a large population of non-English speakers? In many southern border states, because of the influx of monolingual Spanish speakers, being bilingual in Spanish and English is an asset all police departments desire. Many departments do bilingual Spanish recruitments where applicants need to be proficient in both languages to apply. This lowers the overall number of applicants, but again increases the chances of those who have this skill to be successfully recruited. The other benefit of these recruitments is that they allow the departments to be more reflective of the newly diverse communities they serve.

The preceding recommendations used individually or collectively will enhance your ability to secure a law enforcement position. Best of luck!

Michael P. Stein *rose through the ranks of the Escondido (California) Police Department to become the chief of police. Now retired, he has thirty-six years' experience in law enforcement, holds a bachelor's degree in Public Administration, and a master's degree in Human Behavior. Chief Stein is a graduate of the 129th Session of the FBI National Academy and is currently an adjunct professor at Palomar Community College in San Marcos, California.*

 MIND STRETCHES

1. Do you believe your past is an accurate assessment of your employment potential?

2. Who would be a better risk as an employee: candidates who tested the system as juveniles, occasionally having run-ins with the law, or candidates who walked the "straight and narrow," never doing anything wrong, but also never testing their own limitations?

3. What are important benefits of attending college?

4. What volunteer opportunities exist in your community?

5. What do good writing skills say about you? How can you develop them?

6. Name five important attributes an employer might seek from applicants, regardless of the job. How can you develop these attributes?

7. Why is ethics of particular importance to criminal justice and private security?

8. As you look at your past, are there facts that could hurt you as a job applicant? How will you address them to put them in the most positive light?

9. What are your personal and professional strengths?

10. Is it possible to be overqualified? Why or why not?

REFERENCES

Albanese, Jay S. *Professional Ethics in Criminal Justice.* Boston, MA: Pearson Education, 2008.

Bissen, Joe. "College the Second Time Around." *Mpls St. Paul*, August 2006, pp. 140–154.

BusinessWeek. November 2005. Available online at www.businessweek.com/magazine/content/05_47/b3960108.htm.

Mahoney, Mark. "Law Enforcement Recruiting Software." *Law Enforcement Technology*, October 2001, pp. 194–199.

Meese, Edwin, III, and P. J. Ortmeier. *Leadership, Ethics, and Policing: Challenges for the 21st Century.* Upper Saddle River, NJ: Pearson Education, 2004.

Meyers, Mike. "It's Still Worth It." (Minneapolis/St.Paul) *Star Tribune,* June 18, 2006, p. D1.

Perry, Julia N., Mark Scullard, and Norma DiLorenzo. "Are They Up to the Job?" *Minnesota Police Chief*, Spring 2003, pp. 31–37.

Pinizzotto, Anthony J., Edward F. Davis, and Charles E. Miller, III. "Intuitive Policing: Emotional/Rational Decision Making in Law Enforcement." *FBI Law Enforcement Bulletin*, February 2004, pp. 1–6.

Polk, O. Elmer, and David A. Armstrong. "Higher Education and Law Enforcement Career Paths: Is the Road to Success Paved by Degree?" *Journal of Criminal Justice Education*, Spring 2001, pp. 77–99.

Secretary's Commission on Achieving Necessary Skills (SCANS). U.S. Department of Labor, 1991. Available online at http:// wdr.doleta.gov/ SCANS/whatwork/whatwork.pdf.

U.S. Dept. of Commerce News Release. March 2005. Available online at www.census.gov/Press-Release/www/releases/archives/ education/004214.html.

CHAPTER 10

THE RÉSUMÉ: SELLING YOURSELF ON PAPER

Writing a Résumé: Spend time on self-assessment first. Identify all the achievements of your past that illustrate skills. Describe them in active verbs and look for consistencies. That's the clue as to what you should emphasize. A résumé is scanned, not read. It's a sales tool that should give someone a sampling, not details in full.

—*Jean Clarkson*

Do You Know:

➢ What a résumé is?
➢ What purposes a résumé serves?
➢ What seven steps are involved in creating a résumé?
➢ What items to include in your résumé?
➢ What is best left off your résumé?
➢ What three basic types of résumés are commonly used and how they differ?
➢ What is important about the format of your résumé?
➢ What the key is to writing an effective résumé?
➢ What to keep in mind when printing your résumé?
➢ When to send a cover letter and what elements are essential?
➢ The best way to deliver your résumé and what to do after the delivery?

INTRODUCTION

You've spent a lot of time thinking about your goals and yourself, your fitness, education, and attributes. Now it's time to pull all this information together into one of your most important job-seeking tools—the résumé.

Résumé is a French word (pronounced *REZ-oo-may*) that means "summary." Like so many other parts of the job-search process there is more to résumés than many realize. This chapter provides you a working knowledge of the résumé.

WHAT IS A RÉSUMÉ?

Webster's defines *résumé* as: "A short account of one's career and qualifications prepared typically by an applicant for a position." Résumé guru Yana Parker (www.damngood.com) offers a more dynamic definition: "A résumé is a self-promotional document that presents you in the best possible light, for the purpose of getting invited to a job interview. It's *not* an official personnel document. It's not a job application. It's not a 'career obituary'! And it's not a confessional." But it can help get to the next step of the process or keep you out. There's a saying "you only get one chance to make a first impression"; this is particularly challenging when it is on paper (or electronically).

A résumé is a brief, well-documented summary of your education, abilities, skills, experience, and career achievements, which highlights significant aspects of your background and identifies your qualifications for a given job. It is a promotional tool designed to sell you to a prospective employer.

And the sales pitch must work quickly. The *Land That Job!* website (www.landjob.com) states: "Your resumes and resume cover letters can be reviewed and rejected in as little as 5 seconds! Both must communicate your qualifications at a glance." According to *Resume.com*: "The hiring manager will eliminate your resume in less than 10 seconds if it's not the very best in the stack." *Resume Logic* (www.resumelogic.com/index.htm) echoes: "Most staffing managers and recruiters (headhunters) scan and discard each resume in 10 to 15 seconds unless the resume provides them with a compelling reason to flag it for an in-depth review."

PURPOSES OF THE RÉSUMÉ

Krannich (2007, p. 53) contends: "Resumes and letters don't get jobs—they advertise you for job interviews. Writing and distributing resumes lie at the heart of any job search. When done right…a powerful resume and letter clearly communicate what you have done, can do and will do for the future employer."

The résumé serves both the employer and prospective employee. The résumé is important to the employer because it helps weed out unqualified candidates. Employers will use any flaw in a résumé to cut down the number of individuals to be interviewed. Résumés help employers cut through a lot of preliminary questioning about applicants' qualifications and help employers structure their interviews.

The résumé is important to you because it can help get you in the door for an interview. In fact, Barthel and Goldrick-Jones (www.rpi.edu/web/writingcenter/resume.html) assert: "A resume has one purpose: to get you a job interview." Preparing or updating your résumé will also provide the opportunity to consider your skills, qualifications, past experiences, and accomplishments *right now*. If more than six months have passed since you last updated your résumé, you've changed, so too should your résumé. Critically reviewing and updating your résumé will also help you be more prepared and confident for interviews.

Résumés serve a variety of purposes for both the employer and the applicant. A résumé helps an employer by weeding out unqualified candidates, answering preliminary questions about an applicant's qualifications, and structuring an interview. A résumé helps applicants obtain interviews and organizes their experiences, accomplishments, present skills, and qualifications so they may be coherently discussed during an interview.

STEPS IN CREATING A RÉSUMÉ

Creating a résumé is like painting a picture of yourself. From the conception of the idea to the completion of the masterpiece, you need to take seven specific steps.

The seven specific steps to creating a résumé are:

1. Compile all relevant information.
2. Select the most appropriate type of résumé.
3. Select a format.
4. Write the first draft.

5. Polish the first draft.
6. Evaluate the résumé and revise if necessary.
7. Print the résumé.

Creating an effective résumé is time-consuming, hard work, but the results will be well worth it. Without an effective résumé, you are wasting your time applying for most jobs. Even if an agency does not require a résumé, they will expect you to be a "living résumé" at the interview. Get yourself organized before that. Make up your mind to devote several hours to this important document if you haven't created one before, and commit to keeping it current.

COMPILE INFORMATION

Gather all the information that could possibly be included in your résumé. Some will be used; some won't. Painters gather all of their brushes and paints before beginning to work so they aren't interrupted during the creative process. Likewise, you will want to gather all the information you *might* decide to include. You don't want to interrupt the creative writing flow to look up a phone number or address.

 Use the worksheets in Appendix C to organize your résumé information. Flip to the back of the book and place a paper clip at the top of Appendix C to help you locate it quickly while working through this section. Don't cut corners during this first step. Your background makes a great deal of difference. As you compile information, you may be amazed at how much data an employer will need to even consider you.

You'll look at three kinds of information: (1) data you must include, (2) data you might include, and (3) data you should probably not include but should be prepared to discuss. Don't guess at dates; verify them. Don't guess at addresses; check them out if it's been a while since you worked or lived somewhere.

Look first at what *must* be included: personal identifying information, educational background, and work experience.

Personal Identifying Information

Name. Obvious? Yes. But believe it or not, some people actually forget to include their name. In addition, think carefully about how you want your name to appear. Do you want to include your middle name? An initial? A nickname? A title? If you include a nickname, place it following your first name with quotation marks around it, like this: *Robert "Bob" T. Jones.* This lets the employer know what you prefer to be called. Avoid extreme or inappropriate nicknames such as "Killer." Parker advises: "Don't mystify the reader about your gender; they'll go nuts until they know whether you're male or female. So if your name is Lee or Robin or Pat or anything else not clearly male or female, use a Mr. or Ms. prefix."

 How do you want your name to appear on your résumé? Write it on the worksheet.

Address.   It is usually best to give only your home address. Put the street address on one line and do not abbreviate. Put a comma between the street address and apartment number. Put the city and state on the next line and separate them with a comma. Use the two-letter state abbreviation—both letters capitalized and *no* period. Include your zip code, but do not put a comma between the state and zip code.

Example: 123 Third Avenue South, #401
             My Town, MN 55437

 How should your address appear? Write it on the worksheet.

 If you move frequently, you may want to include a permanent address in addition to your present address.

E-mail address: E-mail is no longer a luxury—it is how most businesses now communicate. If you don't have an e-mail address, get one because (1) it makes it easier for prospective employers to contact you and (2) to not have one reflects negatively on your technological skills. Make sure your e-mail address is appropriate. Your name, city, or something innocuous is acceptable; anything silly, immature, or inappropriate, isn't. Unless you are an officer or in the business, avoid e-mail addresses that make you look like a wannabe. Once an officer, few feel the need to advertise it. Stay away from things like copmike@ or deputydawg@. Remember to check your e-mail daily.

Phone Number.   Always include a phone number. Some employers prefer to call rather than write; make it easy for them. Indicate if it is a home, work, or cell number. Many people prefer to not include a work phone to avoid being called at work. Would getting job-search–related phone calls at work cause you any problems? If so, do *not* include your work number. Some people also include the hours they can be reached at a given number. Others put this information in their cover letter.

Example: Work Phone   612-555-9929 (9 A.M. to 5 P.M.)
             Home Phone   612-555-8818 (6 P.M. to 10 P.M.)
             Cell Phone   612-555-2222 (9 A.M. to 10 P.M.)

 Enter your phone number(s) on the appropriate line on the worksheet.

Make sure your home, office, and cell phone messages state they are for you and are not inappropriate. "You know what to do, so do it," as a message doesn't reflect well on you, nor does opening your message with inappropriate music. Just go with, "You have reached the voice mail box for Mary Smith; please leave a message and I'll return the call as soon as possible." (We once called a prospective candidate for an entry-level police job and got the answering machine with the theme music from Dragnet playing in the background and the message: "This is soon-to-be Officer Smith, assume the position and leave a message…or I'll be forced to kick your ass and take your name." We did not leave him a message.)

Answer any phone for which you've left the number every single time, assuming it's a prospective employer. Murphy 's Law dictates that if you think it's a friend and answer with something goofy, it will be the chief following up on your application. Answering with immature, unprofessional, trite phrases like, "Talk to me," or "Yeah?" does not impress; in fact, just the opposite. "Good afternoon, this is Mary Smith." Common sense, right? You'd be surprised.

Did you know there was so much to think about in simply giving your name, address, and phone number?

Education

Information about your education is crucial to your résumé.

 College. List each college attended, city and state, number of years completed, major/minor, unique areas of study, and degree(s) earned. Start with the most recent and work backward. Include any honors, awards, or leadership positions; include your grade point average if it's outstanding.

 Professional Schools. Include the same information as for colleges and include academies here also.

 Internships. Include the place and length of the internship.

 Certificates. Relevant certificates would include first aid, CPR, and the like. Give the year the certificates were awarded and expiration dates, if relevant.

 Other Educational Experiences. Include any relevant seminars, workshops, correspondence courses, and the like.

 High School. Include name, city and state, year of graduation, and grade point average if it is outstanding. Include your high school only if you graduated within the last ten years or if you have no other education to include.

Work Experience

Recall from Chapter 9 that past general employment of any type is valuable in the job search, even if not related to your field. Volunteer experience, work related or not, should also be included on your résumé. Of special importance are the qualifications and skills you bring to the job. You may want to refer to Chapter 9 for attributes most employers are looking for. Your résumé should stress achievements more than education and experience.

 Begin with your present job, or your most recent job if you are not currently employed, and work back in time. Use the worksheet in Appendix C. Make a copy of this worksheet for each job you have had. Use the work experience section to describe your qualities and skills wherever and however you can. If applicable, you might demonstrate these qualities and skills in the education portion of your résumé as well.

Several other areas of information might also be included in your résumé, depending on your background. Even if you decide not to include much or most of the following information, it is important for you to think about it and have it clear in your mind because it could come up during the interview.

Position Desired or Employment Objective

What specific job do you have in mind? Are you open to any position in your chosen field? This information can be very helpful to busy employers as they skim through stacks of résumés. An attractive job candidate is one who knows what he or she wants to do. In fact, to the question: "What is the most common résumé mistake made by job hunters?" Parker replies: "Leaving out their Job Objective! If you don't show a sense of direction, employers won't be interested. Having a clearly stated goal doesn't have to confine you if it's stated well."

 In Appendix C, write down the position desired and, if relevant, your employment objective. An example might be: *Position desired: Entry-level officer with opportunity to provide* _____.

 Tell what you can do for the employer—not what the employer can do for you.

Other Information

Other information that may be put on your résumé includes the following:

 Willingness to travel or relocate, military experience, professional memberships, knowledge of foreign language(s), foreign travel, awards, publications, community service or involvement, interests, and hobbies. Also, list your accomplishments and don't be modest.

 You might also want to include your availability—can you start immediately or do you need a certain amount of time to give notice to your present employer? Can your present employer be contacted?

References

If you get to the point in the hiring process where you are being considered, most employers will want to check your references.

 Choose references now and fill in that portion of the worksheet in Appendix C. Try to have business, professional, and academic references as well as personal references.

Choose your references carefully. Recall from Chapter 8 the advice on selecting references for the background check. Always ask your references if they are willing to provide you with a positive reference. Most people do not include the references in their résumés. You can simply state: "References available on request," and prepare a separate sheet of references to make available to employers who request them. This also keeps your references confidential until a request is made for them.

Photograph

Including a photograph is optional. If a photo could make you stand out in a positive light, consider it. If it might raise any questions, don't. Photos of you doing anything out of the ordinary, unusual, or strange put you in a negative light. If you aren't sure, ask someone. For example, the young police applicant providing a photo of himself holding guns in each hand with his arms crossed never got to explain it; "But I thought police like guns?"

Items to Include

> Items you *must* include in your résumé are personal identifying information (name, address, and phone number), educational experience, work experience, and your employment objectives. You might also include your willingness to travel or relocate, military experience, professional memberships, knowledge of foreign language(s), awards, publications, any community service or involvement, and your availability. You should include a statement that references are available upon request. Whether to include a photograph is debatable. Include a photograph only if it is recent, professional, and presents you in a favorable light.

What *Not* to Include

What not to include is a matter of opinion. While you will *never* lie on a résumé, you will want to present yourself so that even negative occurrences look good for you. If you have to explain them in depth during an interview, that's fine, as long as you get to the interview.

Including too much data is a major fault of many résumés. Not only does this create a document that is so long it won't get read, but you can harm yourself by saying too much. For example, do not state in a résumé why you left past jobs. Newfield (2004) warns: "'Company sold,' 'Boss was an idiot,' and 'Left to make more money' have no place on your résumé." If the reason was somewhat spectacular, for example a series of promotions, put it in, but the presumption will be that you moved upward and onward to better positions. Also, the résumé is not the place to explain difficulties you've had. It is a chance to provide a *brief* overview of yourself, to be expanded on once it has gotten you an interview. Be certain everything you include is relevant and cannot in any way detract.

Personal data is another judgment call that depends on you and the job sought. Hobbies may appeal to some readers because they reflect a balanced life, but may appear superfluous to others. Personal information about your age, marital status, family circumstances, or health usually does not belong in a résumé. Ethnicity, religious affiliation, and fraternal or other organizations belonged to may be helpful, or may not. If in doubt, leave it out.

> Including too much data is a major fault on many résumés. Include the following only after careful consideration:
>
> ➤   Reasons for leaving your current or previous job
> ➤   Salary (previous or desired)
> ➤   Age, marital status, and family details
> ➤   Religious or church affiliations
> ➤   Race, ethnic background, nationality
> ➤   Political affiliations/preferences
> ➤   Hobbies or special interests

Another reason not to include too much information is because you want to *help* the prospective employer, not make things more difficult. With the onslaught of e-communications, people don't have time to go through lengthy e-mails. The same goes for résumés. Use the amount of space you really need and not one character more.

SELECT THE TYPE OF RÉSUMÉ

When you go fishing you select the bait that will best serve your purpose based on the specific conditions at that particular time and the fish you're after. Likewise, you should have all the "bait" you need to land an interview in the form of the data you have just put together. Now decide how to present it. Three basic types of résumés are commonly used:

➢   Historical or chronological

➢   Functional

➢   Analytical

Each type has a specific format, content, and purpose.

Historical/Chronological Résumé

The historical/chronological résumé is the most traditional and is often considered the most effective. As implied by the name, this style presents information in reverse chronological order, starting with your most recent work experience and moving back in time through your past work experience. The educational and employment information worksheets in Appendix C are organized this way. Both education and employment lend themselves to this style. Always include dates and explain any gaps in the chronology.

The historical/chronological résumé is easy to read and gives busy employers a familiar form that can be quickly read. It is the best format to use when staying in the same field. It is not the best format if you have little related experience. Use a chronological résumé if:

➢   You have spent three or more years with previous employers and have not changed jobs frequently.

➢   You are seeking a position in the same field in which you have been employed.

➢   You have worked for well-known, prestigious companies.

➢   You can show steady growth in responsibilities.

See Appendix D for a sample chronological résumé.

Functional Résumé

The functional résumé stresses experiences and abilities as they relate to the job you are applying for rather than a chronological listing of past employment. Dates do not receive as much attention. Hofferber (2004) suggests:

> If you've held a number of different or unrelated jobs during a relatively short period of time and are worried about being labeled as a job-hopper, the functional résumé (also known as a "skills-based format") could

be the answer for you. This format can also work well for those entering the workforce for the first time or after a long absence (such as recent grads with no formal work experience, stay-at-home moms or dads now seeking outside employment, or caregivers who have spent a year or more treating an ill or aging family member). It could also be a good choice if your prior work experience is more relevant to your current job target than what you're doing presently.

This style emphasizes a candidate's strengths in key skills categories and maximizes scant work experience while minimizing irrelevant jobs, employment gaps, and reversals. Use a functional résumé if:

➤   You are seeking a job in a field new to you.

➤   You have been unemployed for more than three months.

➤   Your responsibilities are complicated and require explanation.

➤   You can point to specific accomplishments on your last job.

➤   You are competing with younger applicants.

See Appendix D for a sample functional résumé.

Analytical Résumé

The analytical résumé stresses your particular skills. It is especially helpful if you are changing career goals but you have obtained necessary skills and qualifications from your present and past jobs. It lets you stress those skills and talents instead of your work history. Dates are usually omitted, but past jobs and experiences are referred to at some point. Again, you must determine if this approach can best reflect your particular abilities. See Appendix D for a sample analytical résumé.

The three basic types of résumés commonly used are the historical or chronological résumé, the functional résumé, and the analytical résumé.

➤   The *historical/chronological* résumé, the most traditional and often considered the most effective, presents information by beginning with the most recent experience and going backward in time.
➤   The *functional* résumé emphasizes your qualifications and abilities; minimizes irrelevant jobs, employment gaps, and reversals; and maximizes scant work experience.
➤   The analytical résumé is appropriate if you are changing career goals and stresses *skills* and *talents* instead of past jobs.

What about Creativity?

You may be thinking these three styles are rather boring and want to be somewhat more creative. Think carefully about it. An imaginative or creative approach may be of great benefit, or it may burn you. The positive side of such an approach is that it may set your résumé apart from the dozens, hundreds, even thousands of others, thus receiving the attention it deserves. The negative side of a creative résumé is that it might be the reason the employer is looking for to jettison your résumé, along with any others that do not appear "normal."

 If you decide to use an imaginative/creative résumé, be sure to include all the information any other style would present. If you can do so, you just might be on to something. But be cautious. Unless you have reason to think an employer would find a creative résumé appealing, don't tempt yourself. Criminal justice is a conservative field, so anything unusual risks being viewed as impertinent. A résumé in the format of a "Wanted!" poster might be creative, but do you want to present yourself as a criminal?

FORMAT THE RÉSUMÉ

The format is the layout of the information—what comes first, second, and third. The format should be attractive, businesslike, and professional. Design your format on a sheet of paper and block your material and use headings to guide the reader.

Plan for margins at the top, bottom, and sides of your paper and use white space freely. Will you center your identifying information? Set it flush left? Will you use one or two columns for the bulk of the information? Try to fit all the information on one page. However, if you need two pages, use them. Reducing the font size just to fit everything on one page can become problematic for the employer. Newfield recommends: "If your career warrants a two-page résumé, then go ahead and create a document that reflects the full range of your experience and accomplishments. Don't reduce the type size to such a degree that your résumé becomes difficult to read."

Keep in mind: If your résumé is too long, you risk it not being read; too short, and you risk leaving out relevant information.

> The format of your résumé should be attractive, businesslike, and professional. Not too long; not too short.

Note: Formatting considerations for e-mailed résumés and other computer compatibility issues are discussed later in this chapter.

WRITE THE RÉSUMÉ

The traditional advice for writing an effective résumé has been to use short, action-packed *phrases.*

Short. Omit all unnecessary words. This includes:

➢ Personal pronouns: *I, me,* and *my*

➢ Articles: *a, an,* and *the*

Action-Packed. Write with *verbs,* not with *nouns.* For example, don't say *conducted an investigation*, say *investigated*. Writing with verbs is also shorter than writing with nouns. Look at the following:

> I conducted an analysis of all the incoming calls to the dispatcher, and I compiled detailed analytical reports based on my analysis.

Twenty-two words. Eliminate the pronouns (I, my) and articles (an, the) and use verbs instead of nouns. What you'll get is something like the following:

> Analyzed all incoming calls and wrote detailed reports.

Which statement would you rather read? Which conveys an image of the writer as focused and authoritative?

Phrases. Phrase your writing, watch where lines end, and avoid hyphenating words at the end of the line. For example, read the following:

> It was a difficult job because my boss was a rat-
> her rigid person.

One way to write an effective résumé is to use short, action-packed *phrases.*

Pay attention to effective ads on television and in print. Notice how the words are strung together for maximum effect. You can do the same in your résumé. Try using short "bullet" phrases that begin with a variety of active verbs. Here are some that might fit your experience:

adapted	controlled	hired	planned	selected
administered	coordinated	identified	presented	served
analyzed	decided	improved	produced	set up
applied	delegated	increased	proved	solved
approved	designed	inspected	provided	spoke
arranged	developed	invented	published	supervised
assessed	edited	investigated	recorded	surveyed
assisted	educated	led	redesigned	taught
built	encouraged	managed	represented	trained
chaired	established	modified	researched	updated
completed	evaluated	monitored	reviewed	wrote
conducted	examined	operated	revised	

Parker suggests:

> Fill your resume with "PAR" statements. PAR stands for Problem-Action-Results; in other words, first you state the problem that existed in your workplace, then you describe what you did about it, and finally you point out the beneficial results.
>
> **Here's an example:** "Transformed a disorganized, inefficient warehouse into a smooth-running operation by totally redesigning the layout; this saved the company thousands of dollars in recovered stock."
>
> **Another example:** "Improved an engineering company's obsolete filing system by developing a simple but sophisticated functional-coding system. This saved time and money by recovering valuable, previously lost, project records."

Although the traditional recommendation of writing résumés using verbs is still sound, today's job seekers must also be cognizant of a new résumé rule which Challenger (2000, p. 6) notes as: "Use as many nouns as possible . . . and be as specific as possible." The simple reason for this new rule is the growing use of e-résumés.

Tailoring Your Résumé

As technology advances, so do formats in which employers request résumés. Those using unique formats usually provide sufficient instructions. If you remain in doubt, use your Internet search engine to find directions.

A final suggestion: Tailor your résumé to fit the job. With all the preceding suggestions and choices, you may find it difficult to settle on one "perfect" format or word choice for your résumé, especially if you are applying to a variety of employers. So don't. To the common dilemma: "What if I have several different job objectives I'm working on at the same time? Or I haven't narrowed it down yet to just one job target?" Parker advises: "Then write a different resume for each different job target. A targeted resume is MUCH, much stronger than a generic resume."

As Ortmeier (2009, p. 343) states: "The resume is one of the most important documents in a job search. For the applicant, the resume is a self-marketing tool used to make a first impression worthy of a job interview. For the employer, the resume is a preemployment screening device that is reviewed in less than a minute." Whatever format is requested or most appropriate for you, it needs to be so good it leaves a lasting impression.

EDIT AND POLISH YOUR FIRST DRAFT

First drafts simply don't cut it. Continue to work with it until it has the punch you want. Because employers are busy, say as much as you can with as few words as possible. Spend time refining each phrase. Work at developing brief statements that explain clearly and strongly what your education and experience are, what opportunities you've taken advantage of, and what qualifications and skills you would bring to the job.

You might consider hiring a professional editor or even a professional résumé writer at this point. Services such as www.vault.com can edit your résumé and cover letter for a fee. Using such services will be less expensive if you have completed all the background research, designed a format, and written the first draft.

Proofread your draft. Check the spelling of every word. Check every capital letter and punctuation mark. Some people find it helpful to proofread by going from right to left in each line, looking at each word. Then have a friend whose writing skills you respect check it for you. It is very hard to see your own writing errors. Morem (2001, p. D2) provides the following examples of real résumé gaffes:

➢ "Worked party-time as an office assistant"

➢ "Planned and held up meetings"

➢ "Computer illiterate"

She states: "You want your résumé to generate interest, not laughs: make sure it is error-free, and take the time to step away from it before you proofread and do your final editing."

EVALUATE AND REVISE

 Use the form in Appendix C to evaluate your résumé. Consider both appearance and content. Grade each category as Excellent, Average, or Poor. If a category is poor, decide how to improve it.

PRINT YOUR RÉSUMÉ

You are at the final step. Have your résumé professionally printed or use a high-quality printer. Consider the following:

➤ Buy a quantity of blank 8.5 × 11-inch white bond paper and matching 9 × 12 envelopes.

➤ Print only on one side and use black ink.

➤ Use a type that is easy to read, at least a ten-point size, preferably eleven or twelve points.

➤ If necessary, slightly reduce the font size to assure adequate margins.

➤ Do *not* use all capital letters, script, bold, or italic print. Use graphics sparingly or, better yet, not at all.

➤ Most people prefer a *serif* typestyle. Serifs are the little curves or feet added to the edges of letters to make them more readable. This book uses a serif typestyle (Times New Roman). *Sans serif* typestyles do give a crisp, clean appearance, but are much harder to read. (Example: Arial Typeface—compare p and p, or A and A.)

> Have your résumé professionally printed in black ink, on 8.5 × 11-inch white bond paper. If necessary, reduce the type slightly to assure adequate margins, and use capital letters, script, bold, and italic print and graphics sparingly, if at all.

MAKING IT THE BEST

A résumé is a direct reflection of you on paper. Be sure it depicts you as you want—a professional for a professional job. Everything about your résumé will say something about you. Because employers have to start cutting back the number of finalists, they look for reasons *not* to pursue you as a candidate. For example, typos on a résumé have served as a legitimate reason for disregarding an application for any number of positions. Sometimes, when there are a lot of very good applicants, reasons for getting rid of one résumé and keeping another become, at best, arbitrary.

Put your résumé in an attractive binder or enclose it in an attractive envelope with the name and address of the prospective employer typed. This may say that this particular applicant put that extra effort into the process and should, therefore, be given consideration—an interview. Do not, however, use anything slippery or difficult to file. You don't want your résumé to stand out because it is hard to handle.

THE COVER LETTER

Never send a résumé without a cover letter, even if the employer has asked you to send a résumé. Cover letters should be individually typed, addressed to a specific person and company or department, and signed. Anything less will be ineffective.

Keep your cover letter short and to the point. It is a brief personal introduction of the "you" embodied in your résumé. Don't repeat résumé information. Entice the reader to want to find out more about you. Make clear in your opening paragraph the type of résumé submission:

➤ Unsolicited. If so, give a reason for selecting this particular employer.

➤ Written as a referral or from personal contact, for example, "My mechanic told me your department was looking for qualified security officers."

➤ Written in response to a job advertisement.

Avoid starting every sentence with "I." *Never* start with: "I am writing this letter to apply for the job I saw advertised in the paper." BORING! Focus on the reader. More effective would be something like this: "Your opening for a police officer advertised in the Gazette is of great interest to me." Isaacs (2004) offers the following advice about cover letters:

> Your cover letter is the first thing employers see when they open your materials. Avoid these 10 mistakes, and make your first impression an impressive and lasting one.
>
> **Don't Overuse "I."** Your cover letter is not your autobiography. The focus should be on how you meet an employer's needs, not on your life story. Avoid the perception of being self-centered by minimizing your use of the word "I," especially at the beginning of your sentences.
>
> **Don't Use a Weak Opening.** Job seekers frequently struggle with the question of how to begin a cover letter. What results is often a feeble introduction lacking punch and failing to grab the reader's interest. Consider this example:
> - **Weak:** Please consider me for your sales representative opening.
> - **Better:** Your need for a top-performing sales representative is an excellent match to my three-year history as a #1-ranked multimillion-dollar producer.
>
> **Don't Omit Your Top Selling Points.** A cover letter is a sales letter that sells you as a candidate. Just like the résumé, it should be compelling and give the main reasons why you should be called for an interview. Winning cover letter strategies include emphasizing your top accomplishments or creating subheadings culled from the position ad. For example: "Your ad specifies . . . and I offer . . ."
>
> **Don't Make It Too Long or Too Short.** If your cover letter is only one or two short paragraphs, it probably doesn't contain enough key information to sell you effectively. If it exceeds one page, you may be putting readers to sleep. Keep it concise but compelling, and be respectful of readers' time.
>
> **Don't Repeat Your Résumé Word-for-Word.** Your cover letter shouldn't just regurgitate what's on your résumé. Reword your cover letter statements to avoid dulling your résumé's impact.
>
> **Don't Be Vague.** If you're replying to an advertised opening, reference the specific job title in your cover letter. The person reading your letter may be reviewing hundreds of letters for dozens of different jobs. Make sure all the content in your letter supports how you will meet the specific needs of the employer.
>
> **Don't Forget to Customize.** If you're applying to a number of similar positions, chances are you're tweaking one letter and using it for multiple openings. That's fine, as long as you are customizing each one. Don't forget to update the company/job/contact information—if Mr. Jones is addressed as Mrs. Smith, he won't be impressed.

Don't End on a Passive Note. Put your future in your own hands with a promise to follow up. Instead of asking readers to call you, try a statement like this: I will follow up with you in a few days to answer any preliminary questions you may have. In the meantime, you may reach me at (555) 555-5555.

Don't Forget to Sign the Letter. It is proper business etiquette (and shows attention to detail) to sign your letter. However, if you are sending your cover letter and résumé via e-mail or the Web, a signature isn't necessary.

Keep your letter short—one page. Be direct in requesting an interview. Send the letter to a specific person and use that individual's title. You can usually get this information by calling the agency or department, asking who is in charge of hiring, and asking for the spelling of that person's name and official title. The little time this takes can pay big dividends.

As with your résumé, be sure to carefully proofread the cover letter. Morem (p. D2) reports: "A recent survey by the Society of Human Resource Management found that more than 80 percent of human resources professionals spend less than one minute reading a cover letter; 76 percent said a typo or grammatical error would remove an applicant from consideration."

> *Always* send a résumé with a cover letter. Cover letters should be individually typed, short and to the point, addressed to a specific person (including his or her title) and a specific company or department, and signed.

An effective format for a cover letter is the full-block style—everything begins at the left margin. The parts of the letter should be as follows:

> Your name
> Your address (street number, street name, and apartment number, if applicable)
> Your city, state, and zip code
> Your phone number(s) with area code
> Your e-mail address
>
> The date you are writing
>
> The name of the person you are writing to
> That person's title
> The name of the company/department
> The address of the employer
>
> Salutation (Dear . . .):
>
> Opening paragraph—why you are writing.
>
> Second paragraph—provide some intriguing fact about yourself as a lead into your résumé.
>
> Concluding paragraph—ask for an interview and state where you can be reached.
>
> Complimentary closing (Sincerely, or Yours truly), (Skip four lines—sign in this space)
>
> Typed name
>
> Encl: Résumé

Notice the spacing between the various sections. Notice the capitalization and the colon following the salutation and the comma following the complimentary closing. The importance of a cover letter on the front end and a follow-up after the résumé has been submitted cannot be overstated. A sample cover letter is given in Appendix E.

Half (2008) suggests that although you may think your résumé and cover letter are terrific, chances are you could probably improve on them:

> Take a close look at your résumé and cover letter. Do they sell your skills and qualifications? Make sure that, instead of simply listing your previous duties, you detail your accomplishments and contributions in previous roles. So rather than saying, "Wrote one high-tech column for company intranet each week," try, "Wrote weekly high-tech column for company intranet that increased readership by more than 200 percent and helped employees better utilize company systems." This will show a prospective employer exactly how your work improved the bottom line and why he should hire you.
>
> Also make sure your materials are targeted. Research the company before responding to an ad to determine how your qualifications can meet its business needs. In addition, read through the job description and include specific terms from it in your résumé and cover letter. Doing so will demonstrate to a hiring manager that your skills are a good fit for the position as well as increase the likelihood that your documents will be flagged as promising by résumé-scanning software.

SENDING YOUR RÉSUMÉ

Mail your cover letter and résumé unfolded in a 9 × 12 envelope. Everybody else's is going to be folded and crinkled. Résumés that travel flat are going to look better than all the others. As one employer commented: "When I looked for résumés, the easy ones to find are the flat ones. They stand out in the pile of folded résumés." Also, mail your letter and résumé to arrive in the employer's office on a Tuesday, Wednesday, or Thursday.

One final suggestion—consider using certified mail, with a return receipt requested. Not only will you eliminate those nagging doubts about if it got delivered, but again, it says something to the employer about the kind of person you are. Here is a candidate concerned enough to make sure it arrived. That's the kind of attention to detail a lot of employers are looking for.

You may think you need to send out only a few résumés, but the reality is: "Finding a job is a numbers game. A hiring manager may receive countless résumés for an open position. That's why it pays to spread a wide net. And while you want to keep in mind your goals, it may be unwise to hold out for the 'perfect' job, which you might not find—or which might not even exist" (Half, 2008).

Electronic Submission and Faxing of Résumés

Sending material electronically is good—it makes a statement that you possess computer skills that today's employers desire—but keep the following in mind:

➤ Always keep a copy of anything you send, should you need it in the future.

➤ Make sure your electronic communiqués appear every bit as professional as those submitted in hard copy. Begin with a proper salutation (Dear "recipient") and finish with a professional closing (Sincerely).

➤ Never use electronic communication simply because it is easier. Use it only because the employer requested it or you believe an electronic submission will be viewed positively.

➢   Clearly state the purpose of your e-mail in the subject line (Application for job posting . . .).
      Never leave the subject line blank, as many antispam filters delete such "unannounced" e-mail.
      Furthermore, it may be considered rude or careless to not inform the recipient of the nature of your
      correspondence—they likely will not recognize your name and may simply delete the file without
      opening it.

➢   Do not assume electronic communications are always received. Servers go down, systems crash,
      antispam programs interfere—following up on all electronic correspondence is crucial in ensuring
      the intended recipient did, indeed, receive your material.

Converting e-mailed résumés or other documents to .pdf format lets you send more material quickly and
allows the recipient to open it more quickly. Electronic communications has spawned its own etiquette,
or "netiquette." E-communication should be brief; however, being overly brief risks taking on the
appearance of text messaging with cryptic abbreviations. Just because you know what something stands
for doesn't mean the recipient does, especially if they are of another generation.

Comedian Jim Gaffigan does a routine about how lazy people have become because e-mail is so easy:
"That's a symptom of being lazy when you can't quite reach the shift key."

Think carefully before faxing your application materials. It's old technology that has mediocre resolution,
causing them to succumb to scanned documents.

HAND DELIVERING YOUR RÉSUMÉ

It's always a good idea to hand deliver a résumé if possible because it allows the employer to associate
your name with a face and makes a statement about how important this job is to you. Dress well and
look professional when delivering your résumé. Even if you don't get to the boss, you will make a good
impression on the staff person accepting it. These people can have a great deal of influence on their
bosses. Don't let your guard down because you aren't dealing directly with upper management. When you
drop your material off, it is another opportunity for you to emphasize that you really want the job. Keep in
mind many secretaries and receptionists are gatekeepers. Establishing a positive contact with the person
taking your résumé (or answering the phone) may also help you get that interview.

FOLLOWING UP

Be sure to follow up. The follow-up is another opportunity to prove what kind of person you are—the
kind they should hire! A day or two after you have mailed or hand delivered your résumé, write a brief
letter to the employer. Recognize that the employer will be busy and only a short letter stands a chance of
being read.

Confirm that you delivered your résumé and thank the employer for the opportunity to participate in
the hiring process. Even if this merely gets stapled to your résumé without getting read initially by the
employer, or gets forgotten by the employer who might read it, it is something that just might catch
the attention of the interview committee when your résumé surfaces. If they are looking for reasons to
keep some and get rid of others, this could be the reason yours stays in the running. The cover letter and
follow-up support the résumé much like bookends. See Appendix E for a sample follow-up letter.

Hand deliver your résumé if possible to enable the employer to match your name with a face. Dress well and look professional when delivering your résumé. A day or two after you have delivered your résumé, follow up by writing a brief letter to the employer confirming the delivery of your résumé and thanking the employer for the chance to participate in the hiring process.

A business column called "Ask Matt" poses the question: "Is it appropriate to follow-up on résumés sent by E-mail? Many businesses do not have contact names when applying via E-mail, just a general HR listing, so whom should I send a follow up to?" Matt Krumrie (2007a) responds that yes, it can be appropriate, but quotes Farhan Farooqui: "Watch for E-mail boxes set up to only take E-mail resumes—where no one actually replies to that E-mail. It's always appropriate to call the company and request to speak to someone in staffing or recruiting directly."

Another "Ask Matt" column addresses thank-you letters (2007b): "We couldn't count the number of times that a letter of appreciation caused great things to happen for candidates. Thank you letters should express appreciation for time spent in the interview, highlighting key points of the interview and job. It's also a good time to mention you're looking forward to the next step in the hiring process. Make sure it has a personalized touch and sounds sincere. Then, reiterate how you can add value…or how excited you are with potentially joining the new company."

Krumrie also quotes Brad Konik: "Handwritten thank you letters are still the preferred since it reflects your willingness to put in the extra time and effort. E-mails are certainly acceptable but can easily be overlooked and may be interpreted as being the easy way out…(but) an E-mail thank you is better than none at all. Keep track of everyone you interview with or who helps you along the way. Send thank you notes to anyone directly involved with the interview or hiring process. Keep in mind the thank you letter won't be the sole reason you get hired, but it could be what separates equal candidates, or gives you an edge in a highly competitive job market."

Basic good manners seem to be at such a premium now that even something as simple as a follow-up letter or thank-you can make you stand out. Whether you feel a follow-up thank-you letter or card is appropriate, failing to follow up is as egregious as not providing a cover letter. But *don't* become a pest. Too many letters or calls can just as easily land you in the "no" pile, identified as overly eager or unable to exercise enough common sense to know when it's "too much."

FOR MORE HELP

Bookstores and libraries have dozens of texts on résumé writing, each with its own particular advice. Other sources of information and assistance may be found online—search under the keyword "résumé." The references and URLs at the end of this chapter provide a start if you want to go into this topic in more detail or from other perspectives. If you are in college, your computer career center can be of help.

CONCLUSION

One of your most important job-seeking tools is the résumé. A résumé is a brief, well-documented summary of your education, abilities, skills, experience, and career achievements, which highlights significant aspects of your background and identifies your qualifications for a given job. Its main purpose is to sell you to a prospective employer. But don't overdo it. Including too much data is a major fault of many résumés. And remember, always include a cover letter with your résumé, even when delivering the résumé in person.

AN INSIDER'S VIEW

THE RÉSUMÉ: A BALANCE OF MODESTY AND SELF-CONFIDENCE

Gil Kerlikowske

Former Police Commissioner
Buffalo (New York) Police Department

The law enforcement field offers a wide variety of employment opportunities. Police agencies operate with a number of specialists in areas such as finance, computer technology, planning and education as well as enforcement officers. Having hired individuals for these positions has given me an opportunity to review thousands of résumés. I have also served on search committees for CEOs. Nothing can be of more importance than the quality of the application and résumé submitted.

The cover letter should be specific to the individual job you are interested in. Photocopies and generic cover letters are an automatic turn-off to reviewers. The letter should be addressed to an individual, not "Personnel Department" or another title. Match your qualifications to those requested in the advertisement and keep the letter to one page. A balance between modesty and self-confidence is what you are striving for. If the letter shouts out how outstanding you are, the reviewer might question your sincerity to be a team member. On the other hand, you want to stand out from the hundreds of other applicants.

There are several types of résumés and numerous books to guide you in developing your individual résumé. If you have experience in the criminal justice field and are interested in a more senior position, I would recommend a style that illustrates experience and accomplishments. An applicant who is new to the field and is looking for an entry-level position should opt for a style that emphasizes their interest, education and dedication.

The résumé should also fit the specific qualifications the job requires. Length depends upon your experience and age. One to two pages is sufficient for entry-level positions and no more than four to five pages for management and executive positions. Education and specialized training (dates, course titles and degrees, of course) in an easily read style are a must. Where they are included is another style question; however, large-type headings for Education, Experience, Training, etc. make it easy to scan the résumé and check off important qualifications.

If you do not meet minimum qualifications, it is generally not worth your effort to apply for the position. Individual jobs just have too many applicants who do meet the requirements. However, if you know other positions you may be qualified for are going to become open, I suggest you meet with someone in that division to discuss your interest. Having someone in the department know your name and interest may be the extra push that helps you land the job you want in the future.

One automatic disqualifier for me has always been information that is not completely accurate. Most employers are careful to make sure individuals have the degrees and experience they claim. Areas of experience are more subjective. The rule of thumb is to be cautious in stating your qualifications. For example, if you once filled in for a crime prevention officer at a community meeting, do not cite experience as a crime prevention specialist.

Finally, photographs, copies of diplomas and other material are not necessary in an initial application. After you make the cut, those items may be requested. My personal feeling is that newspaper and magazine articles about you are self-serving. In the second or third phase of the employment process these materials, if they are focused on a program or unit you worked in or managed, are acceptable.

The employment process is different in every locality and can be frustrating and time-consuming. Professionalism and perseverance will be your greatest allies in finding the job you desire. And remember, nothing can be of more importance than the quality of the application and résumé submitted.

Gil Kerlikowske *is the former police commissioner for the Buffalo (New York) Police Department and has twenty-six years' experience in criminal justice. Prior to working in New York, Commissioner Kerlikowske was the chief of police in Fort Pierce, Florida, for four years. He holds an MA in Criminal Justice.*

 MIND STRETCHES

1. Imagine you have been assigned the task of reducing an extremely large pile of résumés to a more workable number. Regardless of the position, what are five reasons you can think of to get rid of applications right away?

2. What are three things you might look for that would make a résumé stand out as being worth taking time to look at further?

3. Paint with words the picture you want your résumé to make. Use three words. Use six words.

4. How can you liven up your résumé?

5. What might be dangerous about preparing a résumé that is too creative? What benefits might result?

6. What attributes do you have that will impress an employer?

7. What concerns do you have about your qualifications that you will need to consider in preparing your résumé?

8. What are five power verbs you associate with yourself?

9. Which résumé style could work best for you? Why?

10. What unique ways can you present your résumé?

REFERENCES

Barthel, Brea and Goldrick-Jones, Amanda. The Writing Center, Rensselaer Polytechnic Institute. Available online at www.rpi.edu/web/writingcenter/resume.html.

Challenger, John A. "Surprize! Resume Rules Have Changed." *Bottom Line Personal*, March 15, 2000, p. 6.

Half, Robert. Robert Half International, 2008. Available online at http://msn.careerbuilder.com/custom/msn/careeradvice/viewarticle.aspx?articleid=1237&SiteId=cbmsnty41237&sc_extcmp=JS_1237_today1&GT1=23000&cbRecursionCnt=1&cbsid=808776ed16d54cedafde66b75a0ece9b-262083042-R4-4.

Hofferber, Karen. "Breaking Tradition with a Functional Resume." Monster Career Center, 2004. Available online at http://resume.monster.com/articles/functionalresume.

Isaacs, Kim. "Ten Cover Letter Don'ts." Monster Career Center, 2004. Available online at http://resume.monster.com/coverletter/donot/.

Krannich, Ron, and Caryl Krannich. *No One Will Hire Me*, 3rd ed. Manassas Park VA: Impact Publication, 2007.

Krumrie, Matt. "Ask Matt" (Minneapolis/St. Paul) *Star Tribune*, February 4, 2007a, p. W1.

Krumrie, Matt. "Ask Matt" (Minneapolis/St. Paul) *Star Tribune*, November 25, 2007b, p. W1.

Land That Job! Available online at www.landjob.com.

Morem, Sue. "Don't Make Mistake of Erring with Résumé." (Minneapolis/St. Paul) *Star Tribune*, November 13, 2001, p. D2.

Newfield, Peter. "Ten Resume 'Don'ts.'" Monster Career Center, 2004. Available online at http://resume.monster.com/dosanddonts/resumedonts.

Ortmeier, P. J. *Introduction to Security Operations and Management*, 3rd ed. Pearson Upper Saddle River, NJ: Prentice Hall, 2009.

Parker, Yana. Damn Good Resume Guide. Available online at www.damngood.com.

Resume.com. Available online at www.resume.com.

Resume Logic. Available online at www.resumelogic.com/index.htm.

HELPFUL WEBSITES

http://10minuteresume.com
http://eresumes.com
http://collegegrad.com

CHAPTER 11

PREPARING FOR NOT GETTING THE JOB

Accept that some days you're the pigeon and some days you're the statue.

—*Roger C. Anderson*

Do You Know:

➢ What you can do to prepare for and effectively handle rejection in your job search?
➢ Why a support system is beneficial?
➢ The importance of maintaining a positive attitude?
➢ What emotions are part of the sequential reaction to loss and change?
➢ What feelings follow the transition curve?

INTRODUCTION

It's hard to get a job in these fields! It is most unusual for a person to get the first job for which they apply. And because the job market today is changing so rapidly and downsizing is more prevalent than ever, you will find an increasing number of people competing for work. You should gain comfort in knowing that the vast majority of successful applicants were eventually successful because they had a lot of experience in the application process. In a negative situation, many people fail to take advantage of a great opportunity to gain from it. Energy *is* present, albeit uncomfortable, and can be rechanneled in a positive direction.

Although the bulk of this book deals with how to get a job, this brief but important chapter deals with *not* getting a job—a realistic part of any job search. As Bolles (2008, p. 37) states: "Many if not most people find at times in their lives that the job-hunt is nothing but a long dreary process where, at the end, you may indeed find acceptance (a job). But prior to that it's a series of seemingly endless rejections." You need to know how to deal with failure in order to continue onward. You may want to reread this chapter when you get that first, almost inevitable, rejection, to reassure yourself that your feelings are normal and that you must go forward.

HANDLING REJECTION

Many adages apply to not obtaining something, and with good reason. We all experience rejection. Think about it: For every individual hired, many more did not get hired for that job. Everyone in the job-search market will face rejection; that's reality. You may hear similar sentiments following a less-than-successful interview:

> There must be something better around the corner.
> They didn't deserve you. Besides, they're probably all jerks anyway.
> You can do better than that place.

These statements may be true, and you will no doubt hear them from your friends and family. After all, they want to support you. You will agree, of course, but inside you may be thinking things like:

> I knew I could never get that job. I'm no good.
> Everyone else is better than me. I'll never get a job.
> I should never have gone into this profession. Etc., etc., etc. . . .

If you are not careful, this negative "self-talk" might overwhelm you and become a self-fulfilling prophecy. If you get to the point that *you* don't believe in yourself, why should a *potential employer* believe in you? Remember, success comes in "cans"—failure comes in "can'ts."

Tell yourself everyone must take their share of rejection. Sure, some take a little more, some take a little less, but everyone takes it. It's not just part of the job search, it's part of life. If you understand ahead of time the reality of rejection and are prepared for it, when the first one hits you, it's not likely to knock you down so hard. And if you're one of those fortunate few who hears "yes" on the first try, way to go! You beat the odds on this one. For the rest of us, each "no" we hear brings us one step closer to that "yes," as long as we don't give up.

How many résumés you can expect to send out to get an interview, and then how many interviews you can expect before getting a job depends on the job sought, the overall economy, and the local hiring climate. It also depends on your qualifications and the effectiveness of your job-search strategy.

No one ever said job hunting was easy. For all practical purposes, job hunting will have to be a full-time job itself, at least for awhile. If it isn't full-time time-wise, it will be energy-wise. But, in the beginning, you'll probably believe rejection could never happen to you. This is the case with older, experienced people who find themselves looking for work after being successful thus far; as well as the younger, so-called "entitlement generation," who assume because everything else has come easy, finding work will, too.

It's similar to the "It Can Never Happen to Me" syndrome frequently heard in discussions of officer safety. The idea is that an officer's daily existence would be too difficult if he or she thought that harm or perhaps death was lurking around every corner. Officers instinctively develop the "It Can Never Happen to Me" attitude in order to continue on with their day-to-day lives. To a certain degree it helps prevent them from becoming hopelessly paranoid. Problems arise, however, when care is not taken. Police, corrections, and security officers must accept the natural risks associated with their jobs, but they must also be prepared and they must be realistic. Similarly, job applicants must balance the risks. If you know you're going to be rejected, why even try? This is what happens to some job seekers who start out feeling they will never be rejected. Two or three rejections turn them into defeatists who simply go through the motions.

Consider the applicant who has become so defeated that after several "thanks but no thanks" letters, when he woke up on the morning of an interview and found that it was raining, the weather became the last straw. He decided to stay in bed. This would-be police officer made it easy for the employer to weed out one more applicant. Who does this applicant really have to blame for this failure?

Success is getting up one more time than you fall down (author unknown). Make up your mind right now to accept the facts of job seeking.

➤ Fact #1: Criminal justice, private security, and related fields are *very* popular, sought-after, competitive jobs.

➤ Fact #2: You're up against many, many applicants—many with experience and college degrees.

➤ Fact #3: Eventually you will get hired WHEN you're right for the job.

The benefit of having to repeat the application process is that you will improve each time. The downside is that it can cause you distress. Although rejection doesn't feel good to anyone and is understandably discouraging, whether you will turn that energy into a positive force or let it drag you down is a decision only you can make.

To prepare for and effectively handle rejection in your job search, be aware that it does happen to just about everyone and that the only ones who fail are the ones who stop trying. Avoid negative self-talk and never lose faith in yourself. Each "no" brings you closer to a "yes."

Bolles (pp. 26–27) describes the "rejection shock" experienced by many job hunters searching for that elusive "yes":

> Most of us don't understand the nature of the job-market until we bump our head or stub our toe on that nature. High school or college doesn't prepare us for it. Only out there amid the hard-knocks of life do we begin to slowly and painstakingly piece this information together, usually completing the task by the time we're, oh, 65 or 70. Earlier than that, the way the job-market behaves may come as a stunning surprise. Our response is usually shock.

To avoid this damaging loss of self-esteem from the shock of having to look for work, sometimes after being gainfully employed most our lives, it is crucial to be realistic, know the odds you are working against, and maintain a positive attitude.

REMAINING POSITIVE

Because successful job seeking takes persistence, of all the attributes you must develop, remaining positive and motivated are the most crucial. You can and, in fact, must turn the negative energy from rejection into positive momentum. Rather than giving up, become determined to strive that much harder, knowing you are stronger and more polished. Nineteenth-century German philosopher Friedrich Wilhelm Nietzsche stated, "What does not destroy me makes me stronger."

Learning that you can endure makes rejection less onerous and allows you to keep trying. No one likes to fail, but even top corporations have learned that to not fail is to not try. The July 10, 2006, cover story of *BusinessWeek* was, "How Failure Breeds Success: Everyone fears failure. But breakthroughs depend on it. The best companies embrace their mistakes and learn from them."

Having more than 10,000 failed experiments before succeeding at inventing the light bulb, Thomas Edison understood the importance of not giving up as part of the road to success: "I am not discouraged, because every wrong attempt discarded is another step forward." No one likes to be turned down, which can be perceived as failure, especially for a desperately wanted job. It does not get any easier the second, third, or sixth time. In fact, the more you are turned down, the heavier it may weigh on you. But, like Edison, it's understanding and managing your response to disappointment that helps you move forward—stronger, better, and eventually more successful.

Maintain a positive attitude. To deal most effectively with that most common part of job hunting—rejection—keep the following basics in mind:

➤ Go into the process understanding the norm is to send out many résumés to get an interview, and interview many times to get a job.

➤ Not getting this job does not mean you deserve to be banished from the planet. It simply means you did not get this one job. Another job is just around the corner (trite, but true). Avoid the temptation to believe that a particular job is your one-and-only dream job. If you are convinced only one job suits you, you are closing the door to other opportunities. Some people report finding a better job, even career, because their "dream job" didn't work out.

➤ If you need help, *ask for it!* No law says you must go it alone. If you are not confident about your job-seeking skills, seek help. If you get discouraged or depressed, seek help.

➤ Most important—keep trying. You've come this far. It is no time to give up. *Listen* when everyone tells you that you can get a job. You can. Just give yourself time.

Take advantage of everyone else's understanding of discouragement and build a support system. It helps to talk, and you will be surprised by how many people have experienced similar rejection.

> Support systems are valuable because they allow you to talk out your frustrations and realize you are not the only one who has ever felt rejection—everyone else has experienced it, too. People in your support system may be able to share what worked for them in getting past their rejection.

Do not be afraid to get support and help if you need it—professional or otherwise. Frustration and disappointment are normal, but do not let it get the best of you. Negative feelings can become overwhelming, and they can also be self-perpetuating. Feeling depressed and gloomy often leads to deeper feelings of depression and gloominess. Besides not feeling good, they can sap so much of your energy that your interview skills become less than adequate, and you will not perform as needed.

Employers are very aware of how much competition you have—they have to sit through all those interviews! What would happen if you went into your tenth interview exhausted and depressed and the next person after you was upbeat and positive because it was only their first interview? Presenting the same energy and freshness during your tenth interview that you possessed during your first one will not only leave a positive impression on the interviewer but will also help fuel positive feelings in yourself. You have a choice: You can come out of the interview feeling even worse because you *knew* you were mopey and unenthusiastic, or you can come out feeling great because you gave it your best shot.

In short, if you do not deal with the uncomfortable feelings that go along with rejection, you will eventually come to believe that you do not deserve to be hired, and it will show. Pick up and press on.

Remaining positive is crucial to a successful job search. A positive attitude leaves a favorable impression on an employer, and it helps fuel positive feelings in yourself.

To help handle the sense of failure you may feel when your job search seems to lead only to rejection, keep in mind the words of Bill Gates (2000): "Once you embrace unpleasant news not as negative but as evidence of a need for change, you aren't defeated by it. You're *learning* from it."

LEARNING FROM THE PROCESS

Ask prospective employers who turned you down what could have made a difference. If approached in a nonthreatening way, people will usually be honest and open. Employers at one time were seeking employment themselves and so they understand. Perhaps they may be so impressed you wish to better yourself it could give you an advantage if you apply there again.

Bolles (p. 13) states: "As job-expert Richard Lathrop observed long ago, the person who gets hired is not necessarily the best person for the job, but the one who knows the most about how to get hired." Recognize that, sometimes, the fact you didn't get a particular job may not have had anything to do with you. There may have been factors at play beyond your control, and even if you had done everything right, that specific job was not meant to be yours.

NORMAL REACTION TO LOSS

The fear of the unknown is always the worst. Since it helps to know what to expect, here's a brief explanation of what many people experience when they lose something (such as a death in the family, a ruined relationship, or a lost job opportunity). Called the *sequential reaction to loss and change,* it describes how many people *normally* act when losing something important. If you get a rejection, you may feel the following, in roughly this order:

➢ Denial

➢ Anger

➢ Sadness

➢ Hopelessness

➢ Disorganization

➢ Withdrawal

➢ Reorganization

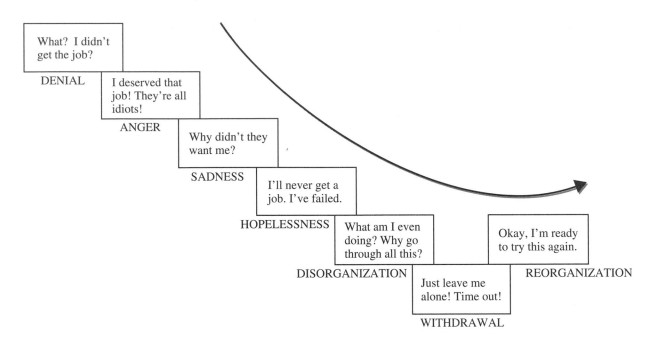

FIGURE 11–1   Sequential Reaction to Loss and Change

This sequential reaction to loss and change is illustrated in Figure 11–1.

Denial. This is the "It can never happen to me" phase, and it's completely normal. It hasn't quite sunk in yet that you didn't get the job. Denial helps by keeping you from getting too hurt from rejection(s). It can be harmful, however, if you don't move on or get too hung up on that rejection (possibly thinking that this is the only job in the world for you). Accepting the loss is a necessary step on the journey in order to continue on with life.

Anger. Once you have accepted the rejection, the understandable response is anger. "I wanted that job! I deserved that job! They won't get away with this! The process is unfair!" These things may be true, but the fact is you did not get the job. Staying angry too long will, at best, depress you and, at worst, drive you to do something you may later regret, like writing a nasty letter, making a nasty phone call, or paying a hostile visit to the employer. It's in your best interest to not burn bridges, should another opportunity arise there in the future. The anger must be dealt with, and the challenge is to find an appropriate outlet.

Sadness. After the anger subsides, you may feel sad. Sadness can run from a mild case of the blues to a bout with deep depression. It depends on many factors and reflects the absolute need of a strong support system as you seek work. Don't beat up on yourself too much if you feel down. Who doesn't after rejection? Many people tend to ignore it because being sad is not their style. However, rather than fight it, accept it, draw some energy from it, and move on. If it becomes overwhelming to the point of your being unable to continue the job search, or if it begins to seriously affect other areas of your life, get help. You need to work through the sadness, but not let it consume you and keep you from moving on.

Hopelessness. Hopelessness may occur as the feelings of anger and depression subside. The hopelessness may seem overwhelming, but it is a normal part of adapting to rejection. The natural assumption after one or more employers reject you is that you are unemployable, and that no one wants you. This is not true. It simply means those jobs did not work out. You have to keep going, which isn't always easy because of the natural progression of feelings.

Disorganization. At this point you may want to continue on, but nothing seems to fit anymore. You may find it hard to organize your time or your thoughts. You may spend time haphazardly reading help-wanted ads and making futile attempts to schedule a productive day. Frustration may set in, and you may simply give up.

Withdrawal. Wanting to give up or withdraw is also natural. It is understandable that you are frustrated, uncomfortable, and wanting to simply quit. This is how your psyche lets you rest, regroup, and get ready to jump into the battle again. Rather than fight the desire to withdraw, help it along. Get away from job hunting for awhile. Go to a movie, take a long walk, or even go on a vacation. Retreat and regroup, but do not withdraw by skipping scheduled interviews or by showing up and not putting forth your best effort. If you need a break, take it.

Reorganization. At last! You have worked through the normal feelings associated with being rejected. Here is where you are getting closer to the pot of gold at the end of the rainbow. Having worked through the previous emotional stages, you're now ready to get back out there and get that job.

> The progression of feelings involved in the sequential reaction to loss and change are denial, anger, sadness, hopelessness, disorganization, withdrawal, and, finally, reorganization.

Nathan and Hill (2005, p. 27) describe a similar pattern they refer to as *the transition curve,* characterized by the following chain of reactions:

> *Shock, denial:* Unable to believe that it has happened. "You're joking!" A feeling of emptiness, perhaps numbness.
> *Euphoria:* Making the best of it, and minimizing the reality of the change. "Now I've got time to . . . paint the house, take a holiday . . .—I didn't like the job anyway."
> *Pining:* Hoping that the job will come back—an unrealistic expectation that the next job will be exactly the same.
> *Anger:* Blaming someone—"I never could work with him (my boss) anyway." "They should have . . ."
> *Guilt:* Self-blame—"They didn't choose me because I wasn't up to it /did something wrong."
> *Apathy:* A sense of powerlessness and hopelessness as the reality sinks in.
> *Acceptance:* Letting go of the past, and the emergence of a new energy.

Nathan and Hill's transition curve is illustrated in Figure 11–2.

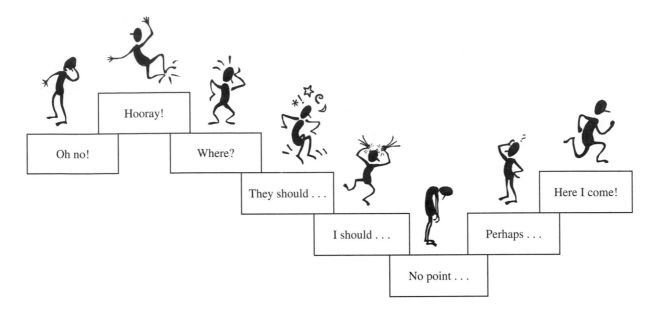

FIGURE 11–2 The Transition Curve

SOURCE: Robert Nathan and Linda Hill. *Career Counseling,* p. 28, © 2005 by Sage Publications, Inc. Reprinted by permission of Sage Publications, Inc.

> Another common progression of feelings following rejection are those of the transition curve, namely, shock or denial, euphoria, pining, anger, guilt, apathy, and acceptance.

Regardless of the intensity of the feelings you experience following rejection, how long it takes you to work through the negative feelings depends on the seriousness of the rejection. The first rejection is not as bad as the second once you understand it is part of the process and brings you one step closer to achieving your goal. The more rejections, or the more important a job is to you, the more extreme your reactions may be. Remember: Accept the inevitable and understand that this is how it is going to feel. There is strength in self-awareness. As George Bernard Shaw says: "Better keep yourself clean and bright; you are the window through which you must see the world."

One positive result from your job-seeking journey, especially the jobs you didn't get, is the strategy you'll develop to effectively cope with life's disappointments. It's hard to imagine at the time, but you will be a better, stronger person for these experiences.

But even with the good that comes from the process, financial challenges might cause you to question if you should keep up the search or just take any job to pay the bills. Even people new to the workforce need an income, but being without a job or underemployed can seriously affect people with even more obligations. Dealing with finances while job searching can compound frustrations and fears. Weston (2008) provides the following tips for managing finances while job searching:

➢ *Get your head on straight.* Stay positive.

➢ *Schedule your job search.* Treat it like a job.

➤ *Let people know how to find you.* Stay connected.

➤ *Stay covered.* Keep adequate insurance.

➤ *Apply for unemployment benefits.* Don't let pride stand in your way.

➤ *Track your spending.* You can live on a budget.

➤ *Get your priorities straight.* Stick to your budget.

➤ *Conserve your cash.* Live within your budget.

➤ *Use your home equity with caution.* Don't sell yourself short.

➤ *Raise cash.* Consider part-time or temporary work to tide you over.

➤ *Identify emergency sources of aid.* Have a secondary plan.

➤ *Consider volunteering.* Adds to your résumé, constructive use of time, and networking is always good.

CONCLUSION

The knowledgeable, prepared applicant understands and accepts that *everybody* experiences these negative feelings when they lose something they want. To prepare for and effectively handle rejection in your job search, be aware that it does happen to just about everyone and that the only ones who fail are the ones who stop trying. Avoid negative self-talk and never lose faith in yourself. Each "no" brings you closer to a "yes." But whatever setbacks you may experience, "nos" you may hear or rejection you may feel, DO NOT GIVE UP!

> *You may be disappointed if you fail, but you are doomed if you don't try.*
>
> —*Beverly Sills*

AN INSIDER'S VIEW

EACH FAILURE IS ONE STEP CLOSER TO SUCCESS

Timothy J. Thompson

Vice President
Verification, Inc.

Accomplishing your employment objective is often not in your control. Any decision to hire involves many factors. Since you're looking at the situation of *not* getting the job offer, let's analyze the hiring process to understand why you sometimes don't have control. As discussed in previous chapters, the hiring process involves three main areas:

➤ Education—what you've been taught
➤ Work history—what you've done
➤ The interview—how you appear

One other additional component of the hiring process is vital in employee selection: *who* is doing the hiring. If you know someone involved in the hiring process or are related to the president of the company, your chances of getting the job are obviously many times better than those without such connections.

How the hiring is done and by whom often differs greatly from agency to agency and firm to firm, making it hard for applicants. To be properly prepared, you must research the hiring process as well as the position. The process may involve a simple application to a company president or personnel manager or may be much more complex, involving panels and boards. Because the process is not uniform, the people doing the hiring are not always proficient at employee selection. Many do not have practical experience to adequately evaluate the ability and qualifications of applicants. Police commissions and selection boards are good examples of such lack of practical experience. All too often the hiring groups are made up largely of community laypeople, lacking professional credentials in the field for which applicants are applying. Even city managers and personnel directors sometimes lack experience in hiring to make good choices.

So where does this leave you? Well, when the candidates appear on paper to be equally qualified (i.e., their educational credentials and work history are very similar), the selection comes down to an interview and personalities. With so many variables operating, no one can pick a favorite. But if you have an outstanding résumé, you can make yourself appear more qualified than the rest. How? Consider these guidelines.

Your résumé should reflect information pertinent to the position for which you are applying. Entry-level positions should generally be a page or two, tops, but should contain information necessary to qualify for the position. Employers have neither the time nor the interest to read lengthy résumés for entry-level positions. In these cases, the cover letter will help sell your qualifications.

For non-entry-level positions where prior experience is desired or required, additional information can be added to the résumé and cover letter. This information should include specific experiences and accomplishments but, again, should be brief. If you are applying for a management position, your résumé can, and in some cases should, include as much information as possible regarding your background, education, experiences and achievements. However, this information should be compiled in an easy-to-read format with appropriate headings and short paragraphs. Employers seeking managers want to know as much about the applicant as possible before the interview. This is why telephone interviews are becoming more popular with personnel recruiters. It is better to have the information already prepared on your résumé than to have to think about it when someone calls. And your chance of getting that call improves the more the recruiter is impressed with your submitted credentials.

I have discovered that my ability to conduct interviews and effectively examine applicants' backgrounds to determine job suitability has dramatically increased with experience. Unfortunately, many management people, selection boards, firms and the like lack adequate experience to hire effectively. It is no wonder many people are performing jobs for which they are unsuited. It is also no wonder that perhaps you and your talent are being overlooked. Even when you have done all your homework, researched each position, individualized your application and résumé for the job, looked for inside people to help and prepared for each interview separately, you still may not get the position.

It is easy to become frustrated, bitter and resentful when you have worked so hard to prepare and you feel so confident in your ability to perform the job—given the chance. Remember, you are seeking employment in extremely popular fields, and you have plenty of competition. You do not have to give up, however. You *will* get a job that is right for you. And it may come when you least expect it. I know how frustrating it is to get rejection letters. I have a file full of them. I want to share from my experience some do's and don'ts related to the feelings of frustration and hopelessness involved in being rejected for a job.

DO

➤ Develop a support system. It is important to have an avenue to vent your feelings. Find an understanding friend who will listen while you express these feelings.

➤ Keep networking. The more people you know, the better your chances of learning about job openings. Often when you least expect it, a job will appear. Just ask some friends and acquaintances how they got their jobs.

➢ Look for alternatives. Often people get tunnel vision when looking for jobs, limiting themselves to one particular area when in fact they have abilities in many areas. You may want to be a police officer, but what about other possibilities such as being a U.S. Marshal, a state fraud enforcement officer, a postal inspector, an FAA enforcement officer, an FBI secret service agent and on and on.

➢ Consider relocating as an option if possible.

➢ Use the Internet for your job search.

DON'T

➢ Don't spend every minute worrying about your job situation. Take time for other things, especially recreation. Remember, a job often appears when you least expect it.

➢ Don't give up. Talk with friends. Acquaint yourself with other people in your chosen field. Join associations.

➢ Don't make compulsive decisions. This is no time to make major changes in either your employment situation or your lifestyle. Do not, for example, pack up and move to Florida because you believe more job opportunities exist there, unless you really want to live in Florida. Nor should you buy a house or new car because you think it will make you feel better.

Hang in there. Press on. You *can* and *will* land that job.

Timothy J. Thompson *is a vice president for Verifications, Inc., a private detective agency. Mr. Thompson holds private detective licenses in more than twenty states. He is also a security trainer and security consultant performing security audits and assessments.*

His background includes more than twenty years in public law enforcement, serving as police chief for seven years, and nineteen years in the private sector, holding top management positions with Canterbury Downs Racetrack, Shakopee, Minnesota (security director); the Thoroughbred Racing Protective Bureau, Fairhill, Maryland (special agent); Minnesota Timberwolves, Minneapolis, Minnesota (arena manager and human resources director); and the University of St. Thomas, St. Paul, Minnesota (director of public safety and parking services). His experience includes managing, investigating, assessing needs, designing and planning security departments and communications centers, and writing policy and procedure manuals. He also has extensive knowledge in electronic security equipment as well as access control and card systems, risk management, and parking services.

 MIND STRETCHES

1. What benefits can come from *not* getting a job?

2. Why is it helpful to understand the sequential reaction to loss and change and the transition curve?

3. Why is it harmful to ignore negative feelings arising from a rejection to an application?

4. Why would someone ignore these feelings?

5. Do you think applicants for criminal justice or security jobs are less likely to deal with their feelings? Why?

6. Why do you think unsuccessful candidates might lash out at an employer who didn't hire them? Could this ever be successful?

7. Is there ever one perfect job?

8.   Is there danger in believing there *is* one perfect job?

9.   Who is included in your support system? How can you best use them?

10.   Can you think of "failures" or "losses" in your life that actually benefited you?

REFERENCES

Bolles, Richard Nelson. *What Color Is Your Parachute? A Practical Manual for Job-Hunters & Career-Changers.* Berkeley, CA: Ten Speed Press, 2008.

Gates, Bill. *Business @ the Speed of Thought: Succeeding in the Digital Economy.* New York: Warner Business Books, 2000.

"How Failure Breeds Success: Everyone Fears Failure. But Breakthroughs Depend on It. The Best Companies Embrace their Mistakes and Learn from Them." *BusinessWeek,* July 10, 2006. Available online at www.businessweek.com/magazine/content/06_28/b3992001.htm.

Nathan, Robert, and Linda Hill. *Career Counseling.* Newbury Park, CA: Sage Publications, 2005.

Weston, Liz Pulliam. "A Survival Guide for the Unemployed." *MSN Money,* 2008. Available online at http://articles.moneycentral.msn.com/SavingandDebt/LearnToBudget/ASurvivalGuideForTheUnemployed.aspx?page=all.

SECTION THREE

JOB-SEEKING STRATEGIES

A wise man will make more opportunities than he finds.

—*Francis Bacon*

You've decided what you're looking for in a career. After closely examining your personal characteristics, you have found a fit. You've created an impressive résumé to demonstrate that fit to potential employers, and you're prepared to handle rejections. You're ready. Where to find jobs and how to get them is the focus of this section. Chapter 12 looks at the application process. It takes you through various strategies for locating job openings and making your availability and interest known. It discusses the importance of the application form and the role of your résumé, and it reviews the testing process.

If all goes well to this point, you will be invited for a personal interview. The basics of presenting yourself for an interview are the focus of Chapter 13—how to dress, communicate, and follow up. Chapter 14 takes a closer look at the all-important interview process and what to expect from it. Figure S3 illustrates the steps you've already completed and what lies ahead.

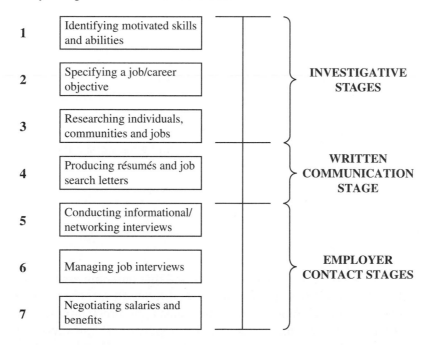

FIGURE S3   Job-Search Steps

SOURCE: Ronald L. Krannich. *Change Your Job, Change Your Life*, 9th ed. Manassas Park, VA: Impact Publications, 2005, p. 101. Reprinted by permission.

CHAPTER 12

THE APPLICATION PROCESS:
FINDING AND APPLYING FOR JOBS

(1) Regard job hunting as a real job—and expect that it, like any other job, demands time, persistence, and discipline. (2) Recognize that while you can get a good job through ads or employment agencies, competition for jobs that are advertised tends to be fierce. (3) Apply directly to an employer even without any hint there is a job opening. Positions constantly become available and it's wise to be on a good list. (4) Try to get as many job interviews as you can and concentrate on smaller firms. (5) If you can see a layoff coming, start looking for a job while you are still working. (6) Expect to be discouraged. Guard against anger, apathy, or feeling defeated.

—Sylvia Porter

Do You Know:

➢ What you must identify before beginning your job search and how many hours you should spend each week looking for work?

➢ Which ads to read in the classified section of the paper and in which papers to look?

➢ What specialized periodicals to review?

➢ How the Internet can help?

➢ The variety of other places to check for leads on job openings in your field?

➢ The importance of looking and acting your best during any contact with a potential employer?

➢ How to make contact with a prospective employer by mail?

➢ What networking is and how important it is to your job search? With whom you should talk?

➢ Why it is important to never "burn your bridges"?

➢ What the entire application process usually involves?

➢ What information the application form usually asks for and what impact the Equal Employment Opportunity (EEO) guidelines have had on these application forms?

➢ The importance of follow-up?

INTRODUCTION

You have to *work at finding work*. Serious job searchers find that pursuing employment requires as much, if not more, effort than a full-time job and that a well-thought-out strategy is essential. A well-developed search demands action. Unmotivated, unenthusiastic, undirected individuals will miss opportunities and are easily identified and weeded out by employers. Employers are looking for that *special* applicant who exudes drive, energy, and genuine enthusiasm. Develop your strategy so you not only maintain the energy necessary to pursue your career goals, but so your energy *shines brightly* to employers.

Don't just plan to look for work. Chase it! Hustle! Scramble! Be creative! Have fun! Turn what can be a frustrating experience into a personal challenge. Each disappointment, each new challenge, is part of the training that will let you succeed. *Get what you want!* Let the process feed you, not defeat you.

Although these jobs appear conservative, employers still want enthusiasm and look for it in applicants. The way you pursue employment throughout the process reflects the kind of employee you will be. Do you put your all into each step in the process or commit only minimal energy? Some people choose a safer, but less effective, route which has been called *playing not to lose*: "Avoiding situations where we might lose, fail, be emotionally hurt, or be rejected" (Wilson and Wilson, 2004, p. 23). *Playing to win*, on the other hand, "means consciously choosing to experience those situations that will help us grow . . . it means going into those situations wholeheartedly, committed to going as far as we can with all we have" (Wilson and Wilson, p. 25).

DEVELOPING YOUR JOB-SEARCH STRATEGY

To keep on track—physically, emotionally, and intellectually—you have to develop a strategy. The first step is to determine *what* you are looking for. The unemployed are frequently asked, "How can you not have a job? Hundreds (thousands) are advertised for!" This may be true, but take a closer look. You are not going to apply for every job advertised. Somewhere between *actuarial* and *zookeeper* are the jobs you will consider.

Begin with the questions: "What do I want? How do I get it?" If nothing short of police officer will satisfy you, do not apply for private security positions. On the other hand, might a position as an armored-truck driver, for instance, be a good stepping-stone to lead you to your end goal? Unless you are desperate for money, taking a full-time position of no interest or value to your career goals could result in several problems. For example, say you start applying randomly, get a job in an unrelated field, and eventually quit for a job you probably should have waited for in the first place. This could make you look like a "job jumper," create hard feelings with that employer when you leave, and maybe result in a negative reference.

This doesn't mean you should sit at home unemployed until you get your dream job. For a variety of reasons, including financial and emotional, it is frequently much easier to get a job when you have a job. What is important is to identify what you want before going after it. Then, if you are completely employment-free, you must dedicate yourself to finding work as if the search itself was a full-time, forty-hour-a-week job.

Bolles (2008, p. 8) points out: "Researchers discovered, some years ago, that while a typical job hunt lasted around 14 to 19 weeks, depending on the economy, one-third to one-half of all job hunters simply gave up by the second month of their job hunt. They stop job hunting. (Of course, they have to resume, somewhere further down the road, when and if things get really desperate.)" The reasons vary: lack of immediate results, discouragement, fatigue. But job hunting takes time, knowledge, and a strategy. And the more time you invest, the more knowledge you have about how to get a job and the better your strategy, the more likely it is you'll find a job sooner.

It is important to identify what you want before going after it. Then you must make job hunting a full-time commitment, spending thirty-five to forty hours a week actively searching for work if you are currently unemployed.

WHERE TO LOOK FOR JOB OPENINGS

The sources to consider when searching for work are numerous. A basic part of your job-search strategy is to learn what sources to best leverage for leads. Some may produce more than others, but relying on just one source is a mistake. Sometimes the least expected source has what you need. Your options include checking newspaper want ads, specialty periodicals, and job postings on the Internet; visiting government employment service offices and college or university placement offices; networking with family, friends, and acquaintances; making personal inquiries at potential employers' places of business; and contacting prospective employers by phoning or possibly e-mailing them.

Newspapers

Begin with perhaps the most traditional place to look for employment—newspaper want ads. After watching the local papers daily for several weeks, you will identify the generally accepted procedure employers in various fields use to advertise for employees. Ads for law enforcement positions, for instance, are usually placed in the Sunday paper, under the heading of "police." Private security positions generally appear under the heading of "security." Is this how it is always done? Of course not.

Think creatively. Ads for police officers could appear under such headings as "law enforcement," "public safety," or "officer." Corrections positions may appear under "prisons," "jails," "guards," and the like. Security jobs may appear under the title of "risk management" or "loss control." Take time to familiarize yourself with all the possible headings your job could fall under and continue to scan the entire listing.

Perhaps a clerk or a secretary placed the ad without knowing anything about the actual job and thought "safety officer," "city employee," or "state employee" would be the best spot. Maybe the ad will appear, accidentally or purposely, on a Tuesday only. Do not let yourself get lazy just because such ads are usually in the Sunday paper under a specific section.

 Under what other headings might a police position appear? List them in your journal.

 Under what other headings might a private security position appear? List them in your journal.

 If considering a related field, under what headings might it appear? Note these in your journal.

Job openings are usually placed in the classified ads that appear in columns, row after row. Take time, however, to also check the display (box) ads used most frequently by corporations. These bigger ads are more expensive, but occasionally a city or private employer that wants to state specific needs or is particularly in need of people will use this approach. Scan *all* the newspaper want ads.

Also consider the possibility of ads appearing in papers other than those published in your particular city. A Minneapolis job seeker, for instance, should check the St. Paul newspaper. The Oakland job seeker should check a San Francisco paper. The Seattle job seeker should be looking in a Tacoma paper. Read the local and neighborhood papers as well as those of surrounding cities.

> Begin your job search with the most obvious place to look for employment—newspaper want ads. Think creatively and scan *all* the ads. In addition to your local and neighborhood papers, check the papers of surrounding cities.

You don't have to subscribe to newspapers to use them. Most are available at libraries and over the Internet.

Many Jobs Aren't Advertised. It is essential to know that many jobs are either not advertised or are actually filled before an ad is placed. How could that be? Probably because an aggressive job seeker with an effective strategy found a way in (long before you ever became aware of the job opening), either by having established a relationship with the employer (perhaps as an intern) or by making the employer aware of their interest before the job opening existed. Frequently, in such cases, an ad is run because of department policy or to meet a legal obligation. Your strategy, then, is to learn about these jobs before these probabilities occur. Just because an employer doesn't yet know a job will open up doesn't mean you should not be trying for it.

Specialty Periodicals and Other Publications

Every field has trade publications. Law enforcement, corrections, and private security have many journals, often containing ads. Such periodicals as *The Police Chief, Law and Order, Corrections Today, The Prison Journal, Corrections Compendium,* and *Security Management* not only contain higher-level position openings, but also contain current information beneficial to individuals applying in these fields.

Other publications deal with more general topics and could contain an ad for your job. For example, magazines that deal with municipal government could contain such ads. Become familiar with a variety of specialty periodicals, including periodicals that only list jobs. One such publication of particular interest to those seeking employment in law enforcement and private security is the *National Employment Listing Service,* which contains only related employment opportunities.

Other specific publications address only city, county, state, or federal jobs. If not contained in such specialized publications, they will usually be posted. If you are interested in a federal job, the *Federal Jobs Register* is a valuable resource. Another source for federal positions or for international positions is the U.S. Civil Service Commission (the address is given at the end of the chapter). *Job Search Guide: Strategies for Professionals,* a U.S. Department of Labor publication, discusses specific steps job seekers should follow to identify employment opportunities.

> Every field has trade publications. Check the specialty periodicals associated with your chosen field, whether it's police work, corrections, private security, or a related criminal justice field.

Again, bear in mind what Bolles (p. 44) found regarding answering ads in professional or trade journals: "This search method . . . has a 7% success rate. . . . 93 job-hunters out of 100 will not find the jobs that are out there if they use only this method to search for them." Despite this dismally low success rate, Bolles points out there is at least one other job-search avenue with a worse track record—the Internet.

The Internet

The successful job seeker will become familiar with Internet job employment searches including finding newspaper ads, articles, discussion boards, and services that can literally come to you. Some are free; some available for a fee. You can access the ever-increasing number of websites available to learn more about a specific company, organization, agency, or even community. Computer bulletin boards and discussion groups are popular for interacting (networking) with others who have similar interests and for finding information on a particular job, agency, or area. Newspapers from across the country can be accessed over the Internet, making it much easier to research job openings in a variety of locations.

Multiple listings, also called "job banks," such as through www.jobbankinfo.org/ can direct you to listings in each state. Other sites can be a gold mine of information. For example, the U.S. Department of Labor Bureau of Statistics is a source many people use to learn about specific jobs. But upon closer exploration there are information-filled links to get even more information about such topics as where to look for jobs, interview tips, and how to consider what work might be best for you www.bls.gov/oco/home.htm.

 Keep a list of helpful sources so you can return to them. Once you start, you'll quickly find that each source provides links to several more.

The Internet has become an increasingly valuable resource, not as much for actual job listings but for researching specific agencies and communities where career opportunities are available.

As the Internet continues to expand, it's worth devoting some time to exploring what is readily accessible.

 Use your search engine for the following terms. Then list five hits (including the URL) that might provide helpful information in your job search:

➤ Résumé

➤ Job interview

➤ Government jobs

➤ Criminal justice careers

➤ Why I can't get a job

➤ (Your own job-seeking related term or query)

Always Check the Source. Just because it's on the Internet doesn't make it credible. Using the Internet not only requires you know where and how to look, but what to believe. Consider the following issues to be aware and cautious of when using the Internet:

➤ *Check the Date*: When was the material posted? Job postings can remain for months, years, or longer after the ad has expired.

➤ *Who Posted It?* It may be the hiring authority or a service. Employers often enlist agencies who receive a fee for their service. Be clear about who pays for any fee.

➤ *What Information Is Requested?* It's not as much a concern if a potential employer asks for information, but if anyone else asks, consider why they want the information, especially if the sites offers anything "free," such as suggestions by e-mail. By obtaining your e-mail, which may be sold to vendors, it's also possible to install spyware on your computer. Consider obtaining a no-cost e-mail account for these searches, such as through Yahoo! or Google. This also keeps the spam you're likely to receive separate from your personal e-mail account.

➤ *Beware of Scams*: Never provide personal information to anyone requesting it on the Internet unless absolutely sure it is a legitimate request; even then, exercise caution. As with any other online requests, never provide information that could be used for identity theft, including your date of birth, Social Security number, bank account, credit card or other financial information, or information that strikes you as odd. Never provide information to any *international sources*. Anyone beyond the physical reach of American law enforcement or other regulatory agencies is a concern because they are not bound by our laws.

➤ *Consider Safety*: Never agree to personally meet someone off-site, and if you feel any communication has strayed from a purely professional basis, dismiss it. Unfortunately the Internet has provided a means for some to seek out people to victimize.

Government Employment and Educational Placement Offices

Because government is the largest employer of all, the serious job hunter routinely checks federal, state, county, and municipal offices regularly (every week or two) for updated job postings. You may be able to subscribe to job listings used by government agencies as well as privately published services. Some are free; others are offered by paid subscription. Sometimes local libraries or a school you attend may have electronic or hard-copy subscriptions you may access for free. When using these types of resources, check them regularly. If you have a special interest in something particular, stop and actually ask, or communicate by phone or e-mail. You don't want to be a pest, but if you do communicate, in person or otherwise, always present yourself professionally.

For students, placement offices at colleges and universities that offer programs in law enforcement, corrections, criminal justice, or private security often post job notices and have excellent employment listing services. Contact the career services office on campus for a list of current openings. These offices also coordinate interviews with agencies looking to hire and have reference libraries or agencies throughout the world.

Networking

With all the benefits from newspapers, magazines, and the Internet, the most important strategy of all is developing personal relationships with everyone who might help; that is, networking.

There is great truth in the saying, "It's not *what* you know but *who* you know." Rarely will this saying be truer than when searching for employment. Family members, friends, neighbors, people you know through church, people whose kids go to the same school as your kids, other soccer moms and hockey dads, the guy at the gym —you can tap all these resources for leads in the job market. And if they can't help, they might know someone who can. Because networking is so important, it is discussed in depth later in the chapter. For now, continue with the discussion on where to look for job openings.

Personal Inquiries

With an overreliance by some on e-communication, and a lack of interpersonal skills and manners by others, taking time to personally inquire or express interest about a job can be a very effective strategy if you:

➤ Are polite to the person at the front desk when asking if there is someone with whom you can speak.

➤ Are prepared to leave your résumé or other information if no one is available.

➤ Never make a personal visit without appearing your best.

➤ Keep the inquiry brief so as not to impose, acknowledging that you understand they are busy and appreciate a moment of their time.

➤ Never leave without thanking everyone with whom you talked.

Telephone Inquiries

Active job seekers put considerably more effort into their pursuit than just browsing through newspaper and Internet ads. You've got to get out there and investigate. An easy, quick, relatively nonthreatening way is to telephone and ask if a certain department, agency, or company has, or expects, any openings. This is known as *cold-calling.*

When making such calls, begin by asking whom you should talk with about possible job openings. Ask if they send out a mailer or have an Internet site for job openings or if you could get on a specific list to be notified for a particular job. With a little polite interaction, you may be able to get an individual notice from the contact person you impressed while inquiring. Even if the contact you made proves fruitless, never hang up without asking if they know of anyone *else* who is hiring. Your goal is to develop an ever-expanding list of resources and contacts.

Other places to check during your job search include the federal, state, county, and municipal personnel offices; your local library for job listing mailers used by government agencies and privately published services; placement offices and employment information resources at local educational institutions and universities; your local telephone directory; employment services and organizations; computer bulletin boards; and government pamphlets and publications. You might also consider making personal or telephone inquiries at companies or agencies that interest you, requesting information about current or anticipated job openings.

ON BEING YOUR BEST

An absolutely essential part of your strategy is to be your best at *every* phase of the job-search process. Because of the natural frustrations of the process, this is sometimes difficult. Yet it is vital that you relate positively, courteously, and respectfully to everyone with whom you come in contact. You may not think the receptionist, secretary, or person who casually strolls up and asks if they can help you is important. They are. You never know with whom you are talking.

If you are making phone inquiries, be away from crying babies, barking dogs, and other noises that could be distracting for both you and the person you're calling. Consider dressing as you would for a personal interview. If you look sharp, you will feel sharp and, in turn, will act sharp, making a better impression than if you were calling while lounging in your bathrobe at 2 o'clock in the afternoon. Besides, you never know if the prospective employer might say something like, "Can you come down right now?" It happens. Also, don't assume your call will be answered by "just a secretary." The boss may answer the phone when the receptionist is away from the desk. Furthermore, many employers come in early and stay later than their administrative staff—phone calls at these times may reap unexpected benefits. Even if it is the secretary or receptionist, they often screen contacts or are certainly trusted enough to be listened to if they think you were rude or otherwise inappropriate.

When making personal contacts, coming across well is especially important. Applicants who drop off résumés while wearing extremely casual attire or something bizarre take a possibly fatal risk. There is always a chance you could meet with someone, even if you meant to only leave your résumé and ask about possible openings. Perhaps the person responsible for hiring will walk by or has told the person at the front desk to send any applicants to see him/her. Maybe a new receptionist or a temporary employee will mistakenly send you into the employer's office. If you are wearing cut-up jeans and lizard-skin cowboy boots, you have damaged what should have been a spectacular opportunity. The prepared job seeker is always ready for the unexpected.

In addition, the first contact person may deliver your message or résumé to the boss *with* an editorial comment. It had better be something like:

➤ This applicant sure was polite.

➤ This person dressed well.

➤ This one seemed like she would fit in.

➤ This is the one who called and was so courteous.

You don't want something like:

➤ Wait until you see this slob.

➤ This guy was really rude just now.

➤ This is the gal who hung up on me last week.

You will likely be talked about after you leave, so make sure the talk is positive. You may also get something more from being polite—the person taking your call or greeting you at the front desk may be willing to give you advice or a tip on future openings. It is also possible they may go tell the boss, "There is someone here you should meet," or even call you with information about a new opening. Because you never know, always be prepared. Even if you feel frustrated, frazzled, and tired, look like this is *the* most important contact you are making. And when anyone anywhere says,

"Feel free to give me a call if you have any other questions," include them in your journal—they just offered to help you!

An essential part of your strategy is to be your best at *every* phase of the job-search process. During phone contacts and especially during personal contacts, dress and act professionally. Expect the unexpected. You may be talking to the boss and not know it.

Being your best applies to other forms of communication as well. Mail or e-mail should reflect upon you positively.

CONTACTS IN WRITING

The importance of appearance in making a good impression also applies to written material submitted in any format because it is a direct reflection of you. Although you may not meet the person doing the hiring, if you supply a résumé, chances are it will at least get looked at. Provide that person with something that interests them, not something that gives them a reason to throw it away. Résumé submission by mail (or e-mail or fax) was discussed in depth in Chapter 10.

Contacting prospective employers by mail is perfectly acceptable. Like telephoning, it is quick, easy, and even more nonthreatening. It may, however, be less effective. Although it may be hard to say "no" to someone in person, it is easier over the phone, and easiest with a letter (usually by dumping it in the circular file). Taking the time to compose a letter and print it to mail, or in the case of a thank-you that is handwritten, similar to good manners, a personal letter or card is always in style and makes a positive statement about you.

Note here the recommendation is *not* "résumé mailing," but "letter writing." It makes no sense to send an agency or company only a résumé. A cover letter makes the process more personal and sincere by introducing yourself and stating the reason you are writing. Whether responding to an ad or merely inquiring about what might be available, include both a cover letter *and* a résumé.

Writing skills are exceptionally important, and here is a chance to shine. To make a favorable impression when you write, consider the following:

➢   Don't provide a letter without a résumé or a résumé without a letter.

➢   Don't submit anything in pencil (and write neatly in ink only if you are absolutely unable to locate anyone who can type it for you).

➢   Don't use sheets torn out of a spiral notebook or lined, three-hole notebook paper.

➢   Don't use the back of a used piece of paper or an old envelope or receipt.

➢   Don't send form letters, especially those designed for another job area.

➢   Don't send copies of letters or résumés that have been copied so many times they are faded and hard to read.

➤ Don't fold your material into strange shapes. Enclose it, unfolded, in a 9 × 12 white envelope.

➤ Don't apply for a new job using stationery or envelopes from your current job, which could be considered theft.

As difficult as it may be to believe, all of the preceding have been submitted, and all have been thrown away without ever allowing the applicant to recover from the negative impression he or she made.

Employers are busy, especially those expected to do more with less and are shorthanded and need to hire more personnel. They will not have time to go through all the applications, so they will look for reasons to throw most out. Foolish applicants provide plenty of justifiable reasons to jettison their letters and résumés. When providing a prospective employer with *anything* in writing:

➤ Make sure it is neat and appears professional.

➤ Make sure it is typed on your own stationery.

➤ Make sure it is personalized for *that* contact. Call to find out to whom it should be addressed and the proper spelling and title.

Proofread it; and proofread it again. Have someone else proofread it. Then proofread it one last time. Improper grammar and typos provide excellent reasons to pitch a résumé. If you don't, or can't, get it right for this very important step in job seeking, what mistakes might you make on the job?

> When providing a prospective employer with *anything* in writing, make sure it is typed neatly on good-quality paper, personalized, and free of errors. Never send a résumé without a cover letter or a letter without a résumé.

Don't use paper and envelops pilfered from a current or past employer.

NETWORKING BASICS

Because the vast majority of job seekers make several applications, you will want to constantly seek new contacts and new possibilities. After being hired, you are likely to change jobs (maybe several times), so you will need to continue to expand your contacts. This process, called *networking*, is *the* most important component of the job search.

Salespeople have effectively used this networking concept for years, calling it "developing leads." You are a salesperson, selling yourself. The process involves setting up a network of resources you will not forget and who will not forget you. It begins with making whatever contacts you already have and taking every opportunity to add to this list. You then use each contact to make more contacts, and more contacts, and so on. For instance, when making a contact at one agency, ask if you should check with anyone or anywhere else. Imagine if each contact gave you two or three other employers' names. You could quickly develop literally hundreds of possible contacts.

What becomes difficult and complex is *how* you develop and organize your networking strategy and to what extreme you should take it. Because networking can, and in fact should, mushroom into many contacts, proceed in an orderly way. This is best done in writing, with a plan in mind. Here's how:

1. Make an initial contact.

2. Document that step.

3. Acquire additional contacts.

4. Document them.

5. Take action.

6. Follow up.

Keep a Complete List of Networking Contacts

Keep a detailed log of everyone you speak with, people who have been suggested to you, or follow-up ideas you generate. A notebook serves this purpose well and can be further divided to include websites, helpful hints, and personal reminders of your strengths to leverage and weaknesses to work on.

For networking, have complete information on all your contacts, including their name; job, rank, or position; full address; phone; e-mail; and website, if applicable. Also make notes about when you contacted them last, when you plan to again, and anything to help you remember what was said or suggested when you did contact them last. If you run into a dead end, you learn it's not a fit or believe they think so, mark it off to save time contacting them again.

A goal of every contact should be to come away with even more contacts. Never leave a conversation, when appropriate, without asking if there's anyone else the person would recommend contacting. And if someone *invites* you to contact them, *do*!

 In your journal, or in a separate networking notebook, list the important information you need to keep track of and organize it into a workable format. Data to be maintained should include:

> Company, agency, department name, address, phone, e-mail
> Names and titles of contacts (spelled correctly)
> What you did
> Other contacts this contact recommended
> What you will do

 Also, have a separate calendar to set up dates you will contact or recontact sources. The first recontact should be a week or two after the initial contact. Follow up every month thereafter, but be sure to recognize the fine line between an assertive applicant sure to be remembered and a pest they want to forget. Strive for a balance.

Pursue your job search positively and energetically. Develop every opportunity to show yourself in the best light. Be creative and learn from each experience. Even the contacts that appear to be unproductive give you a chance to learn more about the market and yourself. If nothing else, you come away from the experience knowing you are tough enough to accept the natural, expected setbacks that prove you are trying.

Networking—the process of connecting and interacting with people who can be helpful to you in your job search—is a crucial element in an effective job search. Place no limits on your network—talk to anyone and everyone.

ON BURNING BRIDGES

No matter what approach to contacting prospective employers you take, be it responding to an ad, phoning, sending a letter with a résumé, sending a fax, e-mailing, or stopping in, *never* leave a door permanently closed behind you. Don't burn any bridges that may eventually lead to a great job.

Some people can be insensitive, unfeeling, and downright rude. You are bound to get tense yourself because job seeking is difficult, but never show any negative feelings to anyone who may affect your future professional life. Don't be rude or vent your frustrations on anyone where you are applying for work, no matter how they treat you. If they treat you badly, it's probably not *you* they are upset with. They are likely just having a bad day. You may well return, *if* you have kept the door open. If you have sworn at someone or otherwise behaved unprofessionally, you might as well cross that resource out of your networking notebook.

This applies after being informed you were not the one selected. The *appropriate emotions* can include sadness and anger. The *inappropriate actions* exhibit sadness and anger. Employers hardly need a disgruntled applicant telling them what a stupid decision they made. You'd never be welcome to apply there again.

So, what should you do, thank them? Exactly. A personal but professional thank-you by an applicant who did not get the job is so unusual that any employer can't help but take notice. You may have been closer to that job than you realized. Not everyone hired works out or wants to stay, so that same position could open up in days, weeks, or months. And if there was a need to fill that position, how do you know there aren't other positions opening up soon as well?

Imagine if you made the foolish mistake, as some have, to call, write, or worse show up in person, to "give them a piece of your mind" only to find out you were their choice for the next position. The process is personal to you, but it's business to them. If you show so little self-control or restraint, it probably says they made the right decision. You made it that far once; don't destroy the way back if given another opportunity, and it happens.

Never burn any bridges. Doing so only removes any opportunities the future may have held for you.

YOU'VE FOUND AN OPENING AND THEY'VE ASKED YOU TO APPLY

Once you've found an opening and have been asked to apply for the position, you can expect to go through several steps, illustrated in Figure 12–1. The order in which these steps occur may vary, but in almost all instances, the first step will be to complete an application form.

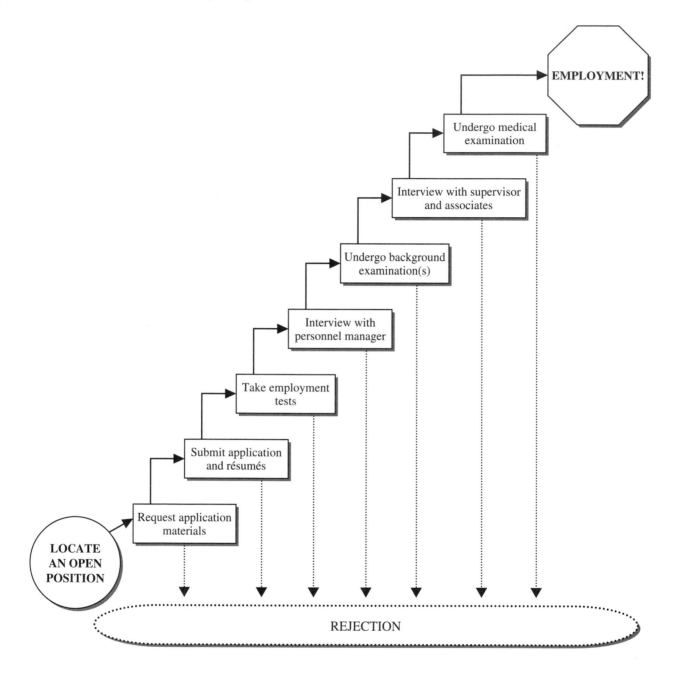

FIGURE 12–1   Typical Employment Process

The application process usually involves completing an application form, taking a series of written tests, having a preliminary interview, undergoing a background check, having a final interview, and taking a medical exam.

The Application

Some application forms are very simple; others are extremely involved. If you are asked to complete the form on the spot, do so neatly using *black ink*—it copies better. If you have done a thorough job on your résumé and are prepared by bringing a copy, you should have all the information you need at your fingertips.

Write legibly using your best *printing*. Write on the correct lines on a form. Sloppiness and inaccuracy on a job application may lead the employer to question your attention to detail and ability to follow instructions. Think before you write so you do not have to erase or cross out information. A high-quality erasable pen is a good investment. you do not understand something on the form, ask. Most of all, be complete.

If they will allow you to take the application home, do so, and type your responses on the form. However, many applicants do not have access to typewriters these days. And trying to format your responses using a computer and running the application form through the printer, hoping everything falls in the right spaces, can be an exercise in futility. Consequently, many forms must be filled out by hand. It is wise to make several copies of the form to practice on, saving the original for your final draft.

Seldom will you be asked to complete an entire application form on-site, but it happens. There may be other components you'll be called upon to write. More employers are requiring on-site written tests so they know you actually wrote whatever they've included in the process.

To be prepared, lessen stress and maintain the appearance of being in control; consider preparing a kit to take with you to every interview or whenever visiting a prospective employer. It could be as simple as including two pens (in case one dries up), a small notebook with the basic information that may be asked (Social Security number, references, etc.), or even personal items like breath mints to help with a dry mouth and a comb. Some opt for a larger folder, but not as large as a brief case, in which extra copies of your résumé and notepaper can be easily accessed. Some people have gone so far as to have personal cards, similar to business cards, printed as a means of quickly and professionally providing your contact information when the opportunity arises. Be prepared to make the best impression possible.

Application forms vary greatly in their complexity and depth, but they usually ask for the same information you gathered in preparing your résumé, so always have a copy of it with you. Although the Equal Employment Opportunity (EEO) guidelines make mandatory responses to questions about ethnic background, religious preference, and marital status illegal, it is usually in your best interest to complete these optional sections.

More departments and agencies are including a written essay as part of the application process, requesting candidates to write two or three pages on a specific topic, such as "Why are you interested in this field?" or "Why are you interested in being hired by this particular agency?"

Take time *before* you apply for a job to write two- to three-page answers to the following questions:

1. Why have you selected this particular field?
2. Why have you selected this particular agency?
3. Who are you? (Write a brief autobiography.)
4. What are your ethical values and how do you apply them at work?

REMEMBER THE MAGIC WORDS—THANK-YOU

Your parents were right. One absolute: *Never* leave a contact without following up with a thank-you, and when doing so in person, with a firm handshake. Not only is this good manners in a world sorely lacking them, but it is also another chance to present yourself positively. The more you can get your name in front of employers, the more they will remember you at hiring time.

You can phone or write your thank-you for the opportunity to interview or to submit your résumé. If you can't decide which way is better, do both. Don't express your thanks to *only* the chief of police or the president of the security company who took time to see you. Also thank the secretary who took time to set up the meeting or greeted you for your appointment. Show them you are thoughtful and courteous, the kind of person they would like working with them. Find out everyone on the interview panel and write a thank-you to them, too.

Always follow up a contact with a thank-you. It demonstrates your good manners and gets your name in front of the employer one more time.

WARNING: TAKE CARE OF YOURSELF

If you think job hunting sounds like a lot of work, you are absolutely correct. Every aspect of the process is emotionally and physically taxing and time consuming. You will be approaching other people trying to sell yourself, knowing the chances of immediate success are slim.

No one likes to hear the word "no." It becomes increasingly difficult to dial the phone, knock on the door, or send the next letter. It is risk taking at the most critical level. You are setting yourself up for a certain number of rejections. It is difficult, if not impossible, to keep from taking the entire process too personally. A rejection does not have to be a failure. Indeed, it can merely be the elimination of another job on your quest to find the job you are looking for.

Rejection can come for a number of reasons. Primarily, there needs to be a match between the candidate and the department. What may be inappropriate for one agency will be a gold mine for another. Rejection may simply mean it wasn't the best match for the department or for *you*.

Take care of yourself. If the whole thing starts to get the best of you, treat it like you would any other job. Set hours, including breaks; plan your days; take an occasional vacation. Finally, recognize the very real need for a support system. Plan time with people who accept and care about you. You can do this informally with family or friends, or more formally by organizing a support group with others in the same position. Such groups work extremely well for sharing support, ideas, and helpful hints. Most important, be sure your strategy allows you to keep at it. The next contact could have a job for you.

TESTING YOUR CAREERING COMPETENCIES*

INSTRUCTIONS: Respond to each statement by circling the number at the right that best represents your situation.

SCALE: 1 = strongly agree
            2 = agree
            3 = maybe, not certain
            4 = disagree
            5 = strongly disagree

1. I know what motivates me to excel at work.   1 2 3 4 5

2. I can identify my strongest abilities and skills.   1 2 3 4 5

3. I have seven major achievements that clarify a pattern of interests and
    abilities that are relevant to my job and career.   1 2 3 4 5

4. I know what I both like and dislike in work.   1 2 3 4 5

5. I know what I want to do during the next 10 years.   1 2 3 4 5

6. I have a well-defined career objective that focuses my job search on
    particular organizations and employers.   1 2 3 4 5

7. I know what skills I can offer employers in different occupations.   1 2 3 4 5

8. I know what skills employers most seek in candidates.   1 2 3 4 5

9. I can clearly explain to employers what I do well and enjoy doing.   1 2 3 4 5

10. I can specify why employers should hire me.   1 2 3 4 5

11. I can gain the support of family and friends for making a job or career change.   1 2 3 4 5

12. I can find 10 to 20 hours a week to conduct a part-time job search.   1 2 3 4 5

13. I have the financial ability to sustain a three-month job search.   1 2 3 4 5

14. I can conduct library and interview research on different occupations,
    employers, organizations, and communities.   1 2 3 4 5

15. I can write different types of effective résumés and job-search/thank-you letters.   1 2 3 4 5

16. I can produce and distribute résumés and letters to the right people.   1 2 3 4 5

17. I can list my major accomplishments in action terms.   1 2 3 4 5

18. I can identify and target employers I want to interview.   1 2 3 4 5

19. I can develop a job referral network.   1 2 3 4 5

20. I can persuade others to join in forming a job-search support group.   1 2 3 4 5

21. I can prospect for job leads.   1 2 3 4 5

22. I can use the telephone to develop prospects and get referrals and interviews.   1 2 3 4 5

23. I can plan and implement an effective direct-mail job-search campaign.   1 2 3 4 5

24. I can generate one job interview for every 10 job-search contacts I make.   1 2 3 4 5

25. I can follow up on job interviews.   1 2 3 4 5

26. I can negotiate a salary 10–20% above what an employer initially offers.   1 2 3 4 5

*SOURCE: Ronald L. Krannich. *Re-Careering in Turbulent Times: Skills and Strategies for Success in Today's Job Market.* Manassas, VA: Impact Publications, 1995, pp. 103–105. Reprinted by permission.

27.   I can persuade an employer to renegotiate my salary after six months on the job.   1   2   3   4   5

28.   I can create a position for myself in an organization.   1   2   3   4   5

You can calculate your overall careering competencies by adding the numbers you circled for a composite score. If your score is more than 75 points, you need to work on developing your careering skills. How you scored each item will indicate to what degree you need to work on improving specific job-search skills. If your score is under 50 points, you are well on your way toward job-search success.

CONCLUSION

Although waiting to hear about a job opening may work once in a great while, you usually must *work at finding work*. It is important to identify what you want before going after it. Then you must make job hunting a full-time commitment, spending a minimum of thirty-five to forty hours a week actively searching for work if you are currently unemployed. An essential part of your strategy is to be your best at *every* phase of the job-search process. *Always* follow up a contact with a thank-you and never burn any bridges. Doing so only removes any opportunities the future may have held for you.

AN INSIDER'S VIEW

LAW ENFORCEMENT JOBS: LEARNING HOW TO GET THEM TAKES THE SAME SKILLS REQUIRED TO DO THEM

John Lombardi

Professor of Criminal Justice and Criminology
Albany State College

Students want to pursue law enforcement positions for a number of reasons. There are also a number of different things a person can do in his or her travels from a student "wannabe" to a real cop, and getting the job is but one of these "rights of passage." This is not a personality contest. It is serious business. I do not believe all students are cut out to be police officers, nor are all police officers meant to be students. However, a student does not have to study law enforcement, but a police officer who aspires to be a professional must become a student of multi-methods of gathering different kinds of information. Dealing with the public, particularly with "street people," is an "art form" more than a science. It is more a pursuit of professionalism through continual training and education than an initial profession after graduating from an academy.

Serving the public is a truly honorable way to make a living, but always place your individual standards higher than those of the public you serve while still regarding them as equals. This is a lot to comprehend. However, if you cannot, it is likely you will be unable to muster the patience to make it through the "gatekeepers" who separate the "wannabe" from the "is." Consider the educational transformation you will experience during the job quest going from student "wannabe" to the world of law enforcement.

TALKING TO POLICE OFFICERS

For me and my POST [Peace Officers Standards and Training] undergraduate students in Minnesota, the search for a job starts early, during their sophomore year. Approximately one of three or four students applies for academy training in Minnesota. Most of my students apply outside the state because it takes less time to find a law enforcement job. Part of their training in their employment search is to speak with various police officers. This offers many benefits.

Scott Harr spent an hour with my criminal procedure class explaining procedures and answering questions from students, since we use his criminal procedures textbook. How does this work? I set up a call to the criminal justice professional, announce to the class who the speakerphone guest is and ask each student to make up at least one good question. The day of class I give the students several more minutes to look over their questions and collaborate with other students. The students are picked at random, come up to the speakerphone, ask their own questions and interact with the speaker. I have found that this opens up quiet students, gives them some confidence in speaking with authority figures and makes sense out of questions they have created from their own perspectives. It takes them away from books and the familiarity of the professor while, at the same time, shows them the overlap and consistency between the professor and what is learned in class and is supported by other criminal justice professionals with whom they speak and gather new information.

STATE APPLICATIONS

Students universally complain about filling out long applications. A simple solution to this for some positions is to request several state employment applications. Fill out one application, perfectly typed. The only spaces left open should be the date and job applied for. Copy this completed application, possibly 100 times. Also, ask that your name be placed on the state job mailing list or visit a state employment office weekly and file as many job applications as you wish. Most people who do this get a positive response relatively quickly. Remember, you will probably switch jobs a few times, according to research data. Consider "positioning" yourself for your second job as you contemplate your first. The first job *is* important but will likely be a stepping-stone along your career path.

TRAINING IN ORAL INTERVIEWS

I have taught a senior seminar in criminal justice that considers oral interviews, what types of questions to consider, possible responses and why, and the impact of what students have studied in college. The students are told to anticipate obvious questions:

➤ "Why do you want to be a police officer?" (Give three reasons including that you want to help people.)
➤ "Why do you want to be a police officer in this department?" (I have heard that your mandatory training opportunities are excellent; your department pays for graduate courses in management; your field training officer program is well-known; etc.)
➤ "What are your strong points?" (I have been trained to be a problem solver, not a problem creator.)
➤ And "stock" hypothetical questions such as "What would you do in a situation that is either impossible or is one in which you surely have not been, as yet, trained?" (Call your supervisor, follow policy and chain of command, etc.)

As you gather information, cast it into question form. This will get you in the mind-set to think on your feet. You must learn to control situations and yourself. You should become sensitive, but sitting and crying for someone does not help that person and does not make you a problem solver. Finding solutions for the person in need is the beginning of helping that person gain control.

If asked, "How has your education prepared you for a police officer position?" the hiring board does not want an academic, laborious listing of your criminal law or abnormal psychology courses. It is more practical and useful to respond with answers concerning an understanding of (1) mandatory training, (2) the difference between formal education and academy training, (3) factors involved in what being a "professional" means, (4) understanding the chain of command, (5) knowing what "1983 actions" are and not being afraid to ask the hiring board what type of 1983 actions their department has and is experiencing and how their academy is responding to the litigation,

(6) officer turnover and promotional list rates for similarly situated individuals in positions for which you are applying and (7) opportunities existing in areas for which you aspire (e.g., tactical teams, violent crimes units, task forces, etc.). Taking "a broader stroke" to responses shows you understand the "bigger picture" and are sensitive to the organization and the environmental impacts on the agency and its budgetary position.

Don't ask questions about salary. That can be found in job descriptions. And it is permissible to walk into an interview with a legal pad listing "solid" questions (e.g., education, mandatory retraining opportunities, outside "inner-city" voluntary opportunities for off-duty officers through various service agencies, etc.). If the hiring board asks you if you have any questions, you will be prepared. You can raise your oral board scores by asking several penetrating questions that allow board members to respond. This shows that you have thought ahead, that you have researched the agency beyond color coordination of uniform and squad car and that you are career-oriented.

SUBSCRIBING TO MONTHLY JOB OPENING LISTS

Local and national job openings can be purchased for a nominal fee. Ask at your local police department for such listings. In addition, investigate the possibilities in states that have high crime rates, as well as police academies that train for particular police jurisdictions (e.g., Florida). In other words, the state will not only train you, but will also help place you once you graduate. It is possible to qualify for 20 police departments or more with one application and then have an agency pay your salary when going through the academy. Check on hiring versus training rates— that is, how many people qualify each year in a particular state versus the number of persons actually hired.

BOOK LISTINGS OF LAW ENFORCEMENT AGENCIES

You can find annual listings of police agencies in the library or through local law enforcement agencies. You might pick agencies geographically and send a brief one-page request for an application, deadline dates and so on. Keep information on each mail-out, whether the agency is accepting applications or not. Call the agency to see if the application was accepted or when applications might be accepted. Write down the name of the officer spoken with and, when calling back, make sure to ask for the same officer.

WORKING OUTSTATE

In Minnesota, people like to stay instate. However, students who really want to be police officers will travel to states that have jobs. As Dr. Darrell Krueger, President of Winona State University, says, "Prepare for your second job." It is prophetic, since many of my students who have not found law enforcement jobs in Minnesota have gone to other states having reciprocity with Minnesota, that is, the student can work in another state as a fully sworn police officer for several years, then return to Minnesota and become a licensed police officer by counting the prior out-of-state police training accepted by POST. These officers simply need to pass a test to avoid the long waiting period of unemployment. This is good, smart business because it reduces loss and increases credentials.

THE MILITARY

The military can be a tremendous opportunity for immediate and future employment. If this is of interest, cultivate the recruiters starting in your junior year. The more a recruiter interacts with you, the more opportunity exists for that recruiter to see traits that would benefit the military occupational specialty for which you wish to contract.

NON–LAW ENFORCEMENT MAJORS

At a law enforcement training workshop, Dr. Jim O'Connor, at the time second in command of the FBI Academy in Quantico, Virginia, stated that within a few years many police departments will forgo the traditional street patrol requirement prior to becoming a detective and do direct hiring of business students into the detective ranks. Why? Because, according to Dr. O'Connor, traditional police training has failed to produce investigators capable of combating complex white-collar crimes that directly affect drug and violent crimes. You should know this as preparation for becoming a law enforcement professional.

EMPHASIS ON CRIME PREVENTION AND SECURITY

A major trend in law enforcement education and training is to include crime prevention and security functions. This is emphasized in many states, such as Minnesota, which has supported the Minnesota Crime Prevention Practitioners Association. This major movement blends the private sector with the public sector. The School of Criminal Justice at Michigan State has blended programs with their business school. The Florida State University School of Criminology has a long tradition of multidimensional methodological interdisciplinary training.

Be prepared to confront more complex issues in the future as an interested "problem solver," not simply a standard criminal justice major or veteran of many police ride-alongs. Even Forrest Gump understood the private sector. You cannot major in criminal justice and not understand the private sector.

TIMING AND SALESMANSHIP

In an employment search, timing is important. So is salesmanship. Do what you love, not just what you like. If all else fails, take second best or whatever is available. This is where "positioning for future jobs" becomes important. Patience is important when you realize that the first job is not what you want, but is doable until the "right one" comes along.

It is easy to seek comfort when the rejection form letters come in. Good people get rejection letters, the same as all others. The difference is that those meant to be police officers are persistent. You have to sell yourself. You buy from salespeople who believe or want to believe in their product. For the same reason you want to help people, the public wants to believe in the concepts you have to sell . . . "serve and protect." These are intangibles until you make them concrete. Each department can function well only if the majority of their officers practice what they preach. And this can happen only if each officer has faith in their ability to sell themselves, to let the public "buy into" that particular offer.

THE PERFECT TRAINING PROGRAM

I am often asked what I would include in the "perfect training program." I would include philosophy, English literature, verbal and written communication, business management, salesmanship and marketing, problem definition, resource allocation, policy development and an evaluation of what you think you'd accomplished after all that. Why? For *awareness*. For prevention of loss and reduction of faulty risk taking. For increasing accurate anticipation. *The same skills used to interpret a poem are used to write an accurate police report. And preventing loss is the same as increasing sales.*

In conclusion, do what you love and getting the job will be the easy part when you look back years later. And if you love what you do, the hard part will rarely surface unless you lose your sense of awareness, presence and problem definition. Love being a problem solver for a simple reason: it takes less effort to sell an idea you love. You are about to go places where most of the public would not go, but do you have what it takes? Would you hire yourself?

John Lombardi, *PhD, CST, CPO, NAPS, IAPSC, is a professor of criminal justice and criminology at Albany State College in Albany, Georgia, where he teaches graduate and undergraduate courses in methodology, crime prevention, and organizations. He earned his PhD from the School of Criminology at Florida State University, has numerous national board certifications, and is the former training director of the criminal justice training academy in Panama City, Florida, and POST coordinator/professor at Minnesota State University in Winona, Minnesota.*

 ## MIND STRETCHES

1.   List as many sources as you can in which employment ads might appear.

2.   Why are many jobs filled without being advertised or filled before the ad appears?

3.   List ten contacts you have available right now through which you could begin networking.

4.   If you were an employer deluged with applications, how would you eliminate 50 percent of them right away?

5.   What errors could applicants make when contacting a prospective employer by mail?

6.   Whether you contact an employer by phone, mail, or in person, what three things would you want that person to remember about you?

7.   What creative things can you do to get the attention of an employer? What possible benefits and detriments can you think of for each?

8.   What strategies will you use to locate employment opportunities?

REFERENCES

Bolles, Richard Nelson. *What Color Is Your Parachute? A Practical Manual for Job-Hunters & Career-Changers.* Berkeley, CA: Ten Speed Press, 2008.

Wilson, Larry, and Hersch Wilson. *Play To Win!* 2nd ed. Austin, TX: Bard Press, 2004.

ADDITIONAL CONTACTS AND SOURCES OF INFORMATION

Career Paths: A Guide to Jobs in Federal Law Enforcement by Gordon M. Armstrong and Frank Schmalleger, Regents/Prentice Hall, 1994. Lists all major federal agencies, criminal justice positions available, addresses, and phone numbers.

U.S. Civil Service Commission
1900 East Street NW
Washington, DC 20006

American Police Beat: Current events pertaining to law enforcement, including job, career, and training opportunities: www .apbweb.com/index.php.

Career Path: A leading site on the Web for job seekers. After selecting a geographical location, the applicant can peruse the major newspapers' classified ads for current openings in that area: www.careerpath.com.

POLICE Magazine: Variety of police-related articles including job listings: www.policemag.com/.

The Police Officer's Internet Directory: Over 1,500 individual home pages of information on law enforcement agencies across the country. Included is a state-by-state breakdown of agencies with current openings: www.officer.com.

On Patrol: Includes free postings of law enforcement opportunities on a state-by-state basis: www.onpatrol.com.

CHAPTER 13

YOUR JOB-SEEKING UNIFORM:
PRESENTING YOURSELF AS *THE* ONE TO HIRE

You never get a second chance to make a good first impression.

—*Will Rogers*

Do You Know:

➤ What the employer's investment is in the hiring process?
➤ What the job-seeking uniform is and what elements it consists of?
➤ What the primacy effect is?
➤ How you can find out the way your present yourself to others and why this information may be useful?
➤ How your attire influences people's perception of you?
➤ Why it is important to begin your job search in good physical condition?
➤ What the purpose of the interview is and how important knowledge is to this purpose?
➤ The importance of follow-up?
➤ What your strategy will be for presenting yourself?

INTRODUCTION

One critical aspect of presenting yourself is in the written material you submit. The importance of written materials was discussed in Chapters 10 and 12. It is emphasized again here because it is a vital part of how you are viewed. Whatever you do, do it well. Don't submit insufficient, incomplete material or anything that doesn't look perfect. Just as "you are what you wear," so *you are what you write.*

Typos, misspellings, poor grammar, erasures, and messy cross-outs tell an employer a lot. You cannot afford to look inept, uneducated, careless, or sloppy. The weeding-out process becomes arbitrary at times, particularly with a number of equally qualified applicants. You may find yourself out of the running for something as simple as a misspelled word on your résumé. This is not necessarily fair, but it is a fact. How you present yourself begins with your written materials. If you do an effective job, you are likely to get an interview. How should you appear at such an interview? What makes up your job-seeking uniform?

In a sense, we *all* wear uniforms, whether they have badges, patches, and whistles, and whether we are actually on the job. A uniform is apparel that makes a statement. The police, corrections, or security officer's duty uniform is designed to make a specific statement: I am in charge! Clothing worn by medical personnel and firefighters are more utilitarian, stating they are ready to help. Similarly, nurses have uniforms that meet their professional needs, as do bus drivers, waitresses, letter carriers, custodians, delivery people, orderlies, flight attendants, pilots, and military personnel.

When matching clothing to a day's work of job seeking, consider: What image do I want to project? What encounters will I have today? What does this sport coat say about me? This dress? This tie? This scarf? These shoes?

THE EMPLOYER'S INVESTMENT

Before getting into the specifics of *how* to present yourself, look first at the situation from the employer's perspective. When hiring, employers are making a significant financial commitment. The typical police agency will spend several thousand dollars on the hiring process alone. After an applicant is hired, it is expected they won't be fully productive for at least the first year of employment, so the agency is expending a year's salary just to cover training and administrative costs. Initial uniform and equipment expenses also cost the employer thousands of dollars more. Furthermore, that does not include the salaries of those who will be doing the training and mentoring to bring recruits to the point of being considered a productive team member.

During hiring, employers are also making an extremely important organizational decision. Employers are hiring someone to represent them to the public. In all areas of criminal justice, private security, and related fields, public perception is critical. Employers can find themselves in serious trouble by hiring the wrong people for these jobs. In fact, employers may face civil lawsuits for "negligent hiring" (holding the employer responsible for hiring unsuitable employees who cause some sort of harm). Combine this with the fact that it is increasingly difficult to fire people, particularly in the public sector, and you can see the importance employers must place on the entire process.

> The employer has a significant investment in hiring the "right" people. In addition to the financial investment, those they hire represent the employer to the public. Also, hiring the wrong people can land an employer in legal trouble via "negligent hiring" lawsuits.

ELEMENTS OF YOUR JOB-SEEKING UNIFORM

Because employers have so much at stake when they hire personnel, and because their decisions are often based on a few pieces of paper and thirty minutes of personal time with you, you must make the most of those pieces of paper and thirty minutes. How you present yourself during an interview is an important aspect of the overall getting-a-job process. Your strategy for presenting yourself must encompass the entire spectrum of how the prospective employer views you. Many factors come into play here. Employers will tell you that although someone may appear spectacular on paper, the interview provides an opportunity to eliminate many candidates.

Appearance consists of the "whole person." The physical self, the emotional self, and the spiritual/ethical self combine to create the balance that makes up "you." If one aspect outweighs the rest or is significantly lacking, you are out of balance and something appears wrong. For instance, police officers may work odd schedules and perhaps compound things by attending school on the side. They may not have sufficient time to exercise regularly. Weight gain or a poor nutritional program could affect their health, making them feel run-down, irritable, and out of sorts. Officers in this situation should reexamine their lifestyles to restore balance.

Employers will try to view the "whole" applicant during the hiring process. Employers will look for high self-esteem, alertness, intelligence, critical-thinking abilities, and humanistic traits. They will also consciously watch for indications of sadistic, brutal, obsessive-compulsive personalities as well as those who might become victims of "groupthink" and "deindividualization" in the face of peer pressure. The obvious difficulty is that what employers get to see represents a small portion of your overall identity. After all, how long does it take for you to get to know another person, even yourself, before acquiring an accurate perception? Certainly more than the thirty minutes spent during the average interview. So if something they see right away causes them concern, that becomes significant.

Your job-seeking uniform is how you present yourself during an interview. It consists of more than just the clothes you put on—your uniform includes how you come off during the initial contact: your grooming; physical condition; grammar and speech; body language, composure, and personality; manners; and enthusiasm, knowledge, and follow-up. It's your total package.

This is a lot of data to present to an employer, particularly in a short amount of time. You must develop a strategy to maximize the opportunities to sell yourself in each area. Properly pursued, you will have more than enough time to provide employers with an accurate picture of yourself. To best understand this, consider the dynamics of the interview process; that is, the elements of the system and the importance of the first few minutes.

THE PRIMACY EFFECT AND WHY YOU HAVE ONLY MINUTES

The first minutes of any interpersonal interaction are critical, for as the quote by Will Rogers at the beginning of this chapter states: "You never get a second chance to make a good first impression." Sterling (2008) stresses:

> Within the first three seconds of a new encounter, you are evaluated…even if it is just a glance. People appraise your visual and behavioral appearance from head to toe. They observe your demeanor, mannerisms, and body language and even assess your grooming and accessories—watch, handbag, briefcase. Within only three seconds, you make an indelible impression. You may intrigue some and disenchant others. This first impression process occurs in every new situation. Within the first few seconds, people pass judgment on you—looking for common surface clues. Once the first impression is made, it is virtually irreversible.

Research supports this conclusion, with studies dating as far back as 1925 by Frederick Hanson Lund, and subsequent psychological research proves first impressions are lasting impression. This so-called *primacy effect* is the concept that initial impressions are perceived as more important than subsequent encounters, or at least remembered longer.

Sterling goes on to advise: "It is human nature to constantly make these appraisals, in business and social environments. You may hardly have said a word, however once this three-second evaluation is over, the content of your speech will not change it. When you make the best possible first impression, you have your audience in the palm of your hand. When you make a poor first impression, you lose your audience's attention, no matter how hard you scramble to recover it."

> It can take as little three minutes for the primacy effect to occur. According to this concept, the first several minutes of a social interaction are crucial to the continuance of the interaction.

You can test the primacy effect theory by asking yourself some questions:

➢   Have you ever sat next to someone on a bus, train, or plane and almost immediately wanted to talk with them? Or instead—decided to quickly get your nose into your book or magazine? Why?

➢   Have you ever had someone come to your door seeking contributions for some worthy cause and known almost immediately that you'd probably contribute? Or cut them short? Why?

➢   Have you ever had a teacher you just knew wasn't approachable to discuss a grade you received? Why?

➢   Have you ever gone into a job interview and known within minutes that you were a strong candidate? Why?

 In your journal, list what turns you off when meeting someone. In contrast, what makes someone come across as interesting or personable?

Sterling says: "You can learn to make a positive and lasting first impression, modify it to suit any situation, and come out a winner. Doing so requires you to assess and identify your personality, physical appearance, lifestyle and goals. Those who do will have the advantage."

How do you come across to others? It is the courageous job seeker who is willing to actually inquire of others how they come across. The especially brave are willing to ask after an interview from which they didn't get hired for honest feedback. Herein lies insight that can change the course of future job seeking efforts.

DIFFICULT INQUIRIES

It is important to understand *how* you come across to others because you can seldom judge this for yourself. How could you know how others perceive you? Do you dare ask? Most people seldom think of this. It's just too risky. But it may be necessary, particularly if you are experiencing repeated rejections. We can all take constructive criticism. If that is what is needed to identify your weak points, take that risk.

For example, one officer left her initial law enforcement career path to go to law school and then returned to seek employment in the police field. Armed with experience, training, and extensive education, she finished second on almost every interview in which she participated. Why? She had to know. So she called several individuals to which she had applied and explained her motives for inquiring—not to criticize, not to take another try at that job, but to understand how she could improve. She was stunned to learn she had not convinced them she did not want to practice law. They were all sure she would stay with them only until a "real" lawyer job was offered to her. Was this *their* fault? Of course not. It was hers for failing to anticipate this reaction and making false assumptions. Her only regret was not taking this step earlier. In this case it worked. She got the next job for which she applied.

Find out how you come across to others by asking. Although it may seem risky, the constructive criticism may help you identify and strengthen some of your weak points, particularly if you've been experiencing repeated rejections.

GETTING TO KNOW EACH OTHER

The goal of the job application and the interview is really the same for both the prospective employer and for you: *getting to know each other*. It would be considerably more fair and accurate if time was unlimited, but it is not. For better or worse, you must deal with the brevity of the process and acknowledge the importance of the first few minutes. This is not all bad, however. If you recognize the elements of the interview, this is actually an ideal amount of time. Now take a more detailed look at each element of the job-seeking uniform, including what comes before and after the interview.

BEFORE THE INTERVIEW

One critical event before the interview might be a phone call to arrange the interview—or even a preliminary telephone interview. Vogt (2004) acknowledges: "Phone interviews can be tricky, especially since you aren't able to read your interviewers' nonverbal cues like facial expressions and body language during the session—a big difference from the typical interview." He further notes:

> Many companies use phone interviews as an initial employment screening technique for a variety of reasons. Because they're generally brief, phone interviews save companies time. They also serve as a more realistic screening alternative for cases in which companies are considering out-of-town (or out-of-state and foreign) candidates.
>
> So the chances are pretty good that, at some point in your job hunt, you'll be asked to participate in a 20- to 30-minute phone interview with either one person or several people on the other end of the line. In many ways, the way you prepare for a phone interview isn't all that different from the way you'd get ready for a face-to-face interview—save for a few slight additions to and modifications of your list of preparation tasks.
>
> Here's what to do:
>
> 1. **Treat the phone interview seriously, just as you would a face-to-face interview.**
> 2. **Have your résumé and cover letter in front of you.** You'll almost certainly be asked about some of the information that appears on these documents.
> 3. **Make a cheat sheet.** Jot down a few notes about the most critical points you want to make with your interview(s).
> 4. **Get a high-quality phone.** This isn't the time to use a cell phone that cuts in and out.
> 5. **Shower, groom and dress up (at least a little).** Odd advice? Perhaps, but focusing on your appearance, just as you would for a normal interview, will put you in the right frame of mind.
> 6. **Stand up, or at least sit up straight at a table or desk.** Again, there's a psychological, frame-of-mind aspect to consider here. But on a more tangible level, research has shown that you project yourself better when you're standing up, and you'll feel more knowledgeable and confident.

Whitten (n.d.) suggests:

> If your phone has a call-waiting feature, consider disabling it the day of the interview. . . .
>
> Remember to speak clearly and listen attentively, just as you would if you were meeting with the interviewer in person. Even though no one can see you, your voice betrays attitudes and confidence. . . .
>
> At the end of the interview, express your willingness to speak with the employer in person.

Ledgard (2004), a senior technical recruiter for Microsoft, offers additional advice:

> *Lose the distractions*! Find a nice, comfortable, and quiet place for your phone interview.
>
> *Define your talking points!* Think of creative stories that highlight your competencies and innovative ideas you have for the job that you want to make sure the interviewer hears. You should still let the interviewer drive the discussion and direction of topics, but these talking points will help you sneak in some of your own flavor, when it's applicable.
>
> *FAQs rule!* No matter the company or job, some questions are frequently asked. Anticipate these questions and answer them in advance. Print out the list and have it handy for reference. Topics you might be asked to cover include: your passions, your strengths, your areas for improvement, a difficult challenge or situation you've encountered on the job and how you handled it, your most proud accomplishment, interest in this job and/or company, and your 5 year plan. Chances are, you'll be asked to expand upon at least one of these subjects during the interview.
>
> *Do you have any questions?* Almost every interview ends with the interviewer asking, "Do you have any questions for me?" Since you know the question is coming, write down two or three questions you'd like to ask ahead of time. . . .
>
> *Self-motivation works!* Okay, this is really silly, but I find this helps me. Type up something that says, "<Your name here>—you are the coolest. You are so smart. This company would be lucky to hire you. You have ALL the power, and YOU ROCK!" Print out this mantra and read it just before the interview begins. Glance back at the words during the interview. I guarantee this will help you maintain your poise and confidence.

Many of these recommendations, such as anticipating questions you'll be asked and preparing questions to ask the employer, will also help you prepare for a face-to-face interview, whether or not a phone interview actually occurs.

INITIAL CONTACT

The interview itself is the brass ring you strive to get. When you get it, you must be on time. Before your interview date, it's important to know exactly where you're going so you can get there on time. Making excuses for a late arrival as an opener for your interview gets you off to a rocky start. When called for an interview, get clear directions on how to get to the interview. Make a trial run of the actual trip so you know how to get there and how long it takes. Plan to arrive at least ten minutes early to allow for traffic delays or parking problems. Murphy's law dictates the later you are, the more delays you'll encounter.

CLOTHING AND GROOMING

Clothes make the person—and get (or lose) the job. Maher (2004) observes with amusement: "So far, no reality show follows the hapless job seeker who mixes plaid and pinstripes and flunks a luncheon job interview by drinking from the finger bowl. Such blunders may be extreme, but no one can deny the importance of making a solid impression on a hiring manager or boss." Like so many other things, the "experts" have made a science of dressing for success. John T. Malloy, who coined the term *wardrobe engineering*, was among the first to stress publicly the link between professional accomplishments and wardrobe in his well-known book *Dress for Success*. His research indicates that your credibility and likeability are immediately established by what you are wearing.

Research indicates that your credibility and likeability are immediately established by what you are wearing.

Few would argue with the research that tells us that people's appearance has a direct impact on how they come across to others and how they will be treated. Since clothing is extremely important, how should you dress for a job interview to make a favorable impression? You have dressed effectively if your interviewers do not even remember what you were wearing. You want them paying attention to you, not your clothing.

It cannot be overemphasized that those doing the hiring for criminal justice and security jobs are likely to be *conservative* because of the work they are in. Regardless of social or pop-culture trends, when a male applicant comes in with long hair, an earring, and a tattoo, those doing the hiring will have already made up their minds before the first question has been asked. It may not be fair or even right, but employers are looking for people who fit their workplace cultural norm, or at least have the awareness to not deviate too severely from it.

In planning an "appearance strategy," begin by identifying exactly what job is being interviewed for. An applicant for an executive position would dress differently than an applicant for a manual labor position. An interview for an officer or first responder position falls somewhere in between. Start with several givens:

➤   The jobs themselves are conservative. Extremists are generally not well received.

➤   The fields are regarded as important and seek to be viewed as professions.

➤   You've got to look the part.

Begin by deciding on clothes that fall between the extremes, that is, conservative. A spangled three-piece suit and lots of gold jewelry is obviously inappropriate. So is a concert T-shirt or a low-cut dress. The consensus is that a conservative, smart-looking, fresh, low-key appearance is most appropriate.

Comfort is a factor. You will not perform up to your potential if you are dressed uncomfortably. If you do not feel good, it will show. Therefore, pick clothing you feel comfortable wearing. You can build on your interview outfit from this point.

A suit is traditional for an interview—for men and women. A suit conveys a statement: The person wearing it is businesslike, is capable of creating a positive image, and is taking the interview and the interviewers seriously. The same can be said for a sharp sport coat with a nice pair of slacks, or a good-looking skirt with a neat blouse or sweater. The final decision is yours, but consider the following:

➤   Is your outfit conservative? Is it comfortable?

➤   Could a suit work to your advantage or disadvantage? (Might a rural jurisdiction view a three-piece suit as "too much"? Might another jurisdiction view a tweed sport coat as "too little"?)

➤   What do you own now? Chances are you feel comfortable in clothing you own. But if you don't own the right apparel, get it and wear it until it becomes comfortable.

➤   Can you afford to buy new clothes for your interviews? Can you afford not to?

➤   How do you think you look? Ask others for honest feedback.

A frequently overlooked area is that of accessories: socks, belt, tie, jewelry, shoes, and so on. In addition to being conservative, use *common sense*. To review a few basics you probably already know:

➤   No hats worn indoors. If you question this, watch people in a restaurant look when someone, regardless of age, fails to remove their baseball caps.

➤   White socks? Absolutely *not*.

➤   Socks that are too short, or droop, or have runs or holes in them? Ridiculous.

➤   Hosiery that's more appropriate for evening or holidays? Hold off for the office party.

➤   An old, cracked, mismatched leather belt? Absurd.

➤   Too much jewelry? Leave it at home.

➤   Still using your father's old clip-on tie? Spend a few dollars for a new one.

➤   Worn-out heels or scuffs on the back of the heels from driving? Replace them.

➤   And don't forget to shine your shoes.

Avoid wearing pins or other jewelry identified with a particular fraternal, religious, athletic, or other group or club, as you risk offending someone participating in the interview and give them something other than your face on which to focus. Do not give them excuses to avoid eye contact. Also avoid loud colors, wild patterns, or any unusual apparel. Seek help from clothing store clerks, who are generally fashion-conscious and can offer advice regarding your clothing needs. Consider other resources when setting up your dressing strategy, such as books and magazines. Such an approach may give you a slight advantage. Finally, since your perception of yourself is too subjective, solicit feedback from someone you trust. Ask them how you look. Hear the answer—good or bad—and make any necessary improvements.

Another consideration is personal grooming. Although these things may seem obvious, before an interview evaluate such things as hair and nail care, makeup, antiperspirants, fragrance, and breath freshness. Some things can be fixed relatively quickly; others may take more time. Some basics change with time; for example, fragrances for men and women, once considered a grooming enhancement, aren't any longer.

Make sure your fingernails are clean and trimmed. Women should use discretion in how long they allow their nails to grow. You don't want a prospective employer wondering if you can type a report or even pick a pen up without difficulty, much less engage in a physical confrontation, if necessary, as part of the job. If you choose to wear nail polish, select something subtle.

Women who wear makeup should choose a natural or professional look, not a dramatic look. Avoid heavy applications of eye shadow or cheek color, and select a lipstick that is flattering but doesn't scream "Read my lips!" Before the interview, make sure there is no lipstick on your teeth. If you're uncertain about how to achieve a professional look with makeup, consult a local department store cosmetics clerk. Women in these positions don't necessarily encourage women to forego their feminity, but as is the case with men, extreme statements are not what you want during interviews.

Know if your antiperspirant works well in anxiety-producing situations. If it doesn't, find a new one! You'll be nervous enough without the added worry of body odor. However, don't overdo it on the fragrance. Go easy on the strong aftershave or perfume. Although most people find body odor offensive, many people are just as offended by strong fragrances. Some people suffer allergic reactions to such smells. In fact, some businesses have "fragrance-free zones" due to allergies. You want to mitigate any risk of being or being perceived as a problem. Too much of anything isn't good for interviews.

Pay particular attention to your breath and oral hygiene. There is no bigger turnoff than bad breath, and many people don't even know when they have it; however, your interviewer will know. Be sure to brush and floss your teeth before an interview, and avoid drinking liquor or eating exotic foods the night before an interview. These things can stay on your breath long after you've ingested them. Furthermore, never chew gum during an interview. As smoking continues to decrease in popularity and acceptance, the lingering smell on the breath and clothing are obvious and detract from your impression. Check yourself in a mirror one final time before entering the interview room. Remember to smile. A friendly smile can be key to the impression you make during those critical first few minutes. Make them feel good when they look at you.

The bottom line is: You are selling something—you! You need the tools to make that sale. If you do not have the proper clothing to make a good impression, buy some, even if it means borrowing money. The loan can be paid back once you get the job. You must appear like someone the interviewers would want representing their city, county, department, agency, institution, or company.

PHYSICAL CONDITION

Closely related to clothing and grooming is your physical condition. Chapter 7 was devoted entirely to physical fitness and its importance. The fact is simple: Few other professions require you to be more physically fit than those of criminal justice, private security, and any of the first responder and related fields. You are not expected to be at your peak for only a few seasons or to compete in a once-in-a-lifetime event like the Olympics. You need to be in top physical condition every day you report for duty. The public depends on it, your partners depend on it, and your life may depend on it. The very nature of the job is stressful. Many first responders die not at the hands of criminals but as victims of their own clogged arteries and unhealthy hearts.

Employers in these fields will notice your physical condition. Every police, fire, paramedic, corrections, and security administrator knows it's hard to keep their officers in peak shape as the years go by. They certainly don't want to begin with out-of-shape officers. It's not good for the employee, and it's not good for the department. Every organization is concerned about its public image. So much of criminal justice and related work is accomplished by easily identified personnel. They are often uniformed and drive marked vehicles. No department wants overweight, unfit officers representing them, nor does the public they serve.

> Your job-search strategy should include being in good physical shape, not only because employers expect it, but because you will feel more confident about yourself. And confidence shows.

Finally, don't smoke. If you do—quit. An increasing number of police departments and private employers are including "nonsmoker" in their initial requirements. Public buildings are also quickly becoming completely smoke-free. Besides the obvious health-related problems, smokers today look out of place, and many feel smokers present a bad image. Further, most smokers don't realize how the odor clings to them. An interview panel of nonsmokers will almost certainly be overwhelmed by the offensive odor of an applicant who smokes. It sends a message you don't want to send.

GRAMMAR AND SPEECH

Individuals employed in criminal justice and security are expected to present themselves like any other professional. As educational requirements for applicants increase, so do standards about communication skills. Use of slang, obviously mispronounced words, or limited vocabulary can embarrass an applicant. Furthermore, people who speak nonstandard English rarely recognize the handicap they carry. Ask someone who speaks "good" (standard) English to listen to you and see if your speech needs improving.

Like physical fitness, communication skills take time to develop. Some people are better communicators than others, and some simply need to brush up in this area. If you need to improve your speech, take classes. Volunteer in ways that require you to interact with the public. Become familiar with a long-standing resource that helps people become better speakers, Toastmasters. This website not only provides information on the organization, but offers valuable speaking suggestions (www.toastmasters.org/). Feeling confident in how you sound will make you feel better, knowing you will be perceived better.

Be yourself. Trying to come off too intellectually or too much like a seasoned professional will be perceived as phony. Don't address your interview panel as though you were giving a stage performance, and resist the temptation to use any professional jargon you think might help you convince the interviewers you're "one of them." You aren't—yet. Present yourself as you are. That's who they want to get to know.

BODY LANGUAGE, COMPOSURE, AND PERSONALITY

The stress associated with the job-search process makes it hard to appear as well as is needed. Stress and anxiety can intimidate you to the point that you sit rigidly upright during the interview, responding with short, one-word responses—the only goal being to live through the interview. Relax, be real, and let them see you. You wouldn't buy a car or house based solely on how it looked from the outside. The same goes for hiring someone.

As important as the words you say is the nonverbal communication exhibited through your body language. As noted by the Life Coaching Studio (2008): "When meeting anyone for the first time 93% of the communication and impression that they make of you will be down to the way that you look, your body language and the sound of your voice. Only 7% will be down to the words that you use." According to Borrello (2001, pp. 23–24):

> As an officer walks through the door and greets the interview panel, interviewers see how he or she walks, moves, shakes their hands and gets seated. Does the officer's posture reflect confidence? Is he or she stiff and nervous? Is his or her handshake solid or like a wet fish? Is the officer's face lacking emotion, with shoulders slumped downward? . . . As the officer speaks, is there any eye contact? Does he or she seem to have physical energy, representing confidence and a willingness to perform?
>
> Does the officer ever smile or display facial expressions showing him or her to have a personality? Are the officer's hands unnaturally trapped in his or her lap, or can he or she comfortably and effectively use gestures to support and add emphasis to words and ideas? This is physical communication at work, and it is very powerful in making or breaking impressions.

MANNERS

Good manners make a great impression. They start with being on time for your appointment. Lateness shows a lack of respect for others' time and might lead the employer to wonder: If you can't be on time for an interview, how can you be on time for work? If circumstances beyond your control are making you run late, call to explain your delay.

Shake hands with and greet each interviewer at the beginning of the interview. Make your handshake an extension of yourself. It can communicate warmth, strength, and confidence. Use a firm, full, deep grip and maintain eye contact. (You might want to ask some friends how they feel about your handshake and, if need be, work to improve it.) Don't forget to smile. In an interview environment, shaking hands and smiling are skills—practice them.

Listen attentively throughout the interview, and do not interrupt the other person in your eagerness to answer their question. Don't argue their position if not requested as part of the process. Finally, never let any contact with a prospective employer end without another handshake and a sincere "thank-you."

ENTHUSIASM

Do you want the job, or do you WANT the job? Employers aren't interested in hiring someone who pursues their work halfheartedly. They want people who greet each day as a unique challenge, make the most of every opportunity, and do a great job. If you meander into the interview and respond casually to questions, why should they hire you? You must show them that you don't just want a job, you want this job with this organization. Let them know why. If you don't, someone else will. It is amazing how so few applicants, when asked why they want the job, exclaim it is because they really want to work here, for this organization. When the interviewer asks if you have anything else to ask or say, you should make it absolutely clear that you really do want this particular job and that you will do a great job for them. Be enthusiastic about it!

KNOWLEDGE

The biggest error applicants make when presenting themselves to prospective employers is misunderstanding what the employer is looking for. In the hiring process, this can be fatal. The purpose of the hiring process is for applicants to present themselves—the only thing the employer is interested in learning about is *you*. However, most applicants go into the process thinking the employer wants to learn how much the applicant knows. If you were applying for a position as a brain surgeon or scientist, what you knew might be of primary importance. But for criminal justice and security jobs, particularly at an entry-level position or at the initial promotional stages, employers recognize that the right kind of person will be able to learn and grow with the job. If you get "hung up" thinking knowledge is all-important and concentrate entirely on memorizing facts, data, laws, rules, and procedures, you have missed the point. Interviewers want to get to know you, not your capacity for memorizing. In fact, this is why the application process is so frightening for most applicants. They worry that they do not know enough, but this is not what employers are looking for.

> The purpose of the interview is for the employer to have a chance to get to know you, not your capacity for memorizing or how much you know.

Depending on what field and position you are being interviewed for, you may need to know certain basics. For example, in Minnesota, a person applying for any law enforcement position must know elementary law such as the use of deadly force applicable and some fundamental Fourth Amendment search and seizure concepts. Ask people who have applied for similar jobs what questions they were asked.

If you don't know the answer, even if you should, don't make it up. And when you don't know, don't panic. Admit it, and tell them how you'd find the answer. They may ask you a legal question, knowing it's very unlikely you'll know the answer, and what they're really looking for is your ability to admit you don't have the answer but that you know where to look for it. Or given a hypothetical situation and asked how you would respond, be able to explain the process you would use to analyze the situation rather than just saying what you would do.

It is also important to know about the organization to which you're applying. Never enter an interview without having first checked out the website of the hiring authority. If the hiring agency has a Web presence, it is here you will likely find their mission statement and other valuable information. For example, you should research and learn details about the follow specifics of a community:

- ➢ Population
- ➢ Racial climate
- ➢ High-profile issues
- ➢ Unemployment rate
- ➢ Type of government system in place
- ➢ Size of the police force
- ➢ If community policing has been implemented
- ➢ Chief's name and how long he/she has held the position
- ➢ Recent increases or decreases in crime statistics

If there isn't a website, the local chamber of commerce may be able to provide up-to-date data. You might also ask if it's acceptable to have a preinterview meeting with the chief or hiring authority to find out more about the agency. It can also serve you well to tour the area you're applying to work in. Stop in and chat with some of the business owners, walk the streets, and drive around. Be able to present yourself as interested enough to get to know the area in which you want to work.

FOLLOW-UP

Follow-up refers to the extra steps taken after the interview, the time when most applicants sit and wait to hear from the employer. Just as you must never leave a contact with an employer without saying "thank you," you must not walk out of an interview never to be heard from again. A single follow-up thank-you letter can give you another chance to show off how well you wear your job-seeking uniform by reviewing such elements as:

- ➢ Grammar
- ➢ Manners
- ➢ Personality
- ➢ Enthusiasm
- ➢ Ability to follow up
- ➢ Knowledge

Six of the nine elements in your job-seeking uniform can be reinforced after the interview. You can also demonstrate again your proficiency with written material, and provide the employer with one more reason to remember your name positively. Imagine the employer sitting with half a dozen or fewer résumés that all look good, pondering a decision. Suddenly you call to say thank-you for the interview. This simple thank-you can tip the scales in your favor. Because hardly anyone does this, doing so can make a tremendous difference.

How you follow up is up to you. Some employers prefer not to be called while they are making a decision. Although a phone call may not be a bad idea, it should not replace a letter. A letter is a necessity. Write to everyone who participated in your interview. Get their names, proper spellings, and titles from the secretary on your way out or call the secretary later to get this information. Remember a thank-you for the secretary, too.

> Always follow up after the interview with a thank-you letter and possibly even a phone call. However, recognize the fine line between being remembered positively and becoming nothing more than a pest. Don't overdue it.

PLANNING YOUR INTERVIEW STRATEGY

Job hunters can gain a competitive edge by mentally rehearsing how a successful interview will go. This technique, which is similar to that used by gymnasts, skaters, divers and other athletes to mentally play out their moves prior to an actual competition, is being advocated by career coaches as a way for job applicants to optimize their interview performances.

As you imagine how your interview will go, start with the beginning introductions and walk yourself through the questions you anticipate being asked. Visualize what you are wearing, how you are sitting and other body language. Picture the faces of the people interviewing you and "practice" (in your mind) making eye contact with them. "Hear" yourself speaking in a confident, easy to understand voice. Have a question or two ready to ask when that inevitable stage in the interview arrives. And prepare your "thank you" and exit strategy.

> Take advantage of what you now know about what to expect during the interview and plan your strategy as to how you will present yourself.

 In your journal, write down your interview game plan. Then when you are done writing, read and reread your interview story until you are able to mentally rehearse it without looking at the words.

What things will you do when first entering the interview room? Who will you meet? What will you say to them? What will they say to you? Remember, this opening scenario is driven by the primacy effect; you have only a few minutes—what impression are you going to make and how?

After initial introductions, the formal interview gets under way. This is your sales pitch scene—you must sell the interviewer on you. What questions are you likely to be asked? How will you reply? How will you present your skills, competencies, experience, and career ambitions? How will you communicate to the employer that you are the one to hire? What can you do for their agency that sets you apart from the other applicants?

As the interview winds down, you will need to deliver a close. Make it positive and upbeat, one the employer will remember favorably. Write in your journal a closing comment or a positive question that might be asked at the end of an interview. Make your statement something you're comfortable saying. Practice saying it. When the interview comes to a close, don't be caught off guard. You want your comment ready to roll off your tongue for the strongest possible conclusion to your interview story. However you close, leave the message loud and clear: "I am sincerely interested in this job and will be the best person you can hire."

All of this takes practice. Practice by yourself, in front of a mirror, with other people, and with prepared questions, and then have people ask you questions they make up.

CONCLUSION

Your job-seeking uniform is just that—how you present yourself during an interview. It consists of more than the clothes you put on, however. Your uniform includes how you present yourself during the initial contact, your grooming, physical condition, grammar and speech, manners, personality, enthusiasm, knowledge, and follow-up. Take advantage of what you now know about what to expect during the interview and plan your strategy as to how you will present yourself. Pick out your job-seeking uniform and put it on before your interview, just to make sure it fits and that you're comfortable in it. The more you wear it, the more natural it will feel. But you must practice putting it on and wearing it to be the most effective. Plan how you will present yourself as *the* one to hire.

AN INSIDER'S VIEW

PRESENTING YOURSELF AS *THE* ONE TO HIRE

Brenda P. Maples

Former Lieutenant
Memphis (Tennessee) Police Department

Whether you are applying for a position with a large law enforcement department or a small department, you will be required to complete a series of testing procedures. This allows the department to glean the best qualified from all the applicants. This battery of tests will probably consist of written, oral and physical agility tests. The testing procedure may vary from department to department; however, at some time during the hiring process you will be asked to come for an oral interview. This is your chance to sell yourself, to make a lasting and favorable impression.

First impressions do persist. Your initial appearance can go a long way toward impressing the interviewer, either positively or negatively. Take a long look in a full-length mirror. If you were running a business, would you hire someone who hadn't put on clean clothes or gotten a haircut in several weeks? Wear your "Sunday go to meetin'" clothes and get a fresh haircut or style so you appear neat. You will feel more poised when you know you look your best.

Don't go into the interview cold turkey. Prepare!! The purpose of the oral interview is to gather information and judge face-to-face interaction. This is an important element of law enforcement work because of the time spent dealing with the public, either as complainants, victims or suspects. You will be continually seeking information from others to make decisions.

An interviewee must be confident but not overly aggressive. An intelligent interviewee should anticipate the questions asked in a typical employment interview and rehearse the answers. To prepare, record yourself on video. This is a helpful way to practice your responses and gain confidence. When you review the video, be aware of any weaknesses or areas in which you might improve. Are you able to communicate effectively in clear and logical sentences? Do you use correct and accurate diction? Many judgments are made about other people's intellectual achievements by the way they talk.

While viewing your video, also be mindful of nonverbal communication. This can include facial expressions, fidgeting, hand and arm movements and lack of eye contact. Try to keep nervous mannerisms under control. Sometimes you say more with nonverbal communication than you realize. After all, how does a good investigator get that "gut feeling" when talking to a potential suspect?

You will be asked questions relating to your experience and any special skills or abilities you may possess. You probably have much more going for you than you think. Try to think of experiences where you demonstrated your abilities and skills.

With all these tips on how to sell yourself during an interview, you're still trying to present your unique self. A phony personality will be spotted by any seasoned interviewer. Sincerity and enthusiasm can go a long way in selling yourself as THE right person for the job.

Brenda P. Maples *(retired) is a former lieutenant with the Memphis (Tennessee) Police Department and has twenty-six years' experience in the criminal justice field. She holds a BS from Middle Tennessee State University and was national president of the Law Enforcement Alliance of America and the vice chair of the Tennessee Peace Officers and Standards Commission.*

MIND STRETCHES

1. What three things have made you feel accepted by another person while attempting to get to know them within the first few minutes? What three things have made you feel unaccepted by another person within the first few minutes?

2. How would you work your responses to Question #1 into the job application process?

3. List opportunities you could create to sell yourself besides the traditional résumé and interview.

4. Why is it important to approach the elements of the interview as a whole rather than looking at the pieces separately?

5. Why is it important to develop a strategy rather than just jumping into the interview process itself?

6. Who could you ask for constructive feedback on how you come across to others by your clothing? Your handshake? Your cover letter and résumé? Their initial reaction to you? Why do you think so few people actually take this step to prepare and improve?

7. Which elements of the interview do you think you need to work on? How will you do so for each?

8. How might videotaping yourself be beneficial in preparing for an interview?

REFERENCES

Borrello, Andrew. "Preparing for the Oral Interview: It's More Than Just Talk." *Police*, January 2001, pp. 22–25.

Ledgard, Gretchen. "Ace That Phone Interview." 2004. Available online at http://blogs.msdn.com/jobsblog/archive/2004/08/04/208403.aspx.

Life Coaching Studio. 2008. Available online at www.lifecoachingstudio.com/sit3.htm.

Lund, Frederick Hansen. "The Psychology of Belief IV: The Law of Primacy in Persuasion." *Journal of Abnormal Social Psychology* 20, 1925, pp. 183–191.

Maher, Kris. "Image Makeovers Can Give Candidates an Added Edge." *Wall Street Journal* Online, July 14, 2004. Available online at www.careerjournal.com/jobhunting/jungle/20040714-jungle.html.

Sterling, Michelle T. *Do You Make Your First Impression Your Best Impression?* 2008. Available online at http://entrepreneurs.about.com/cs/marketing/a/uc051603a.htm.

Vogt, Peter. "Mastering the Phone Interview." Monster Career Center, 2004. Available online at http://interview.monster.com/articles/phone.

Whitten, Chris. "Phone Interview." n.d. Available online at www.jobsfaq.com/interview/phone-interview.html.

CHAPTER 14

THE INTERVIEW: A CLOSER LOOK

Whenever you are asked if you can do a job, tell 'em, "Certainly I can"—and get busy and find out how to do it.

—*Theodore Roosevelt*

Do You Know:

➢ What the definition is of interview?
➢ What purposes the interview serves?
➢ What five types of interviews you may encounter and how they differ?
➢ How likely you'll be able to negotiate your salary?
➢ How you should close an interview?
➢ What the importance is of follow-up?

INTRODUCTION

The interview. It sounds ominous. It stirs two basic fears: confronting the unknown and speaking to others. Fear of the unknown can be paralyzing, as can speaking to others, and both can be worsened by the importance placed on getting to this point in your job search. You are starting out with one very strong advantage: you've done everything right to get this far, and the employer is obviously interested in you. Now is the time to leverage what they already know about you, and more, to land that job.

> A job interview is a meeting between someone who has a job opening and someone who needs a job, at which information is obtained and exchanged.

Job-seeking experts Krannich and Krannich (2007, p. 54) emphasize the importance of the interview: "The job interview is the single most important step in the job search process—no interview, no job. However, many job seekers make numerous mistakes relating to job interview." Krannich and Krannich add: "Like resume and letter errors, interview sins can quickly knock you out of the competition. They are red flags indicating you have 'issues' that the employer does not wish in inherit. Unlike many other job search mistakes, interview errors tend to be both unforgettable and unforgiving" (p. 6).

Important? Yes. Anxiety provoking? Absolutely. But they are a necessary, important part of the process that you can leverage to your full advantage.

PURPOSES OF THE JOB INTERVIEW

As discussed in Chapter 13, the purposes of the interview are for you to find out more about the employer (and the job). But the interview is far more about *them* than you. A good résumé, in addition to the other preparatory material and contacts, is just your ticket into the interview. An advantage of the preliminary phases of the job-seeking process is that you can get outside help, for example, proofreading your résumé. But once you are led into the interview room, you are on your own.

Bolles (2008, p. 83), in his chapter "The Things School Never Taught Us about the Job-Hunt," demystifies some aspects of the interview, noting that while you're assessing whether the job is a fit for you, the employer is "using the interview to find out 'Do I want him or her to work here? Do they have skills, knowledge or experience that I really need? Do they have an attitude toward work that I am looking for? And, how will they fit in with other employees?'"

Many job seekers enter the interview erroneously thinking it's all about them, when in fact it's really all about the employer deciding if you're the one to hire: "If you want to gain important insight, you need to think like an employer. Put yourself in the employer's shoes. What are the principal accountabilities of the job, and what is needed for successful performance? What knowledge, skills, and personal attributes are essential to performance success? These are the questions you must answer before you can expect to formulate a winning interview strategy" (Beatty, 2006, p. 201).

The Purposes—Up Close

The interview becomes especially important because so far you've presented yourself as having attributes the hiring authority is interested in since you've been invited to interview, but now you are clearly under their microscope. Bolles (p. 90) says: "Realize that the employer thinks the way you are doing your job-hunt is the way you will do the job." This is especially the case face-to-face. The personal interview can fulfill several purposes.

The primary purposes of the personal interview are for the employer to:

- Get a look at you.   - Observe how you analyze problems.
- Listen to you.   - Test your people skills.
- See how you perform under stress.   - Test your knowledge.

Looking at You. Employers would no more hire an unknown person than they would purchase a home or a car they had never seen. They want to see what they are getting. Particularly for a job in criminal justice, private security or related fields, you do not want to make a negative impression by presenting yourself in an extreme manner. If hired, you will represent the agency and future clients. Think about it! Rest assured the interviewers will be thinking about it.

The trend in recent years for law enforcement, as well as other first responder positions, has been toward a professionalization of the career. To this end, the PoliceEmployment.com website states:

> It is a given that most interviewers will expect a man to wear a suit and tie, and a woman to wear a dress or a business suit to the interview. Most of the time, an interviewing panel is prohibited from disqualifying an applicant based on what he or she is wearing. However, if you walk into an interview wearing a pair of blue jeans and a tee shirt, they will find some other reason to write you out. You may look good wearing nice casual slacks, but you will look even better to the panel if you wear business attire. You want to project a professional image.

Remember the importance of grooming. Find the restrooms on your way into the building to make that final check: comb your hair, straighten your tie, adjust your slip, zip up your zipper. Anything caught in your teeth? Look sharp. Be sharp. Also get a drink of water.

Most employers think they've seen it all until they hear others' stories. The lists go on and become increasingly astounding. Krumrie (2007, p. W1) offers the following as a reminder that above all, common sense must guide you:

1.   Don't leave your cell phone on, even on vibrate.

2.   Don't smell like smoke.

3.   Don't speak badly about previous employers or coworkers.

4.   Don't focus on the salary and benefits.

5.   Don't fidget, balance talking and listening.

6.   Don't ramble on.

7.   Don't be late, perform a test-drive to make sure.

8.   Don't tell interviewers you have no questions; that shows a lack of interest, curiosity, and depth.

Listening to You.   No matter how great your résumé looks or how sharp you look, employers want to know that you also speak English well. There will probably never be a better test of this than during the job interview. In addition to testing your general grammatical skills, employers want to hear how you sound. PoliceEmployment.com stresses:

> As you answer the questions, speak clearly and loudly. Oral communication is very important in law enforcement. One moment you may be chatting with the public, and the next moment you may be giving forceful verbal commands to a suspect. The panel is assessing your ability to communicate by what you say and how you say it. Speaking in a low tone of voice is not what they want to hear. Meek and mild are not the traits of a good police officer.

This advice holds true for applicants in other areas of criminal justice or related fields, such as corrections, probation, and private security.

If you get uptight during an interview (and understand that everyone does), just be yourself. Do not try to cover up your anxiety by being cute, funny, smart-alecky, or a host of other façades you've probably seen people try when uptight.

What if you sound nervous? Your voice may crack, you may say something you did not intend to, or you may just plain forget where you were or what the question was. Don't panic. It is reassuring to employers to see you as capable of recognizing a mistake and being able to reorganize and continue. Do not fake it. If a major goof occurs, simply proceed as follows:

1.   Take a deep breath.

2.   Admit to the interviewer(s): "This job is really important to me, and I guess I'm more nervous than I thought."

3.   Continue with your answer.

4.   If you don't know the answer, tell them you know where to find it and will. Then do so and follow up by providing it to them.

There is nothing wrong with being honest. If you're really nervous, admit it; your honesty will make a positive impression. Also, take a moment before answering a question, especially if the question is not one you "practiced." What may seem like an eternity to you will likely be only a few seconds. Never answer without thinking through your response. And be sure to answer *their* question, not what you anticipated was going to be asked.

Seeing How You Perform under Stress.   It's no secret; interviews are stressful. Employers know the stakes, and they've all been in your position before. If a candidate doesn't feel some degree of stress, it might indicate a complete lack of interest in the job; however, it is expected you can control your emotions appropriately.

You will not be stress free. In fact, they may not want you to be. Some employers use a specific interview technique called a "stress interview"; the rationale being that the job you are seeking is stressful, so they want to see how you handle stress. Stress interviews are discussed later in the chapter.

Observing How You Analyze Problems.   You may be asked to solve problems but, particularly at an entry-level position, you are not expected to know every answer. For example, an interview for a police dispatcher might include such questions as, "What would you do if . . .?" and then ask something you either don't know or are unlikely to know. Remember that even if there is an answer, in all probability you are not expected to know it. Prospective employers want to know if and how you think.

A good strategy is to begin your answers with your own variation of the "policy/will learn" statement; that is, you understand that every agency or department is likely to have its own policy on how to handle most situations and that you are also eager to learn. For example, if asked, "How would you handle a situation in which you find an open door to an office after hours, and the boss is inside with his partner's wife?" A reasonable answer could be: "Because I have had no previous security experience, that situation is certainly a difficult one. Based on the information you have given me, I would follow the applicable company policy as well as immediately advise my supervisor. In addition, I would anticipate learning how the company would want me to handle such sensitive situations during my training period. If it is not brought up, I will bring it up, if hired, now that you've asked me about it." During such analytical interviews, rather than looking for the right answer the interviewers are interested in the process you use in coming to some conclusions. This includes exhibiting common sense and admitting when you don't know something rather than making something up.

Testing Your People Skills. Your résumé may look spectacular, but if you don't come across as friendly, sincere, and respectful, you will not get the job. No matter how nervous you get, no matter how frustrating the interview is, do not forget basic manners. Let the interview board know you appreciate their time and the challenging questions asked. Shake hands with each interviewer while making eye contact, smile, say "yes" not "yeah," and be personable.

Whether or not the interview is specifically designed to create stress, it will! The "little things" are so easily forgotten. Before the interview, make a list of what you want to do. For example:

➢   Shake hands with everyone when introduced.

➢   Look at everyone personally during your responses.

➢   Thank the group at the end of the interview and again shake each interviewer's hand.

➢   Remember to tell them at some point you are there because you really do want this job.

Thinking about it all ahead of time will put it in your head, making it easier to remember during the pressure of the interview. Like anything else, practice helps you to remember and to do well.

Testing Your Knowledge. As discussed in Chapter 13, the purpose of the oral interview is generally not to test your technical knowledge, as this is better assessed through a written exam. However, you may be asked questions during an interview to check your knowledge in specific areas. For police officers, you could be asked about very basic statutes, for example, the deadly force law. You should be prepared to answer as many of these questions as possible, but do not panic if you cannot. In such a situation admit that you do not know, but that you would look it up in the state statute book, or the traffic code, or wherever the correct answer is found. Do *not* guess; if you draw a blank, admit it. In such a case, you may want to follow up with a letter providing the answer to show you can find the needed information.

Most of the important purposes of an interview can be addressed during one question posed by the panel. A common question for applicants is: "What would you do if you stopped an off-duty officer (police, firefighter, private security) for drunk driving?" Try the "policy/will learn" approach to come up with an answer. For example: "Recognizing that a DWI is a serious offense and that officers are not above the law, I would advise the supervisor and follow company policy." You get the idea. Such a question gives you a chance to appear at your best—or worst.

  Imagine you are an employer seeking to fill the position of a police, corrections, or security officer. An applicant has just walked into the room. List in your journal five things that would turn you off immediately.

  Next, list five things that would strike you positively.

Rather than specific knowledge, you are likely to be asked questions that reveal to the employer who you are, and there aren't that many variations of what you can expect: "Beneath the dozens and dozens of possible questions that the employer could ask you . . . there are only five basic questions you really need to pay attention to . . . which they may ask directly or try to found out obliquely" (Bolles, p. 92). These include:

➢   Why are you here (why do you want this job with this employer)?

➢   What can you do for us (would you become one of the problems or a solution)?

➢   What kind of person are you (will your personality and values help you fit in)?

➢   What distinguishes you from nineteen other people who can do the same tasks that you can (are your work habits better than theirs)?

➢   Can I afford you (can you learn the job quickly and remain productive)?

Bolles (p. 93) goes on to say that even if these questions aren't asked, they are what any employer wants to know: "Anything you can do, during the interview, to help the employer find the answers to these five questions, will make the interview very satisfying to the employer."

 Again, imagine you are the employer. List two variations of each of the five questions above in your journal.

You can prepare further for various questions. Beatty (p. 207) stresses the importance of predicting what the interviewer will ask: "With a little advance forethought and planning, most job seekers will be able to anticipate and predict, with a high degree of accuracy, about 80 to 90 percent of the questions they will face during a typical job interview. This is like having access to the test questions in advance of the exam." Bolles' questions make perfect sense when you think *like an employer*. Just as there are only so many ways they can ask them, there are only so many appropriate ways, even in personal ways, to answer them that best suit you.

Putting it bluntly, the Kranniches tell you to: "Be honest, not stupid." They list general patterns that cause employers concerns from prospective employees:

➢   Lack of tact (being too frank).

➢   Bad attitude (if it's bad in the interview, what will it be on the job?).

➢   Brutal frankness (usually not appropriate in any people-based occupation).

➢   Talks too much (inappropriate behavior that impedes ability to focus).

➢   Self-centered (not a team player and only concerned for themselves).

All of these are easily remedied if the interviewee thinks about the five general areas from an employer's perspective instead of it being "all about them."

You can also anticipate general interview formats you are likely to encounter in the fields discussed in this book so you can practice to be more flexible, and confident, in various situations. Like a ball player, once prepared you'll react faster and better to whatever pitch comes your way.

TYPES OF INTERVIEWS

There are as many theories about interviews as there are theorists because there are so many variables. People put different names on types of interviews and categorize them differently. A type of interview that's gained popularity recently is the *behavioral interview*: "The behavior-based interview is an interview process based on the concept that the best predictor of future behavior is present or past behavior. This concept has a scientific basis. Psychologists have been able to conclusively demonstrate, during the course of a career lifetime, that most people really don't change their stripes. If, up until now, they have always looked and behaved like a striped zebra, they aren't very likely to now suddenly become a spotted giraffe. There is high likelihood that their behavior will remain essentially the same" (Beatty, p. 206). In reality, all interview formats are seeking insight to your behavior, past, present, and future.

Interviews provide employers with a chance to observe you from a variety of perspectives.

The majority of interviews can be classified as:

- Informational
- Mass
- Stress
- "Unnecessary"
- Courtesy

Informational Interviews

This is the "classical" interview, where you are asked to come in so employers have a chance to check you out in the areas previously outlined. These interviews are straightforward. Presumably you enter this interview in a relatively equal position with the other applicants. You have no say about what format your interview will take, so "go with the flow." The interview may be formal, relaxed, or somewhere in between. You may have only one interviewer, or there may be several.

The formal interview is rather rigid, with questions being asked one after another and the interviewers giving little or no response to tip you off as to how you are doing. They purposely do not respond so that you will not have any advantage over other applicants. This can be rather disconcerting, since everyone likes feedback, but just keep going. On the other extreme, you may find yourself caught off guard by the informality of the interview. Your interviewers may be so laid-back, it may seem they don't even care. Although possible, don't let a group that likes to have fun throw you off. In either case, provide your interviewer with as accurate a picture of yourself as possible. Just because you find yourself in a formal setting doesn't mean you must perform rigidly, nor should informality lull you into a false sense of security and cause you to lose your edge.

The informational interview is the classical interview. These interviews are straightforward and are typically one-on-one, although there may be more than one interviewer present.

Mass Interviews

The number of individuals that employers like to interview varies. One or two applicants may be interviewed if they are exceptionally strong candidates, or several people may be asked. Many applicants present themselves so poorly that a general informational meeting can serve to weed out a number of them. "Assembly-line" interviews are hard on everyone, including those conducting the interviews. Applicants seem to melt together, making it difficult to remember each individual interviewer. This is when it is critical to not only provide a very strong interview, but to also pay particular attention to follow-up.

> Mass interviews involve several candidates being interviewed in rapid succession, or in "assembly-line" fashion. In these situations, candidates may blur together in the interviewers' minds, and you must pay particular attention to your follow-up to stand out from the crowd.

Stress Interviews

Here you have good news and bad news. The good news first: "Stress interviews" are not too common in the world of job hunting. The bad news is that criminal justice, private security, and related fields do lend themselves to this type of interview. These jobs involve a great deal of stress, so the approach is justified in order to see how applicants respond under stress. Don't expect these to be comfortable. They are not designed as such. Go into the interview with the commitment that, regardless of the type of interview you are confronted with, you will do your best.

During stress interviews rapid-fire questions give you little time to think about your answers or to regroup before the next question. The interviewer may seem harsh, if not downright mean. Furniture may be placed in unusual configurations; for instance, your chair may be put in a corner—or maybe you won't even have a chair. Be direct by asking where they'd like you to sit or bring the chair to the interview. Logic suggests they don't want you to sit in the corner.

Recognize what the game is—to get you uptight. You should feel tension. In fact, you have much more reason to be concerned if you *don't* respond nervously to this setup. Draw energy from a stress interview and maintain a level of calmness and use the strength that brought you this far. On the job you'll find yourself confronted with similar stress. The interviewers want to be sure you won't become overly defensive, hostile, or panicky. Although many interviewees would tell you that every interview is a stress interview, in fact, few are set up to purposely make you uptight.

> The stress interview's purpose is to make you uptight so the interviewers can evaluate how you handle stress. Rapid-fire questioning, interviewer hostility, and unusual furniture configurations may all be parts of the stress interview.

"Unnecessary" Interviews

Do not be misled or succumb to not doing your best because you think the employer has someone specific in mind for the job, even if that is indeed the case. Public employers usually have to interview several candidates and most private employers will, too. So what? What if the job is offered to someone else? Who's to say that person will accept it? If they do, who's to say it will work out? Most importantly, what if they like you better?

Yes, it is frustrating to be called to an interview merely so the employer can prove he or she has done a search before hiring the predetermined first choice. However, if you do well in the interview, the employer may keep you in mind for the next opening. At the very least, it is a chance to practice your interview skills and find out that you can survive rejection. Both opportunities are valuable.

Because you are unique, you may be the perfect candidate. Never let an opportunity pass by. You have no way of knowing if this job will be the one. A lot can be said for the person who tries, even in the face of adversity.

> "Unnecessary" interviews may be conducted when the position is already filled but policy demands the position still be advertised or that a certain number of people be interviewed. Make the most of this opportunity—no interview is truly needless.

Courtesy Interviews

Never dismiss an opportunity by thinking, "I only got this interview because the chief knows my dad. He did it as a favor to him." It doesn't matter how you got into an interview, just that you did. Once you're there, it's all up to you. All that matters is that now you have the chance to impress the interview panel. Go for it!

> Courtesy interviews may result from "connections," but they are still legitimate interviewing opportunities, so make the most of them.

TELECONFERENCING AND VIDEO INTERVIEWS—A NEW TWIST

Technology is changing the way jobs are pursued and found. Although face-to-face meetings between job seekers and prospective employers are still the most common interview method, videoconference interviews are growing in popularity. Two primary reasons for the increased use of this method are that others beyond the formal process can view the interview and that long-distance applicants can effectively compete for a position without having to travel extensively.

Such "interviews" may consist simply of a candidate's videotaped responses to questions or it may be a "live" interview via video hookups, as is done routinely on the news. Internet technology makes it equally convenient for prospective employees or employers to communicate, interview, and negotiate long distance.

Some additional strategies to optimize this opportunity include applicants presenting themselves in different modes to set off their personality. For example, some questions could be answered in a dress uniform, others in a suit, and yet others more casually in a sweater. A fire service applicant might answer questions with a fireplace or fire truck as a background. This is a chance to plan how to present yourself in the best light and to be far more in control of the situation than in most conventional interviews.

TYPICAL QUESTIONS

Countless lists have been compiled of questions you should anticipate and be prepared to answer during job interviews. You've already looked at the five basic questions typically asked. Although the previous questions can be anticipated by nearly every job seeker in every profession, Hart (2004a) identifies some specific questions law enforcement applicants must be prepared to answer:

1. Why are you seeking a career as a police officer/deputy sheriff?

2. What education and experience do you possess that has prepared you for this career?

3. Describe the worst work situation you have encountered. How did you deal with the problem?

4. How do you feel about carrying a gun and possibly having to take someone's life in the line of duty?

5. What are the sources of stress in your personal and work life? How do you manage this stress?

6. What is your pattern of alcohol use?

7. What types of interpersonal conflict have you experienced in your work life?

8. What steps did you take to resolve the issues?

9. In what area are you looking for a change or self-improvement?

10. What personal qualities and traits do you possess that would make you well-suited for a law enforcement career?

11. What types of situations cause you to feel discouraged? Anxious? Irritated?

12. When have you had to take charge of a situation to quickly resolve a problem or crisis?

13. As a police officer, you pull over a speeding car. It's a friend of yours, and you think he may have been drinking. How would you handle the situation?

These questions call for more than a mere "yes" or "no." In many cases, there is no single "right" answer, but there is generally a right approach. Concentrate on your approach to each question. What would make a good response to each?

 Write a response to each of the preceding questions in your journal.

PRACTICE, PRACTICE, PRACTICE

As with so many things in life, the more one goes through the interview process, the better one becomes at being interviewed. Herein lies the "upside" of interviews that do not result in a job offer. Practice helps.

When you aren't interviewing, practice interviewing with friends, with family, and anyone who will ask you questions or listen to yours. Also, take advantage of opportunities to ask others what questions they were asked, and how they responded. It might be wise to keep a list of these in your journal. The crazier the question, the better—it gets you prepared to think on your feet. Questions like what you do for fun or what your favorite color is won't distract you if you have given them some thought or practiced to the point you can comfortably think spontaneously.

NEGOTIATING

Negotiating is sometimes not possible. The majority of criminal justice jobs are union jobs, or are at least positions that bargain collectively. Therefore, you will have little room to negotiate, particularly at entry-level positions.

Likewise, security positions generally permit little room for you to make demands. As you work your way upward in either the public or private sector, you may find room to negotiate. At almost all entry-level, and even mid-level lateral movements, you could easily appear too demanding if you want too much. Be realistic and recognize the limitations of these careers. If you have specific needs, however, pursue them as far as you can.

> The opportunity to negotiate a salary in these fields, particularly in entry-level jobs, is very limited.

CLOSING THE INTERVIEW

The final impression you make on your way out is also important. Here is an opportunity to shine as the ideal, enthusiastic candidate. The interview is likely to close with the interviewer asking, "Is there anything you would like to ask?" Every other candidate will say something like, "Well, no, not really." This makes you boring and unmemorable. Your strategy should include having several closing questions and statements. Questions to have at the ready, although you don't have to ask them all, could include:

➢ What is your anticipated start date for this position?

➢ Are there any other questions I can answer for you?

➢ Is there anything in addition to my résumé I can provide you?

Similarly, statements you may wish to close with could include:

➢ Thank you all for this opportunity to interview.

➢ My goal has been to convey my genuine interest in this position.

➢ I am truly interested in this job and invite you to contact me if there is anything additional I can provide.

Always leave on an assertive, upbeat, energetic note. Regardless of the words you choose, make sure the message comes across loud and clear: I want this job, and I'll be spectacular at it! One of the strongest conclusions an applicant ever gave me was to simply say, "You'll never regret hiring me!" Don't be too brash or boastful. Make your closing statement brief and to the point. Any last-minute chance you have will be ruined if you drag it out with question after question or statement after statement. As is true throughout your overall strategy, seek a balance.

Because interviews typically end with the question, "Is there anything you'd like to ask or say?" to simply fade away with an answer of "no" is forfeiting a great opportunity. If you do, you'll be categorized as just one of the many interviewed that day.

 List several closing statements you can use when asked if there is anything you'd like to ask or say at the conclusion of an interview and then practice them.

In summary, let the interviewer know that you want the job. You would be astonished by how few applicants ever communicate that they've applied for the job because they want the job!

Close the interview on an appropriate, upbeat note. *Never* close by asking about salary or benefits. Finally, let the interviewer know that you really want the job.

FOLLOW-UP

Punctuate your interest with a follow-up. Follow-up is an easy way to score points during the hiring process because few applicants have developed a strategy that includes courtesy. At the least, send a letter telling the interviewer(s) you appreciate the time and opportunity to meet. Such a letter not only demonstrates politeness but also offers one more chance to impress the employer with your strong points. Anything in addition, within reason, will probably benefit you: "Writing powerful thank-you letters is not just a formality. Thank-you letters are marketing tools that can have tremendous value in moving your candidacy forward and positioning you above the competition" (Enelow, 2004). Droste (2004) adds:

> The thank-you note can be a critical piece of your job-hunting strategy. But should you send it by email or snail mail, handwritten or typed? In this fast-paced computer age, the question baffles even the most sophisticated job hunters. Follow these guidelines to help you through the maze.
>
> **Email Thank-You Notes.** How did the company initially contact you? If you have corresponded with people there via email for setting up the interview and answering questions, then by all means send an email thank-you note as soon as you return from an interview. However, make sure to follow it up with a typed note to show that you are not Mr. or Ms. Casual. Email thank-you notes have one clear advantage over their snail mail counterpart: They can put your name in front of the interviewer on the same day—sometimes within hours—of your interview.
>
> **Snail Mail.** If the company you interviewed with is formal and traditional, use snail mail to send your thank-you note. Should it be handwritten or typed? Typed is standard . . . [but] handwritten notes are appropriate if you'd like to extend your thanks to others in the [department] who helped you out.

She concludes:

> More important is what you say and how you say it. A standard thank-you note should accomplish several things:
>
> - Thank the person for the opportunity to interview with the company.
> - Recap some of the conversational highlights.

- Clarify any information you needed to check on for the interviewer.
- And most importantly, plug your skills. Use the last paragraph as the chance to state, "The job is a good fit for me because of XYZ, and my past experience in XYZ."

Interviewers have short memories. A thank-you note is your final chance to stand apart from all of the others who want the same position.

> *Do not* forget to follow up. Following up helps you score points in the hiring process by demonstrating your courtesy and getting your name in front of the interviewer one more time.

MAKING A DECISION

Making a decision is something you probably can't imagine would be a problem. Selecting from several jobs would be a great problem, right? If this does become your "problem," take your time before deciding. Usually employers are happy to give you a reasonable amount of time to make a decision. The *Occupational Outlook Handbook* (*OOH*) notes:

> Once you receive a job offer, you must decide if you want the job. Fortunately, most organizations will give you a few days to accept or reject an offer. There are many issues to consider when assessing a job offer. Will the organization be a good place to work? Will the job be interesting? Are there opportunities for advancement? Is the salary fair? Does the employer offer good benefits? Now is the time to ask the potential employer about these issues—and to do some checking on your own. (www.bls.gov/oco/oco20046.htm)

If you are a final contender in another agency, you now have a card to play if you haven't heard from them yet. There is nothing wrong with contacting these other employers to let them know you would like to work for them, but you have been offered another job elsewhere. Suddenly you have increased your desirability, since someone else wants you, too.

DANGER LURKS IN JOB OFFERS

Greek mythology tells the tale of seductresses luring sailors towards the dangerously rocky islands of Sirenum scopuli with their music and song. The temptation of these Sirens was too much to resist, resulting in the sailors being killed in the ensuing shipwrecks. Is it coincidence that sailors were once tempted by Sirens much the way you may be by sirens of a different kind?

Without question, some jobs call people because of the excitement and potential of becoming heroes. It's almost too much to resist, especially if you've known for as long as you can remember that's "just what you had to be." But what if it's not? Tieger and Barron (2007, p. 3) stress:

> It's important to find the right job. Despite the universal fantasies of winning the lottery, buying expensive cars and homes, and doing fascinating work with interesting people in exotic places, the sober reality is that most of us have to work, hard, for a long time. If you spend forty to fifty years – not an unlikely scenario – working at jobs you'd rather not be doing, you are in truth throwing away a large part of your life. This is unnecessary and sad, especially since a career you can love is within your reach.

Before you put yourself and an employer through all that is involved with the hiring process, be sure you have given this all-important decision due thought. Even then, beware of jumping at the first offer that comes your way. The fact that you have landed an offer confirms you *are* hirable, so think carefully before taking that first offer. Do not accept it simply because of an underlying sense of desperation. Many job seekers are so desperate for work, or work in a particular field, they accept things without giving it the necessary thought. Getting into a career that's not really a "fit" is unfortunate, but so is accepting a job at an agency you're miserable at, even if you like the work itself.

Realistically weigh as many factors as you can. Ask for honest input from family and friends and talk to people already working at the agency. Ultimately only you can make the final decision to accept a job or keep looking. Beem (2006, p. 115) asks: "What do your instincts say? Does it feel like the right thing?" Beem (p. 115) recommends asking yourself the following when evaluating a job offer:

➢ What is your instinctive reaction to the offer?

➢ Does the money seem right for the job and you personally?

➢ Do the duties seem reasonable and within your ability to do?

➢ Is the employment culture one with which you'd be comfortable?

➢ Are there opportunities for advancement?

Above all, don't set yourself up for unhappiness or failure. Remember, your job-seeking strategies are intended to help you find a satisfying career, not just any job.

A QUICK REVIEW

Review these job interview tips now, and then again when you have an interview lined up (Hart, 2004b):

➢ Call the agency for directions to the interview site, if you are at all uncertain about the location.

➢ Review your application and background statement. Be familiar with key aspects of your education, job history, and driving record.

➢ Research the department—Do your homework! Talk with some law enforcement officers.

➢ Ride-alongs and facility tours can be most informative.

➢ Get a good night's sleep. You will need it.

➢ Look sharp. Dress professionally. Select a conservative suit of clothing.

➢ Minimize jewelry.

➢ Be able to clearly and convincingly state your interest in law enforcement.

➢ Prepare a few relevant questions to ask the Oral Interview Board. This conveys your genuine interest and preparation.

➤   Arrive at least one-half hour early.

➤   Anticipate key interview questions and practice answering them with family members or friends.

➤   Be willing to ask that questions be repeated or clarified if you don't understand them.

➤   Relate to interviewers in a confident, courteous, and respectful fashion.

A FINAL WORD OF CAUTION

Sometimes no matter how well you have prepared and how well you have performed you still don't get the job. And sometimes there's just nothing you could have done differently to change that. The one aspect you can't control is chemistry. You can do your very best, but if the chemistry, or connection, isn't there, it's just not the right fit. Sometimes it's as simple as the employer feeling better about one individual over another. When it comes down to equally qualified candidates, the tie breaker may be something you have no control over—how they "feel" about you. Rather than let any disappointing interview experience cause you to lapse into a state of remorse, use it to draw the energy needed to realize your time will come. It wasn't happenstance that got you this far—it was *you*.

CONCLUSION

The interview is the goal of job hunting. Prepare by anticipating commonly asked questions and practicing your responses to these questions so you aren't caught off guard. Also, prepare a few questions and closing remarks of your own. Close the interview on an upbeat note, affirming you are a candidate worthy of their serious consideration. Never close by asking about salary or benefits, and realize that the opportunity to negotiate a salary in these fields, particularly in entry-level jobs, is very limited. Finally, let the interviewer know that you really want the job. And do not forget to follow up.

AN INSIDER'S VIEW

YOUR TURN TO STAR

Jim Chaffee

Security Director
Fox Entertainment, California

BEFORE THE INTERVIEW

I would suggest you type all correspondence, including your application. One of my greatest "turnoffs" is to receive an application that is not typed. This is not to say I won't look at it, but when you are in competition with a hundred other candidates, every little edge will help.

I don't mean to suggest that if you type all correspondence that's all you need to worry about. Correspondence should be neat and organized and should not contain spelling errors or noticeably improper grammar. Some people have their résumés professionally done, which looks very nice and can be impressive. A résumé does not have to be done professionally, however. With today's computers, a professional-looking résumé can be done with little effort.

Do not include a poorly typed cover letter to go with a professional résumé. This only points out in a glaring fashion that the résumé was done professionally and for obvious reasons. When responding to a job announcement, try to include in the cover letter all your attributes that mesh with what was indicated in the ad. For instance, if the ad listed "map reading" as a desirable trait, be sure to highlight your qualifications and/or experience in map reading. As a general rule, the cover letter should not be more than one page long and should cover what the announcement asked for.

THE ORAL INTERVIEW

There is not a lot you can do to prepare for an oral interview. Unless you know the type of interview and the questions being asked, you are going in blind, so to speak. Don't worry about being nervous. Everyone is. Try not to be overly nervous, though, where your voice cracks and breaks and you perspire profusely.

On the other hand, don't be too relaxed and nonchalant. It does not look good in the interview process to sit back with your legs crossed and your arm draped over the back of the chair. Remember that the interviewers are not only listening to what you have to say, but they are surveying your mannerisms, posture, dress, grooming and the like. The interviewers may not have ever seen you before, and first impressions are lasting impressions.

Absolutely be on time. If you are late for an interview, it is almost like a kiss of death for that particular job. There may always be a reasonable excuse that caused your tardiness, but the burden will be squarely on you to show why you were late. Some examples of reasonable excuses are: "I was robbed, beaten up and sent to the hospital on my way over here," or "I was caught in a flood where several people were swept away, and I ended up saving all of them." If you do have a reasonable excuse for your tardiness, if at all possible telephone and try to let someone know. If you flat out miss the interview and don't call and explain why, you have just indicated your desire not to continue in the selection process.

Do dress appropriately. That does not always mean a suit or sport coat and tie, but it almost always does. Wear conservative clothing without loud colors or patterns. A white shirt, neutral tie and dark suit (gray, black or dark blue) is most appropriate. Do not forget about shoes and socks—you are being evaluated in totality, which includes your shoes and socks. Make sure your shoes are shined and your socks match whatever you are wearing. Try to make sure your entire outfit is color-coordinated and pleasing to the eye. Do make sure you are neatly groomed, for example, that your hair is combed and not too long. Also, women should not wear an overabundance of makeup or perfume.

ANSWERING QUESTIONS

Do not attempt to answer a question when you clearly do not know the answer. It is okay to ask to have the question repeated or to ask for clarification. Look the interviewer in the eyes, but not aggressively. If there are several interviewers, look at them also while answering the question. Try not to fidget.

TRICKS OF THE TRADE

When being introduced to the panel, repeat each interviewer's name. For example, "Good morning (or afternoon), Lt. Adams. Pleased to meet you." Doing this should help you remember each interviewer's name as you go through the process. It is impressive when you can repeat the interviewer's name at some time during the interview. For example, you may need the second part of a question reread, and you could say, "I'm sorry, Lt. Adams, but I did not understand the second part of the question." Try to work in each interviewer's name some time during the process, but don't do it unless it sounds natural.

Be prepared for trick questions that may or may not have anything to do with the job. Sometimes a question may be thrown in just to see what your reaction is. Sometimes it will be a humorous type of question, but be sure that it is before you laugh.

Also, be prepared for the unexpected. During one interview session we placed a lone chair way out in the middle of the room for the applicant to sit in. This very definitely causes stress to the interviewee. We were trying to see how the person coped with the situation. Some sat in the chair very appropriately, and others were obviously very nervous. We even had several drag the chair up to the interview table before sitting down. One candidate just stood and would not, or could not, sit in the chair. Some candidates appeared really perplexed when trying to decide the appropriate action to take regarding the chair.

Always follow up your interview with thank-you letters to the interview panel.

Jim Chaffee *is the security director for Fox Entertainment in California, and the former director of international security for the Walt Disney Company. He has over twenty-eight years' experience in the field of criminal justice, including four years with the United States Air Force Security Police; eleven years as a police officer in Minnetonka, Minnesota; and three years as the public safety director in Chanhassen, Minnesota. Mr. Chaffee holds an MBA and is a certified fraud examiner.*

MIND STRETCHES

1.   Why would a mass interview put you at a disadvantage? An advantage?

2.   How could you make the interview process more enjoyable and memorable for an employer?

3.   At what point during any phase of the hiring process can you become a pest rather than an impressive, aggressive candidate? How can you maintain an awareness of this and prevent it?

4.   What could you do to remain cool during a "stress" interview?

5.   What could you do if you really blew an interview?

6.   What techniques could you use to deal with the understandable stress and anxiety everyone experiences during interviews?

7.   Why should you follow up with an employer you've applied to, even if you take a different job?

8.   List your three greatest concerns about being interviewed. How can you reduce these concerns?

REFERENCES

Beatty, Richard H. *The Ultimate Job Search Intelligent Strategies to Get the Right Job FAST.* Indianapolis, IN: JIST Works, 2006.

Beem, Linda J. *The Geek's Guide to Job Hunting.* Birmingham, AL: Crane Hill Publishers, 2006.

Bolles, Richard Nelson. *What Color Is Your Parachute? A Practical Manual for Job-Hunters & Career-Changers.* Berkeley, CA: Ten Speed Press, 2008.

Droste, Therese. "Notable Thank-You Notes." Monster Career Center, 2004. Available online at http://interview.monster.com/articles/followingup/

Enelow, Wendy S. "Write Winning Thank-You Letters." Monster Career Center, 2004. Available online at http://interview.monster.com/articles/thankyou/

Hart, Mac. "The Firing Line." 2004a. Available online at www.policeinterview.com/firingline.html

Hart, Mac. "Preparing Yourself for Your Police Interview." 2004b. Available online at www.policeinterview.com/prep.html

Krannich, Ron, and Caryl Krannich. *No One Will Hire Me*, 3rd ed. Manassas Park, VA: Impact Publications, 2007.

Krumrie, Matt. "Ten Things Not to Do in an Interview." (Minneapolis/St. Paul) *Star Tribun*e, March 25, 2007, p. W1.

Occupational Outlook Handbook (OOH), 2008–09 Edition. Washington, DC: Bureau of Labor Statistics, U.S. Department of Labor. U.S. Government Printing Office, 2004.

Tieger, Paul D., and Barbara Barron. *Do What You Are*, 4th ed. New York: Little, Brown and Company, 2007.

SECTION FOUR

YOUR FUTURE IN YOUR CHOSEN PROFESSION

The future comes one day at a time.

—*Dean Acheson*

Destiny is not a matter of chance, it is a matter of choice; it is not a thing to be waited for,
it is a thing to be achieved.

—*William Jennings Bryan*

What is the recipe for successful achievement? To my mind there are just four essential ingredients:
Choose a career you love. . . . Give it the best there is in you. . . . Seize
your opportunities. . . . And be a member of the team.

—*Benjamin F. Fairless*

The road to happiness lies in two simple principles: find what it is that interests you and that
you can do well, and when you find it, put your whole soul into it—every bit of energy
and ambition and natural ability you have.

—*John D. Rockefeller, III*

There are no secrets to success. It is the result of preparation, hard work, and learning from failure.
—*General Colin L. Powell*

After landing the job you've worked so hard to get, another challenge begins. How do you not only make certain you keep the job, but also make certain you excel? Chapter 15 addresses this major challenge, Chapter 16 discusses how you can enhance your chances for promotion, and Chapter 17 looks at job loss and starting the job-seeking process all over.

Preparing for the future is another important part of your job-seeking strategy because that's where you'll be spending the rest of your life. It is especially the case with jobs considered in this text that if something goes wrong and you wash out, for whatever reason, it can mark the end of a career before it even gets started. Being the victim of layoffs is difficult enough; being the cause of your own job loss can feel insurmountable.

CHAPTER 15

AT LAST, YOU'VE GOT THE JOB—CONGRATULATIONS!

When you are making a success of something, it's not work. It's a way of life. You enjoy yourself because you are making your contribution to the world.

—Andy Granatelli

Do You Know:

➢   What needs to be done once you get the job?
➢   As you keep trying to do well, what is important?
➢   How to be "appropriate" on the job?
➢   What the likely effects are of "knowing it all"?
➢   Whether it's possible to be "overly enthusiastic"?
➢   How to approach politics on the job?
➢   How to respond to criticism?
➢   Why being yourself is critically important?
➢   How to maintain yourself?
➢   What is meant by "paying your dues"?

INTRODUCTION

By the time you get to this chapter, you will have covered an exceptional amount of material that should give you a genuine edge during your job search, especially when considering the majority of job seekers haven't given it any thought, much less developed an actual strategy. You have taken a look at where to find jobs, how to write a résumé, how to best present yourself, how to interview, how to follow up, and even how to deal with those inevitable rejections.

But wait, the race is not yet over. In a sense, it is just beginning. The only thing expected of the unsuccessful candidate is to be a good loser. But for the successful candidate, the ultimate challenge is just ahead. Getting a job brings a whole new set of challenges, especially in fields where you usually face a six-month to one-year probationary period: "During this critical period, your agency and your fellow cops are checking you out; make sure they like what they see" (Scoville, 2008, p. 10). The recommendations are direct: Put your best foot forward; don't (upset) your training officer; don't confuse responsibility with privilege; roll with the flow and get along; off duty means just that (you aren't a cop 24/7); and make your own luck (Scoville, pp. 11–12). These recommendations apply to anyone new in criminal justice, security, or related fields. "Most young cops who get terminated during their probation period commit career suicide by making bad decisions, using poor judgment, and associating with suspect friends" (p. 10).

Entry-level employees, in particular, are subject to a multitude of unwritten rules. Because criminal justice and private security are fields traditionally closed to outsiders, you have no basis to understand the expectations. You'll learn all too soon that the expectations are extremely high.

Starting a new job is like going to court. It doesn't happen all that often, but when it does, officers are expected to know what to do without having to be told ahead of time. To make an error could be very serious. The same with getting the job. Do you act like the old-timers? Do you act like the rookies? It is imperative that you have at least some idea of what to expect. Call it learning from others' mistakes.

What a bitter disappointment it must be to be successful in the pursuit of your dream job—only to lose it because you don't know what these circumstances demand. Although many job applicants who could probably do the job just fine never get the chance because they cannot interview adequately, the opposite is true as well. Many people who cannot perform adequately get the job because they came across very well during the interview. Being successful in an interview does not guarantee success on the job. You must have some idea of what to expect and what the circumstances demand in order to hold on to the job.

Here's what needs to be done once you get the job:

- Keep trying
- Be appropriate
- Do not be a know-it-all
- Wait until you are asked
- Understand politics
- Accept criticism maturely
- Be yourself
- Maintain yourself

KEEP TRYING

Do not stop putting forth your best effort just because you have the job. If anything, make even greater attempts to fit into the new job than you did to get it. As Abraham Lincoln was fond of saying: "Things may come to those who wait, but only the things left by those who hustle." This is particularly true for those who have not had a professional job before. Criminal justice, security, and related fields jobs are demanding, both in expectations and workload. You will be expected to perform as a professional, even at an entry-level position. Most employers expect you to know the basics; they seldom ask if you do. It is up to you to know when to ask appropriate questions. You'll be expected to learn at a reasonable pace and to show signs of professional development.

Keeping a job takes constant effort. You must not be afraid to ask questions, for not doing so may lead to mistakes that may cost you your job.

BE APPROPRIATE

This aspect of easing into your new job may seem simplistic, but it's not. The job you have landed is very different from most other entry-level jobs such as working at a fast-food restaurant, washing cars, or bagging groceries. The usual horseplay and immature attitudes frequently found at such jobs are simply not tolerated in any criminal justice or security job. These fields are constantly seeking to prove their professional image and demand employees who will help in this mission.

It is hard for new employees to know just what *is* appropriate behavior, unless they have been in the military, police explorers, reserve officers, interns, or have had some other association with the criminal justice or security fields. Few outsiders know what goes on "inside." For a newly hired individual, a conservative, low-key, quiet approach is not only appropriate, but it's key to survival.

The best way to discover what behavior is appropriate is to observe what is happening around you. You will see what behavior is approved of and what is inappropriate. Especially when new in these fields, you want to fit in, not stand out. Younger hires may be especially challenged if they fit the description of the current generation of job seekers described by Armour (2005): "They're young, smart, brash. They may wear flip-flops to the office or listen to iPods at their desk. They want to work, but they don't want work to be their life. . . . (this generation) is much less likely to respond to the traditional command-and-control type of management still popular in much of today's workforce. . .They've grown up questioning their parents, and now they're questioning their employers. They don't know how to shut up. . . that's aggravating to the 50-year-old manager who says, 'Do it and do it now.'"

> Learn appropriate behavior by assuming a conservative, low-key approach, taking the necessary time to observe what is happening around you and what behavior is approved of, disapproved of, and expected.

DO NOT BE A KNOW-IT-ALL

It is frequently easy to tell who is new. They are often overbearing and brash, seeming to go out of their way to show the world they know it all—or at least *think* they know it all. Experienced officers acknowledge there is always more to learn.

Fact: A hierarchy exists in every police and fire department, correctional facility, and security corporation. Entry-level employees, especially *new* entry-level employees, are at the bottom of the ladder. You may never recover from the damage unintentionally done by telling anyone above you how *they* should be doing something. Many rookies destroy relationships with senior personnel (maybe senior by only a year) by telling them how they should do their job.

Maybe the rookie is correct, as rookies have usually received up-to-date training that reflects better ways of doing things and have not had time to develop bad habits. *This is not the point.* You will have plenty of time to do it your own way. Irritate anyone early on and word will spread that you are a know-it-all.

This is not advice to "play dumb." If you are asked for an opinion, give it. If you have to make a decision, make it. Show interest and a desire to learn. It may be difficult to admit to yourself and others that you *are* new and really do *not* know it all.

> Being a know-it-all will likely earn you a negative reputation and delay your being accepted by others in the department, institution, or agency.

WAIT UNTIL YOU ARE ASKED

Officers in law enforcement, corrections, private security, and related fields are in positions of respect. They expect it and generally receive it. Particularly as a new employee, you will get more respect from other employees if you show respect for them. They deserve it and they've earned it. Give them the opportunity to share their wisdom with you.

Make it clear you know you have much to learn, and take advantage of this opportunity to ask questions. Do not, however, ask personally or professionally challenging questions (e.g., "Why would you wear a holster everyone *knows* is dangerous *and* ugly?"). A better way might be to ask what equipment the officer suggests you consider when purchasing your gear.

It will not make a positive impression to say to an officer you are riding with, "My instructor told us to tag every violator for speeding. Shouldn't you have?" Rather, you might ask what other violations could have been written or how the officer decided what to write on that particular stop. Well-thought-out questions are expected of you.

People working in criminal justice, security, and related fields make their living getting lied to by the best. Do not pretend to be interested or ask questions for the sake of asking them. You will be spotted before you get the question completed, and you will be off to a terrible start.

> It is possible to be overly enthusiastic by asking too many questions. Determine this on your own.

Teachers *want* students to ask appropriate questions, but also come to cringe at those always-present students who chronically ask questions for the sake of hearing themselves talk.

UNDERSTAND POLITICS

Every organization has its own politics. *Merriam-Webster's* defines *politics* as: "competition between interest groups or individuals for power and leadership in a government or other group." That is a fitting definition, but the complexities are so deep you can be caught in the political web before ever being aware of its existence.

To understand politics, recognize that politics are impossible to understand. This is an area in which to be particularly careful. Even seasoned veterans can easily fall prey to internal politics. Politics can be a deadly game and should be avoided, especially when you don't know the players or issues. Avoid getting embroiled in personality or agency issues if you have no reason to get involved.

Although many officers are fond of asserting they are not politicians and so are not going to play politics, in reality, we are all politicians to an extent. Whether or not we're a "player" in the politics of our agency, we may become entangled in it.

Although certain people tend to be more than willing to give advice, such advice may not be sound. Eventually you will learn with whom you can talk openly. Some people are willing to share helpful insights, others may well set you up for a fall, and others may be garnering supporters. Some things said innocently may offend someone. *You just do not know,* so don't take a chance. When it involves coworkers and relationships and agency issues, stay quiet and neutral.

Experienced officers learn it is best to never write anything they don't want to show up, because it inevitably will surface. Similarly, it is a good practice to never say things you don't want heard because statements always seem to get repeated. People will tell you things in confidence. An eight-hour shift in a squad car or ambulance, working a cell block or on security duty, lends itself to sharing a lot of thoughts and ideas. Should you make the mistake of telling others what was told to you may cause some serious relationship problems for yourself and others. Never say anything you do not want repeated, and never repeat what is told to you in confidence.

> Do not play politics, do not try to understand politics, and do not get yourself drawn into politics. This is important advice for anyone on the job, but absolutely crucial for a newly hired individual.

ACCEPT CRITICISM MATURELY

A natural aspect of getting into any new job is learning. Considering that most people learn from their mistakes, you, too, should want to learn from *your* mistakes—they present great opportunities. Everyone (yes, *everyone*) makes mistakes at work—especially when new. Employers expect this and would probably feel you weren't trying if mistakes weren't made.

So what's the big deal about making mistakes? The problem is that many people can't deal with thinking they can make mistakes, especially younger people who feel entitled to a job. Whether because of ego, incorrect assumptions about training, or just plain embarrassment, many individuals react inappropriately to being told they did something wrong. Failure to respond appropriately to criticism received at work can negatively affect a critical phase of the new job.

Frequently, part of field training or the probationary period is seeing how recruits or new employees handle criticism. Assuming you learn from your mistakes and are able to prevent them from recurring, what is essential is that you can maturely accept critical comments and process them, hopefully improving as a result. To argue with a trainer or superior is a poor choice for those who have been at the job for only a short while. It could prove fatal for someone on probation. Take advantage of the occasional times someone offers criticism to not only improve the particular skill at issue, but also to make sure the person leaves thinking about how professionally you handled the situation.

One aspect of this process that people often fail to recognize is that offering criticism is frequently as difficult as receiving it. If you accept the comments in a positive way, even thanking the person for the comments, you may well end up scoring far more points than you will ever realize. It would be a serious mistake to get angry, challenge the superior, have a temper tantrum, or go shooting your mouth off to others. In the unlikely event that you genuinely are being harassed or ill-treated, discuss this with the person first, and only then proceed up the proper chain of command to deal with it. In some situations, new employees have, for whatever reason, not hit it off with a trainer. Personality conflicts do occur, as do outright illegal discrimination and harassment. But the real issue will be how you choose to handle it.

> Accept criticism maturely, for such instances provide great opportunities for you to learn from your mistakes. Recognize also that offering criticism is frequently as difficult as receiving it, and by accepting the comments in a positive way, you may score far more points than you will ever realize.

BE YOURSELF

You managed to get the job by being yourself, and you will succeed by being yourself. Don't get down on yourself because you're nervous, afraid, or feel inadequate—we all feel this way when starting new jobs. The first few weeks *are* challenging at any new job. Draw energy from it rather than allowing it to exhaust you. Those working in the fields discussed in this text are used to people trying to manipulate them, and will see this in new hires also. Just be yourself, not what you think others think you should be.

> Be yourself. Starting a new job, particularly in a field you are not used to, is uncomfortable and requires an adjustment. You will become exhausted if you spend energy putting on an act. Save your energy for learning the job.

Peer pressure is always hard to cope with. As a rookie, you will be expected to do as you are told. If you are unfortunate enough to get drawn into negative circumstances, you will face some tough decisions. Under no circumstances should you become involved in actions that violate agency policy or are illegal or unethical. Recognize that to stand by and watch unethical, possibly illegal, behavior is only slightly less devious than actually participating. If you don't think you can resist the temptations from within or without, get out now. Being witness to, hearing about, or having any knowledge of illegal or unethical behavior leaves you without any alternative but to report it.

If you are not happy, do something about it. These jobs are *not* for everyone. If you are unhappy, or if you can foresee problems, admit this to yourself as soon as you become aware of it. Miller (2003) helps put this into perspective: "Since September 11, people everywhere have been re-assessing their priorities and realizing life is too short to waste doing something you don't love. Many will undergo a total re-focus in life because of this. No explanation or repackaging required."

It is unfortunate for people to suffer at jobs they dislike—especially those in jobs that provide the individual with a great deal of power and authority. Perhaps some officers "go bad" by becoming abusive or cynical because the job is just no longer right for them, and it shows. Further, consider that professionals who dislike their work do not have the necessary focus to be safe.

MAINTAIN YOURSELF

Burnout. We've all heard about it. Maybe you've been there. Most of us have at one time or another to some degree or another. When starting a new job, consider ways of balancing it to keep it as attractive as it was when you first heard about it. Don't overdo it; maintain a balance in your life. Keep up your other friendships, activities, and interests. Take care of your physical self: eat right, exercise, and get enough sleep. Take care of your social and spiritual life. This is more difficult when working shifts and schedules that aren't what your family and friends do; it takes effort.

What you do off duty affects how you react on duty. If you become overly tired, out of shape, and fail to maintain healthy family and social relationships, you aren't going to be as effective at work or as safe. The demands of these professions can take a toll on all aspects of one's life. You can often tell the rookie because they don't take days off, eagerly jump at any overtime, and sign up for every off-duty job, limiting the time and energy for outside activities.

> Maintain yourself physically, mentally, and spiritually. Stay current not only with things related to the job but also with things and relationships that interest you outside of work. This helps prevent burnout.

A lack of balance may be moderately uncomfortable or debilitating. Sometimes it can become a matter of life or death. If you need help, get it. Sheehan and Van Hasselt (2003, p. 12), in referring to the terrorist attacks of 9/11, observe:

> These horrific acts harmed all Americans, including thousands of law enforcement officers. Clearly, large-scale critical incidents are stressful, but so are the numerous smaller scale events that so many law enforcement officers encounter on the job. Who can accurately measure the stress caused by being wounded in the line of duty, having a partner killed or injured, shooting another person, seeing abused or deceased children, and witnessing severe motor vehicle accidents? Who can calculate the effects of continued exposure to murders, suicides, kidnappings, hijackings, rapes, and other violent acts that assault the sensibilities of law enforcement officers? Too often, assistance is delayed until officers display maladaptive behaviors, such as excessive drinking, domestic violence, or even suicide.

Careers in law enforcement, fire protection, and security carry a heavy burden of responsibility when compared to most other jobs. It is often easy for new recruits to feel overwhelmed by this and to overcompensate by placing a higher priority on performing their professional duties, to the detriment of all other areas in their lives. Solan and Casey (2003, p. 17) have identified this as "police work addiction" and note: "Certainly, expectations run high in the law enforcement profession. Establishing and maintaining [professional] relationships creates tremendous demands on time, resources, and energy; life balance easily becomes lost." Solan and Casey (p. 17) caution: "While law enforcement professionals should possess a strong sense of duty and responsibility for the public's welfare, they must not forget the well-being of their families, friends, and, most important, themselves."

In examining the phenomenon of police officer burnout (which also applies to the other fields discussed in this text), Hawkins (2001, p. 343) reports: "An important aspect of the burnout syndrome is increased feelings of emotional exhaustion. . . . Another aspect of the burnout syndrome is the development of depersonalization, that is, negative, cynical attitudes and feelings about one's clients. This callous or even dehumanized perception of others can lead the individual to view their clients as somehow deserving of their troubles."

The longer you remain in a job, any job, the harder it is to let go of the benefits (seniority, time off, pay raises, etc.) and the identity of the job itself. You will be much further ahead if you are honest with yourself and leave if the work does not suit you. Similarly, the work may suit you, but the job may not. For a variety of reasons, not every employment opportunity will fit everyone. If you know you want to be a police officer or other first responder, corrections, or security officer, but personalities or any other factors make this particular job less than satisfying, do *not* stay. It is unlikely that things will improve. There *is* a job out there for you, and your job is to find it.

PAYING YOUR DUES

It's uncomfortable and doesn't feel fair. Why should you have to wait to be accepted just because you're new? One answer is simply because that's the way it is in most social or employment situations where others want to get to know you. Another answer is that this is your time to assess the landscape, to better be able to fit in down the road. Acceptance happens when it happens.

Generation differences do exist. Some refer to the current generation of younger job seeks as "the entitlement generation" because they expect to get much without earning it. That's just not how it is in the professions discussed here. Perhaps it's a lingering aspect of the apprentice process, or maybe it's just the amount of time it takes for others to trust and accept you.

"Paying your dues" means taking one step at a time. It means being asked, proving yourself, is the process of being accepted.

In a sense, it is about fitting in from the beginning and getting off to the right start, which provides a firm foundation for the rest of your career. Menegio (2008, p. 34) stresses the importance of fitting in for new employees and developing a positive reputation from the time you start, because who you are and what you do will follow you: "After all, a good or bad reputation can haunt or help you throughout your entire career." Menegio (p. 35) suggests doing this by maintaining balanced relationships on and off the job and avoiding the self-defeating behaviors, such a alcohol abuse: "As a new officer you will be faced with some of the greatest challenges and changes in your life. How you respond to these changes in the first year . . .will affect the rest of your careers."

CONCLUSION

Congratulations! You've got the job! These words will, and should, be a deserved conclusion to a significant amount of work. Relish them. You are well on your way to professional career fulfillment. Don't let your guard down, and don't give up pursuing excellence. Set exceptional goals for yourself, and you will be exceptional.

Your success during the interviews will not guarantee success on the job. You must have at least some idea of what to expect and what the circumstances demand if you want to hold on to the job. Keeping a job takes constant effort. You must not be afraid to ask questions, for not doing so may lead to mistakes that may cost you your job. Work in criminal justice, security, and related fields is important. It is satisfying and says something about you that people working in other fields cannot boast. Congratulations on choosing these fields to pursue employment in and for making the effort to do it well. By maintaining a healthy balance, you can enjoy a career that many continue to find is the best job in the world.

YOUR GAME PLAN FOR EXCELLING ON THE JOB

 Take time *now* to write out, on a *separate* piece of paper you can keep in your pocket or billfold, three goals to help you excel in your new position. Put the paper someplace you will see it often. Let these goals guide you as you embark on your exciting new career. And again, congratulations!

AN INSIDER'S VIEW

SURVIVING PROBATION

Linda S. Miller

Former Executive Director
Upper Midwest Community Policing Institute

Now that you have landed that job, you probably think you can relax. Think again. You are about to undergo a period of the most intense scrutiny you've ever experienced. It's called *probation.* Usually a period of six months to a year, it gives the department a chance to see you in action and to evaluate your work, your judgment and your style of relating to others. You don't have that job wrapped until you "make probation." Think of this period as a time to apply what you've learned in school and what you will learn on the job. Advice from veteran officers as you begin your probationary period would surely include the following:

➤   Don't be a know-it-all. You may have been the star of the academy, but keep it to yourself or you may alienate your colleagues.
➤   Learn the basics well. Fancy shooting or exotic defensive tactics moves won't be of much help to you unless you can also write a good report and make a proper car stop.
➤   Concentrate on report writing. Carry a pocket dictionary if you are not a good speller.
➤   Don't be a "gadget" person. One can often tell a rookie by the surprising number of pieces of equipment hanging from the gun belt.
➤   Watch respected veteran officers do their job and learn from them. Don't, however, adopt their "bad" work habits.
➤   Don't take shortcuts. These are for veterans willing to live with the consequences. You can't afford it.
➤   Don't get a reputation for being too aggressive. You want to be a willing worker, very interested in doing your job, but not a crusader chosen to rid the world of criminals.
➤   Treat the public and your coworkers with respect. Displaying your personal prejudices can be detrimental to your continued employment. Don't make derogatory racial or sexual remarks, even if you hear others doing so.
➤   Try to develop a reputation of being cooperative and nonargumentative. Be a team player.
➤   You may be in social situations with coworkers where alcohol is served. Drink conservatively. You can be sure that what you say and do under the influence of alcohol will be the talk of the department by the next day at the latest. Alcohol abuse is a serious problem in this society and in law enforcement. Most departments will not be impressed with a rookie who displays even a hint of alcohol abuse.
➤   The same goes for sexual behavior. Keep your personal life personal. Above all, don't sleep around with fellow employees.

Remember, your training officer and the department's supervisors have your future in their hands. In many departments, probationary employees can be let go for *any* reason. With a little forethought, you can avoid providing a reason. You have what it takes for the job or you wouldn't have been hired. And the department wants you to "make it" too. They have invested time and money in your hiring and training. They need you to assure them they've made the right choice.

Linda S. Miller *is the former executive director for the Upper Midwest Community Policing Institute as well as a former sergeant with the Bloomington (Minnesota) Police Department. She was with the department twenty-three years, and was a police dispatcher; patrol officer; crime prevention officer; patrol supervisor; and head of the planning, research, and crime prevention division. Sergeant Miller had been a member of the Minnesota Peace and Police Officers Association, the*

International Police Association, the Midwest Gang Investigator's Association, the International Association of Women Police, and the Minnesota Association of Women Police. She was a member of the People-to-People's Women in Law Enforcement delegation to the Soviet Union in 1990. Sgt. Miller is a frequent presenter to community groups and is also an instructor.

 MIND STRETCHES

1. Have you ever been "too enthusiastic" at a new job? Why do you think you were? Did it hurt you?

2. What behaviors have you observed in people in uncomfortable situations (like in a new job)?

3. Why do you think important people often seem so "down-to-earth"? Conversely, why do you think many "not-so-important" people act so brashly?

4. How long does it take to fit in at a new job? What helps you fit in?

5. Have you ever felt pressured at a job to behave in a way you did not feel comfortable? How did you handle this situation?

6. Why do you think people, particularly officers, seem to like to complain or be negative? What traps can this create for new employees?

7. What dangers are there in "taking sides" in an office dispute? How can you avoid becoming involved?

8. Can people who work together get along "too well"? Are office romances good or bad? Can they be avoided, or do they "just happen"?

9. How would you handle a situation in which you knew a coworker was doing something illegal, immoral, or unethical? Would you respond differently if the person was a peer or your supervisor?

10. At what point do you think people stop growing and developing professionally? What opportunities exist to help you maintain your own personal and professional vitality?

REFERENCES

Armour, Stephanie. "Generation Y: They've Arrived at Work with a New Attitude." *USA Today,* November 8, 2005.

Hawkins, Homer C. "Police Officer Burnout: A Partial Replication of Maslach's Burnout Inventory." *Police Quarterly,* September 2001, pp. 343–360.

Menegio, Mike. "Fitting In." *POLICE Recruit,* Winter/Spring, 2008, pp. 30–35.

Miller, Jo. "Life Is Too Short to Waste Doing Something You Don't Love." CareerBuilder.com, 2003. Available online at http://msn.careerbuilder.com/Custom/MSN/CareerAdvice/WPI_LifeIsTooShort.htm?sc_extcmp=JS_wi12_dec03_advice.

Scoville, Dean. "How to Survive Probation." *POLICE Recruit*, Winter/Spring, 2008, pp. 10–12.

Sheehan, Donald C., and Vincent B. Van Hasselt. "Identifying Law Enforcement Stress Reactions Early." *FBI Law Enforcement Bulletin,* September 2003, pp. 12–17.

Solan, Gerard J., and Jean M. Casey. "Police Work Addiction: A Cautionary Tale." *FBI Law Enforcement Bulletin,* June 2003, pp. 13–17.

CHAPTER 16

THE CAREER LADDER:
INSIGHTS INTO PROMOTIONS AND JOB CHANGE

If you can dream it, you can do it.

—*Walt Disney*

Do You Know:

➤ Whether the promotional process differs from initial job seeking?
➤ What changes, besides promotions, may lead to personal and professional growth?
➤ What factors motivate people to seek change in their professional lives?
➤ Which basic job-seeking skills apply?
➤ How important are "off-duty" activities?
➤ What a successful advancement strategy includes?
➤ Whether changing jobs can help or hurt future job-seeking efforts?
➤ If you can ever have "too much" education or education in the wrong area?
➤ When networking is important (other than during the job search)?
➤ How important the oral interview is to the promotional process?

INTRODUCTION

The world of work has changed dramatically over the decades. It is no longer the norm to remain in one career with one employer until retirement. Although there is nothing wrong with that—if a person finds a niche and enjoys doing the same thing daily—the fact is that more and more people are changing jobs and careers, either because they want to—or because they have to.

This chapter provides suggestions on how to prepare for the promotional process and what to expect. For the new job seeker, just *getting* that first job is the dream, but eventually everyone seeks change. For some it is seeking promotions on the way to "the top." For others it is changing within their present agency or looking for opportunities with others. And some want to change professions altogether.

The final chapter discusses the impact of job loss and change, but what about the *desire* to change work or employers? This hasn't been considered the "norm" in a field of work that has involved staying with one agency, possibly seeking internal transfers or promotions. Whether seeking a promotion or other job change, developing a strategy will make the transition more successful.

The basic job-seeking skills and strategies you are developing will also serve you well throughout the promotional process. Promotional interviews are similar to initial job interviews. Regardless of the level of employment you aspire to, you will need to provide information about yourself that presents you as *the* one to promote.

It is important to create a plan. Life itself presents numerous opportunities, as does work. By thinking ahead, you develop not only some ideas of where you want to go in life (and work), but also the ability to recognize the many opportunities that present themselves. Recall how many careers people normally have during their lives. When you consider all the promotions or job changes people experience, it is easy to see how important it is to know how to prepare for opportunities. John L. Beckley, first U.S. Librarian of Congress, put it this way: "Most people don't plan to fail. They fail to plan."

Finally, recognize that in criminal justice, security positions, and related fields, seniority and "paying your dues" can play important roles in promotions.

> Promotion-seeking skills are very similar to the basic job-seeking skills and strategies you are developing. Both scenarios demand you present yourself as *the* one to hire/promote.

PROMOTIONS: WHAT THEY ARE AND WHERE THEY ARE

Traditionally, promotions are considered to be upward moves, usually within the same organization where one is presently employed. Although valid for many promotions, try thinking of promotions in a much broader way. Any promotion is a change, but is every change a promotion? Take it one step further. Obviously, every promotion provides new challenges, but so does every change—even those that don't initially appear to be upward. Consider *any* job change as an employment opportunity. This includes promotions, transfers, and, yes, even demotions or dismissals.

Think about it. Many people who have confronted what appeared to be overwhelming adversity end up saying it was the best thing that ever happened to them. Why? Because they grew from the experience. The bigger the challenge, the greater the opportunity for personal and professional growth. But the other side to "bigger and better" is causing people to reconsider if getting ahead at all costs is their best life strategy.

> Promotions are but one type of change that provides new professional challenges and allows for growth. Often the most adversarial changes, such as demotions or dismissals, lead to the greatest amount of personal and professional growth.

MOTIVATIONS FOR SEEKING CHANGE

The chapter on rejection addresses how you should strive to obtain energy from the process, and how you should control the process rather than let it control you. It *can*, *should* and (eventually) *will* result in growth for you. Laurence J. Peter, creator of the "Peter Principle," is credited with the saying "a rut is a grave with the ends knocked out." And it is this feeling that frequently compels people to set their sights on bigger, better, or at least different, careers. Although previous generations seemed more content to remain at one job, it has become more common for people to follow their desire to find whatever feeds their souls. Or dual working couples can be faced with the challenge of deciding which one might move to a new job and which will follow.

Considerations such as better pay, different working hours, more benefits, or a desire to move to another community motivate people to change jobs. Other reasons may not present themselves as "positive" reasons for the change—downsizings, reorganizations, closings, and even involuntary terminations force people to change. The work world is seeing upheaval past generations did not experience. Layoffs are occurring by the tens of thousands. No job is guaranteed secure forever, even in government and union work, which previously had been considered untouchable.

Another motivation for job change is that people are working longer and, thus, want to enjoy it more. The "I'm just lucky to have a job, any job," attitude of previous generation has in many cases been replaced with a more holistic perspective. Yes, work is important, but it's just one part of life's equation. If a job is negatively affecting your health, marriage, family life, or overall happiness, does it make sense to stay?

> Motivations for seeking change include better pay, better benefits, the desire to find more fulfilling work, the desire to live and work in another community, downsizing, reorganizations, closings, and involuntary terminations. Some of these reasons originate in the individual, and some are forced upon the individual—but all lead the individual to change.

With regard to law enforcement promotions, Hamilton (2004, p. 25) notes the importance of being true to yourself, not just doing what you think others expect you to do: "While it is expected that people aspire to higher levels of job status, not everyone wants to leave patrol and join management." She tells the stories of several officers who faced promotion dilemmas:

> "I was a lieutenant in charge of Violent Crimes when I realized that I had promoted myself out of the job I really wanted to do. I signed on to be a street cop, not pay bills, do evaluations, handle grievances and the like. . . . It is a good thing to want to be a supervisor or commander and I applaud anyone who does. Just make sure it is what you really want to do. While administration is essential, 'real' police work is not done at headquarters." . . .

> Not everyone advances to higher positions, and it's not necessarily because they were passed over for a promotion. [Another officer] made a decision to remain a sergeant at the San Diego Police Department. He found that he liked working with people in the field instead of working behind a desk. He has no regrets.

Whether change results from unanticipated factors or your desire to better yourself professionally, seek a bigger paycheck with improved benefits, or move to a different place, your job-seeking skills will serve you a lifetime.

SIMILAR SKILLS

Take time to reflect on the entry-level job search and the promotional process, and you can see the similarities. In fact, both are going to result in different jobs—new jobs, and the skills you will need are the same:

➢ Cover letters (sometimes called "letters of interest" in the promotional process)

➢ Résumés (now providing more specific training and experience records)

➢ Test-taking skills

➢ Interview skills

➢ An overall positive appearance as *the* one to hire

> The job-seeking skills needed during the promotional process include writing effective cover letters and résumés, taking tests, interviewing, and presenting yourself positively as *the* one to hire or promote.

The changes you will notice as you work on your promotional strategies are simply a fine-tuning of the skills developed earlier. It is through explaining how you have developed professionally and why you want the change that makes this job-seeking process different from an entry-level job search.

INCREASING YOUR CHANCES FOR PROMOTION—PREPARATION IS KEY

Using skills and strategies discussed throughout this book, when it comes time to move ahead you'll be seen as someone who can do more than what you were hired for at the entry level. As you take on new challenges there will be more training, of course, but you will be expected to have certain basics mastered in addition to other traits sought in those promoted. You can prepare for all of these:

➢   Basic understanding and knowledge of the work.

➢   An understanding of the broader system.

➢   People skills.

➢   Future potential.

➢   Drive.

Developing and exhibiting these go hand in hand. It doesn't happen overnight, and a shortcoming for some is trying to do (and expect) too much too soon. Be patient, let it happen on a realistic timeline, do good work, and people will notice.

A basic understanding and knowledge of the work takes a different amount of time depending on the job. Moving up to assistant manager at a fast-food restaurant may not take long, but in law enforcement and other jobs discussed in this book in may take years. Do not rush the process of acquiring the basics because that is what everything else is built on. For example, many agencies promote to specialty positions such as crime scene investigator from the ranks of experienced patrol officers who have mastered evidence processing. It's common for police agencies to require officers to have as much as five years of basic experience before becoming eligible for promotion. This is good; the better a foundation you build, the better prepared you will be for future opportunities.

Because promotions involve doing more, you should demonstrate this capability. For example, in law enforcement, don't be satisfied with just taking the initial call and turning a scene over to the crime lab investigators. Ask questions, follow up, and develop an understanding of what happens after your initial role ends. Follow up on court cases to learn the outcome. If given the chance to help on something different, do it. Show a genuine interest in learning and you will be noticed.

Whatever you're promoted to, it will involve working with different people in different capacities. Those considered for promotion will be expected to have people skills, both with those they serve and those with whom they work. The reality is that in these jobs you'll likely garner some complaints. No one likes getting a traffic ticket, and some violators will lash out at the officer. It's how many complaints and how you deal with them that reflect your ability to communicate. Those occasional commendations from citizens and supervisors help reinforce your abilities. Develop a pattern of doing your job consistently well and being able to communicate with everyone you work with.

Some people are hired for or promoted to certain positions that are not intended to lead to further career development. For example, civilian fingerprint examiners may be hired because they are less expensive than sworn officers promoted to this job. But they are unlikely to be promoted out of the lab because they lack other experience. If you're interested in getting promoted, recognize that employers are looking to advance people who have the potential to continue advancing. In *Who Gets Promoted, Who Doesn't, and Why,* Asher (2007, p. 1) states: "Most people believe that getting promoted is a reward for past performance. This is absolutely false. Employers are not rewarding strong performers for their *past* contributions; they are investing in their *future* contributions." A promotion should be perceived neither as an entitlement nor as an expectation. Hard work, proving yourself, and demonstrating you can contribute at a different level is what makes you a stronger candidate for promotion. Just like background investigators seek out behaviors that can predict future behavior, so do those making promotion decisions. Seize every opportunity to develop and show your leadership potential, and you will be noticed.

Drive. That's the motivation exhibited in doing your best and a willingness to do more than just what's expected. This doesn't mean volunteering for everything or going overboard to be noticed, both of which can be frowned upon in the workplace. It means doing your job and doing it well and taking the opportunity to do more than what's expected.

> Being actively involved in "off-duty" activities such as professional organizations/associations and volunteering demonstrates a commitment to your profession, which is looked upon favorably by promoters.

Stating "the reality is [that] doing your job is not enough to get promoted," Asher (p. vi) lists the subtitle of his book, "10 Things You'd Better Do If You Want to Get Ahead."

1. *Timing is as important as performance or talent.* Understand what the agency needs, anticipate change, and prepare to be the one to best respond to these.

2. *You have to get noticed.* Don't be shy about sharing your abilities and drive.

3. *Lifelong learning is required for lifelong success.* Knowing the basics is important. Knowing how to find information you'll need in the future and at a new position is essential.

4. *All business is sales.* Or in criminal justice jargon, persuasiveness to achieve the mission is what you're selling; oh, and yourself!

5. *You need an ascension plan.* Plan to get ahead by seizing and creating opportunities to develop professionally and get noticed. Simply doing your job, although a great start, isn't enough.

6. *Always make your boss look good.* If you are considered an investment to the agency, you don't want to be viewed as a detriment to the hiring authority.

7. ***Suction—it pays to stand next to superstars.*** Associating with negative people will drag you down; associating with positive people will keep you on top. Developing relationships with those on the move can help move you along too.

8. ***Find guardian angles and benefactors.*** Recognize and foster relationships with those who believe in and support you.

9. ***Move, dammit—and here's why***. Remember the saying offered previously: "A rut is a grave with the ends knocked out." You don't want to be stuck at work. Your strategy should include ways to achieve all of these items on Asher's list.

10. ***Find the right mix of prepared and lucky.*** Ever hear the saying, "The harder I work the luckier I get"? Asher (p. 157) says: "The best way to lobby luck is to be ready for its arrival." It may be luck that a position opens in your agency or elsewhere; it's never just luck if you are ready to act on it.

Entry-level people who think they want only a specific job at one agency doing one thing diminish exponentially their potential for success. They may want that job, but they have no control over when that job might become available or whether that employer will want them. They will never know what fabulous jobs were overlooked by their failure to prepare or failure to open their eyes to other opportunities.

This principle applies to promotional strategies as well. You may presently work for an agency that has traditionally promoted from entry level to corporal to sergeant to lieutenant to captain to deputy chief to chief, but it takes only one change to throw that all out of alignment. For example, it's not unheard of for a consulting agency to recommend a top-to-bottom reorganization, with new positions created, old positions eliminated, and opportunities that hadn't existed one day to be posted the next. You will have a promotional route in mind, but that may be similar to throwing a dart for your first job. Prepare well for the unexpected and your target will become easier to hit.

Most people in criminal justice, security, and related fields retire at the rank at which they were hired. Three common reasons exist for this fact. Some find they are satisfied at that level and choose to stay, which is fine. Others recognize that there are more people than promotions in their agency and, thus, decide it's not worth the effort to try for one of the limited advancement opportunities. Still others choose to stay where they are by refusing to recognize career opportunities beyond their current agency. As but one example, most criminal justice practitioners might look askance if anyone suggested they consider working for Target, the upscale discount retail store. But Target's own crime lab is being inundated with requests from local law enforcement for assistance, creating exceptional opportunities in the private sector that could lead to even bigger and better corporate security opportunities.

A successful advancement strategy includes preparing for the expected and unexpected; *preparation* being the key term.

Broadening Your Experience and Education

Moving up usually requires stepping outside your comfort zone. Take advantage of new opportunities as they present themselves, and avoid spending your entire career in one area. This doesn't mean you are unmotivated or lack drive. It may mean you are one of the truly fortunate who are happy in their work. But if you desire job change, position yourself to be ready to pursue opportunities that present themselves. One sergeant (Hamilton, p. 26) recommends: "Don't stagnate in a position for too long if you want to move ahead. Get experiences in as many areas as possible and if you particularly like one, become a subject matter expert in that field. Whether it is gangs, drugs, firearms, accident investigation, or some other field, your expertise will make you valuable to your department, unit, or section."

Although broadening your experience may not be a problem for people employed in larger agencies, as federal, state, and large municipal agencies permit many opportunities for change, new challenges, and promotional advancement, smaller agencies may demand that the motivated employee take new jobs outside their agency. These changes should be pursued as a part of your plan for achieving your employment goals, just like all other areas of developing your strategy.

Sometimes opportunities present themselves in being involved in a joint-powers task force or being assigned to a specialized effort such as a drug interdiction unit or gang strike force. Some opportunities involve changing employers. Change merely for the sake of change may become self-defeating. If you don't stay at a new job or a new assignment long enough to really benefit from it (or be of benefit to your employer), this may cause understandable concern to those in charge of hiring. It's a tough call, and an individual one, to pursue another opportunity "too soon." Take the time necessary to think through frequent changes.

A word of caution: Ask yourself why you want to change jobs. Job wanderlust might be symptomatic of something entirely separate from a valid reason for wanting job change; it may be rooted in an underlying issue that will follow you from job to job unless it is dealt with. For example, adult children of alcoholic parents or adults dealing with unresolved separation issues from an early age might seek inappropriate or unrealistic things from work to fulfill them. And when work doesn't satisfy these needs, these people go on to another job, and another, and another, eventually finding these changes have not only failed to meet the unrelated need, but have caused them to appear unable to commit to any job long term. Only you know if something like this relates to you; but if it does, deal with it so you can find fulfilling work.

> Take opportunities that further your planned career path, but do not get carried away, jumping from one job to another. Be selective in your moves, or such job jumping may damage any future options in your profession.

Hamilton (p. 26) suggests: "Also think about furthering your education as part of your training and preparation for higher-level jobs. You can often get grants and scholarships or reimbursements from your agency. There's usually some kind of financial help available if the degree you're pursuing can be applied to your job."

> Education is akin to experience—you cannot acquire too much education or education in the wrong area.

IT PAYS TO BECOME A LIFELONG LEARNER

Asher's list included, "Lifelong learning is required for lifelong success." There was a time when the entire world's data could fit in a small newspaper and the amount of new information generated accumulated very, very slowly. Now: "World information may be doubling as quickly as every six months" (Ollhoff, 2008). What does this mean for job and promotion seekers?

Nierenhausen (2008) explains the necessity of being a lifelong learner when it comes to getting hired or promoted: "Regardless of rank, these days you're expected to be able to respond to information voids. These may be in the form of something you want to know or a superior wants you to find an answer to, but you'd better be able to do so beyond shrugging your shoulders or just using Google. Especially if you want to be considered for a specialty assignment or advancement, part of the job, as much as using the traditional tools, is knowing how to stay informed and knowledgeable. That's what information literacy is all about."

Positioning yourself for advancement means more than being able to answer specific questions. A college degree gives you an edge because, even for entry-level applicants, it sets you apart from the competition. In the fields discussed in this text, college experience is becoming more common, even expected (sometimes required by law).

True, the younger you are the more convenient college may be to attend. However, it is easier now than ever before for adults to return to school despite their increased obligations of family and work. In fact, because of the increased desire for more education by adults, most schools see an opportunity in adult education programs. The development and acceptance of online college degree programs virtually eliminates the traditional excuses of not being able to attend traditional college programs—that going to college is "out" because it isn't close enough or the courses offered aren't flexible enough to meet the needs of people working shifts or trying to juggle busy family lives. A degree offered online from a regionally accredited college or university is every bit as good as one provided face-to-face, maybe even better: "If the fact it's offered online makes it accessible to you when it might otherwise wouldn't even be possible to return to school, that's a plus. The fact you can navigate the technology associated with online learning, although exceptionally easy, makes a positive statement about you. And a well-developed online degree isn't second best; especially for adult learners it can exceed what is offered in the traditional classroom. People, especially criminal justice professionals, need accessibility in order to return to school. Online provides that in a proven manner" (Ollhoff).

It is difficult to understand how anyone's education could be viewed negatively, but it may. The two reasons that surface most frequently are a fear by employers the applicant will soon move on to a bigger and better job and the fear of intimidating those "above." Do not fail to acquire advanced education because of what others might think, but be prepared to defend the choice and explain what you will contribute because of your college coursework. If an agency is so determined to remain stuck by not recognizing the benefits of education, you need to ask yourself if that's an agency with whom you want to work. Never stop learning, especially for fear of what others may think. Be it shortsightedness or just plain jealousy on their part, furthering your education is always a sound investment in yourself and your future.

NETWORKING AND OTHER VALUABLE PROMOTION-SEEKING TOOLS

As with the job search, *networking* for a promotion is very important. The more people you know, and the more people who know you, the more it will benefit you. Again, becoming involved in professional organizations and associations is a great way to learn more and to get your name out there.

Networking is as essential to promotion efforts as it is to job-seeking efforts.

Letters of commendation are another tool with high promotion-seeking value. They reflect positive actions in which a candidate was involved and highlight the leadership abilities or management skills sought when evaluating an employee for promotion. Don't be shy about asking for letters. Many people will tell you they appreciate your work but may need some encouragement to document it. You have a responsibility to yourself to do everything you canto best convey your excellence. A good supply of such personal recommendations will put you in a great position to include the best and most applicable for your next effort.

Feedback is always beneficial, particularly for those who have not gotten the promotions they sought. Face it, most people are either too polite or too intimidated to tell an applicant why they didn't succeed. It takes guts to ask for honest feedback, but once you ask for it, you must be willing to accept it.

IMPROVING PROMOTIONAL EXAM PERFORMANCE

Promotional exams are a fact of life in the protective services. Fire service and law enforcement routinely use such exams to help determine which candidates should advance to the next rank. There are no hidden secrets to doing your best on a promotional exam. It's no different than what was suggested for every phase of entry-level job seeking: preparation is the key. Do your best to find out what kind of testing will occur, and seek out material that will help you prepare. If the employer recommends specific books, get them. Preparation also includes reducing stress, getting rest, and eating properly before taking any exam.

IMPROVING PROMOTIONAL INTERVIEW PERFORMANCE

Borello (2004) asserts:

> An officer's performance during the oral interview is paramount because the process is highly competitive. Officers must 'out-score' others also vying for promotion. This is difficult in that candidates may be competing against dozens or even hundreds of other police personnel, many of whom may have greater education or more experience. Police officers and front-line supervisors who have tested in promotional oral interviews or who have sat in on oral interview panels will tell you that the information basics—leadership, risk management, sexual harassment, discipline, etc.—are important, but that having a solid comprehension of this knowledge has little value if candidates cannot articulate that information with professional skill and confidence. Anyone can memorize a definition for leadership. Most can repeat that definition with a little practice and preparation.
>
> Very few can deliver a dynamic well-rounded response that hooks the panel's attention, builds the answer with connective issues, and articulates the information both verbally and nonverbally while exemplifying poise, energy, confidence, and presents a clear nexus to the position being tested for. Studying books, articles, policy, and promotional materials for information is a limited process that will only prepare officers with the internal knowledge they need—"the what"—but falls short in giving officers the communication skills needed to verbally deliver what they have learned—"the how."

Narramore[1] (1991, pp. 161–162) has devised a comprehensive review on how to prepare for a promotional interview:

> The people involved in an interview to evaluate your qualifications try to ascertain three basic facts about you. These are the most important traits you will need to convey to the panel:
>
> ➢ You can handle the job.
> ➢ You will do the job to the best of your ability.
> ➢ You are a manageable team player.

---

[1]Adapted from Randy E. Narramore. "Preparing for a Promotional Interview." *Law and Order,* September 1991, pp. 161–162. Reprinted by permission.

Candidates who communicate to the evaluators "yes" to the above questions will score the highest. You must be able to demonstrate willingness and ability during the interview process.

The first time I competed for the position of police sergeant was a disappointment I will always remember. I felt very comfortable after taking the written examination. I had scored high and was in an excellent position. Because I felt so confident, I did nothing to prepare for the oral interview. I felt showing up in all my glory and answering the questions to the best of my ability would be enough. That was a very big mistake. I finished in the top five overall, but I was not in the winner's circle. I looked back and learned from my mistake. That experience taught me to take that extra step of preparedness for every phase of the testing process.

The interview is the most important part of the promotional process. A successful candidate will make the "question and answer period" an exchange of ideas between law enforcement professionals. Accomplishing this means you are qualified and prepared. . . .

Law enforcement agencies look for specific traits in individual profiles to help determine the type of supervisor a candidate may become. Being more skilled and more qualified does not prove they will be a team player. Education and experience alone does not guarantee they will fit into the scheme of the organization. Several traits are reviewed during an interview: ambition, motivation, communication skills, devotion, conviction, and confidence. . . .

Narramore also addresses the basic "traps" so many well-qualified candidates fall prey to, some of which are so damaging, recovery is next to impossible:

Failure to listen to the question. Every question asked by an interviewer demands a specific answer. Do not ramble on with superfluous responses. Be brief, yet concise. For example, if asked how many years you have been in law enforcement, provide a specific number. However, if you are asked to relate your feelings about illegal drugs, provide a more general answer.

Not taking enough time before answering questions. Do not answer a question immediately. Think about what you are going to say. This gives the impression you consider your responses and do not respond spontaneously.

Answering questions not asked. Answering a question not asked is annoying. When the board wants more information, they will ask for it.

Not being brief and to the point. The board does not want drawn out answers providing little information. If you do not know the answer, don't attempt to deceive the board with flowered responses. Be brief and to the point.

Not turning a negative into a positive. You may be asked a question regarding a negative area of your career, or be asked to discuss a major weakness. Try to turn the atmosphere into something positive. Admit you had a certain weakness, but were able to recognize it and took the steps necessary to correct it.

Being flippant or a joker. Oral boards do not like flippant responses. One improper response could ruin the entire interview.

It is not always the best person who receives the promotion. The ones who receive the promotions are usually those who have qualities of efficiency, hard work, and reliability. If you follow the above suggestions, you will have a much better opportunity receiving that promotion you deserve.

Borello (2003, p. 131) concludes:

Taking the oral interview is an art. The dynamics of interview performance are vast, involving communication skills, understanding how to build rapport, confidence, poise under pressure, job knowledge, seeing the big picture, skilled decision making, advanced preparation, physical and mental energy, and the list goes on.

Promotion is significant, and is often considered the exemplification of a successful and progressive career. Preparing for a promotion should never be taken lightly; it should be treated like an Olympic event.

> The oral interview is the most important part of the promotional process. Prepare for it as enthusiastically as you did for your initial job-seeking interview.

ASSESSMENT CENTERS

A popular trend is to incorporate aspects in the promotional process that more realistically reflect what the job actually entails. The generic term *assessment center* describes a series of job-related scenarios designed to give the employer a sense of how you would perform on the job. It may be the chief administrator and agency personnel evaluating you, or independent evaluators. The evaluators are unlikely to actually be involved, instead observing to get a sense of responses and skills for the position.

Like the unknown dangers facing Dorothy in *The Wizard of Oz*, the unknowns of assessment centers can evoke consternation in the applicant who is used to tests and interviews. However, with preparation and practice, you can use an assessment center evaluation to your advantage. An important part of preparation is to know as much about the position and what is expected as possible; also important is knowing what might occur.

Like so many other aspects of the employment process, the possible variations in assessment centers are almost limitless. There is no way to know every possibility. Even if you don't anticipate a specific scenario, your preparation will help you remain calm but respond effectively.

What Assessment Centers Seek to Evaluate

Assessment centers seek to evaluate specific job-related abilities, which is why these centers are designed for a specific agency and position. Whitcomb (2008, p. 8) provides a more in-depth description of what employers are looking for, with a list of "the top 10 characteristics" (or "C's") of promotable people:

➤ **Character:** Promotable people have earned a reputation as trustworthy, impeccably ethical, conscientious, and open-minded.

➤ **Confidence:** Promotable people take calculated risks, trust their instincts, are optimistic and courageous, and drive past any fears that might hold them back.

➤ **Communication:** Strong communication skills are common to promotable people; they speak with clarity and persuasion. Further, their presentation style is devoid of distractions with regard to appearance, dress, or habits.

➤ **Competency:** Promotable people possess above average position-specific abilities, industry knowledge, and technology skills.

➤ **Connection:** Promotable people have a charismatic ability to connect with others beyond the superficial level and create rapport with managers, internal constituencies, and customers.

➤ **Critical thinking:** Able to see the "big picture" and always maintain a global organizational perspective, promotable people are able to grasp all facets of a situation and make the best decision.

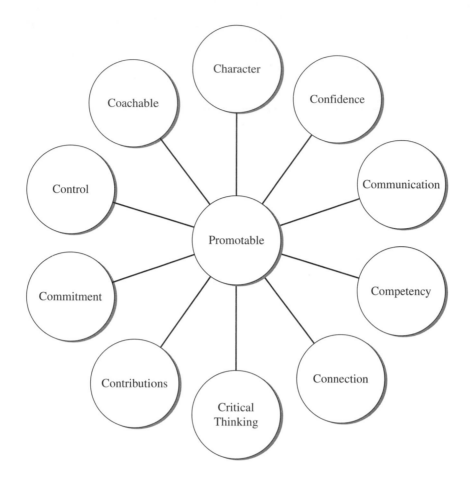

FIGURE 16–1   The 10 C's of Promotable People

SOURCE: Susan Whitcomb. *30-Day Job Promotion, Build a Powerful Promotion Plan in a Month.* Indianapolis, IN: JIST Publishing, Inc., 2008, p. 9.

➤ **Contributions:** Promotable people are results-oriented and make continual contributions that improve the company's bottom line.

➤ **Commitment**: Known for their perseverance, promotable people are committed and never give up.

➤ **Control:** Promotable people control their destiny (without controlling or manipulating others); they act to influence outcomes and do not lapse into powerlessness or passivity.

➤ **Coachability:** Promotable people are open to always learning more; in addition, they are able to implement coaching techniques to develop, grow, and manage others.

Figure 16–1 summarizes these key characteristics.

Although each hiring authority will tailor its process to suit their needs, a core group of exercises appear frequently enough that you should be familiar with them. Not each will be used, and there may be variations. There may even be tasks very particular to that position or employer.

In-basket exercises give you a number of items, which could be in hard-copy or e-mail format, typical of issues the position involves, to see how they are prioritized and acted on. Who is copied on the response is important, too, because it reflects the candidate's awareness of the importance of keeping the proper people in the information loop.

Meeting involvement scenarios may include being called on to facilitate a meeting, participate in a meeting, or even be in a group with no identified leader. Communication and leadership skills are observed during any variation of the meeting component. Depending on the scenario provided, your role may be as leader, participant, or taking charge if there is no leader.

Presentation skills are observed by giving you a topic to present to a specified audience. It could be the agency membership, a governing body, or a community group. It could be videotaped, or you may be asked to record it. The ability to prepare and present a topic is considered in this exercise. A variation of this could be observing you during an actual oral interview or interviews to groups, which would change depending on the makeup of that group (i.e., employees, citizens, etc.).

Problem-solving ability can be observed in a variety of formats. It could occur in any of the formats reviewed here or as a writing exercise prepared by yourself, in which your writing is an important component along with the process you use to solve the problem. Usually these exercises are more concerned with your process than the ultimate conclusion, so expect a scenario with no easy answer.

Role-playing is often used to observe how you would respond in a quasi-realistic personal scenario. This could include dealing with a personnel problem, a disgruntled citizen, or someone above your rank. Interpersonal communication, appropriateness, and how you process and respond to the situation provided are evaluated. Every element of a job could become the focus of role-playing, from a casual conversation with a challenging employee to coordinating a disaster.

Writing skills may be assessed by asking you to write a report, provide internal documentation, or prepare a press release.

In any of the preceding, if all they wanted was a right answer, a traditional test would suffice. By combining various elements to make up their assessment center, employers seek to observe a variety of behaviors and responses that pertain to the position. Mason (2007) includes the following elements as essential to assess in candidates:

1. Decisiveness

2. Judgment

3. Oral communication

4. Stress tolerance

5. Written communication

6. Planning

7. Flexibility

Preparing for an assessment center process can be daunting. The best way to prepare is by doing everything discussed in this book, especially in this chapter. Rather than "cramming at the last minute" to respond to every conceivable scenario that may be presented, you will hopefully have been developing yourself along the way to respond to them because you already know how. Just as with the entry-level candidate, those evaluating people for promotions want to see the "real you." In addition to making the effort to find out what format the process will take, there may be some topics you will want to brush up on.

Because of the popularity of the assessment center approach, a number of books and online resources are available. By using your Internet search engine and simply searching "assessment center," you'll find any number of sources including fee-based online practice opportunities for such scenarios as the in-basket.

CONCLUSION

Because work is such a significant part of life, job satisfaction is vital. Not only do satisfactory jobs provide monetary and other employment-related benefits to enable you to live the lifestyle you desire, but they also help you feel good about yourself.

Promotion-seeking skills are very similar to the basic job-seeking skills and strategies you are developing. Both scenarios demand you present yourself as *the* one to hire/promote. Job-seeking skills needed during the promotional process include writing effective cover letters and résumés, taking tests, and interviewing. Networking and researching the interviewing department or agency are also important elements. Whatever your reasons for seeking a new job or a change in the job you have, your ability to develop successful job-seeking strategies will help you realize your goals. Promotions and professional advancement require a well-thought-out plan that you will implement over time.

AN INSIDER'S VIEW

MAKING THE MOST OF YOUR LAW ENFORCEMENT CAREER

Richard D. Beckman
Former Sergeant (Retired)
Cloverdale (California) Police Department

Let's assume that you have passed all your tests, been appointed to the position of a law enforcement officer, successfully completed the academy and are performing well in your FTO program. Sounds like a dream, sounds like a long ways off, hard to imagine. With a strong set of values, persistence and a good, well-thought-out set of goals, you can do it.

By now you have figured out that law enforcement is not all the glitter and glamour of television, and all your expectations of the job have been shattered or changed considerably. With the academy behind you and your newly gained knowledge as an experienced trainee, you now have a unique opportunity to assess your career, reevaluate your goals based on your newfound knowledge and plan your future.

Law enforcement is a noble profession. We all had different ideas the first time we climbed into the passenger seat of that police car next to a seasoned veteran. With our eyes wide open, we were about to go through a transformation that would affect us the rest of our life. The old standard oral-board answer of, "I want to be a police officer so I can help people," took on a new meaning when you encountered the *real* world. You will learn and see many new things. You will see the worst and the best in people. Remember, we are all part of the same human race. The old adage, "Don't judge a person until you've walked in their shoes," has a lot of hidden meaning to those of us in law enforcement. Don't take things at face value. Look inside things, find out why they happen. Dig deep and you will be surprised by what you find and how it will affect your attitude. As the guardian of the public peace, you will do what is expected of you and do it to the best of your abilities.

Having a strong set of personal values is essential for a successful career. Basic values come from your parents, siblings, life experiences, interactions with others and your inner self. Some of the personal values required of a successful law enforcement professional would fall into the following categories:

Integrity. The lack of integrity destroys the effectiveness of the individual and can affect the entire organization. Integrity is the backbone of what we do and who we are. There is no room for dishonesty in our profession, and any breach of the public trust must be dealt with immediately and severely.

Loyalty. Loyalty is the hinge that ties individuals to their environment and creates the flow of power between employees and management. It is important to understand the prioritization of loyalties and the nuances of loyalty conflicts to be able to make decisions consistent with existing values.

Humility. Humility is one of the strongest values an individual can possess. On occasion where you have erred, nothing demonstrates your positive values so powerfully as a simple, humble apology. You must recognize that errors or failures will occur in life. You must be willing to accept the failure or apology of others if you expect others to tolerate your own human nature. Humility includes the recognition of the need to learn.

Tenacity. Tenacity tempered with patience gives the individual the ability to focus on long-term goals and creates consistency of purpose and successful change.

Courage. Courage is demonstrated most often as the result of a strong personal value system that supports action in the face of adversity. It requires "strength of character" and a strong moral fiber, which denotes a strong sense of values and ethics. Courage is not something that can be taught but comes from combining skills with your entire value system.

Responsibility. To be an effective law enforcement professional, you must accept responsibility for all that occurs in your purview. Responsibility ties directly into integrity and courage and, if you are wrong, humility.

Confidence. Confidence is a state of mind that exists in particular situations when an individual's knowledge or experience dictates a high likelihood of success or acceptable consequences in the event of failure. Confidence cannot be taught, but can be gained through repeated experiences in specific areas of knowledge. Confidence is your tool of survival. Confidence is a key element of a successful career.

Setting Goals. You have obviously set some goals for yourself as you have been successful in your quest for a law enforcement career. Goals are not something you set, attain and forget. To grow in your life and career, you must constantly reassess your goals. You may want to set long-range and short-range goals, such as being an FTO by the time you have three years on the job, or making sergeant within five years. You must work for these goals; they will not come to you. When you reach a goal, set another one. Do not become complacent in your career. Get as much overall, broad-based experience as you can. Don't be afraid to try. Avoid being stereotyped or stuck in a rut. See what you want and go after it, keeping in mind the basic values you have set for yourself and your career.

Expectations. Know what is expected of you at all times. Constantly communicate with your fellow officers about what you expect of each other. Don't be afraid to go to your supervisor and ask what is expected of you. This is an integral part of building your confidence and maintaining your value system.

Survival. During my 30-year law enforcement career, I saw many changes, both good and bad, in our profession. Early on, while driving around solo on those long night shifts, I started playing a mind game with myself that later enabled me to survive encounters that could have been deadly. After each call, as I got back in my car and drove off, I would mentally go through the call and play a "what if" game with myself. What if the guy had a gun? What if the lady attacked me? I would change the scenario several times and play it over in my mind along with my reactions to the situations. What I was doing (unknown to me) was building up a computer program in my mind as to what I would do and how I would react in hundreds, if not thousands, of situations. When confronted with a real-life, deadly encounter, I was (during a 30-second period) able to save the life of a fellow officer, a 17-year-old hostage and take out an armed suspect by reacting to that mental computer program.

Never stop playing that "what if" game, have confidence in your ability and live by a good set of values, and I hope your career will be as successful as mine.

Sgt. Richard D. Beckman *is a thirty-year veteran of California law enforcement, now retired from the Cloverdale (California) Police Department. In 1988 he received the "Police Officer of the Year" award from the International Association of Chiefs of Police for his actions in saving the lives of a fellow officer and a seventeen-year-old hostage. In 1990 he received the Medal of Valor from the Attorney General of the State of California. Sgt. Beckman was referred to as a "true American hero" by President Ronald Reagan. He is a founding board member and president of the Law Enforcement Alliance of America, and travels extensively throughout the country promoting officers', citizens', and victims' rights as well as other pro-constitutional issues.*

 ## MIND STRETCHES

1.   What promotions do you see as being of interest to you now? In one year? Five years? Ten years?

2.   If you were promoting someone, what characteristics would you look for?

3.   Why would "off-duty" actions influence employers?

4.   Name what you are doing now that employers would view favorably.

5.   Name anything they could view unfavorably.

6.   Do you think someone could be "overeducated"? Why or why not?

7.   What schooling do you think could help you in your job pursuits?

8.   Consider those around you who have been promoted. What have they done to benefit themselves?

REFERENCES

Asher, Donald. *Who Gets Promoted, Who Doesn't, and Why.* Berkeley, CA: Ten Speed Press, 2007.

Borello, Andrew. "Promotional Oral Interviews." *Law and Order,* September 2003, pp. 128–131.

Borello, Andrew. *Oral Interview Dynamics.* San Clemente, CA: LawTech Publishing Co., 2004.

Hamilton, Melanie. "How to . . . Get Promoted." *Police,* April 2004, pp. 24–26.

Mason, Don. "The Assessment Center Process." Prepared for the New Jersey Conference of Mayors. Available online at www.njmayornet.com/Spring07Mason.htm.

Narramore, Randy E. "Preparing for a Promotional Interview." *Law and Order,* September 1991, pp. 161–162.

Nierenhausen, Ron, Sgt. River Police Department, MN, Concordia University St. Paul, MN. Personal interview, 2008.

Ollhoff, Jim. Rosemount, MN. Personal interview, 2008.

Whitcomb, Susan Britton. *30-Day Job Promotion, Build a Powerful Promotion Plan In a Month.* Indianapolis, IN: JIST Publishing, Inc., 2008.

CHAPTER 17

JOB LOSS AND CHANGE: THE ROAD LESS TRAVELED

In the middle of difficulty lies opportunity.

—*Albert Einstein*

Success is how high you bounce when you hit bottom.

—*General George Patton*

Do You Know:

➤ What besides death and taxes is inevitable?
➤ How common is job-loss grief?
➤ Why an effective strategy to deal with job loss is needed?
➤ What myths about employment are common?
➤ What basic job-loss survival strategies are needed?
➤ What emotions are normally experienced following job loss?
➤ What depression is? What to do if it occurs?
➤ When you should begin your job search after losing your current job?

INTRODUCTION

The reality is that *getting* a job cannot be fully and properly addressed without discussing loss of that job. A fact of life is that you will lose every job you get, eventually. It will happen to you, as it happens to everyone. It's just one more example of how life is a series of changes accompanied by inevitable losses.

Fact: We will lose every job we ever have. Sometimes leaving a job is unexpected and unwanted, sometimes it's a desired change, and sometimes it's a promotion or a demotion. Eventually it will be retirement. Maybe it has just happened to you, which is why you are focusing on this chapter. However, this is not as grim as it may sound because, like anything else, a well-thought-out strategy will make this ebb and flow of life more manageable.

This chapter is titled *Job Loss and Change* because even desired, positive employment changes are challenging. People often are surprised at the emotions accompanying these changes. In fact, the stress and fear of change prevents some people from pursuing promotions or other job opportunities, or to turn them down when offered. It also keeps some people at jobs they dislike, but not as much as they dislike facing the unknown. This may not make sense now, but it will.

No job is sacrosanct, no job is yours forever, and there is no such thing as job security. Past success, being union, tenured, working for the government or being a really good employee—none of this guarantees you anything. It only takes a downturn in the economy to result in layoffs. No one is immune. Never before have you needed a strategy to deal with change more than now.

Transition is inevitable and job loss is inevitable. It happens to everyone.

THE IDENTITY CRISIS

"Who are you?" said the caterpillar.

"I—I hardly know, Sir, just at present," Alice replied rather shyly, "at least I know who I *was* when I got up this morning, but I think I must have been changed several times since then."
                                                                        —Lewis Carroll, *Alice's Adventures in Wonderland*

It's something you can't imagine until it happens to you. Many put off retirement longer than need be to avoid dealing with it, as do those remaining in tenuous or downright unhappy jobs, hoping for a change that never comes. Even being miserable can be more appealing than not knowing what's on the other side of a job change. Change *is* that intimidating.

Planning for a desired change, including retirement, is one thing. Losing a job you thought was yours "forever," or at least until *you* decided you wanted to move on, is something totally different. In addressing the emotions that follow job loss, Knox and Butzel (2002) note:

There are few things worse than feeling you have failed. You feel pummeled, destroyed, violated, betrayed, terrified, angry, guilty, depressed, vengeful, lethargic, impotent and occasionally relieved and resolute. Your defenses have been shattered.

You have sustained a severe blow, a loss of your very sense of self. And the more closely you identified yourself with the job, the greater that loss. Career failure is unlike any other loss; it is a sudden, brutal destruction of self-esteem. Even the death of a loved one does not attack *our* ego. Mourning for another does not obliterate our sense of self. Career failure often does.

Job-loss grief is a universal experience.

The importance of work and the amount of time spent on it makes it such an integral part of our lives that when we're suddenly without it, we feel as if we're in freefall. The shock of the loss of employment is like falling out of an airplane and can be every bit as terrifying. Lacking experience or a strategy, you tumble earthward with absolutely no control, fearing for your life.

When you're falling out of the plane is no time to learn skydiving. Skydivers have learned to control themselves during a freefall by adjusting themselves and the resources at hand so they *are* in control. They have developed a strategy to manage the descent. They return safely to earth, exhilarated. The key is *control and planning.* Not only do skydivers learn what to do when everything goes right, they have and practice contingency plans for the unforeseen.

The strategies discussed in this chapter apply to any changes in our lives. Even when the change is wanted, there's usually a corresponding loss. Understanding the dynamics of change is a powerful tool because it prevents you from misinterpreting emotions as "signs" there is something wrong that really isn't.

Examples abound. Attend any graduation or wedding, where everyone is (supposed to be) happy, and you'll inevitably see tears. If you ask why someone is crying you're likely to hear, "Because I'm so happy." No, tears are a physical response to emotional sadness, so what's to be sad about? Both the graduate and bride or groom *are* happy to be moving forward with their lives, but there is also apprehension and, yes, sadness about leaving their former identities and security behind. It's not a sign they are making a mistake or doomed for failure; it's a normal response to change.

WHY IS HAVING A STRATEGY SO IMPORTANT?

It is as important to develop a strategy to deal with job loss as it was to get the job in the first place. Why? Because it *will* happen, and it can be significant and downright painful. In fact, according to Rolls (2004): "In the hierarchy of the 20 top stressors in life, losing one's job is #8. It's accompanied in the Top Ten by death (of a loved one), divorce and going to jail! Career and income loss can have serious consequences on lifestyle and health."

Hodowanes (2004) states: "Since you can't eliminate the possibility of a job loss, you should always be prepared to deal with it." This is especially true for those in the professions discussed in this text. These positions carry a significant "identity attachment," with the job becoming the person's identity. The uniform, badge, equipment, and important work become hard to give up.

> An effective job-loss strategy will not only enable you to feel more in control of very difficult circumstances, but it will allow you to move on in a healthy way to the next job or phase of life.

And there *will be* another.

THE MYTHS AND HARD TRUTHS ABOUT WORK

Employment has changed drastically in the past several decades. Yet, despite these changes, people continue to believe in certain myths about employment when they should, instead, be acknowledging some hard truths about unemployment and preparing for the inevitable.

The Myths

> Myth #1: My employment is secure—after all, I got the job, didn't I?
> Myth #2: If I do a good job, I'll continue to be recognized for it and be assured of a secure future.
> Myth #3: Job loss can happen only to someone else—not me.
> Myth #4: Even if it does happen to me, I'll be able to handle it without a problem.
> Myth #5: I'll never retire.

Myth #1: My Employment Is Secure—After All, I Got the Job, Didn't I? What is meant by *secure?* If it means you will always have your current job, this is incorrect. At most you will retire. Or you could be fired. You could be promoted, transferred to another division, or even find yourself on long-term disability after becoming ill or being injured on the job. You might move. But you will *not always* have a particular job just because you once got it. Of course, it is everyone's hope that any particular job will end when *we* want it to. After all, it's *our* job and it belongs to us. It's a part of us, and we're a part of it. But unless you are truly self-employed, you do *not* own your job. Even the self-employed do not necessarily have a job that will last a lifetime.

According to Leider and Shapiro (2002, p. 89): "The idea of a permanent job is obsolete. Your job, today, is never safe! The work world is in constant turmoil. . . . Companies whose names used to be synonymous with security have laid people off in record numbers. . . . These days, nearly everyone will be 'between jobs' at some time."

No one is immune from the possibility of losing their job. And those who think they are may well be most at risk. Job loss is becoming an increasingly familiar scenario and one that must at least be acknowledged. To do otherwise will lull you into a complacency that makes you even more susceptible to risk. Leider and Shapiro (p. 90) caution: "You must be prepared to go job-hunting for the rest of your life. No one owes you a job—not your present employer, not your union, not even if you work for Mom and Dad. It's up to you to create your future. In the 21st century, almost everyone, up through the highest ranks of professionals, will feel increased pressure to package themselves as a marketable 'portfolio' of talents."

Some jobs have shorter durations than others, but that doesn't necessarily make the transition any easier, just expected. Chief law enforcement officers, prison wardens, and city or county managers have notoriously short professional life spans in their positions because of the politics involved. Stanek (2008), corporate trainer for Fortune 500 companies, says it may be as little as four years before your job is eliminated in restructurings or it's hoped "new blood" will propel the company to better times. You are forewarned: It doesn't matter if you are union, senior, government employed, or just really, really good at your job. There *are* circumstances that could, and eventually will, cause you to lose your job. The only question is: How will you handle it?

Myth #2: If I Do a Good Job, I'll Continue to Be Recognized for It and Be Assured of a Secure Future. As just pointed out, *not necessarily*. This is an old paradigm. It's the way things might have been for our parents or grandparents, but it's no longer what employees can expect. In fact, it's just the opposite. A frightening prediction made in 1970 by Alvin Toffler in *Future Shock* anticipated societal change: "In the three short decades between now and the twenty-first century, millions of ordinary, psychologically normal people, will face an abrupt collision with the future. Citizens of the world's richest and most technologically advanced nations will find it increasingly painful to keep up with the incessant demand for change that characterizes our time. For them the future will have arrived too soon."

The future is now. More and more people have had their employment collide with this future, and they *are* in shock. No doubt you know some of these people. And you may well find yourself among them. Cutbacks, downsizing, and other synonyms for *job loss* are occurring not only in corporate America. With the national cry for "Lower taxes!," public sector programs, personnel, and even entire departments, once the bastion of security, are increasingly finding themselves part of the tax-reduction "solution." No shield can fully protect employees from inevitable change—not unions, not job performance, not popularity.

The loyalty once integral in job relationship is no longer. Even those parting company because of downsizing and on very good terms with the employer can be shocked at how they are escorted off the premises without time to even look around one last time or say goodbye to friends and colleagues. Especially in security-related jobs where the employer wants to limit access the person once had to equipment and data, they can literally be left with their belongings in a box with little or no fanfare.

Myth #3: Job Loss Can Happen Only to Someone Else—Not Me. Wrong. Remember, that "someone else" is a "me." And as stated at the beginning of the chapter, *unemployment has become the great equalizer*. It can hit you just as easily as your cousin, your neighbor, or the person you used to sit next to on the train every day on your way to work.

Myth #4: Even If It Does Happen to Me, I'll Be Able to Handle It without a Problem. It is all too easy to judge those experiencing the natural range of emotions resulting from job loss as weak, self-pitying, or otherwise not up to the task. Anyone who has lost a job or experienced any other significant loss will tell you it takes considerable courage to address this change.

Loss and change are a part of life and can actually build character. It is just an area all too often ignored until it is on our front doorstep. Everyone who has "been there" has a whole new appreciation for the intensity of emotions that surface and a willingness to extend an understanding hand to those who will need it.

The Hard Truths

Instead of buying into the myths about work and hoping the "inevitable" doesn't happen to you, Tischler (2001) offers some hard truths to help you "respond to the new era of downsizing without downsizing your dreams":

Truth #1:	*There are worse things than being laid off—like staying in a bad job for "security."*
Truth #2:	*In fact, losing your job may be the best career move you'll ever make.*
Truth #3:	*But don't be surprised if you are unemployed longer than you expected at first . . .*
Truth #4:	*. . . Even though it often pays off to move fast.*
Truth #5:	*By the way, the Internet won't necessarily solve your job-search problem.*
Truth #6:	*You might have to settle for less money too.*
Truth #7:	*And you might find yourself at a more conservative company.*
Truth #8:	*You may also have to consider a different city.*
Truth #9:	*For all the turmoil, never forget that your professional life span is longer than that of most companies.*
Truth #10:	*So your real job is to find what you love and then find a way to do it.* (Return to Truth #1.)

Tischler cushions these harsh realities with some final, more optimistic, words of advice: "Don't forget the most important lesson of all. Markets go up, and markets go down. Digital technologies catch fire and then burn out. But through it all, the defining truth of the business world is that people are still front and center. If you're a talented person with a real passion for your work, you are living in the right times— layoffs or not."

Recall from Chapter 1 that service industries, including social services, legal services, and protective services, are currently among the most rapidly growing occupations in the United States, with this trend projected to continue through 2012. Although this bodes well for those presently seeking employment in criminal justice, security, and related fields, it does not guarantee this trend will last indefinitely, nor does it give you immunity from future job loss. Things change. Be prepared.

DEVELOPING A STRATEGY

As noted, once you've fallen out of an airplane is not the time to learn to skydive. If you are reading this chapter *before* you need it—good for you. But human nature being what it is, you'll probably give it a lot more consideration when you find yourself needing it. Even then, using concepts contained in this chapter, you can get a plan in place quickly and benefit from it.

Basic job-loss survival strategies include:

➤ Building a support network now—for fun, for closeness, for information, and for the future.
➤ Building a "survival nest egg" of at least six months' living expenses, maybe longer.
➤ Balancing your life so your job isn't the only important thing to you to prevent yourself from "losing it all."

As you build your network, consider volunteering for an organization you are interested in.

 List in your journal individuals you want to keep in contact with not only for future job networking, but also because you enjoy them. Can you help any of them now? Can they help you?

 What volunteer opportunities might interest you and might also benefit you in a job search? Your biggest challenge will be making the best use of the time off. Seize the opportunity to reassess where you want to go through your next work.

 How much money would you need if you suddenly lost your job? What financial commitments would you need to keep to ensure security for you and your family?

 What interests or hobbies have you put off due to lack of time or money? If you had six months off right now, what would you do with the time?

Survival strategies set a foundation for you to proceed. A strategy addresses the areas that need to be worked with and worked through: awareness, acceptance, support, putting the past behind you, and, finally, moving ahead.

THE SEQUENTIAL REACTION TO JOB LOSS AND CHANGE

You can't go around the emotions of job loss and change; you must go through them. There is no shortcut. Chapter 11, which dealt with *not* getting a job, discussed the predictable process most people experience when losing something important (see Chapter 11, Figure 11–1). Whatever begins the sequence of emotional, sometimes physical, responses to job loss, the emotions are so universal that we know they've got to be dealt with. Failure to do so will keep you stuck in that phase (e.g., becoming overly angry or sad), and will affect all other areas of your life.

> The normal emotions experienced following job loss are denial, anger, sadness, searching, withdrawal, and reorganization. The sequence in which these emotions occur may vary, and emotions may repeat themselves.

These emotions were explained more fully in Chapter 11, but we'll briefly recap them here:

➤ *Denial* is normally experienced as, "I can't believe this happened to me." The ability to *accept* the loss is a necessary step in being able to continue on with life.

➤ *Anger* is "Why me?" You lost your job—who wouldn't be upset? But don't lash out at those close to you or burn bridges with your former employer. Another opportunity may arise in the future, or your former employer may be called for a reference. Deal with the anger by finding an appropriate, constructive outlet.

➤ *Sadness* is another emotion to expect along the way. Do not ignore it. You need to let yourself feel the sadness so you can work through it and move on.

➤ *Searching* may involve going back to your place of employment, even if only to drive by. You might call or you may hold on to the hope that "they" will come to their senses and ask you, beg you, to come back. It's like survivors going back to the disaster scene—it provides a reality check. Give yourself time to check out the old as you prepare to move on to the new.

➤ *Withdrawal* may be hard for family and friends to understand and may create stress for everyone. Pulling away lets you do your emotional work inside while you step back and assess where you fit into the world now. This takes time, and only you can do it. So when your family and friends see you as more quiet and withdrawn, no one has to worry. It's simply another part of the process.

➤ *Reorganization* is when you've worked through the previous emotional stages and are ready to rebuild. Going through this exhausting set of emotions makes it understandable why people resist change—good or not. Young police officers have difficulty understanding why they keep getting called back to the same address on domestic disturbance calls. "If it's so bad, why doesn't one of them just leave?" The answer is that even as difficult as the situation is, it's known. It's predictable. What's on the other side of that door is unknown. Only when the pain exceeds the risk will change occur.

> All changes, even the most longed for, have their melancholy; for what we leave behind is part of ourselves; we must die to one life before we can enter another.
>
> —Anatole France, writer

Change is hard. To expect anything less is unrealistic. The emotions experienced are normal and natural. By understanding the predictable, normal sequence of emotions, you can harness the energy rather than letting it become debilitating.

Managing the Responses

It is not enough to know and anticipate the feelings you will experience. You must effectively *manage* them as well. This is *not* easy because of the intensity of the emotions and (fortunately) the relative lack of experience most people have dealing with such significant loss. Do not add to your difficulties by letting the emotions overtake you. You will feel anger, but don't make inappropriate, hostile phone calls to or confront a former employer you blame for your job loss. Does this happen? Yes, even to extremes. We've heard about former employees who act their anger out with violence, sometimes even killing former employers and coworkers. It's probably not coincidence that workplace violence is increasing at the same time job loss is increasing across the country.

Nor do you want to take the emotions out on people trying to support you. You're angry. You're sad. The denial factor may keep you from seeing that it's your job loss causing these feelings. Having lost your job, you don't want to lose those close to you, too. It is possible to "grieve other people right out of your life." Here is where you will benefit from objective help, professional or otherwise. Get it!

Understanding, accepting, and managing the emotions associated with job loss is a huge step in moving forward. However, you must guard against one emotion that can be devastating: depression.

DEALING WITH DEPRESSION

The number of people suffering from depression is far greater than people may realize. It can be a miserable state to be in and, left untreated, can become debilitating and lead to illness and even suicide.

> Depression is not about being sad. It's about being in a cloud that casts a dark shadow over everything. The hopelessness associated with it may become devastating.

Those who experience depression know you can't just "snap out of it" or "tell yourself it will all be okay." If it were this easy, no one would be depressed. Allow yourself to feel all of what you are going through. You don't have to like it, but you do need to accept it and to accept help if the feelings become overwhelming.

Perhaps no other group as a whole is less willing to reach out for help than criminal justice professionals or anyone used to being in control and taking care of others as part of their work. After all, they are there to help others, those who can't help themselves. It's surely not the stereotypical police officer or first responder who admits to someone else, much less to themselves, that they need help.

Sadness and depression to some degree *will* result from job loss. It's a normal part of the process. Things can get away from you, so don't try to go it alone. If you were a police, corrections, or security officer, you'd never respond to a call alone if you knew you'd need additional officers and firepower at the scene. You'd never hesitate to call for help on the street, so don't hesitate to call for help now if you need it.

> If you are depressed, get help. It could be a matter of life and death.

Do not rush the process. Dealing with each stage lets you move on to the next. A very successful person caught in job-related change, emerging stronger from it, advises others to embrace each emotion, to accept, learn from, and then move on from it.

Talk to friends, see a counselor or psychologist, join a support group, see a psychiatrist, and get on medication if needed. But whatever you do, GET HELP. It takes a strong, courageous person to reach out in the midst of despair. But you can do it. You can!

Another way to break out of depression is to tackle the job search for your next job.

GOTTA GET WORKING

You know how to get a job. After all, you got the job(s) you no longer have.

> As you move through the emotional steps of job loss, start working at finding a new job when the time is right for you.

 Write in your journal ten ways you can get back in the job search and tactics to deal with the predictable emotions and start networking again.

DON'T MAKE THINGS WORSE

Not working is bad enough, but it will pass, likely sooner than you expect. During this especially vulnerable time you're susceptible to making decisions you'll regret. Taking your emotions out on others, self-medicating and getting a DWI, or not taking care of yourself or your family can exacerbate what was just one problem.

Be cautious about going overboard with cutting expenses. Think things through. For example, once insurance is no longer available from a previous employer it can be temping to go without it, thinking the risk is offset by the savings. Especially families, the 48 million people in the United States without health insurance, are taking a dangerous gamble (Abelson and Freudenheim, 2008, p. A7). One significant medical event could set you back even further. Bad decisions on your part could make the situation much worse and limit options.

 Write in your journal where your savings are and where you could go if you needed money to help you between jobs.

One tactic some people who have lost their jobs seriously consider is a lawsuit against the former employer.

TO SUE OR NOT TO SUE

No one who has lost their job thinks it was fair; it may well have not been. But unless it was illegal, no judge will care. Even then, you need to think about whether a lawsuit is the way to proceed. For some people it's nothing more than a way of striking out in response to a hurtful situation. Others may have a legitimate legal basis to consider.

Employment law is very complex, and a discussion of when a dismissal is illegal is beyond the scope of this book. It depends on your particular circumstances. Do you have a contract? Are you a veteran? What does your employee handbook include? Are you union? And the list goes on. You need legal counsel for answers. But simply because it wasn't fair or you didn't do anything wrong doesn't necessarily warrant legal action.

Even if you have a legal cause of action, consider the consequences of suing a previous employer: What is the likelihood of prevailing? What will future prospective employers think of this action? Will a lengthy lawsuit prolong your agony and prevent you from beginning the healing process? How much might it cost? All these questions need to be considered. A competent attorney will be able to help with this, which is why they are also called counselors at law.

CONCLUSION

Maneuvering through job loss appears to be inevitable. Never forget—it's just a job. If not job loss, you will be confronted with other situations where a solid loss and change strategy will be of help. All endings lead to new beginnings; it just might not seem like it at the time. But you must believe there will be another side—a brighter side, a new job, new opportunities, new friends, a whole new world.

AN INSIDER'S VIEW

JOB LOSS AND GRIEF

Richard J. Obershaw, LICSW, MSW, ACSW

Founder of the Grief Center
Burnsville, Minnesota

Our job is a lot about who we are. When we lose our job, we lose who we *were*—not who we *are*. When we lose our job, we often lose our identity, our security, our friends, our coworkers, our financial security, our sense of accomplishment, our lifestyle, our routine, our sense of productivity, and sometimes we lose the reason for getting out of bed in the morning.

We often select "our work" because of who we *were*. For example, perfectionists seldom take on jobs that can't be done perfectly. If they do, they soon learn to look for another job. Individuals who enjoy people usually select jobs that involve people. During those years at the job we all change. The changes come because of maturational issues in our life as well as situational occurrences. But because of financial factors we seldom elect to leave our first job of choice. We learn to "live with the way I am now in a job that was selected for the way I was then." We adapt by mixing the *new me* with the *old me*.

Then the day comes when someone says you are no longer wanted, needed or capable of performing this job, or your job is eliminated because of (1) a change in the workplace, (2) economic factors or (3) interpersonal differences. It is at this point in our life that we have to once again ask, "Who am I now as an individual and what do I need for a job that matches this 'now' individual?"

This is the process of grief—letting go of the *old me* and learning who the *new me* will be. It is the job of reidentifying the self. After many studies on the topic of change and grief, we have come to learn that the process is somewhat predictable. No one follows the process in exactly the same pattern as others, but the overall general idea may help you understand your "normally crazy" thoughts, ideas, feelings and behavior during this period of reidentifying yourself.

Initially we find it difficult to accept the reality of our loss. Our **denial** system starts to protect us from the stress created by change. It may seem like a bad dream, or we may wish, sometimes out loud, that the old familiar activities will once again return. This may look unhealthy to others around us, but it serves as a buffer for us as we go gently from the *old me* to the *new me*. We may even decide not to tell our family and friends about the job loss because they will want to discuss it. But we aren't ready to deal with a discussion about it because it makes it too real. This denial will fade gently as we become more aware that we can cope with this change in our lives.

As we become more aware of the reality of the loss, we become more aware of the effort it will take to reidentify ourselves. It is at this point we get **resentful** of the effort needed to change, and we find ourselves with a general "anger all over" feeling. We get angry that we have to change. We get angry at the people who get to keep their jobs. We get angry at those who told us our job was ending. We get angry at God, and we get angry at ourselves. Because we are punched in the gut over this loss, we want to punch others. We want others to suffer with us.

Soon we find ourselves feeling quite restless and pacing around the house. Where do we belong? We awaken at the time we normally would to go to work, but find ourselves with no place to go.

Then comes the **search**—we may drive by and around the workplace feeling the need to check out if it's still there for us. We may search our minds and others to come up with the "real reason" this loss has been placed in our lives. We may search to find new meaning in our life without our old job. The term *job search* may also explain why initially we search to find a job—sometimes any job. And, because we find a job we take it—just to end the search and get a job back. These jobs often do not meet our new needs, our changed selves.

Another part of the grief process with job loss is **withdrawal.** We withdraw from our families, friends, former coworkers and often from ourselves. We sleep to withdraw from life and ourselves. We withdraw into television and spend countless hours staring at brain-dead talk shows that help us escape from our own grief and reidentification process. In extreme cases we may withdraw into obsessive-compulsive behaviors, alcohol and other drugs, dangerous hobbies, sexual affairs, excessive spending and even suicide.

If we survive all of the preceding, we begin the process of realizing we are new. Our thinking, our needs and our goals are often new. We start to know the *new me* and become more comfortable being changed. It is at this point we should begin with a true job search that fits the *new us*. If everyone had the financial security to wait this long, life would be easier, but the reality is, jobs are needed to earn money to pay the bills. Perhaps what we need to do is reassess how we choose to live our lives. Is the job where we work about collecting money or is a job about meeting our needs to be who we are?

Richard Obershaw, *LICSW, MSW, ACSW, is an internationally renowned expert on loss and change, grief, and bereavement. He travels extensively, lecturing and consulting on these subjects in addition to his clinical practice. He is also founder of the Grief Center in Burnsville, Minnesota.*

 MIND STRETCHES

1.   If you needed them today, who makes up your support network?

2.   What losses have you experienced? How did you work through the steps?

3.   Why does job loss affect more than just the individual?

4.   Why do you think job loss is more common now than in years past?

5.   Do you think job loss can be harder to deal with than death? Why or why not?

6.   Why do people think job loss can't happen to them?

7.   How would you help yourself if you lost your job today?

8.   Do you have enough resources to get by if you were suddenly out of a job? Where could you go to get financial help until you were reemployed?

9.   If you were to lose your job now, would you say, "That's what I was" or "That's what I did"?

10.   Why do you think some people put more emphasis on their jobs than on the rest of their lives?

REFERENCES

Abelson, Reed, and Milt Freudenheim. "More Underinsured as Economy Sinks." (Minneapolis/St. Paul) *Star Tribune*, May 4, 2008, p. A7.

Hodowanes, Joe. "Negotiating a Smooth Job Exit." Net-Temps, 2004. Available online at www.net-temps.com/careerdev/ index.htm?type=topics&topic=layoff&id=213.

Knox, Deborah L., and Sandra S. Butzel. *Life Work Transition.com: Putting Your Spirit Online.* 2002. Available online at www.lifeworktransitions.com/exercises/stgesloss.html.

Leider, Richard J., and David A. Shapiro. *Repacking Your Bags: Lighten Your Load for the Rest of Your Life,* 2nd ed. San Francisco: Berrett-Koehler Publishers, Inc., 2002.

Rolls, Sonya. "Dealing with Your Loss of Employment." Net-Temps, 2004. Available online at www.net-temps.com/careerdev/ index.htm?type=topics&topic=layoff&id=101.

Stanek, Susan. Bloomington, MN: Inspiring Results (company). Personal interview, 2008.

Tischler, Linda. "10 Hard Truths About Layoffs." *Fast Company*. Boston: Gruner and Jahr USA Publishing, June 2001. Available online at www.fastcompany.com/articles/2001/06/10truths.html.

ADDITIONAL CONTACTS AND SOURCES OF INFORMATION

How to Plan, Negotiate, and Take the Break You Need without Burning Bridges or Going Broke, by Hope Dlugozima, Henry Holt, 1996.

CareerBuilder.com—Provides a Layoff Survival Kit including discussion boards where people can commiserate and share job-hunting tips.

FastCompany.com—Serves people's individual career needs with six custom-built Career Zones. Each Career Zone contains Web-only stories, interactive tools, expert opinions, and valuable connections to help Fast Company readers get ahead in the new economy.

JobHuntersBible.com—Richard Bolles, author of *What Color Is Your Parachute?,* guides career changers and suggests what to do once they've exhausted Internet job sites.

JobSearching.org—Sponsored by the Professionals in Transition (PIT) support group, this site helps the unemployed cope and retool skills.

Monster.com—Has suggestions for stress management and repositioning yourself in a tough market.

EPILOGUE

In three words I can sum up everything I've learned about life. It goes on.

—Robert Frost

A beginning. An end. A new beginning. This describes life, including your working life.

Work. It's much more complex than most people realize. Work can feed our souls, but it can also destroy them. Striking a balance in life is what "success" may well be. Home, family, education, faith, health, recreation, and work. Unfortunately, many people allow, knowingly or otherwise, the work component to overshadow the others, causing an imbalance that can affect every aspect of life. The danger in letting work define you was encapsulated well by E. L. Sopow during a discussion with the author (Harr) in Vancouver, Canada, about work, job loss, change, and resilience:

> Most people have come to equate what they DO with who they ARE. This means when they lose their job they experience two out of the three forms of death—death of self-image and death of hope. And in some unfortunate cases, the third form of death—clinical—is also a consideration. We might learn from biology rather than business school when it comes to dealing with death. Nature has survived 3.8 billion years by facing a crisis with enhanced communications, increased connectivity, and cooperation leading to evolution. We are not cogs in a machine. We are a network of complex, adaptive systems.

From an evolutionary perspective, the ability to adapt to a changing environment is a prerequisite for survival. Presently, the world of work seems, more than ever, a world of change. Adaptation may be one of the best strategies for success or, at the very least, survival in the work environment. You can't afford to get caught up in what was, assuming things will always remain the same. They won't and they can't. It's just not the nature of things. In fact, the definition of "security" as it relates to the workplace has changed to such a degree that some argue it's gone altogether. "Employment security" is now best defined as having a well-thought-out strategy to adapt to change, to be secure with change.

Dr. Susan Stanek, training and development consultant, endorses the plan of people developing a *dual* career path to better prepare themselves for job change. Whether people tire of a primary job or find themselves needing another job, having the education and training to fit into another position is a wonderful means by which to adapt. This approach has served many people well, whether they found themselves estranged from their original position, by their own decision, or taking advantage of early retirement, yet not ready to quit contributing to the world around them in some way.

Through reading this book and completing the exercises within, you have had the opportunity to do far more than merely learn to write a résumé. You have had the opportunity to develop ideas on where you would like your work life to take you. You've been encouraged to consider the necessity of balancing the many aspects of life, including work, and you've prepared yourself for the changes you will surely face. Some of them will be good and some won't. All will contribute to make up the person you are, and that, unquestionably, is of great value.

Work. It is so much a part of our lives. It deserves careful consideration. *But in the end, remember, it's only a job!*

APPENDIX A

IACP POLICE CODE OF CONDUCT*

All law enforcement officers must be fully aware of the ethical responsibilities of their position and must strive constantly to live up to the highest possible standards of professional policing.

The International Association of Chiefs of Police believes it is important that police officers have clear advice and counsel available to assist them in performing their duties consistent with these standards, and has adopted the following ethical mandates as guidelines to meet these ends.**

Primary Responsibilities of a Police Officer

A police officer acts as an official representative of government who is required and trusted to work within the law. The officer's powers and duties are conferred by statute. The fundamental duties of a police officer include serving the community; safeguarding lives and property; protecting the innocent; keeping the peace; and ensuring the rights of all to liberty, equality and justice.

Performance of the Duties of a Police Officer

A police officer shall perform all duties impartially, without favor or affection or ill will and without regard to status, sex, race, religion, political belief or aspiration. All citizens will be treated equally with courtesy, consideration and dignity.

Officers will never allow personal feelings, animosities or friendships to influence official conduct. Laws will be enforced appropriately and courteously and, in carrying out their responsibilities, officers will strive to obtain maximum cooperation from the public. They will conduct themselves in appearance and deportment in such a manner as to inspire confidence and respect for the position of public trust they hold.

Discretion

A police officer will use responsibly the discretion vested in the position and exercise it within the law. The principle of reasonableness will guide the officer's determinations and the officer will consider all surrounding circumstances in determining whether any legal action shall be taken.

---

*Adopted by the Executive Committee of the International Association of Chiefs of Police on October 17, 1989, during its 96th Annual Conference in Louisville, Kentucky, to replace the 1957 code of ethics adopted at the 64th Annual IACP Conference.

**The IACP gratefully acknowledges the assistance of Sir John C. Hermon, former chief constable of the Royal Ulster Constabulary, who gave full license to the association to freely use the language and concepts presented in the RUC's "Professional Policing Ethics," Appendix 1 of the Chief Constable's Annual Report, 1988, presented to the Police Authority for Northern Ireland, for the preparation of this code.

Consistent and wise use of discretion, based on professional policing competence, will do much to preserve good relationships and retain the confidence of the public. There can be difficulty in choosing between conflicting courses of action. It is important to remember that a timely word of advice rather than arrest—which may be correct in appropriate circumstances—can be a more effective means of achieving a desired end.

Use of Force

A police officer will never employ unnecessary force or violence and will use only such force in the discharge of duty as is reasonable in all circumstances. Force should be used only with the greatest restraint and only after discussion, negotiation and persuasion have been found to be inappropriate or ineffective. While the use of force is occasionally unavoidable, every police officer will refrain from applying the unnecessary infliction of pain or suffering and will never engage in cruel, degrading or inhuman treatment of any person.

Confidentiality

Whatever a police officer sees, hears or learns of, which is of a confidential nature, will be kept secret unless the performance of duty or legal provision requires otherwise. Members of the public have a right to security and privacy, and information obtained about them must not be improperly divulged.

Integrity

A police officer will not engage in acts of corruption or bribery, nor will an officer condone such acts by other police officers. The public demands that the integrity of police officers be above reproach. Police officers must, therefore, avoid any conduct that might compromise integrity and thus undercut the public confidence in a law enforcement agency. Officers will refuse to accept any gifts, presents, subscriptions, favors, gratuities or promises that could be interpreted as seeking to cause the officer to refrain from performing official responsibilities honestly and within the law. Police officers must not receive private or special advantage from their official status. Respect from the public cannot be bought; it can only be earned and cultivated.

Cooperation with Other Officers and Agencies

Police officers will cooperate with all legally authorized agencies and their representatives in the pursuit of justice. An officer or agency may be among many organizations that may provide law enforcement services to a jurisdiction. It is imperative that a police officer assist colleagues fully and completely with respect and consideration at all times.

Personal/Professional Capabilities

Police officers will be responsible for their own standard of professional performance and will take every reasonable opportunity to enhance and improve their level of knowledge and competence. Through study and experience, a police officer can acquire the high level of knowledge and competence that is essential for the efficient and effective performance of duty. The acquisition of knowledge is a never-ending process of personal and professional development that should be pursued constantly.

Private Life

Police officers will behave in a manner that does not bring discredit to their agencies or themselves. A police officer's character and conduct while off duty must always be exemplary, thus maintaining a position of respect in the community in which he or she lives and serves. The officer's personal behavior must be beyond reproach.

APPENDIX B

ASIS SECURITY CODE OF ETHICS*

PREAMBLE

Aware that the quality of professional security activity ultimately depends upon the willingness of practitioners to observe special standards of conduct and to manifest good faith in professional relationships, the American Society for Industrial Security adopts the following Code of Ethics and mandates its conscientious observance as a binding condition of membership in or affiliation with the Society:

ARTICLE I

A member shall perform professional duties in accordance with the law and the highest moral principles.

Ethical Considerations

I-1   A member shall abide by the law of the land in which the services are rendered and perform all duties in an honorable manner.

I-2   A member shall not knowingly become associated in responsibility for work with colleagues who do not conform to the law and these ethical standards.

I-3   A member shall be just and respect the rights of others in performing professional responsibilities.

ARTICLE II

A member shall observe the precepts of truthfulness, honesty and integrity.

Ethical Considerations

II-1   A member shall disclose all relevant information to those having a right to know.

II-2   A right to know is a legally enforceable claim or demand by a person for disclosure of information by a member. Such a right does not depend upon prior knowledge by the person of the existence of the information to be disclosed.

II-3   A member shall not knowingly release misleading information, nor encourage or otherwise participate in the release of such information.

ARTICLE III

A member shall be faithful and diligent in discharging professional responsibilities.

---

*Reprinted with permission from the American Society for Industrial Security.

Ethical Considerations

III-1   A member is faithful when fair and steadfast in adherence to promises and commitments.
III-2   A member is diligent when employing best efforts in an assignment.
III-3   A member shall not act in matters involving conflicts of interest without appropriate disclosure and approval.
III-4   A member shall represent services or products fairly and truthfully.

ARTICLE IV

A member shall be competent in discharging professional responsibilities.

Ethical Considerations

IV-1   A member is competent who possesses and applies the skills and knowledge required for the task.
IV-2   A member shall not accept a task beyond the member's competence nor shall competence be claimed when not possessed.

ARTICLE V

A member shall safeguard confidential information and exercise due care to prevent its improper disclosure.

Ethical Considerations

V-1   Confidential information is nonpublic information the disclosure of which is restricted.
V-2   Due care requires that the professional must not knowingly reveal confidential information or use a confidence to the disadvantage of the principal or to the advantage of the member or a third person unless the principal consents after full disclosure of all the facts. This confidentiality continues after the business relationship between the member and his principal has terminated.
V-3   A member who receives information and has not agreed to be bound by confidentiality is not bound from disclosing it. A member is not bound by confidential disclosures made of acts or omissions which constitute a violation of the law.
V-4   Confidential disclosures made by a principal to a member are not recognized by law as privileged in a legal proceeding. The member may be required to testify in a legal proceeding to information received in confidence from his principal over the objection of his principal's counsel.
V-5   A member shall not disclose confidential information for personal gain without appropriate authorization.

ARTICLE VI

A member shall not maliciously injure the professional reputation or practice of colleagues, clients or employers.

Ethical Considerations

VI-1   A member shall not comment falsely and with malice concerning a colleague's competence, performance or professional capabilities.
VI-2   A member who knows, or has reasonable grounds to believe, that another member has failed to conform to the Society's Code of Ethics shall present such information to the Ethical Standards Committee in accordance with Article XIV of the Society's Bylaws.

APPENDIX C

RÉSUMÉ WORKSHEETS

Name: _____

Current Address: _____

Permanent Address: _____

Phone Number(s): _____

E-mail: _____

Colleges: _____

_____

Professional Schools: _____

_____

Internships: _____

_____

Certificates Held: _____

_____

_____

Other Educational Experiences: _____

_____

_____

High School: _____

EMPLOYMENT HISTORY
(Note: Make as many copies of this page as you have had jobs so you can complete one page for each job you've had.)

Dates Employed: From _____ to _____

Employer: _____

      Address: _____

      Phone/E-mail: _____

      Supervisor: _____

Position/Title: _____

Responsibilities: _____

_____

_____

_____

_____

Skills Acquired: _____

_____

_____

_____

_____

Achievements/Awards: _____

_____

_____

_____

Salary (NOT included in résumé): _____

Reason for Change (NOT included in résumé): _____

_____

Position Desired/Employment Objective: _____

_____

_____

Other information that may be put in your résumé includes the following:

Birth Date: _____ Height: _____ Weight: _____

Health: _____

Travel (willing to travel?): _____

Location (willing to relocate?): _____

Military (service, dates, rank, honorable discharge): _____

_____

Reserve status: _____

Professional Memberships (committees served on, awards): _____

_____

_____

_____

Foreign Languages (read, write, speak fluently): _____

_____

Foreign Travel: _____

_____

Awards: _____

_____

Publications: _____

_____

Community Service/Involvement (organizations, offices held, etc.): _____

_____

Interests/Hobbies (avocations, nonbusiness pursuits): _____

_____

Availability (immediate or extent of "notice" required): _____

Present Employer Contact: _____
(Is present employer aware of your prospective job change? May the employer be contacted?)

Salary Desired: _____
(NOT included in résumé, but know what you'd expect.)

BUSINESS/PROFESSIONAL/ACADEMIC REFERENCES:

Full Name: _____

     Position: _____

     Address: _____

     Phone/E-mail: _____

Full Name: _____

     Position: _____

     Address: _____

     Phone/E-mail: _____

Full Name: _____

     Position: _____

     Address: _____

     Phone/E-mail: _____

PERSONAL REFERENCE:_____

Full Name: _____

     Relationship (neighbor, teammate, etc.): _____

     Address: _____

     Phone/E-mail: _____

RÉSUMÉ EVALUATION CHECKLIST

CATEGORY	Excellent	Average	Poor	How to Improve
APPEARANCE:				
Is the format clean?				
Is it easy to follow?				
Are headings effective?				
Does it make the reader want to read it?				
CONTENT:				
Do my qualifications stand out?				
Is the language clear and understandable?				
Have I used short phrases?				
Have I used verbs (action words)?				
Is it brief and to the point?				
Are all important skills and qualifications included?				
Does it create a true picture of me?				
Is irrelevant personal information left out?				
PROOFREADING:				
Is it error-free?				
Spelling?				
Punctuation?				

SAMPLE RÉSUMÉS

Historical/Chronological Résumé

WILLIAM A. SMITH
10 South First Street
Minneapolis, MN 55404

Home Phone: (612) 555-5650 / Cell: (612) 555-3333
Work Phone: (612) 555-9123

PERSONAL   Date of Birth: 6/3/84, 6′ 0″, 175 lbs. Married, one child. Will relocate.

EDUCATION

2002–2006   NORMANDALE COMMUNITY COLLEGE
                   Bloomington, Minnesota
                   Associate Arts Degree and Law Enforcement Certificate.
                        Member of football team.
                        Photographer for school paper.

2002   BLOOMINGTON HIGH SCHOOL
                   Bloomington, Minnesota
                   High school diploma. Honor student.
                        Member of football team.

**WORK
EXPERIENCE**

2003–present   SECURITY OFFICER
                   Dayton's Department Store
                   Minneapolis, Minnesota
                   Hired as store detective. Duties include plainclothes observation of retail sales
                        area to observe and arrest shoplifters. Assist in loss prevention seminars
                        for store employees.

2002–2003   WAITER
                   Fancy Joe's Burger Joint
                   Bloomington, Minnesota
                   Hired as dishwasher. Promoted to busboy and then waiter. Duties as waiter
                        included taking customers' orders, delivering food and beverage items to
                        the table, and assisting other wait staff.

References available on request.

Functional Résumé

WILLIAM L. SMITH
10 South First Street
Minneapolis, MN 55404
Home Phone: (612) 555-5650

Personal Data: Date of Birth 6-3-85, 6′ 0″, 175 lbs., Single.

Objective:

Position as a law enforcement officer.

Work History

2007–present	Southdale Shopping Center Edina, Minnesota
Security Officer:	• Hired as uniformed security officer. Duties include patron assistance, emergency first-aid response, enforcement of property rules and statutes. Assist in training new employees by providing presentations on company rules and state criminal statutes. Frequently appear as witness in court cases resulting from my position. Work with the area law enforcement officers hired to assist during holiday seasons. Act as company representative to Minnesota Loss Control Society.
2005–2007	Kenny's Market, Inc. Bloomington, Minnesota
Office Worker:	• Hired as assistant to the vice president. Duties included typing, filing, and telephone reception. In charge of confidential employee records. Assisted in organizing the company's first loss prevention program.

Education

2005–2007	BA, University of Minnesota, Minneapolis, Minnesota.
2003–2005	AA, Law Enforcement Certification, Normandale Community College, Bloomington, Minnesota.
2006	Emergency Medical Technician Registration, Hennepin County Vo-Tech, Eden Prairie, Minnesota.

References available on request.

Analytical Résumé

WILLIAM L. SMITH
10 South First Street
Minneapolis, MN 55404
Home Phone: (612) 555-5650 / Cell: (612) 555-3333
Work Phone: (612) 555-9123

Job Objective: Apply my proven ability in loss prevention.

Qualifications:

- Retail Security: Have developed knowledge and skills in the profession while employed as loss prevention officer for several retail stores. In addition to providing undercover and plainclothes loss prevention services as a store detective, have provided extensive training on the subject to store employees. Excellent performance reviews at each position. Continued increases in apprehension statistics. Received "Employee of the Month" award six times for excellent work as a security officer.

- Supervisory Skills: Promoted to supervisor of 17 loss prevention officers at most recent position. Duties included training, delegating duties, and scheduling. Performance statistics for the crew increased significantly.

- Organizational Skills: All jobs have required detailed activity reports. Hands-on experience using computers to organize data. Often provided oral reports to supervisors.

Employers

2006–present	Donaldson's Department Store, Edina, Minnesota.
2005–2006	Tom Thumb Stores, Inc., St. Paul, Minnesota.
2003–2005	Automobile Club of America, St. Louis Park, Minnesota.

Education

2006	Associate of Arts and Private Security Certificate, Normandale Community College, Bloomington, Minnesota.

Other

2007	Participated in organization of 2007 American Industrial Security Association National Convention.

References available on request.

APPENDIX E

SAMPLE COVER LETTER AND FOLLOW-UP LETTER

Sample Cover Letter

Ms. Jane Smith
1234 Second Street
Los Angeles, CA 90017

September 15, 2008

Lt. Pat Jones
Mytown Police Department
1234 First Avenue
Denver, CO 80203

Dear Lt. Jones:

I am responding to your ad in the *Los Angeles Times* for the position of police officer. With an AA degree in law enforcement and three years' experience as a reserve officer with the Los Angeles Police Department, I am ready to enter the law enforcement profession and hope it will be with your department. A résumé highlighting my background, qualifications and experience is enclosed.

I will call you the week of September 29th to make sure my résumé was, indeed, received and to arrange for a personal interview. I will look forward to talking with you then.

Sincerely,

Jane Smith

Encl. Résumé

Sample Follow-Up Letter

Mr. Scott Anderson
1234 Second Street
Boulder, CO 23456

July 17, 2008

Protection Plus Security
1234 First Avenue
Denver, CO 12345

Attn: Mr. Ronald Smith,
         President

Dear Mr. Smith:

Thank you for the opportunity to participate in the hiring process for the position of security officer. I delivered my résumé to your office yesterday and am sorry to have missed you.

I remain extremely interested in the position and look forward to the possibility of being considered for the job. Please call if you need any further information.

Very sincerely,

Scott Anderson

AUTHOR INDEX

337

SUBJECT INDEX